MEDIEVAL LAW

MANCHESTER
UNIVERSITY PRESS

Manchester Medieval Studies

SERIES EDITOR Dr S. H. Rigby

SERIES ADVISORS Professor J. H. Denton
Professor R. B. Dobson   Professor L. K. Little

The study of medieval Europe is being transformed as old orthodoxies are challenged, new methods embraced and fresh fields of inquiry opened up. The adoption of inter-disciplinary perspectives and the challenge of economic, social and cultural theory are forcing medievalists to ask new questions and to see familiar topics in a fresh light.

The aim of this series is to combine the scholarship traditionally associated with medieval studies with an awareness of more recent issues and approaches in a form accessible to the non-specialist reader.

ALREADY PUBLISHED IN THE SERIES

The commercialisation of English society, 1000–1500
Richard H. Britnell

Picturing women in late medieval and Renaissance art
Christa Grössinger

The politics of carnival
Christopher Humphrey

Chaucer in context
S. H. Rigby

MANCHESTER MEDIEVAL STUDIES

MEDIEVAL LAW IN CONTEXT
THE GROWTH OF LEGAL CONSCIOUSNESS FROM MAGNA CARTA TO THE PEASANTS' REVOLT

Anthony Musson

Manchester University Press
Manchester and New York
distributed exclusively in the USA by Palgrave

Copyright © Anthony Musson 2001

The right of Anthony Musson to be identified as the author of this work has been asserted by him in accordance with the Copyright, Designs and Patents Act 1988

Published by Manchester University Press
Oxford Road, Manchester M13 9NR, UK
and Room 400, 175 Fifth Avenue, New York, NY 10010, USA
http://www.manchesteruniversitypress.co.uk

Distributed exclusively in the USA
by Palgrave, 175 Fifth Avenue, New York, NY 10010, USA

Distributed exclusively in Canada
by UBC Press, University of British Columbia, 2029 West Mall, Vancouver, BC, Canada V6T 1Z2

British Library Cataloguing-in-Publication Data
A catalogue record for this book is available from the British Library

Library of Congress Cataloging-in-Publication Data applied for

ISBN 0 7190 5493 1 *hardback*
ISBN 0 7190 5494 X *paperback*

First published 2001

08 07 06 05 04 03 02 01   10 9 8 7 6 5 4 3 2 1

Typeset in Monotype Bulmer
by Koinonia, Manchester
Printed in Great Britain
by Biddles Ltd, Guildford and King's Lynn

For 'T

CONTENTS

	PREFACE	*page* ix
	LIST OF ABBREVIATIONS	xi
1	**Towards a psychology of law**	1
	The role of ideology	3
	The contexts of law	9
	Law in the mind	18
2	**The professionalisation of law**	36
	The intellectualising of the law	37
	Towards an identity as a profession	44
	Men of law and legal ethics	50
	Judges and lawyers in society	61
	Centre and periphery	65
	Perceptions of the legal profession	69
3	**Pragmatic legal knowledge**	84
	Family and household	85
	Communal obligations	88
	Court attendance	95
	Church attendance	101
	Experience of office-holding	103
	Book learning and literacy	120
4	**Participation in the royal courts**	135
	Availability	137
	Actionability	149
	Accountability	160
	Accessibility	163

CONTENTS

5 The role of parliament   184
    The high court of parliament   186
    The legal personnel of parliament   189
    The regulation of everyday life   207

6 The politicisation of law   217
    Seeing and hearing the law   218
    Legitimacy through the law   232
    The world turned upside down   241

             SELECT BIBLIOGRAPHY   265
                          INDEX   269

PREFACE

This book is intended as both a history of judicial developments in the thirteenth and fourteenth centuries and as a contribution to the intellectual history of the period. Its genesis was my concern that in charting the evolution of English justice one needed to try and ascertain what people actually thought about the law and how this influenced their actions and how they themselves were able to bring about alterations in the law and legal thinking. It therefore aims to provide a new perspective on the period by examining the contextualisation of law within society and by revealing a theology, ideology and psychology of law. To do so in an accessible and stimulating way has also been my aim throughout. In writing this study I am indebted to the other scholars working in the various disciplines into which I have ventured. I owe particular thanks though to Dr Michael Clanchy, Professor Mark Ormrod and Dr Chantal Stebbings, who have patiently read and commented upon drafts and listened to me expounding ideas. I am also grateful to the conference delegates, colleagues and students upon whom some of these ideas have been tested and for the feedback I have obtained. My single-mindedness in researching and writing this book has entailed domestic and personal sacrifices and I am eternally at the behest of those who have allowed me the space to continue along the lonely path.

A.J.M.
Exeter

ABBREVIATIONS

AJLH   *American Journal of Legal History*
BIHR   *Bulletin of the Institute of Historical Research*
Brand, *Origins*   P. Brand, *The Origins of the English Legal Profession* (London, Blackwell, 1992)
CCR   *Calendar of Close Rolls*
Clanchy, *Memory*   M. T. Clanchy, *From Memory to Written Record: England, 1066–1307*, 2nd edn (Oxford, Blackwell, 1993)
CLBCL   *Calendar of the Letter Books of the City of London*, ed. R. R. Sharpe (London, John Edward Francis, 1899–1907)
CPMR   *Calendar of Plea and Memoranda Rolls*, ed. A. H. Thomas (Cambridge, Cambridge University Press, 1926–32)
CPR   *Calendar of Patent Rolls*
EELR   *The Earliest English Law Reports*, ed. P. Brand, Selden Society, 111 & 112 (London, 1996)
EHR   *English Historical Review*
Foedera   *Foedera, conventiones, litterae etc. or Rymer's Foedera, 1066–1383*, ed. A. Clarke *et al.* (London, Record Commission, 1816)
JBS   *Journal of British Studies*
JLH   *Journal of Legal History*
JMH   *Journal of Medieval History*
Learning the Law   J. A. Bush and A. Wijfells (eds), *Learning the Law: Teaching and the Transmission of Law, 1150–1900* (London, Hambledon Press, 1999)
LHR   *Law and History Review*
LQR   *Law Quarterly Review*
Musson, *Public Order*   A. Musson, *Public Order and Law Enforcement: the Local Administration of Criminal Justice, 1294–1350* (Woodbridge, Boydell Press, 1996)
Musson and Ormrod, *Evolution*   A. Musson and W. M. Ormrod, *The Evolution of English Justice: Law, Politics and Society in the Fourteenth Century* (Basingstoke, Macmillan, 1998)
OJLS   *Oxford Journal of Legal Studies*
P&P   *Past and Present*
Powell, *Kingship*   E. Powell, *Kingship, Law and Society: Criminal Justice in the Reign of Henry V* (Oxford, Clarendon Press, 1989)

ABBREVIATIONS

Return of Members   *Return of the Name of Every Member of the Lower House of the Parliaments of England, Scotland and Ireland ... 1213–1874*, Parliamentary Papers (London, 1878)
RP   *Rotuli Parliamentorum* (London, House of Lords, 1783)
RPHI   *Rotuli Parliamentorum Hactenus Inediti*, ed. H. G. Richardson and G. O. Sayles, Camden Society, 3rd series, 51 (London, 1935)
RS   Rolls Series
SCCKB   *Select Cases in the Court of King's Bench*, ed. G. O. Sayles, Selden Society, 55, 57, 58, 74, 76, 82, 88 (London, 1936–71)
SR   *Statutes of the Realm* (London, Record Commission, 1810–28)
SS   Selden Society
TRHS   *Transactions of the Royal Historical Society*
YB   *Year Books* (Selden Society and Rolls Series)

1

Towards a psychology of law

THE dates 1215 and 1381 mark significant turning points in English history. As is well known, they were both years in which the reigning monarch came face to face with rebellious subjects whose demands they were forced to acknowledge. Separated by nearly two hundred years, the two situations contain some basic similarities, but the differences are also significant. Although King John faced dissension among the leading barons and knights in 1215 the rebellion itself was essentially peaceable (even if civil war erupted not long afterwards). In 1381, by contrast, the young King Richard II confronted an angry crowd of peasants and townsfolk amid scenes of death and destruction. John acceded to the rebels' demands by drawing up a great charter of liberties recognised by the Crown (the document later known as Magna Carta). Richard II made far-reaching promises of change in order to save the day, and charters freeing villeins from customary services were drawn up. Nevertheless, unlike those of 1215, the actual demands of the 1381 rebels were not incorporated into any binding document (they appear only in the texts of chroniclers). Significantly, both kings were reluctant to be bound by their undertakings: John sought a papal release from Magna Carta, while Richard II soon revoked the charters of manumission. While it is obvious that the two kings were dealing with very different classes and types of people, the themes underpinning the Peasants' Revolt were deeply rooted and well articulated. Why was there this sudden burst of feeling? From where had the ideas welled up? What had happened in the intervening years?

This book sees the crucial dynamic in this changing world as being the growth of 'legal consciousness'. The product of legal culture and experiences (at the level of both the individual and groups within society), 'legal consciousness' can be seen both as an active element shaping people's values, beliefs and aspirations and also as a passive agent providing a reserve of knowledge, memory and reflective thought, influencing not simply the development of the law and legal system, but also political attitudes. The law in some form or other touched the lives of the entire population of medieval England. Focusing on the different contexts of law and legal relations, this book aims to shift the traditional conceptual boundaries of 'law', portraying both the law's inherent diversity and its multi-dimensional character. Indeed, this study emphasises the need to see law (or 'The Law') not simply as an external mechanism regulating daily life, but as an integral part of the way in which social relations were actually lived out and experienced.

By offering a re-conceptualisation of the role of the law in medieval England, this book aims to engage the reader in new ways of thinking about the political events occurring during the thirteenth and fourteenth centuries. It considers the long-term effects of John's encounter with forces questioning royal government and provides a new explanation for the dangerous state of affairs faced by the boy-king during the Peasants' Revolt over a century and a half later. The book puts forward the view that the years subsequent to the signing of Magna Carta yielded a new (and shifting) perspective, both in terms of prevailing concepts of 'law' and 'justice' and with regard to political life in general. Reissued at intervals in the years after 1215, Magna Carta enshrined aspects of custom and provided a model for legislation. Yet significantly, it can be seen to have reached beyond the purely legal content of its chapters, becoming (along with a duty to uphold the common law) the touchstone of good governance and symbolising a body of 'rights' applicable to all. Magna Carta evolved from certain deeply held notions and beliefs about law and government and, in turn, it created in people's minds expectations concerning royal justice and the king's authority: expectations as to what the law was enabling or providing; how royal authority was exercised; how the legal system operated; and how redress could be achieved.

In terms of the substantive law and the operation of the judicial system, there is a significant contrast between the early thirteenth century and the late fourteenth century, one which serves to underline the constructive, evolutionary process occurring over the two centuries. As will be demonstrated over the course of successive chapters, there was a decisive shift during the thirteenth and fourteenth centuries not only in the number of actions and types of procedures, but also in the nature of the judicial agencies and the personnel staffing them. These changes coincided with – and indeed predicated the development of – a distinctive legal profession, and emphasised the participatory role (either as jurors or as litigants) of members of particular communities. Alterations in substance and scope also affected (and were influenced by) the contexts in which the law developed and was administered, the way which it was perceived and the criteria by which it was judged.

As a critical analysis of developments occurring over the two centuries, this study adopts a holistic and interdisciplinary approach that reflects the cross-cultural trends and qualities inherent in the law. The law as an object of inquiry is pursued in terms of its interaction with other crucial areas of everyday life, notably the political, economic, social and religious spheres. In order to develop this interpretative framework, attempts have been made to register the communication of ideas and understand the internalisation of symbols by employing evidence of a literary, dramatic and visual nature and by adopting modes of thinking currently being developed in cultural history, art history, psychology, sociology and anthropology. By taking advantage of the perspectives afforded from the standpoint of other disciplines, by looking at historical periods more thematically, and by asking the right types of questions of material realistically susceptible to cross-cultural analysis, illuminating comparisons can be drawn and conceptual breakthroughs made in pursuit of the role of law in history.

In so doing, this book moves beyond the somewhat restrictive or myopic view of the law and legal institutions afforded in many conventional interpretations and espouses the aims and values of the 'new legal history': a historiographical and methodological revisionism that has developed apace over the closing decades of the twentieth century. A key platform in this approach has been exploration of the interface between the legal and the social. Revitalising historical thought and bringing a veritable renaissance to the writing of legal history, the new 'movement' has significantly altered perceptions of law and society, particularly for those studying the early-modern and modern periods.[1] This in itself is only part of a wider movement in social history.[2]

The role of ideology

This book takes as its starting point the need for a conceptual basis for an understanding of law in history and so seeks to explore the role of ideology in both law and politics. This chimes conveniently with the requests made over the last decade by proponents of a 'new constitutional history' of late medieval England that historians should focus not just on the tangible elements of royal government, its administration, patronage and personalities, but also on ideas, mentalities, values and principles.[3] Several writers have already underlined the centrality of the law to medieval society (from both a local and national perspective) and have stressed the importance of ascertaining and assessing the influences on – and attitudes towards – the policies adopted by the Crown, especially concerning matters of public order and social control.[4] Indeed, consideration of contemporary views of kingship and aristocratic authority in terms of values and expectations has proved a useful 'tool' when examining the functioning of medieval government in the reigns of Henry V and Henry VI.[5]

Yet, significant and illuminating as such studies may be, to be concerned solely with elite ideologies, the views and guiding principles of landowners and lawyers – in effect the governing classes – runs the risk of creating a rather rarified, one-dimensional model of political involvement and negates the whole reasoning behind the search for 'discourses', modes of thought and silent voices.[6] An attempt must be made (however difficult) to draw upon a wider context of political and legal involvement, to engage with surviving sources (and their subtexts) in diverse ways and to seek to penetrate the ideas, beliefs and attitudes of people operating in different spheres from that of the comparatively well-studied gentry and lawyers: those with urban and mercantile interests, the lesser clergy, wealthy peasants and smaller landowners (both free and unfree).[7] In order to appreciate the drama and tensions of political events, we need to ask some basic questions. As one commentator has suggested, we should display 'a curiosity about what drove the rebels [in 1381], about what they thought and what they wanted'.[8]

Ideology itself has been described as a 'difficult, slippery and ambiguous concept'.[9] It is perhaps best thought of as comprising strategy, motive, attitude and commitment – as being the justificatory dimension of a particular culture based on patterns of belief and value. The rhetoric employed or the expression of certain ideas can often provide vital clues towards perceiving the relevant thought-structures, particularly when claims are made about the nature or condition of society and the direction in which it is perceived to be heading. As 'matrices for the creation of collective consciousness', ideologies can evolve naturally among the lower echelons of society, the socially subordinate and inferior sectors, as much as in socially superior or dominant ones. Such claims should not be seen as purely class-related nor restricted to a literate intellectual elite, but applicable to overlapping and interactive social groups.[10]

The construction of an ideology, however, presupposes the formation and operation of the requisite driving 'consciousness'. Consciousness should perhaps be regarded as the thoughts and feelings that exist in the mind which have been translated into attitudes, but have not yet been refined into an ideology. In other words, an ideology stems from the ordering, rationalising, contextualising and articulating of conscious thought. It is important for historians to have at least a basic understanding of the mental processes at work since it enables them not only to identify and extrapolate possible influences on an individual or a group of people, but also to hypothesise as to the ways in which the individual or group perceived events and relationships and how their perceptions may have accorded with or, indeed, differed from reality.

Analysis of the mental processes behind conscious and unconscious thought demonstrates how information about the human environment is accumulated and how experiences themselves are processed, adjusted, transformed and stored before being reproduced and recalled. The most prominent function of consciousness is held by neuro-physicists to be the construction and rearrangement of mental 'schemata' when stimulated to do so by an external (and often complex) situation. The experience is stored and remains 'unconscious' until stimulated either accidentally or through a deliberate attempt to recapture the memory. Generally the individual will not take in every minute detail of a situation, but create instead a general impression from which the probable details are then reconstructed. The conscious reconstruction of a past event held in the memory may of course be (or result in) a misconception of the original event or experience. It has also been shown that recollection is accompanied by the emotions associated with the occasion. The psychological manifestation of this process is the creation of an 'attitude', perhaps a feeling, the effect of which is then justified by the mind in the process of remembering.[11] As F. C. Bartlett pointed out in his influential study on theories of memory:[12]

> The need to remember becomes active, an attitude is set up; in the form of sensory images or, just as often, of isolated words, some part of the event which is to be remembered recurs, and the event is then reconstructed on the basis of the relation of this specific bit of material to the general mass of relevant past experiences or reactions, the latter functioning, after the manner of the 'schema', as an active organised setting .... In many cases, when the material had to be dealt with at a distance, as in remembering, the dominant features were the first to appear, either in image form, or descriptively through the use of language. In fact, this is one of the great functions of images in mental

life: to pick items out of 'schemata' and to rid the organism of overdetermination by the last preceding member of a given series. I would like to hold that this ... could not occur except through the medium of consciousness .... The theory brings remembering into line with imagining, an expression of the same activities ... it gives to consciousness a definite function other than the mere fact of being aware.

Assessing the functioning and effects of an intangible concept such as consciousness obviously presents difficulties, especially as it comprises inner experiences not easily discernible except in an external manifestation. It would be wrong, however, to adopt the attitude that, if it cannot be measured precisely it does not in fact exist or the general context of thought cannot be explored.[13] Psychologists and anthropologists regard conscious perception as constituting an act of recognition – a conceptual alignment based on previously stored cultural patterns: '[T]hinking, conceptualisation, formulation, comprehension, understanding or what have you consists not of ghostly happenings in the head but of a matching of the states and processes of symbolic models against the states and processes of the wider world.'[14]

Medieval life, as with life today, was lived or experienced within a complex of relations. Some of these relations, be they legal or social, could be called external or objective relations and important in determining the nature of a particular society: they were hierarchic, gendered, subordinating and empowering in ways that the individual was unable to affect and into which he or she was cast at birth. These objective sets of conditions and social practices should not of course be regarded as the sole influences on the individual or indeed as the final determinants of a society's profile. Social relations can also be regarded as having an internal or subjective element. This might be perceived from the way a particular life is lived, how the individual reacts within a given culture, and how he or she contends with and constructs different languages and discourses. It is the overall 'experience', however, which forms both the individual and collective senses of 'consciousness' and enables people to appear to act with purpose and intention when viewed within a historical setting.[15] The impact of the ideological dimension of law, therefore, should be measured in terms of the law's influence on people of all walks of life and especially in their relations with other individuals and groups.

We should not necessarily think in terms of there being a single or universal ideology among the lower orders or assume that the dominant or governing classes themselves espoused the same ideology. There are other problems as well: we should be careful how we attribute an ideology or interest to a particular group. What may appear as a homogeneous group sharing the same ideology, may in fact be a disparate collection of people with diverse interests who give the illusion of operating as a collective. The Peasants' Revolt of the 1381, for instance, involved many people in the uprisings, some of whom were genuine peasants, but others were townsfolk, merchants and members of the gentry who had their own interests in fomenting rebellion. Moreover, as the Baronial Wars of the mid-thirteenth century illustrate, there could be a multiplicity of ideologies, sometimes competing, sometimes shared both *within* and *between* social groups and as such these ideologies could be concerned with reform, revolution or simply preservation of the status quo. There is also the temptation to view ideology as a positive affirmation of direction or with regard to considered goals: it can in fact disguise failure or loss of orientation. To some extent this may have been experienced after the civil wars of 1263 and 1322, or in 1327 following the deposition of Edward II, as the newly disorientated and demoralised groups sought a fresh, meaningful symbolic framework. The extent to which the disoriented could latch on to new ideas or embrace a different set of guiding principles (or in fact failed to do so, as the case may be) may of course say much about the success or failure of the succeeding administrations.

Ideologies of law are themselves multi-dimensional and operate on a number of different levels. In the medieval period it was possible for them to be articulated in both legal and essentially non-legal sources. They could stem from elements of a legal text (such as a statute, law report or treatise) or a judicial pronouncement (either a decision in a court case or an elaboration of legal rules) and they could arise from the association or fusion of different ideological elements (such as philosophical, religious, political, even satirical texts or quasi-legal documents). Institutions forming the royal judicial and administrative machine and other bodies, such as parliament, the county, urban and manorial courts, the Church, and the universities, could also create and disseminate ideology by providing an interface for the communication and exchange of ideas, beliefs and opinions. The actors themselves, whether legal professionals, litigants or those for whom (and upon whom) the law was enforced, as participants in the processes and thus creating the dialogues of law, were also eminently capable of reflecting upon and discussing their views and experiences.

The determining features of ideology are not wholly psychologically based: a pivotal role is played by culture. This study explores the ways in which the culture and life experiences enjoyed (or suffered) by medieval people informed their sense of law; and conversely, the manner in which their sense of law informed attitudes and aspirations, and consequently their life experiences. Some explanation of the term or concept of 'legal consciousness' is required. This phenomenon is regarded as having a definite function and is examined and employed as a term in both a specific and a general way. It is used in a narrow sense (Chapter 2) with reference to the advanced or refined legal consciousness redolent of the nascent legal profession. Indeed, it represents an obvious common feature of those steeped in the languages of the law, its rules and processes. Their primary viewpoint was determined by the various texts and practices associated with their privileged education and livelihood and it was they who, in turn, contributed to the intellectualising of the law and the espousal of ethical standards of professional behaviour. 'Legal consciousness' is also used in a broader sense to describe the reserves of knowledge and thought of those who experienced the law and legal institutions in everyday life, who participated in the legal culture, on whom it created an impression and for whom it provided an integral part of social relations (see Chapters 3 and 4). A coming together of these two forms of legal consciousness can be seen in the way that it infused and influenced both the institution of parliament and events occurring within the wider political arena (see Chapters 5 and 6).

In choosing the word 'growth' – a word imbued with active or developmental overtones – in the explanatory sub-title, 'The growth of legal consciousness', it is not intended to imply that before 1215 any form of legal consciousness was inert or dormant and that in some simple way over the course of nearly two centuries it gradually became a recognisable and important force for change. Historians writing on the Anglo-Saxon and Anglo-Norman periods have stressed the fact that concepts of law were strongly held and that people 'wrote, spoke, and thought in terms of law and laws'.[16] The difference between the periods should be seen in qualitative terms as regards the facilitative nature of legal consciousness. As psychologists and neuro-physicists have stated: to acquire a particular concept does not involve an increase in knowledge or mental faculties, rather it indicates that the information has been re-categorised and generalised.[17] In other words, a key element in the growth of legal consciousness was the ability to process, adjust and learn from past experiences and events. The shifting views in law and politics should be seen in terms of the mental readjustments being made over time by individuals and groups.

In the century and a half after Magna Carta, the nature of 'legal consciousness' changed in England: it became in some respects more focused and concentrated as people assimilated concepts of law and responded by thinking, talking and writing about them, and as the experience of law itself became more diversely spread across the population. Legal consciousness should be regarded as a complex phenomenon enabling people to reformulate their ideas and general opinions on the basis of their existing experiences and in accord with new legal opportunities. The process itself could be intermittent, though, rather than constant, depending on the nature of internal reflection and the stimulus of external events. The idea of 'growth' as encapsulated in the sub-title, therefore, is to be given a wide definition and considered as carrying connotations of germination and expansion (spreading, deepening, broadening, increasing) as well as elements of accumulation, maturation and evolution.

The contexts of law

The complexity of the medieval experience of law should be seen as a key component in the growth of legal consciousness. As A. L. Brown notes, 'English law was more elaborate than the law in any other kingdom in Europe at that time'[18] – one might add, both in terms of substantive law and with regard to its legal systems. Contrasts are inevitably drawn with the systems of law existing on the Continent at this time, but some commentators maintain that the perceptible differences, such as they were, should not be overdrawn: it was not so much the laws themselves which differed as the approaches to (and legal thinking behind) them and approaches to record-keeping.[19] Medieval England was graced not simply with a single, monolithic form of law, but several distinct types of law, sometimes competing, occasionally overlapping, invariably invoking different traditions, jurisdictions and modes of operation. Indeed, the variety and range of application was the main and remarkable characteristic.[20] In order to appreciate the diversity and variability of the English judicial scene, and the co-existence of different forms of legal relations, it is necessary to provide a fuller explanation of the forms of law in existence.

There were three main legal traditions operating in the country during the thirteenth and fourteenth centuries: common law, canon law and customary law, which were based on the justice dispensed by the various royal courts, the ecclesiastical courts, and the customary (or local) courts respectively. The 'common law' (while not a contemporary term as such) emerged from the knitting-together of customs and practices existing in Anglo-Saxon and Anglo-Norman times with the considerable administrative innovations put forward in the twelfth century under Henry II. As a body of rules and processes that was authorised by the king, it was intended to be applied in standard or 'common' form across the realm to guard against regionality and arbitrariness.[21] Canon law formed the governing principles and rules ('canon' in Greek) of the Western Church and therefore extended not only throughout the realm, but beyond it. Comprising first and foremost a body of papal decretals and promulgations, it also made use of the Roman civil-law tradition to provide a complex (though flexible) amalgam of traditions and procedures covering issues such as ecclesiastical discipline and morality. It was confusingly referred to by jurisprudential treatise writers as 'ius commune' (the 'common law') to distinguish it from provincial (ecclesiastical) legislation and local custom.[22] Customary law, by contrast, was theoretically multifarious and non-uniform in its applicability in that it consisted of local urban and village practices that were interpreted according to local 'custom' or convention. This was not usually a clearly articulated and systematic body of law, but a flexible collection of principles and habits deriving from (and adapted by) folk memory and the decisions made by the court and the body of the community.[23]

In addition to the three categories outlined above there existed other important specific types: statute law, forest law, the law of the march, the law merchant, maritime law and martial law. Some of these had links with the common law, customary law and Roman civil law, but were in some way separate or effectively hybrids of several traditions in that they were designed to fill gaps in the regulation of life that were not possible using the rules and procedures of the three main systems of law. Statutory legislation, sometimes referred to as 'new law' or 'special law', initially comprised pronouncements on a range of matters issued by the king and his council. With the growing supremacy of parliament during the fourteenth century, statutes rapidly became a second tier of law to be enforced in the royal courts in addition to the existing and evolving common law. As a reflection of this change in status and volume, the content also altered: taking on the regulation of human life and behaviour as well as confirming practices in existence.[24]

The area of jurisdiction covered by the forest laws was comparatively large: by the thirteenth century a quarter of England was covered by the royal forest. Accordingly, the laws of the forest were designed to protect the king's deer, trees and other woodland by-products as well as providing for a system of administration. They stood apart from the common law in that the laws themselves always contained an arbitrary element and the punishments (particularly for poaching) were disproportionately harsh.[25] The law of the march combined a recognition of the difficulties involved in maintaining law and order on the frontiers of the English realm (especially when they were actual war zones) with an acceptance of the necessity for the co-existence of – or an amalgamation with – neighbouring traditions and customs.[26] The codification in 1249 of the 'laws and customs of the march' provided the basis for border law in the Anglo-Scottish march, though the corpus was significantly developed under Edward III and consolidated in Richard II's reign.[27] The law pertaining to the Welsh marches was shaped and defined by voluntary charters in various lordships (such as Gower and Maelienydd), the subject matter being fairly similar from one to another.[28] No specific body of border provisions seems to have been in operation in Ireland, though it appears that inhabitants on the fringes of settled areas were allowed to come to agreements with individuals from the hinterland over compensation for wrongs suffered.[29]

Mercantile law, although not a definite code of laws, comprised a composite body of traders' customs that were applicable internationally and based on natural law principles of good faith and plain justice.[30] While there were some points of connection, its doctrines and procedures differed from both those of the common law and (to a lesser extent) the customs of boroughs. The laws were designed to provide swift justice and overcome problems which might confront and deter a foreign merchant seeking redress, such as local prejudice or an unfamiliarity with both the local and national customs. In this, as well as providing remedies for the ramifications of international trading, they were essentially trans-national in character.[31] The problems posed by differing legal traditions were also potentially faced by sailors who were in dispute with men of other nationalities. However, various bodies of maritime law had emerged, the earliest written forms dating from the late twelfth and early thirteenth centuries. The *Consolato del Mare* was widely used and favoured in the commercial centres of the Mediterranean, but the maritime law relied upon by English sailors comprised an international body of rules (operated in the later fourteenth century through the Court of Admiralty), based partly on civil law and partly on the Laws of Oleron and the Laws of Wisby.[32] The 'law of arms' (certainly up to the mid-fourteenth century) was an ill-defined body of military customs covering a range of matters related to arms and warfare occurring both within the realm and beyond the sea. The procedures used did not follow common law and judgments were often summary. The hereditary Constable and Marshal of the Royal Household exercised jurisdiction in disputes over indentures, traitors, prisoners and ransoms (later through the Court of Chivalry), though jurisdiction over matters of discipline and armorial bearings was also accorded to constables and captains holding summary courts in the field.[33]

While the various systems of law can be isolated for analysis, they did not in practice inhabit such discrete categories. Customary law by definition, as particular local practices and commonly held assumptions, provided a basis for most, if not all, forms of law. The English common law itself was, according to *Bracton*'s 'Introductio' at least, a generalised and standardised form of custom. Indeed, it was usually referred to as the 'customary law of England' or the 'law and custom of the realm'. Moreover, the dominant perception of the supreme, unadulterated common law, which has been reinforced down the ages by historians of the common-law tradition, is something of an illusion. Civil-law concepts in fact permeated many areas of law and politics and were utilised not only in ecclesiastical matters, but in the prerogative courts (notably the courts dealing with Admiralty and Chivalry business), in international law and in Anglo-Scottish border law.[34]

As was suggested above, within the different jurisdictions there were considerable overlaps and mutual benefits as well as elements of competition and exclusivity. The Court of Chivalry, for instance, was censured in fourteenth-century parliamentary petitions (and restricted by statute in 1384) for encroaching on matters which arguably ought to have been tried at common law, despite the fact that there was clearly a jurisdictional overlap when dealing with cases of debt which related to military contracts or appeals of treason in time of war.[35] As a multifarious body of customs, border law in Wales was influenced not just by English common law, but by the indigenous Welsh law (*Cyfraith Hywel*), the impact of which was particularly noticeable in the northern Welsh marches, especially in criminal law and in the rules relating to land transactions.[36] In the counties neighbouring the Scottish border, Northumberland, Cumberland and Westmorland, the common law was habitually complemented, supplemented and occasionally even overridden by the law of the march.[37]

The common law was itself influenced by other forms of law. Some early contractual actions – such as deceit for sale of goods without warrant or with false warranties of quality, and the action of *assumpsit* for contractual negligence – resemble or have their models in the law merchant.[38] Similarly, while there is evidence that the customary courts responded to the practices of the royal courts in that they copied some of the forms and procedures used at there, the traffic of ideas and forms was not all one-way. The practices in some manorial courts (and notably Chester city court) pre-empted the statute *Quia emptores* (1290) with its use of grants of surrender and admittance when transferring land,[39] while certain common-law writ actions (such as *mort d'ancestor* and *cui in vita*) likewise had similarly phrased counterparts in use in the manorial courts.[40] The city of London (and some other local courts) also prefigured the central courts in providing remedies for negligent fire-keeping, negligent handling of animals and certain breaches of contractual duty.[41] The continued vitality of the customary courts and the range of actions and business they entertained not only point towards an intimate relationship with the royal courts, but a significant role in the formation of legal attitudes.

Although technically spiritual and temporal were separate and distinct entities, in practice the ecclesiastical and secular spheres proved to be permeable in a number of ways. Indeed, the institutions of Church and state mutually influenced each other's development in that they continually mixed or exchanged practices, personnel and ideas.[42] First, there are indications that the king's courts encroached on a number of areas of the Church's traditional jurisdiction. Benefices and appurtenances became subject to secular law and the royal courts provided the forum for disputes concerning the patronage of livings, as well as their land and income.[43] The king's courts also appear to have accepted some disputes involving testamentary and matrimonial matters (including adultery), and through statutory legislation and judicial examination exhibited a concern for aspects of parenting and childcare – traditionally the preserve of the Church.[44] This was matched by the ecclesiastical courts occasionally moving outside their normal concern for morality and personal conduct in trying to usurp areas of secular law such as debt litigation. Cases concerning petty debts were generally heard in the manorial and borough courts, but many instances came before the ecclesiastical courts. Restrictions on the reach of the secular arm also featured in the alternative sanctions (or relief) afforded those criminals who – by reaching the sanctuary of a church and remaining there – were allowed to abjure the realm, or who upon conviction in the king's court were able to avoid capital punishment by (successfully) claiming benefit of clergy and transferring to the 'softer option' of ecclesiastical jurisdiction. In addition to jurisdictional competition, parallel jurisdiction was exercised in inheritance matters, instances of invalid marriage, and in bastardy cases (where there was a possibility of opting for either lay or episcopal procedures).[45] Sometimes litigation was brought in both courts at the same time.[46]

There were also overlaps in terms of personnel. Half the royal judges were clerks in holy orders, at least until the laicisation of the judiciary, which became widespread in the fourteenth century.[47] This could cause some conflicts of conscience. William Raleigh, a senior royal judge before becoming bishop of Norwich and then Winchester, sided with the barons in their refusal to recognise legitimation by a subsequent marriage, which Pope Alexander III had espoused as canon law.[48] The principal officials of royal government and of the later fourteenth-century prerogative courts of chancery and exchequer chamber, the chancellor and the treasurer, were frequently drawn from the episcopate. Similarly, senior Church leaders were involved in local justice. Bishops, abbots and prioresses, as lords of temporal possessions, controlled manorial or honorial courts at which they sometimes, though not generally, presided in person, exercising responsibility for criminal and customary law.[49] Examples of spiritual incumbents whose authority stretched over a vast territory include the bishop of Durham, ruler of the Palatinate of Durham, and the abbot of Bury St Edmunds, whose lands covered nearly half a county. The peace commissions of the later fourteenth century also reserved positions for spiritual leaders in recognition of their place in local society, though the appointments were purely honorific and such figures rarely, if ever, sat at actual sessions. The peculiar nature of the Scottish frontier, however, may have been an exception since it is clear that Bishop Appleby of Carlisle, one of the royal wardens of the march, was expected to perform his duties and turn up to court sessions (known as days of the march) in spite of his reservations at the weight of business and its suitability for a clergyman.[50] Also in the context of border peace commissions, one of the first appointments to the post-1344 style 'quorum' for the march area in 1373 was the civil lawyer, Master John Appleby, dean of St Paul's Cathedral in London.[51]

The religious side influenced the secular world of law both in terms of substantive legal principles and in the psychological overlap between law and morality. In addition to their invocations of divine law, biblical quotations and elements of sermonising, some legal texts of the thirteenth and fourteenth centuries blend the languages of religion and law often using the term 'sin' (either the Latin *peccatum* or the French *pecche*) as interchangeable with 'offences, injuries, wrongs'.[52] With a number of thirteenth-century and early fourteenth-century judges trained in the 'learned laws' at one of the universities, or at least having some knowledge of the maxims of Roman law, it is not surprising that some of the principles with which they were familiar should influence their thoughts when considering their native law. Maxims of canon law such as *volenti non fit injuria* (to a willing person no injury is done) – now firmly embedded in the common law of tort – and *nemo obligatus ad impossibile* (no one is obliged to do the impossible) were cited by Chief Justice William Bereford in about 1310.[53] Moreover, the chancery's gradual development as a 'court of conscience' owed much to the procedures followed by lawyers of the ecclesiastical courts. 'Leaving matters to the conscience' was a frequent recourse among lawyers seeking reconciliation among litigants, such as Agnes atte Hull and John Weston, who came to the Ely Consistory Court in a marital suit in 1376. The willingness of the chancellor to take decisions based 'in equity', in other words on fairness and right, was also influenced by the *Denuntiato Evangelica* (a canonical device that enabled someone suing in certain secular matters to have the defendant face trial after two admonitions). It was felt that petitioners had a right on grounds of conscience to have secular causes brought before the church courts so as to ensure the upholding of natural law. Equity itself was founded on the medieval notion that 'right' and 'law' could not be overlooked without endangering the soul and thus formed the basis for a more discretionary, morally-based form of justice.[54]

A moral dimension to law was also invoked through preaching and other Church teaching. The Church's views on guilt and the state of a someone's soul in the eyes of God engendered concern for 'spiritual manslaughter', which was delineated by canonists as a category of homicide, but distinguished from 'corporeal homicide' in that it was regarded as inhabiting the world of thought, intent and impulse. Misunderstandings (on the part of the compilers of penitentials and vernacular manuals for clergy) of the canonists' distinctions could give rise to a conflation of, for example, deadly hate and deprivation of food, which (in the minds of thirteenth-century reformers) led to 'spiritual homicide' being seen as a social crime against the poor and oppressed.[55] In the fourteenth century, many churchmen put forward the belief that since recourse to the legal system symbolised the collapse of normal obligations of Christian brotherhood, those who represented the human face of the law (and whose professional life in fact depended on litigation) must be stirring up animosity within society since they stood to gain by it. John Wycliffe, for example, was particularly vehement against the moral reprehensibility of formal dispute settlement.[56]

The institutional aspect of law (in all its various forms) is clearly an important and necessary area to consider. Nevertheless, it was only one of the contexts affecting legal relations and the legal world-view. The concepts and strictures of the different systems of law were frequently abrogated, circumvented and supplemented by alternative means of dispute settlement and more informal sanctions. The importance of extra-judicial forms is demonstrated, firstly, by the popularity of arbitration as a way of settling disputes: a method whereby all parties could be pacified rather than one humiliated or punished. Negotiation and private treaties were actively encouraged among the gentry and members of the nobility,[57] but also widely employed by merchants as a means of achieving compromise in trade and commercial disputes.[58] Settlements made outside the courtroom – or 'lovedays' as they were known – were equally favoured by the less affluent parts of society and took place even at the borders of the kingdom, where they were sometimes known as 'days of the march'. Undoubtedly a key resource (either as natural recourse or in last resort), arbitration or mediation embodied a significant response to a breakdown in relations in potentially providing for amicable and non-confrontational approaches.[59]

Informal pressures towards compromise and conformity were also employed behind the closed doors of the gilds, misteries and religious confraternities.[60] The Gild of the Assumption in London, for example, expressly forbade members from embarking on court action against each other before the gild had had an opportunity to settle the argument.[61] The Pepperers' Fraternity of St Antonin, similarly, placed pressure on members not to submit disputes against fellow members to a public court (unless a felony had been committed) and established their own private court within the trade to which differences could be brought for arbitration and settled swiftly and cheaply.[62] Private settlement within the bounds of the family, affinity or work association was probably a natural and necessary first step – one that should be kept in mind – to avoid bringing disrepute upon a particular community. Where the private failed, more public methods of shaming, including expulsion or exclusion, might be considered.[63]

Again, we should not regard the formal judicial apparatus and extra-legal methods as incompatible or mutually exclusive. Nor were out-of-court settlements and informal sanctions viewed simply as an alternative. Non-institutional forms, significantly, operated both *within* and *beyond* the legal order of the state. Indeed, the motives behind their employment and the particular forms they took relied in part on the very existence of an established legal system; and litigants recognised the benefits of utilising both law courts and arbitrament. For instance, initiating litigation might be seen simply as a preliminary stage in the arbitration process; and could be threatened or continued if the parties were unable or unwilling to agree suitable terms. Moreover, arbitration was sometimes recommended in commercial cases when, in the opinion of the judges, it was the best option for the parties. Lawyers were often chosen as arbitrators or were employed as the architects of a settlement. Indeed, professional vetting of the arbitrament was recognised as a prerequisite to ensure that the agreement was legally sound and unchallengeable in the courts.[64] In mercantile arbitrations there was often an implicit relationship with the common law in that a sanction against a resumption of hostilities or one party reneging on the negotiated treaty was found in the arbitrators' imposition on both parties of heavy sums (bonds), which were enforceable at common law (or later in chancery).[65] Occasionally, the stylised gathering of supporters for a loveday was misinterpreted (accidentally or deliberately) as a form of conspiracy or armed violence and could result in the presentment of one or both sides at forthcoming judicial sessions.[66] Even outright violence could prove the basis for a defence (against a scold, for instance) or in combination with arbitration be regarded as litigation by other means, thereby eroding the distinction between orderly law and disorderly violence.[67]

Another important facet of medieval life involving an essentially non-institutional exhibition of legal concepts, one frequently overlooked by those focusing solely on the law and legal system, was that twilight zone or interface between law and anarchy, namely 'misrule'. Misrule, in the form of symbolic inversion or transgressive actions, appears to have been a significant and well-established element in the medieval psyche. It characteristically found expression in the *marginalia* of illuminated manuscripts, and in dramatic and literary works.[68] But it was also exhibited in 'real life' situations in the ceremonies and customs associated with urban and village life, especially carnival festivities and religious or civic processions. As conscious, expressive behaviour, misrule in these situations usually involved an intermingling of social categories and presented an alternative to commonly held codes and values. Social historians and anthropologists have generally regarded inversion and transgression as a conservative phenomenon: a safety mechanism for society, allowing dissident elements to 'let off steam'.[69] Although some writers consider the phenomenon to have more radical overtones, believing that subversion was allowed in order that it could be contained more effectively,[70] it has been suggested that in fact these two interpretative models are limited and overlook not only the complexity of the different customs and the flexibility of their symbolism, but also the *range* of possible functions and the specific *context* (in terms of timing, location, setting and historical background) in which a given custom or behaviour trope appears. Indeed, in examining the political and social context in which misrule occurs we should not divorce it from other conventional forms of action and we should at the same time be prepared to regard it, firstly, in terms of wider strategies employed by groups within society and, secondly, as part of a meaningful social dialogue incorporating more flexible notions of negotiation and exchange.[71]

Where does this leave our over-arching sense of a context for law? Is the phenomenon of misrule reconcilable with the apparatus of law and order? It is, when seen in the context of a perspective that views social control and dispute settlement as existing and operating within a continuum: legal institutions and concerns for public order would represent one end of the spectrum; and informal sanctions, private forms of ordering and misrule would stretch towards the other end. This model allows for a multiplicity of forms within the concept of law, and allows for diverse and overlapping forms and methods.

Law in the mind

The aspects encompassed or touched by the law – aspects outlined above – represent the building blocks for an over-arching sense of the law in context, forming a gateway to an understanding of people's direct experience of law in medieval times. We can also gain some insight into the way law was indirectly experienced (and the mental world of law) by examining the different ways in which 'law' was communicated both to individuals and social groups and by attempting to decipher the 'code' by which their experiences (and the information gleaned from them) were actively recorded and replayed. Research work in the semiotics of law has suggested that law has the capacity to impinge on consciousness in subtle and widely diffuse ways through the media of language, image and symbol: 'Law is a material presence, a visual structure of everyday life, a heritable form of repetition which comes to constitute in a very real sense part of the nature of things .... It is through symbols, its forms of appearance, its phenomenality, its emblematisation of persons and of public space that law makes itself felt.'[72]

Medieval life was redolent with image and symbolism. One has only to look at the margins of medieval books, stained-glass windows or the texts of writers and preachers alike to become aware of the emphasis upon image and the imagination employed through pictorial narratives, mental pictures and clever literary analogies.[73] It is more than probable, therefore, that people in the Middle Ages were more alive to the inflections and nuances of iconography than we are today. Indeed, it has been argued that the way people's minds worked and the connections they made have changed significantly.[74] We should not underestimate, therefore, the scope of the visual dimension and its capacity to heighten legal consciousness. The formative influence of visual imagery in the promotion of law in all its aspects, and its reception by those who encountered it not only in the routine judicial context, but also as an inherent component of contemporary life, should be emphasised.[75]

The clearest mental impressions may have been formed from the public spectacle afforded by the law and lawyers in operation. The advent of the royal justices in a particular venue for judicial sessions was heralded by prior proclamation and much preparation in the town. There was undoubtedly a procession of the justices and their clerks, who would have made a fine spectacle complete with banners and their distinctive form of dress. This is illustrated nicely in a descriptive scene in the mid-fourteenth century poem *Winner and Waster*:[76]

> Another banere es upbrayde with a bende of grene,
> With thre hedis white-hered with howes one lofte,
> Croked full craftyly, and kembid in the nekke:
> Thies are ledis of this londe that schold our lawes yeme.

[Another banner with a green band is unfurled/With three white-haired heads with lawyers' caps above them/Curled very skilfully and combed at the neck/These are men of this land who should guard our laws.] In some towns, such as Chester, a horn was sounded to indicate that judicial sessions were in progress; in others the ringing of bells may have heralded to all their start.[77]

The parading of prisoners (especially those charged following well-publicised crimes) and the public nature of the executions at the end of the sessions sent a strong signal of justice in action. While the hanging (and occasionally burning) of men and women may have been a way of demonstrating status and authority, the figure left on the gibbet may also have been designed to act as a deterrent.[78] The gathering of crowds of ordinary people to watch and cheer at the gruesome fate of traitors was itself redolent both of the attitude of awe, respect and fear which the Crown wished to inculcate and the way in which the public at large could be attracted by or drawn into such events. People watched the beheading and hanging, the drawing of the bowels and entrails and the quartering of the body. Following this the head would be put on public display and then, symbolically, the traitor's remains would be dispersed to the 'four corners' of the kingdom. Each action was in itself referential in some way. The significance of the decollation lay in his status as an outlaw and a traitor,[79] while the burning of the entrails was in respect of their believed role in producing blasphemous thoughts. Such a fate befell the Scottish rebel, William Wallace, in 1305. His remains were then escorted northwards in procession and deposited at Newcastle, Berwick, Perth and Stirling. The punishment, decidedly brutal (and one which impressed even medieval chroniclers), was clearly designed to deter people from rebellion.[80]

In court itself, particularly at the royal courts at Westminster, a rather different quality – an air of ritual and mystery – would have been observed by lay persons attending in the capacity of litigants or jurors.[81] Lawyers and judges, who appeared to be the 'priests' of the law – its guardians and interpreters – were clothed in distinctive special vestments: the serjeants sporting the close-fitting coif (similar to a white skull cap, but tied beneath the chin) and wearing robes of rayed (striped) or parti-coloured material; the (non-clerical) judges wearing the same, but probably also having a tabard and hood.[82] They communicated in forms of language that made comprehension difficult for some both linguistically and intellectually: by employing perhaps as many as three languages (English, French and Latin) and by reciting complicated rhetorical formulae.[83] The celebrants would also have observed certain procedures and maintained positions of strict hierarchical deference within the court itself. In Westminster Hall the justices sat on a raised bench with the clerks positioned at a table below them. The court furniture was also important, with the use of a wooden bar as a means of physically separating the justices from the parties, who would have to approach the bar to speak.[84]

The quasi-religious aspect of the legal world was further enhanced with the use of sacred oaths and gospel books. Before writing became common, gospel books or valuable objects (such as swords, knives or horns) were taken and preserved as symbols of a property conveyance.[85] Indeed, technical rites such as ceremonial transfer or conveyance were as much a part of the substantive law and legal procedure as exemplifying its mystery. The assertion of a right of entry, for instance, a necessary first step in an assize of novel disseisin, had by the later fourteenth century become largely symbolic, so that in one case a baby (the rightful heir) was positioned at the entrance to a house until the uncle (the disseisor) came home; while in another case, the court regarded it as sufficient demonstration of intention (once entrance through the main door had been prevented) for the plaintiff to have got half-way through a window.[86]

Trial by battle, although it was an obsolete option in English 'civil' cases, retained its symbolic nature as a 'supernatural' ordeal in those 'criminal' cases where a felon had turned king's evidence and also in the procedure of Anglo-Scottish border law.[87]

On a slightly different level, the legal space was imbued with symbolism of its own. Whether it was a court session or an arbitration, the venue and its architectural or locational features carried an underlying significance. There were a number of things to take into consideration: whether the occasion merited formality or was best served by informality; whether it was essentially a public or a private matter. The significance of an event could alter depending on whether it took place in the enclosed space of a building or out of doors in the open. If it were held indoors, importance might be attached then to whether the building was dedicated primarily to sacred use or was designed for secular purposes. Churches were regularly used for secular business in medieval times, providing a venue for meetings and at times a place for the writing-out of judicial writs.[88] The atmosphere of a church, however, added much-needed solemnity or a religious dimension to an arbitration or court proceedings. In 1364, for example, an arbitration award between a purser and a saddler was pronounced in the church of St Thomas of Acres in London.[89] Naturally there was some blurring of the resonances: sessions held outdoors were not necessarily synonymous with informality. Court sessions were sometimes held outside, often under an ash or an oak tree (the latter a traditional symbol of solidity, age and wisdom).[90] Sessions held outdoors readily invoked images of natural justice – Louis IX of France was famously portrayed as dispensing justice under an oak tree at Vincennes[91] – and it was a concept effectively employed in popular literature when it was said that true justice was available only in the natural world of the greenwood.[92] Natural features such as a river were also capable of imbuing metaphorical overtones. A 'loveday' held in Lancashire in 1350 at a place called 'Lovesbridge' suggests that the two sides met on their respective sides of the river (at what may have been a traditional location for settlement of disputes) and then symbolically bridged the divide.[93]

The choice of venue did not necessarily involve a deliberate or noticeable distinction between 'public' and 'private' spheres. The very nature of a court session (wherever it was held) was that it was open to all to attend, view and hear, even though the matter might essentially be a private one. This too was often the way in an out-of-court settlement. Although it was in fact a private treaty, the reconciliation might be held outside for all the world to witness, or if inside, open to or reported to an audience, thus becoming a public act of recognition.[94] The similarities between this and the private arrangement turned public event that usually enshrined the solemnisation of marriage vows would not be lost on contemporaries. The similarity between various words and phrases used in land charters and those in marital contracts (especially the *habenda et tenendi* – 'to have and to hold' – in the marriage vows) is also significant.[95] Both the arbitration treaty and marriage contract were pronounced in a church and so there would be a familiar mixture of 'sacred' and 'secular' associations. Indeed, when marriage broke down or one of the parties misbehaved, a public shaming in full view of the community was often the Church's main recourse. In the thirteenth century this usually took the form of a whipping at least three times around the church or the market place, though in later years the penance was 'softened' to walking in procession dressed in penitential style and carrying a candle.[96] The observation by a wider audience than the immediate parties was thus an important element both in legal and religious spheres. Moreover, it demonstrates that the elements common to dispute settlements and marriage were given similar treatment while nevertheless operating in different contexts. Then again, just as marriage contracts were sometimes formed clandestinely (albeit using familiar forms of words and ritual),[97] reconciliation in disputes was not necessarily in public. In some cases the arbitrator's actual award was for the parties to sit down to a (presumably private) meal together or go for a drink together in the tavern, invoking traditional symbols of friendship.[98] The implications did not stop there, however, since a meal had quasi-religious resonances, while the drink in the tavern also offered a public view of renewed relations.

The written word was a powerful symbol of the influence of the law. While in the thirteenth and fourteenth centuries the possession of documents and charters in some cases reflected the ability to read and/or write, the possession of books and documents was more obviously a mark of status. The size and intricate ornamental design of some statute books signifies that they were what we would term 'coffee-table' books or the medieval equivalent of a set of the *Encylopaedia Britannica* – mainly there for show and only occasional referred to – but such volumes were probably viewed as possessing an inherent (perhaps even sacred) authority that was passed on and shared by the book's owner.[99] The symbolic power of the law stretched more especially to documents such as Domesday Book, Magna Carta and (possibly) the Statute of Winchester (see Chapter 6). These texts were appealed to for the perceived rights, freedoms and customs that they purportedly contained and extolled (whether or not they actually enshrined such rights even remotely in the form that it was evidently believed they did).

Images could also encapsulate concepts of power and rights: the indent of the great seal of the king, which embellished even the humblest writ, utilised a double-sided image: on one side the seal portrayed the king enthroned in all his majesty (signifying law-giving), while on the reverse it showed the king riding as a knight (signifying military might).[100] Seals were used to authenticate documents and symbolically reinforced documentary proof (which could be inadequate without one). The importance of a charter could be enhanced (and duly recognised) by an impressive number of seals attached to it. Outside official circles, seals were regularly used by ordinary people, who were perfectly capable of distinguishing the (hated) 'green wax' used in exchequer documents.[101] The sword was a symbolic instrument of conquest and when produced (in a predominantly oral culture) could authenticate the acquisition of property as much (if not better in some people's minds) than seals or charters. By the 1290s, Earl Warrene's brandishing of 'an ancient and rusty sword' during Edward I's inquiries into franchise holding (according to the well-known story) may not have cut much ice in terms of proving his right to his lands, but it appealed graphically to a memory image and a time when title to property could be proved by possession of a sword.[102]

Another interesting example can be found in the way a document's accompanying artwork (which was supplied by the recipient soon after the document was written) could effectively enhance its authority. Using subjects of symbolic or heraldic significance, the illustrations manifested the aspirations and achievements of both corporate bodies and individuals.[103] A royal charter awarding hunting rights to Roger Pilkington in 1291, for example, is framed by realistic pictures of birds, animals and trees – clearly descriptive of and signifying the privileges being granted in the document.[104] Marginal images in the Morgan Register of Writs, which are placed opposite examples of chancery writs, directly represent the legal rights contained in the text of the writ. For example, the right of free fishing is depicted by a pond and two green hills, while a little man chopping down a tree with an axe refers to the writ initiating an action against someone preventing him (the owner of the book) from exercising his right of cutting timber.[105] Charter decoration was used during the Hundred Years War by both the English and French kings as a form of royal propaganda, with claims and counter-claims expressed through iconographic symbolism.[106]

In a more general sense, the common law possessed an aura and identity arising from its nature as custom and practice. In the same way that customary law, the 'remembered' custom of the local community engendered a sense of 'the way things were done', the common law too, where necessary, relied on the memory of the oldest and wisest men in cases where there was no documentation or the record was for some reason distrusted. By accommodating the fact that what the human memory recorded was not necessarily the historical truth (although it is important that it was believed to be) the common law thus was able to retain a certain flexibility as to how things were done, allowing for changes in perception and fading memories. It was on this basis that the limit of legal memory at any one point was considered to stretch back for about a hundred years (the range covered by the oldest living person). The period before this was accordingly known as 'time out of mind'. The artificiality of 'legal memory' became apparent when the statutory limit on how far back chronologically this period extended ceased to be updated. In statutes of 1275 and 1293 Edward I set the limit of legal memory for his reign as being 3 September 1189 (the date of Richard I's coronation). At the end of his reign it was not altered (and is still fixed at 1189 today) because a new reliance on documentary evidence rather than human memory made updating it no longer so crucial.[107] Nevertheless it created by default a fictional time by which matters of ownership, possession and usage were (and are) theoretically judged. This in turn helped to foster notions of the tradition and timelessness of the common law.

The idea of English common law as an 'ancient law' was not just something invented by legal historians of the seventeenth and eighteenth centuries, such as Coke and Blackstone, to buttress their stand on the common law as a distinctive form of law. It was a notion very much current in the Middle Ages. This can be seen, for example, in the words judges and lawyers used to describe the law, contrasting statute law ('novel ley') with common law ('ancien ley'). A concern for legal continuity, and an interest in the old laws, is apparent also in the work of chroniclers, such as Andrew Horn, and the writers of treatises such as the *Mirror of Justices*.[108] In his manuscript compilations, for instance, Horn introduces and explains the laws from the Anglo-Saxon period up to the reign of Edward I in order to justify historically the law the contemporary courts were applying. His *Annales Londinienses*, like the annals of many monastic chroniclers before him, incorporate documents bearing witness to civic precedents to provide what one historian has described as 'a contemporary record of the triumph of lawful and customary government over the spirit of party, both in England as a whole and in London'.[109] This appeal to the past may have developed out of a genuine regard for and interest in legal tradition, but it may also have grown out of a feeling of dissatisfaction or unease during a period of increasing changes and novelty in the administration of justice.

An essentially unwritten tradition, the common law's individuality and distinctiveness already separated it symbolically and conceptually from the Continental civil-law tradition. This in turn contributed to a sense of geographical and 'national' identity.[110] Scholars working on written law-collections have shown that by emphasising their law's ancient origins and perhaps identifying a fundamental 'law-giver' people could engender and further a sense of community and collective identity, whether it was the Christian Church or an individual kingdom. The argument that indigenous laws and customs could define a people – and in so doing justified their right to retain them – was put forward by the Welsh and the Scots as an ideological platform on which they themselves could unite and as a challenge to claims of English sovereignty in the thirteenth and fourteenth centuries. Conversely, the defining qualities and benefits of English law could also be used to claim cultural and political superiority. It is clear then that law not only 'occupies a crucial role in the mythology and ideology of a people',[111] but acts as a catalyst or dynamic to a consciousness of 'nationality'.

Legal consciousness should not be restricted to the 'active' experiential forum. It also should be considered as taking effect in the unconscious or subconscious, a realm in which experiences, memories, thoughts and aspirations are assigned, jumbled, stored and reflected upon in preparation for recall or recycling.[112] In this context it is important to consider what the medieval sense of history was and whether the past (or a sense of the past) played any particular role in typical attitudes to the present; in other words whether history was felt to have relevance to the contemporary scene; and if so, how it was manifested and to what effect. There are two areas which merit attention here: first, the individual's sense of past and present, lineage and family tradition; and, secondly, the more collective sense of past (and future) happenings as recorded by the various chroniclers or those artists, who, in the illuminated-manuscripts tradition, tried to portray an image of the world and its wider historical context.

During the thirteenth and fourteenth centuries, probably concomitant with the growing importance of having documentary proof in the form of relevant charters, there was a concern for terriers (constructions of family landholdings) and family lineages. The nature of law and landholding rules dictated the way contemporaries looked at their family history (genealogy). The Luttrell Psalter is a good example of a complex constructed image of a man and his family (both ancestral and extended). It is to be seen in the context of the time it was produced and as a document providing both a retrospective on the past and a prospect on the future. It was expressly manufactured at the request (and presumably with the advice) of Sir Geoffrey Luttrell (and in the text there is a portrayal of the owner/patron and an inscription to this effect). Within the manuscript there is also a 'feasting scene' which acts as a horizontal family tree or portrait of lineage. The psalter should be viewed, however, not just in terms of family propaganda, in that it can be seen as revealing or describing their religious, economic, social and political interests and affiliations, but more intimately, as a search for self-identity.[113]

Concern for a family's past might be related to holding hereditary office. The right to act as the King's Champion at coronations was actively (though peacefully) fought over by two related families, the Dimmocks and the Frevilles, both of whom had a common ancestor in the Marmion family and claimed an association with the office as descendants of the champions to the dukes of Normandy. The exercise of the privilege was eventually decided in favour of Dimmock (on the basis of better records and evidence) in the Court of Claims held prior to the coronation of Richard II in 1377 and was deemed to be linked to possession of the manor of Scrivelsby in Lincolnshire.[114] The holding of hereditary office in itself effectively provided men of the present with someone to look back to and emulate. In the 1370s Sir John Basings argued that he ought to have the shrievalty of Rutland because it had been granted to his great-great-great-grandfather, Ralph Normanville in 1202. The time and trouble taken in carrying out the necessary genealogical research is indicative of the value placed on such offices and the sense of continuity they provided.[115]

A person's particular role or standing in the past might affect their perception of the course of actions open to them in the present. In the early fourteenth century, Thomas, earl of Lancaster undoubtedly looked back to Simon de Montfort's stand against the Crown in the mid-thirteenth century. His claim to the hereditary Stewardship of England invoked notions of constitutional and administrative guardianship (arguably reflecting on a more national level the principles of estate management instilled by the burgeoning literature on the subject), while his desire to be the political as well as the territorial heir of de Montfort, not least in his concern to win the support of the knightly class, may have influenced the formulation of judicial policies and his stand on the Ordinances.[116] The advent of civil war (as had occurred in the late 1250s) may not have been entirely coincidental. Similarly, Henry Bolingbroke (the future Henry IV) looked back to his ancestor, Thomas, and equated his own stand against the tyranny of Richard II with his ancestor Thomas's actions against Edward II.[117]

In general, modern scholars have realised that medieval men and women were not interested in history as fact – history as being a true record of events. To them, the significance of the past lay in its possibility for interpretation and its capacity for being understood in terms of – or identified as relevant to – the present. There was no over-riding desire for historical accuracy, fictions were often presented as historical reality (though when recording events occurring in *their* present some authors might genuinely try for a faithful reminiscence) since it was the *exemplary* qualities that attracted them. Indeed, some contemporary scholastic and monastic authors believed that the role of the inquiring mind (and its functioning as part of the processes of rational comprehension) was to overlay a particularised image of the past on to the generalised present. Naturally, there were differing attitudes towards the portrayal of events, and medieval chroniclers or artists employed various methods and genres, but they were essentially constructing what amounted to a conscious ideological text.[118]

The chroniclers knew they were providing a link with the past for the benefit of future generations. They practised a craft as much as any artisan and sought logical continuities and coherent propositions to structure a narrative reminiscence. Their armoury consisted of rhetorical flourishes and the employment of particular words with contemporary resonance in chosen contexts. Prophetic texts were deployed especially, not so much as an indication of the future, but as a form of political discourse, commenting on historical events and the past actions of rulers.[119]

The fact that medieval histories and pictorial images have a particular view of the past, does not mean that we should avoid using them as historical evidence. The importance of the artist's work and that of the chronicler lies not so much in their witnessing and portraying past or contemporary events, but in their capacity to disclose elements of 'popular' culture and the narratives of unofficial discourses through the complexity of their images, symbolic associations and contradictions heaped upon the text. Documents produced for aristocratic culture may often have appropriated, mediated or contaminated the popular. Where it is possible to strip away the surface layers or perceive the elements of a vernacular tradition it is then that something of the 'popular consciousness' can be revealed and reconstructed with a view to understanding the ideological contribution of the non-governing classes to the world of politics.[120]

This chapter has shown the necessity of examining the workings of the mind and the psychological elements of law as a means of identifying the dynamic role of legal consciousness in the prevailing political culture. By emphasising the contexts in which law operated and the ways in which it was represented and understood, it is possible to gain an insight into how law had the capacity to form, affect and direct political attitudes during the thirteenth and fourteenth centuries. The subsequent chapters flesh out the basic thesis by taking particular areas where the conditions are suitable for observing the growth and effect of legal consciousness, namely within the legal profession itself, in the legal relations and obligations experienced by all subjects, in the processes adopted by the law as experienced by litigants, in the active participation of those administering its processes and in the parliamentary forum where problems involving law and justice were aired and solutions reached. The politicisation of the law, examined in the final chapter, is regarded as an inescapable concomitant of the intrusion of law into all areas of society. Law is seen to be a vehicle for royal jurisdiction and royal propaganda as well as providing the catalyst and underlying reason for civil disobedience and popular complaint.

Notes

1 D. Sugarman, 'Theory and practice in law and history: a prologue to the study of the relationship between law and economy from a socio-historical perspective', in B. Fryer *et al.* (eds), *Law, State and Society* (London, Croom Helm, 1981), pp. 70–106; D. Sugarman, 'Writing "law and society" histories', *Modern Law Review*, 55 (1992), 299–301. Sugarman has a very full bibliography of work undertaken in this area.
2 See M. de Certeau, *The Writing of History* (New York, Columbia University Press, 1988); A. Wilson (ed.), *Rethinking Social History* (Manchester, Manchester University Press, 1993).
3 E. Powell, 'After "After McFarlane": the poverty of patronage and the case for constitutional history', in D. J. Clayton, R. G. Davies and P. McNiven (eds), *Trade, Devotion and Governance* (Stroud, Alan Sutton, 1994), pp. 10–13; C. Carpenter, *Locality and Polity. A Study of Warwickshire Landed Society, 1401–1499* (Cambridge, Cambridge University Press, 1992), pp. 2–3: 'It is the search for attitudes and beliefs among landowners who dominated the medieval polity that seems to be the most urgent task for historians of late-medieval English politics.' (p. 3).
4 R. W. Kaeuper, *War, Justice and Public Order: England and France in the Later Middle Ages* (Oxford, Clarendon Press, 1988); Powell, *Kingship*; P. C. Maddern, *Violence and Social Order: East Anglia, 1422–1442* (Oxford, Clarendon Press, 1992); R. C. Palmer, *English Law in the Age of the Black Death, 1348–1381: a*

Transformation of Governance and Law (Chapel Hill, NC, University of North Carolina Press, 1993); Musson, *Public Order*.
5 Powell, *Kingship*; J. Watts, *Henry VI and the Politics of Kingship* (Cambridge, Cambridge University Press, 1996).
6 S. Reynolds, *Kingdoms and Communities in Western Europe, 900–1300*, 2nd edn (Oxford, Clarendon Press, 1997), pp. lvi–lvii, 4–8; R. Horrox, 'Local and national politics in fifteenth-century England', *JMH*, 18 (1992), pp. 401–2.
7 Reynolds, *Kingdoms and Communities*, pp. lxi–lxvi.
8 S. Justice, *Writing and Rebellion: England in 1381* (Berkeley and Los Angeles, CAL, and London, University of California Press, 1994), p. 9.
9 A. Hunt, *Explorations in Law and Society. Toward a Constitutive Theory of Law* (New York, Routledge, 1993), p. 135.
10 C. Geertz, *The Interpretation of Cultures* (London, Fontana Press, 1993), pp. 193–233 (quotation at p. 220).
11 M. Carruthers, *The Book of Memory: the Study of Memory in Medieval Culture* (Cambridge, Cambridge University Press, 1992), pp. 603–5, 611; Geertz, *Interpretation of Cultures*, pp. 80–2.
12 F. C. Bartlett, *Remembering, A Study in Experimental and Social Psychology* (Cambridge, Cambridge University Press, 1932), cited in Carruthers, *Book of Memory*, p. 613.
13 M. Midgley, 'Putting ourselves together again', in J. Cornwell (ed.), *Consciousness and Human Identity* (Oxford, Oxford University Press, 1999), pp. 160–2.
14 Geertz, *Interpretation of Cultures*, p. 214.
15 Hunt, *Explorations*, pp. 251–2.
16 J. Hudson, *The Formation of the English Common Law: Law and Society in England from the Norman Conquest to Magna Carta* (London and New York, Longman, 1996) pp. 2–23; P. Wormald, *The Making of English Law* (Oxford, Blackwell, 1999); Reynolds, *Kingdoms and Communities*, pp. 12–66.
17 Carruthers, *Book of Memory*, pp. 609–10 (considering the work of Robert W. Weisberg).
18 A. L. Brown, *The Governance of Late Medieval England, 1272–1461* (London, Edward Arnold, 1989), p. 101.
19 R. C. van Caenegem, *Judges, Legislators and Professors* (Cambridge, Cambridge University Press, 1987), pp. 1–2; R. H. Britnell (ed.), *Pragmatic Literacy, East and West, 1200–1330* (Woodbridge, Boydell Press, 1997).
20 H. L. A. Hart, *The Concept of Law*, 2nd edn (Oxford, Clarendon Press, 1994), pp. 26–49.
21 Hudson, *Formation*, pp. 16–23, 230–3; P. Brand, *The Making of the Common Law* (London, Hambledon Press, 1992), pp. 79–102.
22 R. N. Swanson, *Church and Society in Late Medieval England* (Oxford, Blackwell, 1993), pp. 140–1, 158–60.
23 L. Bonfield, 'The nature of customary law in the manorial courts of medieval England', *Comparative Studies in Society and History*, 31 (1989), pp. 514–34; J. Beckerman, 'Procedural innovation and institutional change in medieval English manor courts', *LHR*, 10 (1992), pp. 197–252; L. Bonfield, 'What did English

villagers mean by "customary law"?', in Z. Razi and R. Smith (eds), *Medieval Society and the Manor Court* (Oxford, Clarendon Press, 1996), pp. 103-16.

24 T. F. T. Plucknett, *Statutes and their Interpretation in the First Half of the Fourteenth Century* (Cambridge, Cambridge University Press, 1922); B. H. Putnam, *The Place in Legal History of Sir William Shareshull* (Cambridge, Cambridge University Press, 1950), p. 41; G. L. Harriss, 'The formation of parliament, 1272-1377', in R. G. Davies and J. H. Denton (eds), *The English Parliament in the Middle Ages* (Manchester, Manchester University Press, 1981), pp. 45-8.

25 D. Crook, 'The records of forest eyres in the public record office, 1179 to 1670', *Journal of Society of Archivists*, 17 (1996), pp. 183-93.

26 R. A. Griffiths, *King and Country: England and Wales in the Fifteenth Century* (London, Hambledon Press, 1991), pp. 34-5, 66-7; M. Prestwich, 'England and Scotland during the wars of independence', in M. J. Jones and M. Vale (eds), *England and Her Neighbours, 1066-1453* (London, Hambledon Press, 1989), pp. 190-7; C. J. Neville, 'Keeping the peace on the northern marches in the later Middle Ages', *EHR*, 109 (1994), pp. 1-25.

27 H. Summerson, 'The early development of the laws of the Anglo-Scottish marches, 1249-1448', in W. M. Gordon and T. D. Fergus (eds), *Legal History in the Making* (London, Hambledon Press, 1989), pp. 29-42; C. J. Neville, *Violence, Custom and Law. The Anglo-Scottish Border Lands in the Later Middle Ages* (Edinburgh, Edinburgh University Press, 1998), pp. 27-95.

28 R. R. Davies, 'The Law of the March', *Welsh History Review*, 5 (1970), pp. 1-30.

29 G. J. Hand, *English Law in Ireland 1290-1324* (Cambridge, Cambridge University Press, 1967), pp. 34-6.

30 *Lex Mercatoria* in *The Little Red Book of Bristol*, ed. F. B. Bickley (Bristol, W. C. Hemmons, 1900), pp. 57-85 (including differences between law merchant and common law, p. 58); *The Staple Court Book of Bristol*, ed. E. E. Rich, Bristol Record Society, 5 (1934), pp. 31-8; *Lex Mercatoria and Legal Pluralism: a Late Thirteenth-Century Treatise and its Afterlife*, ed. M. E. Basile *et al.* (Cambridge, MA, Ames Foundation, 1998).

31 *Select Cases Concerning the Law Merchant*, ed. H. Hall, SS, 49 (1929); H. G. Richardson, 'The law merchant in London, 1292', *EHR*, 37 (1922), 242-9; J. H. Baker, 'The law merchant and the common law before 1700', *Cambridge Law Journal*, 38 (1979), pp. 295-322. Statute law of Edward I and Edward III regulated some procedural anomalies with regard to debt recovery.

32 Guy Meige, *The Ancient Sea Laws of Oleron, Wisby and the other Hanse Towns* (London, 1686); an abstract can be found in *Social England*, ed. H. D. Traill, 6 vols (London, Cassell, 1895-8) vol. 1, p. 313; G. D. Squibb, *The High Court of Chivalry. A Study of the Civil Law in England* (Oxford, Oxford University Press, 1959), pp. 12-13; *Select Pleas in the Court of Admiralty*, ed. R. G. Marsden, SS, 6 (1894). The Laws of Oleron comprised a collection of judgments from the court of Oleron (an island off the French coast) which were adopted by Atlantic and North Sea traders during the second half of the twelfth century. The Laws of Wisby (a port on the island of Gotland in the Baltic), which may have derived from the Laws of Oléron, were adopted in the mid-fourteenth century.

33 M. H. Keen, 'The jurisdiction and origins of the Constable's court', in J. C. Holt and J. Gillingham (eds), *War and Government in the Middle Ages* (Woodbridge, Boydell Press, 1984), pp. 159–69.
34 B. Tierney, *Religion, Law and the Growth of Constitutional Thought, 1150–1650* (Cambridge, Cambridge University Press, 1982), pp. 20–5; Neville, *Violence, Custom and Law*, p. 59.
35 Squibb, *Court of Chivalry*, pp. 17–20; Keen, 'Constable's court', pp. 159–60.
36 Davies, 'Law of the March', pp. 15–21.
37 Neville, *Violence, Custom and Law*, p. xi.
38 A. K. Kiralfy, *The Action on the Case* (London, Sweet & Maxwell, 1951), pp. 9, 83.
39 *Selected Rolls of the Chester City Courts*, ed. A. W. Hopkins, Chetham Society, 3rd series, 2 (1950), pp. xxxvi–xxxvii; P. Hyams, 'What did Edwardian villagers understand by law?', in Razi and Smith (eds), *Medieval Society*, pp. 54–5.
40 *Select Cases in Manorial Courts*, ed. L. R. Poos and L. Bonfield, SS, 114 (London, 1998), pp. xxxii, xlv–xlvi.
41 Kiralfy, *Action on the Case*, pp. 99–101, 138–9; A. Musson, 'New labour laws, new remedies? Legal reaction to the Black Death "crisis"', in N. Saul (ed.), *Fourteenth Century England I* (Woodbridge, Boydell Press, 2000).
42 Tierney, *Religion and Constitutional Thought*, pp. 10–11.
43 Swanson, *Church and Society*, pp. 142–4.
44 The shortcomings of parenting and childcare were examined, for example, in cases coming before the central courts in 1369 and 1373 (see Palmer, *English Law*, pp. 362–3). Childcare arrangements were also considered in the manorial courts (see Poos and Bonfield, *Manorial Courts*, pp. cxxx–cxxxi, cxxxv).
45 Swanson, *Church and Society*, pp. 146–7.
46 *EELR*, vol. 2, p. 27.
47 R. V. Turner, *The English Judiciary in the Age of Glanvill and Bracton, 1176–1239* (Cambridge, Cambridge University Press, 1985); Brand, *Origins*; N. Ramsay, 'Retained legal counsel, c. 1275–1475', *TRHS*, 5th series, 35 (1985), p. 100.
48 For this issue generally see J. Brundage, *Law, Sex and Christian Society in Medieval Europe* (Chicago, University of Chicago Press, 1987) and R. Helmholz, *Marriage Litigation in Medieval England* (Cambridge, Cambridge University Press, 1974).
49 Musson and Ormrod, *Evolution*, pp. 31–4; W. M. Ormrod, *The Reign of Edward III: Crown and Political Society in England* (New Haven and London, Yale University Press, 1990), pp. 128–30; H. Jewell, *English Local Administration in the Middle Ages* (Newton Abbot, David & Charles, 1972), pp. 61–8. *Halmota Prioratus Dunelmensis*, ed. J. Booth, Surtees Society, 82 (Durham, 1886), p. 133.
50 Neville, *Violence, Custom and Law*, pp. 53–4, 56 (n53).
51 *Ibid.*, p. 58.
52 D. J. Seipp, 'The Mirror of Justices', in *Learning the Law*, pp. 102–4.
53 *YB 3&4 Edward II*, p. 200.
54 M. Bielby, 'The profits of expertise: the rise of civil lawyers and chancery equity' in M. Hicks (ed.), *Profit, Piety and the Professions in Later Medieval England* (Gloucester, Alan Sutton, 1990), pp. 73–4.

55　J. Shaw, 'Corporeal and spiritual homicide, the sin of wrath and the "Parson's Tale"', *Traditio*, 38 (1982), 281–300.
56　*The English Works of John Wyclif*, ed. F. D. Matthew, Early English Text Society, 74 (London, 1880), pp. 182, 299.
57　E. Powell, 'Arbitration and the law in the later Middle Ages', *TRHS* 5th series, 33 (1983), pp. 49–67; I. Rowney, 'Arbitration in gentry disputes of the later Middle Ages', *History*, 67 (1982), pp. 367–76.
58　C. Rawcliffe, '"That kindliness should be cherished more, and discord driven out": the settlement of commercial disputes by arbitration in later medieval England', in J. Kermode (ed.), *Enterprise and Individuals in Fifteenth Century England* (Stroud, Alan Sutton, 1991), pp. 99–117.
59　M. Clanchy, 'Law and love in the Middle Ages', in J. Bossy (ed.), *Disputes and Settlements* (Cambridge, Cambridge University Press, 1983), pp. 47–67.
60　B. R. McRee, 'Religious gilds and regulation of behaviour in late medieval towns', in J. Rosenthal and C. Richmond (eds), *People, Politics and Community in the Later Middle Ages* (Stroud, Alan Sutton, 1987), pp. 108–22.
61　McRee, 'Religious gilds', p. 113.
62　P. Nightingale, *A Medieval Merchant Community. The Grocers' Company and the Politics and Trade of London, 1000–1485* (New Haven and London, Yale University Press, 1995), p. 179.
63　P. R. Schofield, 'Peasants and the manor court: gossip and litigation in a Suffolk village at the close of the thirteenth century', *P&P*, 159 (1998), pp. 34–6; McRee, 'Religious gilds', pp. 111–12; H. Summerson, 'The structure of law enforcement in the thirteenth century', *AJLH*, 23 (1979), 314–15.
64　Powell, *Kingship*, pp. 97–106.
65　Rawcliffe, 'Commercial disputes', pp. 109–10.
66　PRO MS JUST 1/443 mm. 1, 4, 4d, 5 (Lancashire – 1350).
67　Maddern, *Violence and Social Order*, p. 14; B. W. McLane, 'A case study of violence and litigation in the early fourteenth century: the disputes of Robert Godsfield of Sutton le Marsh', *Nottingham Medieval Studies*, 28 (1984), pp. 22–44; S. Butler, '"To speke of wo that is in mariage": attitudes towards spousal abuse in the church courts of later medieval England', unpublished paper presented at 35th International Congress on Medieval Studies, Kalamazoo, 2000.
68　M. Camille, *Image on the Edge: the Margins of Medieval Art* (London, Reaktion, 1992); M. Camille, *Mirror in Parchment: the Luttrell Psalter and the Making of Medieval England* (London, Reaktion, 1998).
69　*The Reversible World: Symbolic Inversion in Art and Society*, ed. B. Babcock (1978); C. Phythian-Adams, 'Ceremony and the citizen: the communal year at Coventry, 1450–1550', in P. Clark and P. Slack (eds), *Crisis and Order in English Towns, 1500–1700: Essays in Urban History* (London, Routledge and Kegan Paul, 1972), pp. 57–85; M. James, 'Ritual drama and the social body in the late medieval English Town', *P&P*, 98 (1983), pp. 3–29; P. Burke, *Popular Culture in Early Modern Europe*, rev. & repr. (Aldershot, Scolar Press, 1994).
70　S. Lindenbaum, 'Rituals of exclusion: feasts and plays of the English religious fraternities', in M. Twycross (ed.), *Festive Drama* (Woodbridge, D. S. Brewer,

1996), pp. 54–65.
71 C. Humphrey, 'The dynamics of urban festal culture in later medieval England', unpublished DPhil thesis, University of York, 1997, pp. 48–60.
72 P. Goodrich and Yifat Hachamovitch, 'Time out of mind: an introduction to the semiotics of common law', in P. FitzPatrick (ed.), *Dangerous Supplements: Resistance and Renewal in Jurisprudence* (London, Pluto, 1991), p. 159.
73 Carruthers, *Book of Memory*, pp. 244–5.
74 F. Watts, 'Towards a theology of consciousness', in Cornwell (ed.), *Consciousness*, pp. 192–3.
75 For a detailed exploration of this see C. Stebbings and A. Musson, *Law and Image: an Historical Iconography of Law* (forthcoming).
76 *The New Pelican Guide to English Literature*, ed. B. Ford, rev. and repr. (London, Penguin, 1997), vol. 1, p. 403, ll. 148–53.
77 *Calendar of County Court, City Court and Eyre Rolls of Chester, 1259–1297*, ed. R. Stewart-Brown, Chetham Society 2nd series, 84 (Manchester, 1925), p. 176; Clanchy, *Memory*, p. 273.
78 Maddern, *Violence and Social Order*, p. 13; R. M. Fraher, 'Preventing crime in the high Middle Ages: the medieval lawyers' search for deterrence' in J. R. Sweeney and S. Chordorow (eds), *Popes, Teachers and Canon Law in the Middle Ages* (Ithaca and London, Cornell University Press, 1989), pp. 220–1.
79 Traditionally outlaws could be beheaded summarily if captured.
80 J. G. Bellamy, *The Law of Treason in England in the Later Middle Ages* (Cambridge, Cambridge University Press, 1970), pp. 39–40.
81 An outsider's view of the courts in c.1290 is afforded in the *Liber Memorandum Ecclesie de Bernewelle*, ed. J. Willis Clarke (Cambridge, Cambridge University Press, 1907); M. Clanchy, 'A medieval realist: interpreting the rules at Barnwell Priory, Cambridge', in E. Attwooll (ed.), *Perspectives in Jurisprudence* (Glasgow, University of Glasgow Press, 1977), pp. 176–94.
82 J. H. Baker, *The Order of Serjeants at Law*, SS, supplementary series, 5 (London, 1984), pp. 68–74: judges who were clerics wore academic copes and hoods.
83 P. Brand, 'Inside the courtroom: lawyers, litigants and justices in England in the later Middle Ages', in P. Coss (ed.), *The Moral World of the Law* (Cambridge, Cambridge University Press, 2000), pp. 107–11.
84 For example: YB 14 Edward II, pp. 33, 49; M. Hastings, *The Court of Common Pleas in Fifteenth Century England* (New York, Columbia University Press, 1947), pp. 28–9.
85 Clanchy, *Memory*, pp. 260, 262, J. Cherry, 'Symbolism and survival: medieval horns of tenure', *Antiquaries Journal*, 69 (1989), pp. 111–18.
86 D. W. Sutherland, *The Assize of Novel Disseisin* (Cambridge, Cambridge University Press, 1973), pp. 148–9.
87 N. D. Hurnard, 'Anglo-Norman franchises', *EHR*, 69 (1949), pp. 436–8; R. Bartlett, *Trial By Fire and Water: the Medieval Judicial Ordeal* (Oxford, Clarendon Press, 1986), pp. 127–52.
88 Nightingale, *Mercantile Community*, p. 190; Brand, *Making*, pp. 175, 180 (a church in York and St Swithin, Candlewick Street in London).

89 *CPMR 1323-64*, p. 278; Rawcliffe, 'Commercial disputes', p. 110.
90 H. M. Cam, *The Hundred and the Hundred Rolls* (London, Merlin Press, 1963), p. 171; R. C. Palmer, *The County Courts of Medieval England, 1150-1350* (Princeton, NJ, Princeton University Press, 1982), pp. 19-21.
91 Clanchy, 'Law and love', p. 53.
92 For example in 'An outlaw's song of trailbaston' in R. B. Dobson and J. Taylor, *Rymes of Robin Hood: an Introduction to the English Outlaw*, rev. edn (Stroud, Alan Sutton, 1997), p. 252. See also A. Musson, 'Social exclusivity or justice for all? Access to justice in fourteenth-century England', in R. Horrox and S. Rees-Jones (eds), *Utopias, Ideals and Institutions, 1200-1630* (Cambridge, Cambridge University Press, forthcoming).
93 PRO MS JUST 1/443 m4.
94 Rawcliffe, 'Commercial disputes', pp. 109-10.
95 M. M. Sheehan, *Marriage, Family and Law in Medieval Europe* (Toronto, University of Toronto Press, 1996), pp. 47-51, 55, 59-61.
96 Helmholz, *Marriage Litigation*, pp. 182-3.
97 Sheehan, *Marriage, Family and Law*, pp. 54-9.
98 Maddern, *Violence and Social Order*, p. 141; B. A. Hanawalt, *'Of Good and Ill Repute': Gender and Social Control in Medieval England* (New York and Oxford, Oxford University Press, 1998), pp. 40, 49.
99 A. Bennett, 'Anthony Bek's copy of *Statuta Anglicana*', in W. M. Ormrod (ed.), *England in the Fourteenth Century* (Woodbridge, Boydell Press, 1986), pp. 1-28.
100 H. C. Maxwell-Lyte, *Historical Notes on the Great Seal* (London, HMSO, 1926). Maxwell-Lyte questions whether in fact all royal writs bore the complete Great Seal, though it is to be presumed that they did.
101 Clanchy, *Memory*, pp. 308-17; P. D. A. Harvey and A. McGuiness, *A Guide to Medieval Seals* (London, Public Record Office, 1996); N. Brooks, 'The organisation and achievements of the peasants of Kent and Essex in 1381', in H. Mayr-Harting and R. I. Moore (eds), *Studies in Medieval History Presented to R. H. C. Davies* (London, Hambledon Press, 1985), p. 260.
102 Clanchy, *Memory*, pp. 35-43.
103 E. Danbury, 'English and French artistic propaganda during the period of the Hundred Years War: some evidence from royal charters', in C. Allmand (ed.), *Power, Culture and Religion in France, c.1350-1550* (Woodbridge, Boydell Press, 1989), pp. 76-7, 80.
104 Clanchy, *Memory*, p. 292.
105 M. Camille, 'At the edge of the law: an illustrated register of writs in the Pierpont Morgan Library', in N. Rogers (ed.), *England in the Fourteenth Century: Proceedings of the 1991 Harlaxton Symposium* (Stamford, Paul Watkins, 1993), pp. 7-8.
106 Danbury, 'Artistic propaganda', pp. 79-97.
107 Clanchy, *Memory*, p. 152; P. Brand, '"Time out of mind": the knowledge and use of the eleventh- and twelfth-century past in thirteenth-century litigation', *Anglo-Norman Studies*, 16 (1994), pp. 37-54.
108 Seipp, 'Mirror of Justices', pp. 89, 108-12.
109 J. Catto, 'Andrew Horn: law and history in fourteenth century England', in R. H.

C. Davies and J. M. Wallace-Hadrill (eds), *The Writing of History in the Middle Ages* (Oxford, Clarendon Press, 1981), pp. 367–91 (quotation at p. 375).
110 For what follows and more specific references see Reynolds, *Kingdoms and Communities*, pp. 250–76; R. R. Davies, 'The peoples of Britain and Ireland, 1100–1400. III: Laws and customs', *TRHS* 6th series, 6 (1996), pp. 1–23.
111 Davies, 'Laws and customs', p. 6.
112 Hunt, *Explorations*, pp. 120–1.
113 Camille, *Mirror in Parchment*, pp. 49, 79–81, 93–105.
114 L. G. Wickham Legg, *English Coronation Records* (London, Archibald Constable, 1901), pp. 140, 159; G. E. C. Cokayne (ed.), *The Complete Peerage of England, Scotland, Ireland, Great Britain and the United Kingdom*, rev. edn V. Gibbs *et al.*, 12 vols (London, 1910–59), vol. 8, pp. 513–14.
115 Ormrod, *Edward III*, p. 157; P. Morgan, 'Making the English gentry', in P. R. Coss and S. D. Lloyd (eds), *Thirteenth Century England: V*, Proceedings of the Newcastle-upon-Tyne Conference, 1993 (Woodbridge, Boydell Press, 1995), pp. 22–4.
116 J. R. Maddicott, *Thomas of Lancaster, 1307–1322* (Oxford, Clarendon Press, 1970), pp. 118–19, 166–8, 180–2, 292; E. King, 'Estate management and the reform movement', in W. M. Ormrod (ed.), *England in the Thirteenth Century*, Proceedings of the 1989 Harlaxton Symposium (Stamford, Paul Watkins, 1991), p. 1.
117 S. Walker, 'Political saints in later medieval England', in R. H. Britnell and A. J. Pollard (eds), *The McFarlane Legacy: Studies in Late Medieval Politics and Society* (Stroud, Alan Sutton, 1995), pp. 83–92; M. Bennett, *Richard II and the Revolution of 1399* (Stroud, Sutton Publishing, 1999), pp. 55, 154.
118 J. Coleman, *Ancient and Medieval Memories* (Cambridge, Cambridge University Press, 1992), pp. 454–9, 528–9, 546, 558–9, 570–1, 597.
119 L. Coote, 'Prophecy and public affairs in later medieval England', unpublished DPhil thesis, University of York, 1997, pp. 14–19.
120 Camille, *Mirror in Parchment*, p. 275; W. M. Ormrod, 'In bed with Joan of Kent: the king's mother and the rebels in 1381' in A. Diamond *et al.* (eds), *Medieval Women: Texts and Contexts in Late Medieval Britain* (Turnhout, Brepols, 2000), pp. 277–92.

2

The professionalisation of law

THE emergence of a distinct legal profession was one of the defining features of the development of law in the period 1215–1381. The thirteenth and fourteenth centuries witnessed a veritable explosion in judicial business which consequently brought a strong demand for the services of those who, in the fourteenth century, were known by a new generic term of 'men of law'. In response to the precocity of this 'consumer demand' and with a corresponding growth in the technicality and complexity of the law, there naturally arose those who concentrated on particular areas of legal practice or who performed a more specialised task, such as pleading in court or judging cases. The diversification observable among those purporting to be 'men of law' and the sheer numbers of people offering their services was to a certain extent a reflection of the provision of legal education. The noticeable expansion in practitioners spurred further efforts in this area. It also necessitated the development of forms of control over those working in the law, and the regulation of their conduct once they had started to practise. Taken together, these elements represent the hallmarks of a profession in that they betray an overriding concern over quantity, quality and conduct. While we should not regard the formation of the profession as being necessarily complete at this time or its forms of regulation as wholly effective, these attempts are indicative of contemporary perceptions of the legal profession as representing a significant body of people who not only played an important role in society but who, because of their knowledge and position, had a special duty towards it.

This chapter examines the extent to which the professionalisation of the law inculcated and encouraged ways of thinking about the law and legal practice. It looks, first, at the provision of legal education and the growth of an intellectual domain and, secondly, at avenues of promotion or advancement within the profession and its sense of identity and collegiality. There follows, thirdly, an assessment of the profession's ethical awareness, focusing on the conduct of judges and standards of behaviour within the profession as a whole. The chapter then investigates the relationship between the legal profession and the wider population, especially the position of judges and lawyers within society. It also discusses the relationship between lawyers at the centre and those in the regions, demonstrating that there was a wider definition of the legal profession than is frequently recognised. Sixth and finally, it considers how 'popular' perceptions of judges and lawyers (as portrayed in contemporary art and literature and in the complaints brought against 'men of law') affected the development of the legal profession as these perceptions became part of the mental 'baggage' to be contested and contended by lawyers of the period. In particular, in this respect, it addresses the apparent hatred of – and general violence against – the profession that was exhibited in 1381 and examines the effect in terms of the immediate and long-term implications for the legal profession.

The intellectualising of the law

In the 'preface' to his revised version (compiled during the 1240s and 1250s) of the influential treatise 'On the Laws and Customs of England' which bears his name, Henry Bracton criticises the judiciary of his day – those greater men who are 'foolish and insufficiently instructed, who climb the seat of judgment before learning the laws' – for perverting the laws and customs by deciding cases more by their own will than by the authority of the laws.[1] It is not clear whether Bracton had particular individuals within his sights or whether he simply intended a general condemnation, perhaps as justification for the book's existence and its format. Nevertheless the statement implicitly reveals a concern for the importance of legal education and the application of judicial power provides an exhortation to the nascent legal profession to think about its duties and raise its standards.

This section assesses the implications and veracity of Bracton's indictment and its applicability to the legal profession as a whole for the period under review. In particular, it examines the provision of both formal and informal legal education, the growth of an intellectual side to law and the development of 'professional' attitudes towards work as a practitioner. While it is upon the common lawyers that we naturally tend to focus, we should resist the temptation to regard them as totally distinct from the civil and canon lawyers, or indeed to think that the form and methods of education in the 'learned laws' (as they were called) existed in a completely separate sphere. The revival of interest in Roman law in the twelfth century provided for an infusion of concepts and principles which is observable in the pages of *Glanvill* and in particular Magna Carta.[2] Furthermore, it should be emphasised that the training given – in the common law, civil law and canon law – provided a shared foundation in legal principles (even if they differed in substance) which could be absorbed both by intending practitioners and by those who did not in fact go on to practise law.

Education in the 'learned laws' was available at Oxford from the late twelfth century and in Cambridge (at least in canon law) from the early thirteenth century, though some English students may have gone abroad to the law schools in Paris or Bologna.[3] The study of Roman law was regarded as an essential complement to canon law, so much so that – by the fourteenth century – contemporaries thought of the two as representing a *ius commune* (a general common law) and candidates for a canon-law degree had to show substantial study of civil law.[4] A university education, however, was not a requirement for practice in the ecclesiastical courts in England until 1274. Thereafter, the attainment of a series of academic thresholds was insisted upon for advocates. In 1281, a minimum of three years of lectures in canon and civil law was required in order to practise. For those wishing to practise in the Court of Arches, this was increased to four or five years' study in 1295, when it was also stipulated that attendance at the court (to learn the customs and practices of the court) was expected. By the early 1340s the degree of bachelor of canon or civil law was demanded as a prerequisite for advocates.[5]

Special provisions for students in law were made at the English universities through endowments and benefactions, particularly in the fourteenth century. Both universities benefited financially on the death of royal justice Gilbert Rothbury as he had bequeathed 250 marks for a loan chest at Oxford and founded the 'Roubery Chest' at Cambridge.[6] In 1361 Michael Northburgh left money for the maintenance of scholars in both canon and civil law at Oxford. Two Cambridge colleges were founded with the manifest aim of giving an education in law. Edward II founded King's Hall stipulating that it should form 'a cradle of civil law studies within the Cambridge *studium*', while Bishop William Bateman founded Trinity Hall in 1350, providing for twenty scholars, of whom ten were to study civil law and seven, canon law.[7]

The educational materials used for the study of the common law owed much to the Roman law tradition and to the methods of teaching developed in the universities. Indeed, given that formal education in the common law was in its infancy, it would be strange if there was no overlap in the underlying notions and frameworks used to convey training in legal principles and practices.[8] *Bracton* itself is infused with Roman law concepts and distinctions to the extent that it should be seen as a synthesis of both traditions.[9] Similarly, the exercises in disputation using *quaestiones* found in surviving treatises (see below) and tracts on pleading that are in Latin (rather than law French) are redolent of the methods used in the university law schools.[10] The lecture with its series of problems (questions) and a disputation in which the student was encouraged to take part in fact represented standard academic exercises of the sort found in theology faculties. The format was simply translated by university lecturers into the discipline of law. When the legal problem was revealed, the question was posed *queritur quid juris?* (query: what is the law?). This was followed by a close analysis of the problem (including the definition of terms). The issues raised were then stated and argued for and against. The common-law lecturers merely exchanged the Roman law content for a course based on forms of writs and pleadings.[11]

Although it is really only from the mid-1270s that we have direct evidence for the existence of oral instruction in the common law, a prohibition on anyone teaching 'laws' (*leges*) – issued by the mayor and sheriffs of London in 1234 – may indicate that some form of training in the common law was available in and around the City at a much earlier date.[12] Access to the courts and the royal justices together with the availability of possible 'course texts' certainly provide circumstantial evidence of law teaching in the early thirteenth century. Parts of *Bracton*, for example, were available from the early 1220s and then revised during the 1230s, while a set of 'questions to the court' (*quaestiones curiae*) intended to stimulate discussion and disputation survive in the contemporary Exchequer Red Book.[13] The intervening period is more obscure, but it is possible that some form of training continued to be provided, even if on a purely informal basis. An informal, practical education was always a feature of training in the common law and is probably exemplified most readily in the way judge's clerks learned through their immersion in the plea rolls and attendance at sessions held by their masters.[14]

The survival of manuscript lectures and 'do-it-yourself' manuals is symptomatic of a growing awareness of the need for oral and written instruction in law. The main works on law and procedure were *Glanvill* (a textbook written 1187–89 and revised in about 1229), applicable to the system as it stood in the late twelfth century, and *Bracton*, which was not so much a textbook as a legal 'summa' or compendium. In addition, a number of treatises were compiled especially to meet the rapid expansion in the ranks of men desiring legal training (at least at a fairly elementary level) over the course of the later thirteenth and fourteenth centuries. Some of these, such as the *Mirror of Justices*, *Britton* and *Fleta* are in effect revisions or updated versions of *Bracton*.[15] The provision of texts and lectures on such areas as how to conduct litigation (*Brevia placitata* and *Casus placitorum*), on writs (*Natura brevium*) and how to compose them (*Modus componendi brevia*) and the procedural rules applicable to actions in the king's courts (*Fet asaver*) fulfilled some of the demand for legal education which developed from the 1270s onwards.[16]

More advanced courses and materials were available for those who aspired to the elite world of pleading. In fact from at least the late 1280s it is apparent that there was a body of students known as 'apprentices of the bench' (learning from observing proceedings in the court rather than being tied to an individual serjeant as would be the case with a traditional apprenticeship) who in 1291 were provided with a special vantage point in the courtroom ('en le cribbe') from which they could listen to and study the proceedings.[17] Such was the number of students taking part that permission for the construction of a second crib was requested from Edward II in 1310.[18] The apprentices were clearly afforded a special status in the court and it may have been that they were also provided with other privileges and facilities.[19] The judges themselves took part in the instruction of apprentices, providing comments on points of law to the assembly while the serjeants were consulting with their clients.[20] Chief Justice Bereford, for instance, is reported as ironically telling a serjeant that he was obliged for his challenge 'not for the sake of us who sit on the bench, but for the sake of the young men (*les joevens*) who are here'.[21]

This body of advanced students was able to take advantage of other educational aids and opportunities. The compiling of law reports (examples of interesting cases occurring in the eyre and the central courts to form what are known as the Year Books), which began from at least the late 1260s, provided another way of teaching and assimilating law. In lectures based on these law reports, the factual situation was set out first so that the student could understand the nature of the case. Then the ingredients of the pleadings, the directions in argument taken by the serjeants and the opinions of the judges were expounded, before the items to be noted were summarised.[22] The dictation of reports and the addition of comments by both teachers and their pupils indicates not only that these manuscripts were regularly used as a form of teaching aid, but also that, in making notes, both the teacher and the learner were reflecting on the points being made. By the 1340s, commentaries on the statutes and learning exercises of the kind used in the Inns of Court (and which were forerunners of the 'readings' provided in the Inns) were also offered, which enabled students to focus on single (or closely related) points of law and to gain practice in making counts and defences and engaging in oral argument.[23]

Differences in course content and institutional formality should not obscure the influences that the Roman and canon-law traditions had upon the common law, nor the similarities in the educational aims and methods. Nor should it be assumed that the education of common-law practitioners was solely in that type of law. Knowledge of the 'learned laws' was occasionally required in common-law practice, or a principle or maxim might be quoted in court by way of illustration.[24] Such versatility was also a necessary part of work in government and diplomacy, especially where international relations turned on the understanding and interpreting of (non-domestic) legal questions and issues, as in the Treaty of Paris of 1259 or Edward III's claims to France in the 1340s.[25]

The growth of legal education was an important element in the development of law as an intellectual domain. Lawyers clearly had to think about and discuss the problems they encountered when interpreting and applying the law, and at times needed guidance on the best way to present their argument or on what was likely to be the most successful approach to adopt when confronted with an unusual legal situation. Intellectual cogitation and reflection could occur in private or more publicly within a group of associates. In this respect the collegiality of the profession was undoubtedly a significant factor in the transmission and communication of legal ideas, while the courts and the Inns offered a natural forum for the discussion of points of law or procedure arising from strange or difficult cases.[26] Private reading and reference was aided and encouraged through the provision of legal literature in the form of individual treatises and manuals, but also through collected notes on cases and the production of statute books. The latter, which achieved wide dissemination through a pool of commercial copyists, generally comprised a textual core of statutes from Magna Carta up to and including Edward I's great enactments, a section devoted to apocryphal texts (pseudo-statutes or those of uncertain origin) dating from the same period and a third part, which housed instructional treatises (such as *Hengham Magna* and *Parva* and *Placita corone*). These books were handy, pocket-sized volumes that were tailored to suit the needs of the practitioner and usually contained some blank leaves so they could be updated. By the later fourteenth century they were often indexed and included the statutes promulgated up to 1321, which were organised chronologically.[27]

The breadth of the lawyers' experience, knowledge and reading is sometimes revealed in the arguments used in court, comparisons with other areas of law, and in the citation of cases, especially where points of interest are recalled from cases before the eyre justices or at provincial assize sessions.[28] The misquotation, wrongly-attributed statutory provision or half-remembered citation is,[29] however, as illuminating as the lawyer giving the correct one in that it reveals the emphasis placed on memory and the pressure under which many lawyers worked. The apparent ignorance or lack of erudition betrayed on occasion by some men of law was nevertheless compensated for by a growing concern for the provision and subsequent consultation of accurate and authoritative texts. In court, judges asked to see a copy of the relevant portion of a statute,[30] while judicial officers such as Andrew Horn, the chamberlain of London's Guildhall, carried out research in order to correct legal records and obtain reliable statements of the law.[31] Many judges carried their plea rolls around with them and this provided a ready store of past cases for the public record and for private reference. Geoffrey Scrope kept some rolls in York and some in London.[32] When Shareshull retired from his post at king's bench in 1361, he handed over to Henry Green, his successor as chief justice, 'rolls, records, processes and indictments and all other memoranda touching the king's bench' stretching back to 1339. There were also seventy-five bags and 189 boxes full of indictments, bills and items that had been sent into or related to the court.[33]

The reporting of cases, in particular, provided a fund of information and example that proved useful not only for the student, but also appealed to experienced practitioners, who were able to use them for their own record or to refresh their memory concerning a case.[34] There seems to have been a growing awareness among the judges and serjeants of the royal courts that they might refer to points of law argued in previous cases, and that the information could indeed be relevant, if not crucial, for the outcome of a case in progress. This trend should be coupled with a growing reliance on the written word for evidence and, moreover, litigants' desire for consistency. The circulation of details concerning how things had gone in X's case could cast doubt on the integrity, not to say the infallibility, of judges if the decision was the reverse in Y's case.[35]

The concept of binding precedent is something with which every modern common lawyer is thoroughly conversant. Indeed it is a doctrine upon which the common-law system is based, complete with its own rules and method of application. At this date there was no formal structured theory imposed on the courts. For many judges (at least in the twelfth and early thirteenth centuries when the details of court sessions were not recorded either formally by clerks or informally by other lawyers) each case was to be approached individually and dealt with on its own merits.[36] Even with the advent of court record-keeping, the rolls themselves rarely reveal general statements of legal principles, and even where they do it is difficult to pin down the authority to any single judge owing to the impersonal language of the court record. It is unlikely that early thirteenth-century judges consciously saw the judgments of their forbears as influencing the way they approached the cases before them.[37] It is noticeable, however, that specific reference was made to the concept of precedent in court proceedings as early as 1287. 'On what basis should we give judgment: under the ancient laws customary in the time of those who preceded us, or under the laws alleged by you and others?', one justice in the court of common pleas asked.[38] Indeed, there were signs that the benefits of precedent, in providing for certainty, uniformity and consistency, were appreciated. Bereford (when a serjeant) made clear his belief in the same year: 'I have seen it adjudged before you yourself; and there ought to be one law for all people in this kingdom'.[39]

The medieval Year Books provide some indication that cases were cited and discussed in court by counsel and judges alike.[40] To what extent, though, did citation help a case or influence a decision? In highlighting particular cases, were the serjeants merely offering examples of situations that were similar or analogous or were they in fact suggesting that the decision be followed on the basis of its standing as authoritative law (which was in turn based on the judgment-giving court's hierarchical status)? Cases cited in court were sometimes discussed in detail and their applicability tested. In 1340, for instance, William Thorpe (then a serjeant) introduced a case ('For John Rednesse in a similar case'), which was then distinguished by one of the justices, William Shareshull ('In that case Not so here'). Thorpe cited it again to back up his argument ('witness the case of John Rednesse'), but Shareshull rebuffed him with further detail from the case ('and John Rednesse came two years after').[41] Furthermore it is clear that judges were influenced by previous decisions: in 1308/9 Staunton J. acknowledged some form of precedent 'that the writ lies against strangers is shown by the case of *John of Studley v. Bishop of Winchester*'.[42] The naming of specific judges who made a particular decision, presumably on the basis of their reputation and learning, was also a means of underlining its authority as good law.[43] While some concept of precedent clearly obtained and its value was felt in bolstering arguments and justifying decisions, it was probably as respect for the 'old law' in a changing world that it psychologically drew its power. The dangers of allowing precedent to dominate all decision-making, however, was felt by Shareshull, who while demurring from too much judicial innovation, believed that 'right' remained a powerful influence. 'No precedent is of such force as that which is right.'[44]

The longevity of tenure enjoyed by the justices of king's bench and common pleas and their previous service to the court as serjeants obviously facilitated a strong sense of collective memory and an awareness of past decisions. Individual judges were also known to have excellent memories. William Herle (chief justice of common pleas, 1327-29, 1331-35) was highly regarded in this respect. In fact through special training and the use of mental indices, lawyers were able to develop capacious memories. Many must have possessed the ability to arrange information and revise it mentally (the technique of *cogitatio*) and call upon it as it was needed for argument or decisions in court.[45] The various resources open to 'men of law', including dedicated study, communication with each other and their own experience, thus formed the basis of an intellectual domain in which they participated and from which their professional lives benefited. Education in legal forms and training in the ability to apply theoretical knowledge to a practical context lay at the heart of the emergence of the legal profession.

Towards an identity as a profession

In many ways the legal profession of the thirteenth and fourteenth centuries may appear to us as an amorphous, multifarious group of practitioners. They did possess a common identity in a general sense because the profession relied upon a shared ethos among those who were increasingly referred to in the parliamentary business of the fourteenth century and in the literature and sermons of the period as 'men of law'.[46] Such people were defined by the way they utilised their literate and communicative skills for a particular endeavour in the law and possessed a training capable of coping with (indeed one that was stimulated by) the clarity and intellectual rigour demanded by the technicalities of substantive law and its all-dominating procedures. More significantly, over the course of the two centuries a number of elements combined to provide the legal profession (or parts of it at least) with a distinct identity, certainly (in spite of some similarities and shared assumptions) an identity which marked it off from the Church and from other professions and trades. A lot depends of course on whether the profession is viewed from an external standpoint, an outsider looking in, or alternatively, from an insider's point of view, one which focuses on its internal arrangements and characteristics. Each view results in a different perception. The 'external' view is advanced by the extent to which the profession registered public attention through the outward trappings of display and organisation (costume, conspicuous consumption and relations with other groups). The 'internal' opinion-forming factors rest on intangibles such as opportunities for promotion and advancement and the sense of collegiality which built up as a result of work and (where applicable) from the communal living arrangements.

The legal profession should not necessarily be regarded as a body possessing or desiring the same identity. The bifurcation of the legal profession into attorneys and pleaders (forerunners of the solicitors and barristers familiar today) emerged largely as a result of career choices between generalisation and specialisation, between acting for the client in aspects of litigation and pleading his case before the judges. This was not in fact a differentiation exclusive to the common law, since their counterparts 'proctors' and 'advocates' were also available in the church courts.[47]

Royal concern at the expansion of the 'lower branch' must be presumed to have provoked an initiative to tighten up on the number of attorneys in practice and, by implication, their conduct. Regulation of the number of attorneys was attempted by the Crown in an ordinance of 1292, which prescribed a maximum of 140 attorneys in circulation and set quotas for every county accordingly.[48] A test of professional competence may have envisaged as a requirement for membership of the select county group. This would have offered a modicum of quality assurance over professional education, but the whole scheme appears never to have got off the ground. Indeed, there is no evidence that the royal government seriously embarked on a systematic limitation in the number of attorneys through the quota system in this period.[49] Regulation of the size of the profession, at least of this branch, did not occur: either the political will was lacking or there were practical difficulties in enforcing the ordinance. This is in contrast to successful limitations on the number of canon lawyers (both proctors and advocates) allowed to practise in the main ecclesiastical courts, which were imposed in the Court of Arches in 1295 and in the northern province sixteen years later.[50]

A natural limitation or self-selection process occurred to an extent with the 'upper branch'. The level and complexity of argument required by the serjeants pleading in the central courts was undoubtedly a defining aspect and a reason why they came to be regarded as the elite of the profession. A further refinement within the ranks of common (ordinary) serjeants was the call to the order of serjeants-at-law. The creation of a new serjeant-at-law was a very ceremonial affair marked initially by the giving of gold, a custom which by the mid-fourteenth century had taken the form of a gift of gold rings. Thomas Morice, for instance, common serjeant of London in the 1350s, who then became a pleader in the court of common pleas in 1362, bequeathed to St Paul's Cathedral in 1368 'five gold rings which were left over when I gave gold in the lord king's court, and which I promised then but did not hand over'. There was also an elaborate feast, attended by the great and the good, which some commentators likened to a coronation banquet.[51] Like assuming knighthood, however, the expense involved in the ceremony, combined with the need to maintain the trappings of the order, meant that many would-be serjeants-at-law (who felt that their practice was not sufficiently stable or lucrative) decided to remain common serjeants or apprentices-at-law.[52] Royal preferment visited upon distinguished serjeants-at-law resulted in appointment as a king's serjeant.[53]

At the apex of the profession were the royal judges. Over the course of our period the route for promotion to the bench changed considerably. Under Henry III it was not unusual for the clerks serving judges (particularly the keeper of the rolls and writs) to move up to the bench or become eyre justices. Such 'judicial dynasties' were created in the cases of Martin Patteshull, William Raleigh, Roger Thirkleby and Henry Bracton. Other famous judges of Edward I's reign, such as Ralph Hengham and Hervey Staunton also followed this route. Hengham, for example, was the protégé of Giles Erdington, serving as his clerk from 1258. By 1269 Hengham was an assize justice and was promoted to the court of common pleas in 1273. Staunton, who was a clerk in common pleas, became a judge there in 1306 after a stint as eyre justice (1302) and justice of assize (1303–6).[54] Some of the non-clerical judges appointed in the thirteenth century (and later) either had links with the exchequer or had served extensively in local administration.[55] Although both lay and clerical judges continued to be appointed through these channels, from the 1290s the men elevated to the bench tended to be those who were pleading in the central courts. Judges were thus to be regarded as skilled practitioners of the top rank. The regularisation of this avenue of promotion is observable from the fact that in Edward II's reign two-thirds of the serjeants followed it, while in the period 1315–77 three-fifths of all king's serjeants reached the bench.[56] By the mid-fourteenth century, upon attaining promotion to the bench a judge was normally dignified by being knighted (sometimes as a banneret) and also presented with robes befitting his social status from the royal wardrobe.[57]

A key feature in royal justice towards the end of the thirteenth century and into the fourteenth, and one that distinguished the band of common lawyers from the civil and canon lawyers, was laicisation. The change was not, however, a move from a bench filled exclusively by men in holy orders to a completely non-clerical bench. Not all early thirteenth-century royal judges were clerks. There was a coterie of professional judges who were laymen, among them Simon Pateshull, who came to prominence under King John.[58] The main question is, why did laicisation not occur earlier than it in fact did? Although the Third Lateran Council legislated in 1179 against ecclesiastics sitting as secular judges, the lure of professional advancement through the law was obviously intense. Indeed, Henry II encouraged the employment of a mixture of clerics and laymen on judicial panels. Under Henry III, the issue of the involvement of clerical justices in secular cases was part of a wider campaign for the withdrawal of clergy from secular government. There were arguments put forward by Richard Grant, archbishop of Canterbury and Robert Grosseteste, bishop of Lincoln, among others, against the intermixing of temporal and spiritual responsibilities and the sin encountered by taking part in secular judgments (particularly judgments of blood) either directly as an employee of the royal courts or indirectly through the exercise of franchisal jurisdiction.[59] Some of the greatest judges of the thirteenth century were men in holy orders and, despite the prohibition on participation in judgments of blood, men like William Raleigh had such cases adjourned especially for their hearing.[60] In a reversal of this theme, a late thirteenth-century diocesan statute from the bishop of Exeter prohibited laymen from practising in the ecclesiastical courts on the grounds of the impropriety of their dealing with spiritual causes.[61]

By the late thirteenth century, lay judges and lawyers were replacing their clerical colleagues in the royal courts and in positions of legal service. The justices of assize, who under the Statute of Fines (1299) assumed the duties of gaol delivery, did not actually sit at trials if they were in holy orders, their position being taken by local justices.[62] Under Edward II, only one of the five chief justices of king's bench was in holy orders and by 1327 clerical justices holding positions in the central courts had virtually become a thing of the past.[63] This was not a phenomenon just among the judiciary. The accounts of various religious houses demonstrate that between the 1310s and the 1370s there was a complete shift in the pattern of retaining legal counsel: common lawyers were displacing the canon lawyers.[64] In part, this change was not purely as a result of the policy on clerical involvement, but a social phenomenon, a consequence of the greater provision of education in the common law, itself fuelled by the sheer numbers of men willing to acquire legal skills and the increasing opportunities afforded in the rapidly expanding area of legal administration.[65] In terms of the laicisation of the judiciary, the avenue of promotion from serjeant to the bench may explain the hold that common lawyers gained on appointments. The knighting of judges was of course a reflection of the secularisation of appointments. For religious bodies pursuing litigation in the royal courts it also made sense to retain the services of knowledgeable common lawyers and then conduct all litigation through them.

Laicisation was a trend which significantly altered the attitudes and perceptions of both the profession itself and outsiders. Within the profession, there was a new concern for financial security and a concomitant emphasis on reward for services rendered. Coupled to this was a recognition of the advantages to be had from possessing knowledge and skills that were increasingly in demand and which, in turn, made the lawyer a valuable and essential commodity. Clerics, for instance, had previously been awarded benefices in return for their services. With this option no longer available (or only to those royal clerks and a minority of lawyers who were in holy orders), justices became reliant upon their official salaries (with which the Crown was often considerably in arrears), the retainers paid by magnates and religious houses and other fees and perquisites proffered for legal advice. Similarly, men of law sought remuneration from their clients in return for their services (either in court or in a managerial or advisory capacity) in the form of money, sometimes property, or benefits in kind. Retention on a permanent basis, a writ of annuity and the receipt of robes or livery were particularly desired (indeed, a necessity for men of consequence) as they provided the practitioner with an element of financial security, stability and social status. The writ of annuity was in the nature of a freehold, while the association with a particular body or household could provide the benefits of patronage.[66] Although these were private financial arrangements for professional services, such relations were perceived by those outside the profession as engendering unwholesome alliances.

The legal profession earned a further source of external recognition and a sense of identity within it from the development of a distinctive costume. While its clothing may not have been so different from other forms of medieval dress in the thirteenth century, by the following century a significant shift had occurred. It is apparent from an Oxford decree of 1358 that learned men considered it 'both decent and consonant with reason that those whom God hath made eminent over laymen through inward adornments should also be outwardly distinguished from laymen by their habit'.[67] The costume worn by thirteenth- and fourteenth-century lawyers differed from common dress primarily in its length and in the quality of its material. From at least the fourteenth century, long rayed or parti-coloured robes, hoods and coifs (close-fitting skull-shaped white caps with the corners drawn together and tied under the chin) were generally worn by pleaders. Although the coif was worn as early as 1305, it may not as yet have been an essential part of the costume, since they are omitted in an illustration for which the artist was given specific instructions to depict 'deus pledeurs'.[68] From the middle of the fourteenth century, though, coifs were equated with the order of serjeants-at-law. Judges dressed in similar robes, but usually wore a tabard (*collobium*) with wide elbow-length sleeves above the cassock and hood. By the end of the fourteenth century the tabard had been adopted by the serjeants, and judges wore a cloak or mantle instead.[69]

Although there were obvious similarities in outlook and training, a visual distinction was discernible between lawyers in holy orders and their lay colleagues in terms of the costume worn and its colour. Following laicisation, this in turn created noticeable differences between common-law practitioners and canon lawyers. In the early thirteenth century, Innocent III prohibited the wearing of red or green clothes and garments with sleeves rather than copes, while in 1281 English clergy were forbidden to wear coifs. A late thirteenth-century copy of *Bracton* depicts the clerical judges wearing academic *capae manicatae* (long-sleeved copes) and *pilei* (close-fitting black felt caps), while the lay judges have long gowns and coifs.[70]

By the late fourteenth century, the legal profession bore many of the hallmarks of a profession. Structurally, the legal profession had a hierarchy and an elite, tests of competence and avenues of promotion. Unlike other professions or trades, however, whose members were governed by a gild, lawyers were not at this time subject to the institutional control later exercised by the Inns of Court. Matters of internal discipline, such as the upholding of standards of behaviour within the profession, were handled by the courts. The functions of the Inns of Court (and chancery) were initially restricted to providing residential accommodation for lawyers, clerks and apprentices. These hostels acquired an educational role during the mid-fourteenth century and although they possessed as yet no formal status through charters of incorporation, they were clearly societies promoting a collegiate ethos. The common instructional undertaking and the form of communal living undoubtedly contributed to a strong sense of professional solidarity among the future judges and practitioners. By the end of the 1380s, however, certain Inns (the Middle Temple, Inner Temple and Gray's Inn) had gained a superior status as they were the sole source of the upper echelons of the bar, creating a distinction between the inns of the men of court (apprentices of the Bench) and the inns of chancery clerks.[71]

There were sufficient characteristics of a profession to mark them out to historians and contemporaries, but the boundaries should not be over-drawn: the blanket identity should not mask the differences within the profession nor obscure the overlaps with other professions or groups in society. Many 'men of law' were engaged in tasks outside the immediate legal sphere. Moreover, in many ways common lawyers had much in common with academic and ecclesiastical communities in their forms of dress, living arrangements and in intellectual pursuit. In this sense then it would be possible to speak of a shared consciousness or sense of community among the intellectual elite.

Men of law and legal ethics

The ethical behaviour and general conduct of members of the legal profession was the subject of deliberation and official scrutiny in the profession's early years. This was partly a symptom of the Crown's desire for accountability among its servants, but also evidence of a genuine concern for impartiality in judicial circles and the prevention of practices that would serve to undermine the operation of the law. In order to try to prevent judicial wrongdoing and ensure that practitioners were not behaving unethically a number of safeguards were initiated in the thirteenth and fourteenth centuries. This conscious thought about the effect of the actions (or inaction) of judges and lawyers, and the framing of rules of conduct accordingly, can be seen as a reflection of the growing intellectualism of the discipline and a move towards greater professionalism.

The main restraint on misbehaviour was the psychological, spiritual and chivalric device of an oath: an appeal to honour and a pledge of good faith, backed up by the foundation of religious belief. In the Middle Ages the swearing of an oath had an aura of sanctity, indeed such a pledge was usually described as *sacrum juratum* (sacred oath). Oaths were generally taken on gospel books, which were sacred objects in themselves.[72] Shareshull handed over 'the Book on which oaths are sworn', which he had in his possession, when he retired from the post of chief justice.[73] Oaths played an important part in the integration of society: they had a central place in the exercise of government and the law, and by the fourteenth century (if not before) were required from justices, pleaders, jurors, witnesses, and officials at all levels.[74]

Royal justices took some form of oath on appointment from at least the late twelfth century onwards. According to the earliest surviving example (in *Bracton*), probably in use during the third decade of the thirteenth century, their obligations were of a fairly vague nature: the first two clauses concerned the straightforward diligent exercise of their duties as the king's justices. The third one, however, enunciated a particular ethical standard in the performance of these duties: the royal judge was to uphold 'right justice' (*rectam justiciam*) and swore to do so (in what is a far-sighted recognition of human fallibility) 'to the best of his ability' (*pro posse suo*). An additional element was introduced around 1257 when it was required that royal justices (and barons of the exchequer) swear that they would not accept, either directly or indirectly, any gift or service (excluding customary hospitality of food and drink) from anyone whom they knew was a litigant in a case they expected to deal with.[75]

In the later years of Henry III's reign – or possibly at the beginning of Edward I's – a remodelling of the judicial oath occurred. In contrast to the previous versions there was a more comprehensive promise with an explicit concentration on standards of judicial conduct. The justice swore:[76]

> to do justice to the best of his ability to all as well poor as rich ... not to disturb or respite justice against right or against the law of the land either for the great or the rich, nor for hatred nor for favour nor for the estate of anyone nor for a benefit, gift or promise given or to be given to him nor in any other way; but loyally to do right to all according to law and custom.

By the 1290s, it is clear that the same judicial oath was taken by *all* royal justices (including local gaol delivery justices) on their admission to office and that the complaints of judicial misconduct arising at the end of the previous decade had correspondingly influenced its content. Though similar to the one recorded in 1278, there were significant differences. It contained a promise not to receive anything (except food and drink) *without the king's permission* and, more significantly, a clause designed to prevent complicity in misconduct by putting the onus on an individual to dissuade his colleagues from embarking on or continuing with any perceived wrongdoing. If he failed in this respect he was bound to report it to the king's council or, in the absence of an appropriate response, to the king himself.[77] The terms of the oath also extended to the Justice of Chester as evidenced by the oath used at the installation of Richard Mascy to the position in 1299.[78] In 1307 the oath for royal counsellors contained a clause specifically for members of the judiciary[79] and in 1317 the judges were urged to make sure that they did not deny anyone justice.[80]

The 1346 Ordinance of Justices focused on the actions and behaviour of those exercising power in a judicial capacity,[81] enshrining in statute law standards of conduct applicable to the pursuance of their duties. The oath prescribed under the ordinance was itself remarkably similar to its thirteenth-century predecessors in its emphasis on equal justice to rich and poor alike and its prohibition of reward (either in cash or by way of a gift or anything from which profit might be gained). Hospitality in the form of meat and drink was again exempted provided that it was of negligible value. There was equally a duty placed on those in a position of judicial responsibility to inform the king of any 'damage or disherison'. A significant divergence from earlier oaths was the onus placed on justices when holding office to accept neither payment nor robes from anyone but the Crown. To make up for this restriction on earnings the king agreed to increase the judges' salaries and there is evidence from the wardrobe accounts that they were provided with new robes (in the royal livery) for both summer and winter.[82]

The seriousness with which the Crown viewed any transgression of these solemn undertakings can be gauged initially from the nature of the punishment envisaged. In 1257 the sanction against a judge's violation of his oath was dismissal from his position and forfeiture of a year's wages.[83] Ninety years later, the stakes had been raised considerably. It was not merely his judicial position and wages which could be lost: upon conviction the offender's lands, goods and even his life were placed at the king's will.

This insistence upon standards of judicial conduct could only be effective if there was widespread recognition of the level of behaviour that was expected and the remedies for breaches or injustices that could be claimed accordingly. An important element in the desired success of the ordinance of 1346, therefore, lay in the requirement that it be published openly and exhibited in such places in his bailiwick as the sheriff thought appropriate. Relief was also offered: anyone who thought that they had a grievance under the ordinance concerning the misdemeanours of judges and local officials could complain to the assize justices or pursue the matter in chancery before the chancellor and treasurer. The king was thus encouraging his subjects to scrutinise and report upon the ethical behaviour of royal servants performing judicial functions with an eye to benefiting both the complainant and the Crown: to ensure that justice really meant fairness and that miscreants were not allowed to continue in office unless the king willed otherwise. The ordinance of 1346 was reaffirmed by Richard II in 1384, perhaps to allay doubts over judicial impartiality and show the king's commitment to justice.[84]

Lawyers

A generation or so after the death of Bracton it is apparent that the Crown and judiciary were aware of the potentially disruptive effect of the behaviour of certain members of the nascent legal profession and of the negative impact this could have on public confidence in the judicial system. Regulation was initially confined to a somewhat unspecific professional obligation formulated in the Statute of Westminster (1275),[85] but was more fully developed, at least with regard to fees and retaining, in the Ordinance of Justices (1346). The 1275 legislation created a duty on legal practitioners not to mislead the court or litigants, and established harsh penalties for demonstrable malpractice: imprisonment for a year and a day, together with complete disbarment or permanent suspension from practising. In practice the statute's enforcement was left to the judges, who, through their presidency of the courts, elaborated on its terms to provide norms of professional behaviour equating to an ethical standard. It appears that serjeants and professional attorneys alike were expected to conform to this code, and to observe it whether they acted in the customary or royal courts. The existence of this private regulatory code and, indeed, its practical application is confirmed by instances of professional misbehaviour coming to the attention of the justices either during a trial itself or as a result of complaints brought against court personnel by disgruntled litigants.[86]

Analysing such evidence it is possible to see certain key precepts at work in the courts. A serjeant-at-law owed a primary duty of loyalty to his client.[87] He was not allowed to leave the client's service before the conclusion of litigation unless informed that his services were no longer required or the client failed to pay his fee. There was also a continuing obligation to the client once the particular case in which he was retained had finished:

the serjeant could not be employed by his client's opponent without the former's permission, nor could he appear against his client in subsequent litigation. Secondly (in line with the 1275 statute), he was under a duty not to deceive the court and was liable to be punished if he made an untrue statement in court or advised his client to sue more than once on the same matter. Thirdly, a serjeant's general conduct was subject to scrutiny, whether he was pleading for a client or undertaking his own business. Wasting the court's time or persisting with an unconvincing argument were particularly frowned upon and received discouragement.[88]

A professional attorney was similarly bound in terms of his relations with clients. It was expected, for instance, that he would exercise due diligence in his preparation and handling of the case: obtaining the necessary writs and ensuring that there was a minimum of delay in pursuing the various stages of litigation. Like the serjeant, he was under a continuing obligation to his client and could be punished for deliberate fraud, negligence or incompetence. There were also obligations in respect of a client's opponent (such as taking account of legitimate grounds for absence and not suing in default), a duty to third parties, and to the court itself (such as following the correct procedures).

The fact that this code of professional ethics emerged out of, and may be effectively reconstructed from, the breaches of good conduct exposed in court does, of course, provide direct evidence that abuses continued to occur. But how rife was such malpractice? While the relative infrequency of such cases cannot in itself be taken to indicate that levels of integrity were high and misconduct kept in check, they do demonstrate that blatant deviation from the acceptable standards of good conduct was acknowledged and punished by the courts. Indeed, if anything, it suggests that the judiciary regarded conformity to a code of ethics as a necessary corollary to professional status and to the 'special relationship' which lawyers enjoyed with the courts. Allegations were usually tried by juries of fellow professionals and the punishments reflected the seriousness with which each particular breach was viewed. If the conduct point arose during the trial itself, a warning or some form of judicial guidance might be given. In other instances men were fined (the money being split between the client – as a form of compensation – and the royal coffers) or spent brief periods in gaol (which would undoubtedly affect their reputation and curtail their earning capacity). Others were punished by temporary suspension, by receiving the statutory period of imprisonment, or (in really serious cases, where perhaps a forged writ had been used or an entry in the plea roll had been falsified) by permanent suspension from practising in court.

The evidence compiled by Dr Brand relates mainly to the thirteenth century. It is clear, though, that the courts remained concerned for practitioners' ethical behaviour and, as cases appearing in the court of king's bench reveal, the provisions of the First Statute of Westminster were still being enforced in the mid-fourteenth century. In 1347, for instance, John of Chester, an attorney, received the statutory term of imprisonment (a year and a day) and was barred from practising in the royal courts for deceit and falsity. In 1352 John of Luddington was required to swear before the chancellor that he would not come within twelve leagues of the king's court, that he would not give counsel to anyone in prejudice of the Crown's interests nor act as attorney for anyone.[89] Dissatisfied litigants also began to use other remedies against their legal representatives, couching their complaints in terms of negligence in carrying on the profession of attorney or pleader. In 1345, Cristian de Bury, an attorney, was charged with deceit and trespass on the allegation that he had been engaged to plead an action of debt in the Sheriffs' Court in London and when the action came before the jury he failed to plead.[90] In 1382 a common pleader in London was sued for deceit on the complaint that he had advised his client badly and then advised another party.[91]

It can therefore be said with some assurance that there was definite concern within (and outside) the legal profession during the thirteenth and fourteenth centuries that the law should be upheld and its practices revered. In addition to competence, a reputation for probity was paramount for employment (and of course for re-employment) in the sphere of court activity. Trustworthiness was also a necessary prerequisite for appointment in a number of other legal contexts, such as arbitrations and enfeoffment to uses. The frequency with which lawyers were called upon to act as a feoffee in the late fourteenth century, for example, suggests that landowners relied upon practitioners to perform their duties in good faith.[92]

Judges

The justices' oath placed on them an onus to intervene and use their discretion where it mattered. A practical manifestation of the judges' role in this respect might be using their discretion to assign counsel to poor litigants and thus counteract any advantage which a litigant of higher status might wield.[93] This might be particularly pertinent in the case of a poor litigant unable to provide the customary gifts for judges and jurors. The capacity to look at an individual's situation and go behind the strict letter of the law to the underlying morality characterised the term in office of several judges of the period and was a vital factor in the beginnings of 'equity' and the chancellor's 'court of conscience'. Towards the end of Edward I's reign, for example, royal judges Staunton, Hengham and Howard were quite prepared to override a statute where hardship might result.[94] A couple of years later, Bereford appeared willing to act likewise 'because of the hardship that will ensue'.[95] Staunton refused to let a woman lose her dower through a tenant's deviousness, and by distinguishing between the heir's inheritance and his purchase achieved 'justice' for her.[96] Weyland also sought to make equitable decisions (*Je regarde en ce cas un equite*).[97]

Bereford in particular must have gained a reputation for his humanity. He was not averse to urging counsel to admit a fact that had not been proved if it rescued the situation ('You must not allow conscience to prevent your doing law'). Where he felt unable to intervene, he made it clear that that, in his opinion, good faith was on the losing side ('It is a dishonest thing for an honourable man to demand what his predecessor has released').[98] Bereford's sense of fairness and proportion included the suggestion that lack of proof in writing (now) was not necessarily detrimental to a claim ('Would you have his estate and the estate of his wife perish because he has no charter? It may be that he had a deed which is lost, but thereby he has not lost his right').[99] Although the judges just mentioned were predominantly men of the late thirteenth and early fourteenth centuries, there were others in the mid- to late fourteenth century who carried this spirit forward. Stonor, for instance, was of the opinion (in a case coming before him) that 'by conscience and the law of God it would be against reason' for the plaintiff to be disinherited.[100] Mowbray, similarly, believed the law (judicial decisions) needed to be in accord with 'reason' and to remedy 'mischief' (injustice).[101]

Where there were complaints about royal judges, the Crown was not slow to act. The dismissal in 1289–90 of eleven members of the higher judiciary (three from the court of king's bench and four from common pleas, including the chief justices of both benches, as well as four justices in eyre) following allegations of misconduct could be seen as a defining moment in the early history of the judicial profession.[102] Their convictions in what have been referred to as 'state trials' and the subsequent imposition of substantial fines totalling at least £20,000 (equal to almost a whole year's normal income for the Crown) appear to signal corruption on a grand scale. In what amounted to another aggressive strike at the judiciary almost sixty years later Edward III sacked a total of seven of his judges, dismissing such eminent figures as William Shareshull, Richard Willoughby and

John Stonor, as well as John Shardlow, Robert Sadington and John Inge. Robert Scarborough initially appeared to have survived the cull and formally remained in office as a king's bench justice until suddenly on 5 August 1341 his right to act in any judicial capacity whatsoever was suspended.[103]

When examining the official responses to allegations of judicial corruption that surfaced during the thirteenth and fourteenth centuries it is necessary to bear several points in mind. We should resist the temptation of judging medieval justice purely from a modern ethical standpoint and should instead consider the extent to which judges in fact aimed to provide impartiality. Rather than taking these dismissals at face value as necessarily indicating a manifest lack of ethics among the higher judiciary, it is instructive to analyse the particular contexts and discuss the similarities and differences that emerge from the two events. We must also seek to understand the complicated political and social framework within which royal justices operated. Once we approach the actions of the judiciary on their own terms, we have to sift through the obfuscations of hyperbole (some of it contemporary, some of it more modern) and bias in an attempt to reach a more balanced view. Any criticisms made ought to distinguish individual wrongdoing from that attributable to the entire judiciary. Finally, attention should be paid to the outcome of the particular judicial 'crises' and the capacity of the judicial system to alter its practices as well as rehabilitate its personnel.

Royal punishment took the form of a 'short, sharp shock'. In the 1290s judges suffered a brief spell in prison which was attenuated by payment of an 'agreed' sum for release. The level of fines was then related not to the seriousness of the offences, but to the judge's ability to pay. Ralph Hengham, the former chief justice of king's bench and probably the wealthiest man on the bench, was required to pay possibly as much as 10,000 marks. For the few actually convicted, the scale of fines in the fourteenth century was no less slight. Richard Willoughby was fined a hefty sum (1,200 marks with a recognisance bond of 2,200 marks), but his punishment also (and unusually) included the humiliation of being paraded before the oyer and terminer justices in the various counties they visited.[104] Only Thomas Weyland, chief justice of the common bench (1278–89) was disgraced and allowed to abjure the realm, but this, it should be emphasised, was for complicity in a murder and unrelated to his judicial activities.[105]

Reconciliation with the king and rehabilitation into royal service was more protracted in the thirteenth-century example than in the fourteenth-century one. Although the failure to restore the justices sooner may have in fact reflected subsequent changes in the administration of justice following the suspension of the eyre and/or new recruitment practices, it was ten years before Hengham was re-appointed to the king's council and eleven before he took up judicial office again. Other disgraced colleagues such as William Brompton and Master Thomas Siddington were eventually re-employed in the king's service in the late 1290s, but did not serve in the central courts. Thomas Weyland perhaps surprisingly enjoyed a pardon and was allowed to return to England, but he, like most of the other justices did not live out the century. It may appear significant that two justices (Hopton and Leicester) were never rehabilitated, but in fact both men were accused of only very limited wrongdoing and achieved some measure of exoneration. In the mid-fourteenth century the situation was remarkably different. Restoration generally came within a couple of years. Stonor, Shareshull and Shardlow were swiftly re-instated and were sitting in the court of common pleas again during 1342. Willoughby returned to royal service after two years in the wilderness and enjoyed a long spell as justice of common pleas (1343–57). Only Inge was not fully pardoned until 1344, though this was far sooner than he could have expected sixty years earlier. No charges were ever brought against Stonor and Shareshull; equally, although he lost his seat at the bench, Sadington was merely transferred to the exchequer bench, apparently without any accusations levelled against him.

The nature of the proceedings in the two eras was also quite different. Even though the allegations concerned for the most part the misdeeds of royal servants acting in their official capacity, the so-called 'state trials' of 1289–90 were in fact civil proceedings based on private complaints. With the exception of action taken against Weyland (which, as mentioned above, was unrelated to his official position) there was no hint of criminal prosecution by presentment or indictment, nor was there any mention of public interest, nor an attempt to maintain that the Crown was a party. In fact, if the trial of Willoughby (chief justice of king's bench in 1332, and 1338–40) is a representative example, the 1340–41 proceedings could more aptly be named 'state trials'. His appearance (in the custody of the mace bearers) before the special oyer and terminer commission headed by Robert Parving (very recently elevated to chief justice of king's bench), Robert Sadington (chief baron of the exchequer) and William Scot (newly appointed chief justice of common pleas) was 'by clamour of the people' without any indictment or private suit. Indeed, Parving's assertion that this was how the king was 'informed' brought back memories of Edward

II's reign when notorious deeds could be punished without proper trial by judgment on the king's record (see Chapter 6). While this was clearly not the line being adopted, the general accusation (that he had perverted and sold the laws as if they had been oxen or cows) was nevertheless allowed to stand without any requirement for one of the normal modes of prosecution. A salient feature of Willoughby's trial, though, was his vigorous defence of his conduct, challenging both the substance of the accusations and the way in which they were brought.[106] Some of the thirteenth-century judges also mounted credible defences of their positions.[107]

Interestingly, the higher judiciary were not the only victims in the two royal purges. In 1289 various senior royal officials (including Adam Stratton, a chamberlain of the exchequer) were the subjects of complaints and punished accordingly.[108] In 1340 the chancellor and the treasurer were the main targets and they and a number of other government and household officials were removed and accused of corruption.[109] While the coincidence should not absolve the justices from any provable wrongdoing, it does nevertheless draw attention away from their apparent isolation as a body supposedly with questionable standards of behaviour. Similarly, in 1381, although lawyers were singled out, there was also considerable discontent about the behaviour of royal officials.

It should be remembered that according to contemporary political theory, the judges owed their position to the king (*judices non habentur nisi per regem*) and as the king's servants could be appointed or dismissed at will. An element of arbitrariness, therefore, was to be expected at times of political stress. While the strong element of surprise in the Crown's actions (in 1289 and 1340) undoubtedly gave the judicial profession a sharp jolt, it is difficult to determine whether the impact was anything other than short-term. In employment terms, absence from royal service may have placed a brake on their income (assuming the king was not substantially in arrears with payments as was often the case) but fees could presumably be earned in private practice by giving advice to clients. With regard to professional standards, the purge of 1289 undoubtedly provided a valuable precedent for Edward III and in the years immediately following both instances the threat of further measures may have hovered menacingly over holders of judicial offices. It is significant, however, that there was no royal interference with the composition of the courts during Edward II's reign despite the complaints in the Ordinances of 1311 (cc. 13, 14) about 'evil counsellors'.[110]

The only other judicial dismissals in the period between Magna Carta and the Peasants' Revolt were isolated occurrences: Henry of Bath (a senior justice of king's bench) in 1251, William Inge in 1317, William Thorpe in 1350 and Henry Green (chief justice of king's bench) and William Skipwith (former common pleas justice and exchequer baron) in 1365. It is instructive to examine the context and effect of their alleged wrongdoing. Henry of Bath was accused of 'stuffing his purse' and ambidextry (receiving gifts from both parties) and it was said that he had appropriated more than £200 of lands as a justice in eyre. Following an investigation, Henry III was persuaded to reinstate him in 1253 through the intervention of the justice's wife (a member of the Basset family) and the earl of Cornwall.[111] William Inge was dismissed abruptly in the middle of Edward II's reign when he was accused of corruptly acquiring the manor of Woodmanstern in Surrey. While he lost his position, he did not forfeit royal favour and there is no indication that anything was actually proved against him.[112]

The relatively brief period between Edward III's *en masse* removal of officials in 1340 and the Ordinance of Justices of 1346 and the high-profile dismissals of 1350 and 1365 suggests that the lesson had not been learned. Although there was ultimately a change of heart in terms of his punishment, Edward III's treatment of Thorpe indicates a definite concern to stamp out any allegations of corruption and that, in order to uphold his 'anti-sleaze' campaign, he was prepared to make an example of someone as exalted as his chief justice. The magnates and representatives of the royal household who sat on the commission together with its enrolment in parliament suggest that such misdemeanour was viewed seriously. Edward III may even have taken it as a personal breach of trust.

The charge levelled in 1350 against Thorpe, who faced an oyer and terminer commission headed by the earls of Warwick, Arundel and Huntingdon (and which also included the steward and chamberlain of the household) was that he had gone against his judicial oath and accepted bribes amounting to £100 at king's bench sessions held at Lincoln. Thorpe confessed, and though he initially faced the fierce penalty of being hanged, drawn and quartered and having his lands confiscated (as set out in the Ordinance of Justices), he was snatched from the jaws of death and disgrace when judgment failed to be carried out and the case was removed to chancery. The chancellor and treasurer were ordered personally by the king to search all the records and rolls relevant to his period as chief justice and his actions in other judicial capacities under the supervision of Shareshull, the new chief justice, and one of the clerks of king's bench. The records of the case were then set out for parliament in February 1351. In the event, Thorpe was pardoned in 1351 by the king 'in gratitude for his previous services'.[113] Rehabilitation came almost immediately. Thorpe deserves some credit for pleading guilty rather than raise technicalities or objections (though we do not know the state of the evidence against him). The threat of death itself appears to have turned into a clever psychological ploy on the part of the king: by sparing Thorpe, not only was he able to retain the services of a valued judge for use in his courts, but also secure the penitence, obedience and unswerving future loyalty of a powerful man.

The reasons for Green's and Skipwith's removal from office in 1365 cannot be ascertained from the surviving rolls, though the chronicler, Knighton, enigmatically describes them as 'heinous breaches of trust'.[114] Whatever they were, the former chief justice seems to have disappeared from public life completely and then died four years later.[115] William Skipwith was re-appointed to the common pleas bench at the end of Edward III's reign, and served for a further twelve years (1376–88).

Return to royal service was obviously a feature of the dismissals, but often rehabilitation meant service in a slightly different capacity. William Thorpe, for instance, took up a position as a second baron in the exchequer in 1352. Robert Scarborough, after his suspension in 1341 was restored to royal service in 1344 as chief justice of the justiciar's bench in Ireland.[116] Ralph Hengham, erstwhile chief justice of the king's bench in the late thirteenth century, moved across to the court of common pleas at the beginning of the fourteenth century. Redeployment as opposed to permanent removal enabled the king to continue to make use of a judge's undeniable skills, but at the same time maintained at least in appearance (and perhaps in litigants' minds) the air of enforced absence. The king's desire for accountability was also signalled by the significant reduction in the number of justices appointed to sit in the court of common pleas (from nine in 1340 to three immediately after the dismissals).[117] Codes of conduct and self-regulation by the courts heightened consciousness of the perils of misbehaviour. Such measures also contributed to a sense of identity within the profession (in terms of duties specific to men of law), but effectively signalled to those outside it the profession's capacity for incompetence and wrongdoing.

Judges and lawyers in society

Judges and lawyers operated in a wider context than the immediate one offered by the courts or their legal practices. Most, if not all, possessed lands and private local interests, and were immersed in the local social and economic world. Many lawyers admired and sought to emulate the lifestyles and values of the landowners or merchants they represented or judged. Their earnings (and in some cases accumulated wealth) were usually ploughed into land or capital ventures. Over the course of their lengthy careers in the law, men like Bereford, Scrope and Shareshull were able to build up considerable estates. Bereford had thirteen manors and tenements scattered in nine counties.[118] By contrast, Scrope's lands were accumulated predominantly in Yorkshire,[119] while Shareshull's estates lay mainly in Staffordshire and Oxfordshire.[120] Men of law in holy orders could also build up a considerable income from benefices. A contemporary perception of a judge's 'worth' in the late fourteenth century is afforded by the rates of assessment detailed in the Anonimale chronicle for the 1379 poll tax, for which judges ranked higher than the baronage.[121]

To what extent, though, did judges possess influence within – and therefore impact upon – the consciousness of county society? How did ordinary lawyers fit in to the social and economic network? Where the evidence allows, the impact of lawyers within provincial society can be gauged from their acquisitions and their relationships with other shire residents. Practising lawyers, such as the Scrope brothers, were often 'self-made' men, their status and estates acquired as a consequence of their own labours. Since many of them came from comparatively humble backgrounds, they were unlikely to receive a social or financial advantage from inheritances, but in some cases may well have aspired to a place in the county elite. Some, such as Shareshull, made astute marriages and achieved social or financial advancement.[122] Successful serjeants achieved status through elevation to knighthood, which by Edward III's reign came as a matter of course on promotion to the bench.[123] Deliberate efforts, however, were made on the part of 'men of law' to disguise the fact that they owed their status to their professional know-how and to present themselves publicly as part of gentry society. The blurring of distinctions was increased further by the fact that some lawyers came from gentry families and were therefore already a part of landed society.

The Crown's practice of appointing judges and serjeants of the central courts to assize circuits and oyer and terminer commissions in areas where their own private interests lay, where they themselves held lands or had family or other connections, proved to be a double-edged sword. Royal government obviously deemed it appropriate that the justices should have some local knowledge of the area under their jurisdiction. An appreciation of the balance of power in the region, of the ascendancy or decline of particular families, of the topography and customs, was probably a vital factor in trying to achieve a just outcome. It provided an opportunity for the government to temper its 'centralising' tendencies, presenting on the bench what might be seen as a familiar, local face. It could be useful to have the respect of other landowners, though decisions concerning landholding might be something from which the justice (as landowner in the region) eventually benefited, probably not directly in the sense of profiting from the settlement, but possibly indirectly with regard to subsequent relations (whether legal or social).

However, if disputes occurred between friends, neighbours or business associates, they needed to rely on the judge being impartial. By the later fourteenth century this was something that exercised the minds of the parliamentary commons. In 1375 there was a request from them that lawyers should not be appointed as assize justices in their home county, as it was feared they were too closely associated with the people there and their judgments might accordingly be biased.[124] The Crown invited specific complaints on the matter, but a statute was not issued until 1384,[125] nearly ten years later and only following the backlash against royal justice exhibited in 1381. Even then the effectiveness of this provision was minimal. It was manifestly ignored and the circuit personnel remained virtually unchanged.[126]

The 1375 petition suggests that relations between lawyers and their neighbours may have been strained at times and their motives distrusted. Although lawyers may have been respected because of their knowledge of the law and their influence in the courts, nevertheless as a result of their own landholding and activities they inevitably became embroiled personally in property disputes with neighbours and other local landowners.[127] Status within the realm, as in the case of judges, could inhibit actions against them. The bishop of Worcester's council, when deciding whether or not to proceed against Ralph Hengham, came to the conclusion that 'he is of the king's council wherefor it is not expedient to proceed against him'.[128] Yet, litigants were not always so reluctant or afraid to sue a judge. Cecily de Beauchamp brought a writ of entry against William Inge in 1317 and succeeded in recovering her land.[129] Similarly, Mabel, widow of William Grimbaud, was able to reclaim her dower in the manor of Houghton in Northamptonshire against Henry Spigurnel.[130]

Obviously, relations with neighbours were not always confrontational. Land transactions (including exchanges) took place between lawyers and other landholders and there was mutual witnessing of charters. The retaining of lawyers for advice and assistance, which over the course of the thirteenth and fourteenth centuries was increasingly regarded as a necessity both for individuals and corporations, may have brought about closer relations, resulting in friendships subsisting outside their official connection. Judging from their letters to each other, John Stonor and the bishop of Exeter enjoyed a close association.[131] Links established prior to a man of law's rise to serjeant, and before a serjeant's elevation to the ranks of the central court judiciary, frequently remained intact and could even be strengthened as a consequence of the new position.[132] Although the justice retained by the abbot in *A Gest of Robyn Hode* ('I am holde with the abbot ... both with cloth and fee')[133] might be thought of as working under an exclusive arrangement, in reality both judges and lawyers had a plurality of associations, and rarely did they give anyone their sole, overriding allegiance.

Another feature of the judges' position within society (though it was not necessarily linked solely to connections within their home regions) was an interest in commercial investment and a capacity for moneylending.[134] The latter occupation (shared with some other leading royal servants, some of whom were churchmen) may have endeared them to those in temporary need of funds, but it made them unpopular with those whose 'cash-flow' problems were more serious or long-term and whose debts might be called in.[135] As was common for the period, many lawyers put their money into religious devotion by founding perpetual chantries, either out of genuine spiritual concern or as a means of purchasing the respect of posterity.[136] Clerical lawyers tended to make financial investments in education and culture, endowing churches, colleges and schools or making bequests of their specialist books to institutions.[137] Hervey Staunton, for example, made significant endowments to found and support Michaelhouse in Cambridge (later subsumed into Trinity College).[138]

Lawyers were able to influence the people around them – and those with whom they sought connections or were associated – in other perhaps less obvious, more intangible ways. Travelling around the country, as they frequently did, lawyers provided an important channel of communication: they were bearers of news, gossip and information. In 1290 Solomon of Rochester was able to inform the prior of Christ Church, Canterbury of the queen's death and about the preparations being made for her funeral as well as details about the king's movements.[139] Notions of 'worship' and 'good lordship' were important concomitants of service and retaining, which would have proceeded from formal and informal ties. An awareness of the advantages in knowing a man with legal knowledge and judicial influence meant that acquaintances with judges and lawyers were likely to be cultivated. The bishop of Exeter gave fees of £2 to William Bereford and Hervey Stanton in 1309 for their advice and assistance, as well as for their benevolence and many graces shown in the past and, he hoped, still to be shown in the future.[140]

The desire to belong to a network or affinity may also have been a factor in lawyers' minds, as well as attracting in turn individuals (as servants, retainees, or associates) to their orbit.[141] Marriage alliances in particular were a way of achieving reciprocal benefits for the families concerned. Geoffrey Scrope's daughters, Beatrice and Constance, for instance, both married into the Luttrell family.[142] The very presence of judges and lawyers in a region and, indeed their recruitment from a particular county could make a difference in the treatment that area received and in the way it perceived itself. In the fourteenth century, Yorkshire provided significant numbers not only of royal clerks, but also lawyers and judges, among them men such as Thomas Ingleby, William Finchdean, John Doncaster and the Scrope brothers.[143] The impact of lawyers exercising jurisdiction as landowners could be felt at the very local level. Some judges, such as John Stonor and Geoffrey Scrope, took a close interest in aspects of estate management and were engaged in elaborate agricultural operations.[144] Absence from estates for long periods of time could, however, give rise to instability and uncertainty in the locality.

Centre and periphery

While the centralisation of justice and the professionalisation of the law can give the impression that all changes were derived from the centre, the lawyers practising in the central courts were not divorced from the prevailing concerns of the regions and were just as much members of provincial society as their clients. Indeed, it was the localities outside London which then fed the centralised Westminster system of common law with most of the cases it dealt with. Furthermore, the demand for legal services was not restricted to the Westminster courts and in many instances stemmed from the need for advice and representation locally. Not only were the personnel of the courts drawn from all parts of the country, but many of the cases initiated may have been rooted in local issues.

The various sub-groups or branches within the profession had different aims and attitudes depending on their role, expectations and stake within the practice of law. Some operated on the fringes of the law, but were nevertheless recognisable for their own distinctive contribution. Before the thirteenth century, the standard method for giving parties notice to appear in the court was through an oral summons rather than service of a royal or viscontiel writ. The task of summoning was performed by 'criers' (*criatores*), who were presumably literate and who according to *Glanvill* were required to inform the parties openly and proclaim the summons itself in a public place, usually the county court. Although by the later Middles Ages summoners working in the common-law system had become fictitious persons, the practice of voicing the summons lasted at least until Edward I's reign.[145] The ecclesiastical court's equivalent (deputed by the dean or archdeacon) was required to make the citation to the defendant in person in the presence of two witnesses or publicly during mass in his parish church. The ecclesiastical summons was certainly voiced in the thirteenth century, and although it is difficult to know how long this practice continued, a late fourteenth-century summoner is portrayed (rather unflatteringly) in Chaucer's *Canterbury Tales*.[146]

The role played by scriveners and their ecclesiastical counterparts, notaries, as legal intermediaries between the public and the law, also deserves consideration. There were notaries public operating in England by the 1280s, though the court of king's bench noted that they were a breed whose name had only recently been heard in the realm of England. In the early fourteenth century the usefulness of trained notaries was apparent in ecclesiastical circles. However, the growing demand for legal proofs, exemplifications of title deeds and records of legal processes enabled them to become more established in the public mind. While some may have served mainly as copyists in diocesan registries and the ecclesiastical courts, by the later fourteenth century unattached notaries public were increasingly compiling legal instruments for private clients and offering advice on legal matters.[147] The term 'scrivener' was not in common usage in the thirteenth and early fourteenth centuries, but by 1373, it is apparent that scriveners in the city of London had become a guild or company with their own set of ordinances which had been approved and enrolled by the mayor and corporation. An expansion in the numbers of men engaged in the craft of writing was, like the notaries, dictated by the growing desire for documentation, charters, wills, enfeoffments to uses, bills and petitions, sealed bonds and other legal documents. It was in this context that they became indispensable to less well-off people in London and in the provinces, and perhaps as a first port of call for those who could not afford to engage an attorney.[148]

As drafters of legal documents and recorders of pleas and judgments, chancery or justices' clerks were ideally placed to advise on what legal action could be taken or to comment on proceedings. Some senior clerks appear to have involved themselves in a range of judicial functions and to demonstrate an understanding of current law and practice.[149] In towns there was a special position for lawyers, the common clerk or recorder, who in addition to making a record of – and testifying to – local custom (which it was said he did by word of mouth at his peril), acted as legal adviser to the mayor and aldermen. The civic records of York indicate that the recorder was required to be 'sachaunt de la ley' and was elected by common assent.[150]

The activities of the legal profession were increasingly complex and diverse. Although the training required for each professional branch differed in its focus and intensity, there could be considerable overlap among those who undertook the tasks of 'attorney' and 'pleader' and indeed those who exercised a judicial function depending on the type of court they appeared in and the location in which they were employed. Some men acted as attorneys in the central courts and were also pleaders in the county courts.[151] Pleaders in the Westminster courts frequently appeared as justices of assize and gaol delivery in the provinces.[152]

The employment of local men of law as justices in the regions was an important feature of the judicial system. In the early thirteenth century, commissions were issued to four justices (called 'four knights'), who sometimes included a bench justice, for the assizes and gaol delivery. Opportunities in local justice and shire government increased exponentially during the second half of the thirteenth century as a result of the reforming zeal of the baronial movement of 1258 and the process of resettlement after the civil war. The so-called 'four knights' system continued to operate for the assizes and gaol delivery until 1293. In the reorganisation of the circuits and their personnel in the wake of the statute of 1293, local men (with some exceptions) were rarely commissioned to hold assizes. The period following the demise of the eyre was a key period during which the expertise of local men was relied upon. The popularity among litigants of special oyer and terminer commissions (whose panels included local justices) and the government's use of general ones (again some having local input) provided an important outlet for legal knowledge and judicial experience. With the growth in confidence of the office of keeper of the peace (who in addition to some military functions heard complaints about serious crimes and breaches of the king's peace in the county), this became a channel for the judicial powers of local men as a counterweight to the assize and gaol-delivery circuits staffed by central court justices. Local men continued to play a major role in gaol delivery up until the 1330s, by which time they were regularly enjoying oyer and terminer powers as justices of the peace.[153]

The office of estates steward was obviously attractive to many administrators and men of law. With the benefit of hindsight, it is possible to observe that some men fulfilled the role of steward or bailiff at the start of their legal career, before going on to be serjeant or rising further to become a judge. Some serjeants, such as William Bereford (steward of the abbot of Ramsey, 1287-88 and 1293-94) and John Shardlow (steward of the abbot of St Edmunds, 1323-24) served in this capacity in spite of (or in addition to) their work in the central courts.[154] As the servants of secular and/or ecclesiastical landowners, men appointed as stewards often fulfilled important public duties for the king in the shire.[155] Although the Statute of Lincoln (1316) barred stewards from holding office as sheriff,[156] many were engaged in gaol-delivery work in the early fourteenth century,[157] and continued their judicial involvement in the royal courts through appointment as keepers/justices of the peace. William Cheltenham, the steward of the Berkeleys in Gloucestershire,[158] sat on numerous judicial commissions in the mid-fourteenth century, from assizes and commissions of the peace to commissions on forged currency and weights and measures.[159]

Education in legal matters was not restricted to those who were destined to practise in the central courts.[160] There were many opportunities for people to acquire the knowledge and skills useful for work in county administration, in estate management and in private practice. Some men were fortunate enough to have financial provision made for their studies. An indenture drawn up in 1323 relates how Richard Bruche, who in later life became a coroner of Lancashire, was to be provided with a year's schooling at Oxford followed by a four-year apprenticeship at the court of common pleas, enabling him to acquire accounting and notarial skills before embarking on a more advanced legal education.[161] It is clear, however, that the instruction available in and around the courts at Westminster - and later in the Inns of Court and chancery - did not represent the sole source of legal training. A medieval 'business school' operating in Oxford offered a more elementary law course, but one eminently suited to those wishing to be schooled not only in letter-writing and methods of accounting, but in writing and speaking French and various forms of legal work, including the drafting of charters. The curriculum for the conveyancing course, which was running in the late thirteenth century (and possibly earlier), included teaching on the four kinds of estate in land, the nine principal parts of a deed, detailed instruction on drawing up charters and the factors that might vitiate them. The lecturers (identifiable from surviving manuscripts) provided glosses and specimens on a number of the forms and by the later fourteenth century also included tuition on bonds, acquittances and enfeoffment.[162]

Schooling could be enhanced or supplemented by reading legal texts, from which informal instruction might also be gained. As noted above, the thirteenth century witnessed a flourishing of handbooks and treatises on legal and administrative matters. Some were aimed primarily at the upper end of the professional spectrum, but others were designed for the generalist, especially the steward and the county justice. As professional administrators the former required knowledge of land tenures, pleas and the intricacies of estate management.[163] Treatises, such as *The Court Baron* (composed c.1265) and *How to Hold Pleas and Courts* (composed in c.1272), provided detailed instructions about local courts and templates for potential administrative and judicial encounters ('roleplays'). *Placita Corone* was a text providing precedents on appeals of felony, certain defences and the general conduct of criminal trials at gaol delivery.[164]

A working knowledge of the statutes was obviously considered relevant (if not vital) to the legal work of practising lawyers and officials. Private reference to the *statuta Angliae* was provided by statute rolls, which were commercially produced around the turn of the fourteenth century. Statute books, which soon eclipsed the earlier roll format, were widely available by the 1350s and could be produced to order. They usually contained a number of the common-law treatises mentioned above and other contemporary documents in addition to Magna Carta and important Edwardian statutes, such as the Statutes of Westminster II and Winchester (1285).[165]

Perceptions of the legal profession

The antipathy and extreme violence exhibited towards the legal profession during the Peasants' Revolt, which included the targeting of both central and local lawyers and selected assassinations,[166] offers a 'popular', if very physical, expression of attitudes to law in the late fourteenth century – one that clashes with the dedicated picture of professionalism and intellectual rigour that is preserved in the legal records and which marked the great bulk of the legal profession's work. Views on the legal profession were expressed in a number of different ways and forms. For instance, lawyers were subjected to both oral and physical assaults. Contempt-of-court actions reveal vituperative outbursts and disrespectful attitudes towards counsel and judges,[167] and (although in fact it is difficult to distinguish between assaults on them as public servants and personal attacks arising from private quarrels not directly related to their legal work) individual lawyers were also victims of acts of violence.[168] Such expressions may have been the views of individuals, but frequently they struck a chord with a wider audience. This suggests that there may have been an underlying perception of lawyers and judges, which was lodged in people's minds and remained there despite any good (individually or collectively) that the legal profession might do. The fact that feelings against lawyers run as strong today (at least in jest) as they did in the Middle Ages must surely confirm that the love/hate attitude itself needs to be addressed as well as its influencing factors. What were the general perceptions of the legal profession? What were the reasons for them and how did they change over time?

Greater opportunity for expression undoubtedly aided the focusing of perceptions. The nascence of the legal profession coincided with – and was boosted by – developments in literacy and record-keeping, a flourishing of the arts, and new religious concerns. The physical expression of feelings was a manifestation of what over the course of the period could be termed a growing 'tradition' of comment and complaint, reflecting the state of the world either as it was, or as it was believed to be, or in its least flattering terms so as to maximise sympathy or remedial action. The concern was given voice either in legal form, in bills and petitions, or in literary form, in poems and songs, or couched in terms of theological dogma, in sermons and addresses. The portrayal of the legal profession in contemporary literature and art can provide a useful insight into how they were received in the world at large, or at least how writers and artists thought their audience would identify with and respond to their work. To rely solely on such evidence, however, and accept it uncritically as forming an accurate, unbiased picture would be unrealistic. Its historical value depends on knowing who was providing the 'portrait', the perspective from which they were operating and with what knowledge or agenda they approached their subject matter. It is important to address the motives of the person (or persons) responsible, whether their discourse was intended to be didactic, satirical, polemical or remedial (or indeed a combination of these).[169] Attitudes and expectations can equally be guessed, hinted at or revealed from the information that (either knowingly or unwittingly) contemporaries have provided.

Some attitudes may have been founded on jealousy or disapproval of the lifestyle or ostentation associated with the law and its practitioners. A perennial view of the law (and one still prevalent today) was that everyone involved in its operation made considerable sums of money from the fees paid by litigants. The earning power of judges and lawyers made them targets for those who regarded them simply as 'fat cats', without necessarily discerning the reality. While some judges, such as Hengham or Scrope G., did manage to earn vast amounts, it was usually as a result of very hard work or shrewd investments. In fact the Crown was frequently in arrears with judges' salaries, which until 1346 had remained frozen at the same level for at least the last eighty years, and were themselves 'absurdly low', a fraction of what could be earned by counsel.[170] In comparison with attorneys, the fee-scale for serjeants was generally higher, but they were not all grasping fee-earners as the poet Langland would have us believe, in a satirical passage in the Prologue to *Piers Plowman*:[171]

> Seriantz it semede that serveth at þe Barre
> Pleded en for penys and poundes þe lawe
> And nat for love of Oure Lord vnlose here lyppes ones.
> Thow myghtest betre meten myst on Malverne Hulles
> Than gete a mum of here mouth at moneye be shewed.

It would no doubt raise a few wry smiles among those lawyers who had a successful practice, but not necessarily apply across the board. It is easy to make gibes at lawyers' expense when everyone knows they charge for their services to finance their livelihood. Chaucer's Serjeant-at-Law is not quite the same easily-condemned, stock literary character, nor are we required to make moral judgements. The satirical comments are subtly mixed with admiration for his professional skills. We are told that 'of fees and robes hadde he many oon' (emphasising his connection with landowners) and he regards everything as 'fee simple' (in monetary terms), but he obviously has a busy practice and the words 'fee simple' themselves (referring to a technical term in land law), taken on another level, point towards 'his science' and 'high renoun' and remind us not only that legal knowledge was essential, but also that reputation was important.[172]

Laicisation may have brought the issue of the payment of justices to a head. The trappings of wealth were more observable when lands were purchased and estates built up in the provinces. Lawyers who wanted to appear to be part of landed society in turn contributed to a blurring of distinctions and a belief in collaboration between justices and landowners. Close relations with landowners were a natural corollary of the advances in legal process, but were frequently portrayed as having sinister implications, even though the receipt of money, or another form of gift from an individual, was not necessarily an indication of corruption. Although we cannot know for sure, in the vast majority of cases (especially where the law was clear or the facts straightforward) it was unlikely to advance a cause significantly or prejudice a reasoned judgment in court. In societies where gift-giving is customary and polite, it is the proportionality that matters, not the mere fact of reward or apparent sweetener.[173] High-profile examples of serious misdeeds arising from a close proximity of relations, such as those of John de Molyns and royal judge, John Inge, however, may have underlined people's fears and undermined their belief in the impartiality of royal justice.[174]

Venality was a major theme of the complaints against the legal profession. Langland's well-known character, Lady Meed, is a personification of the bribery or payment for reward that he felt riddled and demeaned the legal system.[175] The leaders of the 1381 revolt also invoked this theme in verses that were circulating at the time: a royal justice utters the motto, 'speak, spend and speed', with the implication that the oral complaint or court room pleading will only achieve success or its desired end with the help of monetary payment.[176] The 'popular' perception of justice apparently had not caught up with changes in judicial standards as both Murimuth and the Bridlington chronicler (probably closer to government sources) were of the opinion that despite the dismissals in 1350 and 1365, the problem in the later years of Edward III was no longer the perversion of justice through the bribery of judges, but a 'new malice', another manifestation of corruption: perjury by jurors.[177] The adoption of venality as a theme of complaint against the legal profession itself marked a shift in attention from the Church and testifies to the new influence of the law and its institutions.

The chronology of perceptions is interesting. Henry III tolerated close relations between his nobles and leading members of the judiciary. The granting of fees and robes was a natural expression of their relationship.[178] Although the money and possessions acquired by lawyers over the course of their lives were commented upon in the thirteenth century,[179] it was not until later in the century that the connection between justice and wealth was made explicitly in *A Song on the Venality of the King's Judges*. The misdeeds of the royal judges (in 1289) were a topic of sufficient notoriety to be included in chronicles and dramatised in the 'Story of the Passion of the Judges'.[180] The complaints concerning lawyers 'on the take' seem to have coincided with the period when many members of the profession were 'on the make'. It is not surprising that by the fourteenth century the abundance of lawyers should be accounted for in some way either by those jealous of their new-found wealth and acquired social status or those who were in fact critical of them precisely because they were 'self-made' men. The *Scrope v. Grosvenor* case in 1385, a dispute about arms heard in the Court of Chivalry, highlighted the contemporary feeling among some in the upper stratum that lawyers were socially inferior: Richard Scrope was told that he could not be a 'gentilhomme' because his father had been a lawyer.[181]

In many ways, lawyers were the victims of their own success. They could be increasingly identified as a distinct body of professionals, who possessed their own ethos and intellectual goals. Legal education (as well as accommodation) in the Inns of Court and chancery was beginning to supplement formal and informal instruction around the courts, while corresponding reading-matter suitable for legal practitioners was increasingly available. By the 1380s the senior ranks of the profession, judges and serjeants, were visually distinctive in their forms of dress and organisationally in their elite grouping and avenues of promotion and advancement. As the guardians and propagators of arcane knowledge and possessing certain specialised skills, they prospered from the opportunities for satiating consumer demand for legal services. Although some attempt was made at limiting the numbers of practitioners, and formal ethical regulations were in place, the profession was in fact governed by market forces on the strength of competence and probity. A lawyer would not succeed professionally, or would be vilified and suspended from practice (or disbarred as in the case of John of Chester mentioned above), if he lost sight of these requirements.

We must be careful not to judge lawyers solely on the basis of the contemporary literature, which does not let the legal profession speak for themselves nor appraises them on their own merits. Rarely are the considerable skills in assimilating the world of the law, in understanding legal procedures and communicating legal ideas, exhibited in the surviving legal records, taken into account. Roger Thirkleby's incorruptibility and value as a judge (and his appearance to a knight in a vision) were recorded by a chronicler, while a sketch of William Herle's character, underlining not only his morality and intellectual qualities, but the confidence he inspired, appears in a letter patent.[182] Nor is there a full appreciation of the different facets to their judicial work or the other side to their legal careers: the compassion and favourable use of discretion, the piety and good deeds. Two of the justices named in the *An Outlaw's Song of Trailbaston* (c.1305) appear to have been respected by the author, who describes them in terms of their piety and concern for the poor. They are clearly contrasted with two of their colleagues, whose discretion, it is implied, was unlikely to be exercised in the litigant's favour.[183] Some indication of the way lawyers viewed themselves – or how they wanted to be remembered – can be gleaned from their concern with the physical and mental image that would remain after their death. Sculptured or carved effigies on tombs, money left for good causes and for masses and prayers for the dead send out mixed impressions of awe and piety, temporal and spiritual desires.[184] The value placed on the services of lawyers by at least some satisfied clients and the lawyers' cultivation of a self-image, reflecting the way they perceived themselves or intended to influence public perception, is an interesting alternative or corrective to the otherwise pervasive picture of incompetence, venality and corruption.

Perceptions of the way justice operated, while not necessarily reflecting reality, could not easily be changed. Caricatures of the law's personnel may have captured popular imagination and often spoke louder than the honesty and upholding of justice to which most judges probably aspired. But in considering such evidence, matters of social and literary form should be taken into account. Lawyers disturbed the traditional hierarchy of society because they could make their own way up it. They clearly could not be idealised in the way that Chaucer idealises the Knight and the Poor Parson: a poor lawyer was simply an unsuccessful one. Perceptions of judges and lawyers may also have been based as much on misinformation and misconceptions. Although oaths were a commonplace in medieval society, ordinary people may not have realised that judges took them or, indeed, that they swore to uphold justice and avoid being prejudicial to any litigant. Some allegations of conspiracy and corruption (brought under the Ordinances of Conspirators of 1293 and 1305) were, as Dr Brand has shown, based on a misunderstanding of the legal situation and a confusion over (or reluctance to accept) the role of the lawyer.[185] Administrative difficulties and a reliance on the correct procedure may have been at the root of adjournments or delays in proceedings, especially in cases where there was a decision not to proceed because the other justices were not present.[186]

The wholesale dismissal of judiciary, though partly political, did bring to light misdeeds of a minority and highlighted the insecurity that could face royal officials. The loss of reputation when esteem in legal circles was paramount probably did not do much for public confidence. Although there are as yet no statistics to show how common lawyers' misdeeds were, the fact inquiries brought these things to light and the faults were acted upon (rather the findings being suppressed) is a plus for the system and for its ability to police itself within a statutory and regulatory framework. But confidence in the integrity of the judiciary and in the legal system as a whole was not easily rebuilt. Was corruption sufficiently widespread at all levels of royal justice that it threatened to undermine the whole system? Such a question cannot be answered in statistical terms, but it should be emphasised that the strength of the medieval legal system lay in its capacity to move with society and to respond to those criticisms which were justifiable and which cast its reputation in a bad light. Some allegations of corruption were in fact symptomatic of cultural changes occurring within the system as a whole or reflected the pervasive nature of the law and the increasingly diverse and complex activities of the legal profession. The problem therefore concerned expectations of law and the legal profession rather than simply changes in the standards of professional behaviour.

Between 1215 and 1381 major changes occurred marking the professionalisation of the law. During the fourteenth century a distinct generic group became perceived and delineated through the use of the term 'man of law'. This group comprised many generalist practitioners, but had a clear apex of experts in the serjeants and judges of the central courts at Westminster. During the period the profile of lawyers altered and it became an increasingly non-clerical profession. Significantly, as a result of advances in the provision of legal education, it was a book-learned profession at every level down to the summoner. In terms of identity, it was the royal common lawyers who dominated the profession rather than the university-educated jurists of Roman law jurisdictions. The conduct of men of law was monitored by the courts in accordance with statutory ethical guidelines. It was also monitored in Commons' petitions and more informally in sermons and literary works. There was thus definite concern exhibited both within and outside the profession for men of law to abide by a recognised code of ethical behaviour, be it of 'official' or 'popular' design. Moreover, the Crown did react to public opinion: in 1381, following obvious criticisms of the way justice was administered, the Commons requested that a select committee (comprising two judges, two serjeants and four apprentices) examine the workings of the law.[187] By the 1390s the retaining of judges was much less common.[188] The legal profession also provided social advantages since in the same way that clergy could achieve promotion to the nobility and inner political circles, so it was a conduit for clever men to progress in society, achieve positions of influence and enter the aristocracy.

Notes

1 *Bracton on the Laws and Customs of England*, ed. S. Thorne, 4 vols (Cambridge, MA, Harvard University Press, 1968–77), vol. 2, p. 19.
2 Powell, *Kingship*, pp. 25–31; R. Helmholz, 'Magna Carta and the ius commune', *University of Chicago Law Review* 66 (1999), pp. 297–371.

3   L. E. Boyle, 'The beginnings of legal studies at Oxford', *Viator*, 14 (1983), pp. 279–358; Paris did not have a faculty of civil law; Bologna had civilians as well as canonists. For fifteenth-century English students, see R. J. Mitchell, 'English law students at Bologna in the fifteenth century', *EHR*, 51 (1936), pp. 27–87.

4   J. A. Brundage, 'The canon law curriculum in medieval Cambridge', in *Learning the Law*, pp. 183–4.

5   Brand, *Origins*, pp. 145–6, 149.

6   *SCCKB*, vol. 6, pp. xxx–xxxi.

7   C. T. Allmand, 'Civil lawyers', in C. T. Clough (ed.), *Profession, Vocation and Culture in Later Medieval England* (Liverpool, Liverpool University Press, 1982), p. 160.

8   J. H. Baker, *The Legal Profession and the Common Law* (London, Hambledon Press, 1986), p. 9.

9   P. Brand, 'Legal education in England before the Inns of Court', in *Learning the Law*, pp. 56–7.

10 Brand, 'Legal education', p. 58; P. R. Philbin, 'The *Excepciones Contra Brevia*: a late thirteenth century teaching tool', in *Learning the Law*, pp. 133–56.

11 *Readings and Moots of the Inns of Court in the Fifteenth Century*, ed. S. E. Thorne and J. H. Baker, SS, 71 & 105 (London, 1954–90), vol. 2, pp. xvi–xix.

12 *Close Rolls, 1234–37*, p. 26; Brand, 'Legal education', pp. 52, 57.

13 Brand, 'Legal education', pp. 56–8.

14 R. V. Turner, *The English Judiciary in the Age of Glanvill and Bracton, c.1179–1239* (Cambridge, Cambridge University Press, 1985), p. 213.

15 *The Mirror of Justices*, ed. W. J. Whittaker and F. W. Maitland, SS, 7 (London, 1895); *Britton*, ed. F. M. Nichols (London, 1865); *Fleta*, ed. H. G. Richardson and G. O. Sayles, SS, 72, 89, 99 (London, 1955–84).

16 Details of manuscript and published versions of these treatises can be found in Brand, 'Legal education', pp. 76–80.

17 *YB 2 & 3 Edward II*, pp. xv–xvi; Brand, 'Legal education', pp. 62–4.

18 PRO MS SC 8/189/9409 printed in *YB 3 & 4 Edward II*, p. xlii.

19 P. Brand, 'Observing and recording the medieval bar and bench at work', SS, 1998 Selden Society Lecture (London, 1999), p. 17.

20 For example: *YB 5 Edward II*, p. 90: 'And I say something for the young men that are around us' (*et jeo die une chose par les jeones qe sont environ*) followed by a mini-lecture on avowry for services. See also *YB 12 & 13 Edward III*, p. 170.

21 *YB 3 Edward II*, p. 36.

22 P. Brand, 'The beginnings of English law reporting', in C. Stebbings (ed.), *Law Reporting in England* (London, Hambledon Press, 1995), p. 7. For examples see *EELR*, vol. 1, p. 151 and vol. 2, pp. 205–6.

23 Baker, *Legal Profession*, pp. 11–16; Brand, 'Legal education', pp. 66–9.

24 For example: *YB 33–5 Edward I*, p. 471; *YB 3 & 4 Edward II*, p. 200; T. F. T. Plucknett, *Statutes and their Interpretation in the First Half of the Fourteenth Century* (Cambridge, Cambridge University Press, 1922), pp. 37–8; Brand, 'Legal education', pp. 73–4.

25 D. J. M. Higgins, 'Judges in government and society in reign of Edward II',

unpublished DPhil thesis, University of Oxford, 1986, pp. 100–1; C. Taylor, 'Edward III and the Plantagenet claim to the French throne', in J. Bothwell (ed.), *The Age of Edward III* (Woodbridge, York Medieval Press, 2001).

26 P. Brand, 'Inside the courtroom: lawyers, litigants and justices in England in the later Middle Ages', in P. Coss (ed.), *Morality and the Law* (Cambridge, Cambridge University Press, 2000), pp. 100–1; R. D. Groot, 'Teaching each other: judges, clerks, jurors and malefactors define the guilt/innocence jury', in *Learning the Law*, pp. 17–32; B. H. Putnam, *The Place in Legal History of Sir William Shareshull* (Cambridge, Cambridge University Press, 1950), p. 118.

27 D. C. Skemer, 'Reading the law: statute books and the private transmission of legal knowledge in late medieval England', in *Learning the Law*, pp. 113–32.

28 For example: *YB 15 Edward III*, p. 386 (*Thorpe*: 'witness the case of Gervase Bray in the third year of the present king'); *YB 16 Edward III*, pt 1, p. 74 (*Pole*: 'and this you might have seen at York between the Lord of Mowbray and John de Haveryintone' – *YB 9 Edward III*, Mich. no. 43); *YB 14 & 15 Edward III*, pp. 82, 96 (W. Thorpe refers to an oyer and terminer case and an assize at Beverley), 114 (*Thorpe*: 'and so it was adjudged in the Northampton eyre').

29 For various examples see Plucknett, *Statutes*, pp. 37, 103–6. Note also in Chaucer's *Canterbury Tales* the Man of Law's distortion or misinterpretation of sources; see S. H. Rigby, *Chaucer in Context* (Manchester, Manchester University Press, 1996), p. 90)

30 *YB 2 & 3 Edward II*, p. 33; *3 Edward II*, pp. 75–6.

31 J. Catto, 'Andrew Horn: law and history in fourteenth-century England', in R. H. C. Davis and J. M. Wallace-Hadrill (eds), *The Writing of History in the Middle Ages* (Oxford, Clarendon Press, 1981), pp. 367–87.

32 *CCR 1323–7*, p. 2.

33 *SCCKB*, vol. 6, pp. 128–9.

34 Occasionally it is the reporter who has got things wrong: Plucknett, *Statutes*, pp. 106, 112.

35 Some reports are arranged topically collecting together different cases of a similar nature (*YB 3 Edward II*, pp. xxx–xxxi).

36 Clanchy, *Memory*, p. 97.

37 R. V. Turner, *Judges, Administrators and the Common Law in Angevin England* (London, Hambledon Press, 1994), pp. 205–7.

38 *EELR*, vol. 2, p. 349.

39 *Ibid.*, p. 293.

40 *YB 15 Edward III*, pp. 160, 260, 350,

41 *YB 14 Edward III*, pp. 246, 252.

42 *YB 1 Edward II*, p. 109.

43 *YB 11 & 12 Edward III*, pp. 412, 498, 612.

44 *YB 19 Edward III*, p. 376; Putnam, *Shareshull*, pp. 105–6.

45 M. J. Carruthers, *The Book of Memory: a Study of Memory in Medieval Culture* (Cambridge, Cambridge University Press, 1992), pp. 99, 109, 154, 205–6, 212–13: it was expected of canon lawyers that they had committed to memory the entire set of Decretals.

46 For example: *Ancient Petitions Relating to Northumberland*, ed. C. M. Fraser, Surtees Society, 176 (Durham, 1966), pp. 115–16; *SR*, vol. 1, p. 301; Chaucer, 'Man of Law's Tale' in *Canterbury Tales*.
47 *Select Canterbury Cases, c.1201–1301*, ed. N. Adams and C. Donahue, SS, 95 (London, 1981), pp. 22–3.
48 *SCCKB*, vol. 6, pp. lxiii–lxiv.
49 Brand, 'Legal education', pp. 74–5.
50 Brand, *Origins*, pp. 149–51.
51 J. H. Baker, *The Order of Serjeants at Law*, SS, Supplementary Series, 5 (London, 1984), pp. 94–5, 99.
52 M. Powicke, *Military Obligation in Medieval England* (Oxford, Clarendon Press, 1962), p. 68.
53 *SCCKB*, vol. 7, pp. xxx–xxxii; xxxix–xl.
54 Turner, *Judges*, p. 199; Higgins, 'Judges in government', pp. 4–5.
55 Turner, *Judges*, pp. 200–1; *SCCKB*, vol. 7, p. xxix.
56 Higgins, 'Judges in government', pp. 6–7, 10; *SCCKB*, vol. 7, p. xli.
57 *SCCKB*, vol. 6, pp. xxiv–v.
58 Turner, *Judges*, pp. 199–204, 218–20.
59 *Ibid.*, pp. 166–76.
60 *Ibid.*, p. 177. As bishop of Winchester, however, he issued diocesan legislation against clerics holding secular judicial office and also forbade priests to study civil law (*Ibid.*, pp. 163–4).
61 Brand, *Origins*, p. 152.
62 See 27 Edward I c. 3 (*SR*, vol. 1, pp. 129–30); Musson, *Public Order*, pp. 95–7.
63 Higgins, 'Judges in government', pp. 7, 10–11.
64 N. Ramsay, 'Retained legal counsel, *c.*1275–1475', *TRHS*, 5th series, 35 (1985), p. 100.
65 *SCCKB*, vol. 7, p. xxix.
66 J. R. Maddicott, 'Law and lordship: royal justices as retainers in thirteenth and fourteenth century England', *P&P* supplement, 4 (Oxford, 1978), pp. 11, 18, 24.
67 Baker, *Serjeants at Law*, p. 67.
68 *SCCKB*, vol. 1, pp. xci, cxxvii.
69 Baker, *Serjeants at Law*, pp. 68–73; J. H. Baker, 'History of gowns worn at the English bar', *Costume*, 9 (1975), p. 15; J. H. Baker, 'A history of English judges' robes', *Costume*, 12 (1978), pp. 27–8.
70 Baker, *Serjeants at Law*, p. 69 and n. 5.
71 Baker, *Legal Profession*, pp. 3–4, 7.
72 Clanchy, *Memory*, p. 256.
73 *SCCKB*, vol. 6, p. 129.
74 A. Padoa-Schioppa, 'Conclusions: models, instruments, principles', in A. Padoa-Schioppa (ed.), *Legislation and Justice* (Oxford, Clarendon Press, 1997), p. 354.
75 P. Brand, *The Making of the Common Law* (London, Hambledon Press, 1992), p. 149.
76 *Ibid.*, p. 150: Dr Brand notes that although the oath first appears in letters close of 1278 directed to the eyre justices, it is possible that it had already been used by

other royal justices and its recording was merely coincident with the reorganisation of the eyre which occurred in 1278.
77 *SCCKB*, vol. 1, p. lxiv; Brand, *Making*, pp. 150–1.
78 Printed in *SCCKB*, vol. 5, p. cxvii.
79 *SCCKB*, vol. 1, p. lxiv.
80 *CCR 1313–18*, p. 514.
81 The requirements of the oaths extended equally to the barons of the exchequer, the justices of oyer and terminer and to the justices of assize and gaol delivery.
82 See 20 Edward III (*SR*, vol. 1, pp. 303–6); *SCCKB*, vol. 6, pp. xxii–xxiv.
83 Brand, *Making*, pp. 149–50.
84 See 8 Richard II c. 3 (*SR*, vol. 2, p. 37).
85 See 3 Edward I c. 29 (*SR*, vol. 1, p. 34).
86 For this and the following three paragraphs, see Brand, *Origins*, pp. 120–37.
87 For the oaths of serjeants-at-law and king's serjeants, see *SCCKB*, vol. 7, p. xxxii.
88 Judges did not always need to control pleading by using words: a wink or a nod could suffice (*YB 4 Edward II*, pt 1, p. 132).
89 For example: *SCCKB*, vol. 5, pp. 45–7, vol. 6, pp. xxxviii–xxxix, 54–6, 62.
90 *CPMR 1323–64*, p. 218: Cristian de Bury was acquitted.
91 *CPMR 1381–1412*, pp. 16–17.
92 N. Ramsey, 'What was the legal profession?', in M. Hicks (ed.), *Profit, Piety and the Professions in Later Medieval England* (Gloucester, Alan Sutton, 1990), p. 65.
93 J. A. Brundage, 'Legal aid for the poor and the professionalization of law in the Middle Ages', *JLH*, 9 (1988), p. 173.
94 *YB 33 & 35 Edward I*, p. 380.
95 *YB 1 & 2 Edward II*, p. 33.
96 *YB 4 Edward II*, pp. 25–6.
97 *EELR*, vol. 2, p. 254.
98 *YB 1 & 2 Edward II*, p. xix.
99 *YB 2 & 3 Edward II*, p. 171.
100 *YB 13 & 14 Edward III*, p. 97.
101 *YB 15 Edward III*, p. 126. Technically Mowbray was not a judge at the time he made this remark, but it illustrates his thinking. He became a justice of common pleas in 1359.
102 For detailed discussion of the events, see Brand, *Making*, pp. 101–12; N. M. Fryde, 'Edward III's removal of his ministers and judges, 1340–1', *BIHR*, 48 (1975), pp. 159–61.
103 *CCR 1341–3*, p. 269.
104 Fryde, 'Removal of judges', pp. 157–8.
105 Brand, *Making*, pp. 131–2.
106 *SCCKB*, vol. 6, pp. xvi–xvii; *YB 14 & 15 Edward III*, pp. 258–63.
107 Brand, *Making*, pp. 109–10.
108 *Ibid.*, p. 103.
109 Fryde, 'Removal of judges', pp. 156, 159.
110 Such allegations could not have referred to the judges in any case as there were only two men raised to the bench in the first four years of Edward II's rule, neither

of whom was a chief justice (and so did not hold high office) nor did they appear to be unsuitable in any way. In fact the reforming barons' influence over appointments was quite limited, and changes in the personnel of the courts were generally the result of promotions and transfers within the court hierarchy or arose from natural retirements (Higgins, 'Judges in government', pp. 20–2).

111 Matthew Paris, *Chronica Majora*, ed. H. Luard, RS, 7 vols (London, 1872-84), vol. 5, pp. 213-14.
112 Higgins, 'Judges in government', p. 14.
113 See *CPR 1350-4*, pp. 30, 61; *CCR 1349-54*, p. 277; *RP*, vol. 2, p. 227; *CFR 1347-56*, p. 266; *SCCKB*, vol. 6, pp. xxv–xxvi.
114 *Chronicon Henrici Knighton vel Cnitthon Monachi Leycestrensis*, ed. J. R. Lumby, RS, 2 vols (London, 1889-95), vol. 2, p. 121.
115 *SCCKB*, vol. 6, p. xxvi.
116 *SCCKB*, vol. 6, p. xviii: Robert Scarborough had previous links with Ireland since he was chief justice of common pleas there in 1332.
117 There was an increase in the number of personnel in common pleas from about 1343, but apart from reaching a total of seven justices in 1348, by the mid-1350s and thereafter it was generally a panel of four or five.
118 C. P. Cottis, 'Sir William de Bereford, c.1250–1325', unpublished BLitt dissertation, University of Oxford, 1958, pp. 1–10; Higgins, 'Judges in government', p. 147.
119 B. Vale, 'The profits of the law and the "rise" of the Scropes: Henry Scrope (d. 1336) and Geoffrey Scrope (d. 1340)', in Hicks (ed.), *Profit, Piety and the Professions*, pp. 98–100.
120 Putnam, *Shareshull*, pp. 1–8.
121 Vale, 'Profits of law', p. 91.
122 Putnam, *Shareshull*, p. 7.
123 Not all desired, however, desired the rank: John Bousser opted not to assume knighthood (admittedly some time before his promotion to the bench) and was distrained accordingly (Higgins, 'Judges in government', p. 192).
124 *RP*, vol. 2, p. 334 (75).
125 8 Richard II c. 2 (*SR*, vol. 2, p. 36).
126 E. Powell, 'The administration of criminal justice in late medieval England: peace sessions and assizes', in R. Eales and D. Sullivan (eds), *The Political Context of Law* (London, Hambledon Press, 1987), p. 59; A. J. Verduyn, 'The attitude of the parliamentary commons to law and order under Edward III', unpublished DPhil thesis, Oxford University, 1991, p. 179.
127 For example: Putnam, *Shareshull*, pp. 4–5, 8, 147, 281 n.152.
128 From the Register of Godfrey Giffard cited in Higgins, 'Judges in government', p. 226.
129 *YB 8 Edward II*, pp. xlii–xlvi, 216–20; *YB 9 Edward II*, pp. xl–xliii; *YB 10 Edward II*, pp. 148–58; *YB 11 Edward II*, pp. 213–16.
130 *CFR 1272-1307*, p. 463.
131 *Register of John de Grandisson, Bishop of Exeter, 1327-69*, ed. F. C. Hingeston-Randolph, 2 vols. (London and Exeter, 1894-8), vol. 1, pp. 210, 235-6;

132 Maddicott, 'Law and lordship', pp. 19, 21, 24; Ramsay, 'Retained legal counsel', p. 102.
133 R. B. Dobson and J. Taylor, *Rymes of Robin Hood: an Introduction to the English Outlaw*, rev. edn (Stroud, Alan Sutton, 1997), pp. 75, 86.
134 *SCCKB*, vol. 1, p. lxxviii; Higgins, 'Judges in government', pp. 177–8.
135 Vale, 'Profits of law', p. 99; R. B. Pugh, 'Some medieval moneylenders', *Speculum*, 43 (1968), pp. 274–89; R. H. Bowers, 'From rolls to riches: king's clerks and moneylending in thirteenth-century England', *Speculum*, 58 (1983), pp. 60–71.
136 Higgins, 'Judges in government', p. 203; Turner, *Judges*, p. 149.
137 Allmand, 'Civil lawyers', p. 171.
138 Higgins, 'Judges in government', pp. 203–4.
139 Maddicott, 'Law and lordship', pp. 30–2.
140 *Register of Walter de Stapeldon, Bishop of Exeter, 1307–1326*, ed. F. C. Hingeston-Randolph (London and Exeter, Bell, 1892), pp. 44, 378.
141 R. Horrox, *Richard III: a Study in Service* (Cambridge, Cambridge University Press, 1989), pp. 1–13, 18–26; Higgins, 'Judges in government', pp. 207–11, 218–20.
142 M. Camille, *Mirror in Parchment: the Luttrell Psalter and the Making of Medieval England* (London, Reaktion, 1998), pp. 93–5, 105.
143 J. L. Grassi, 'Royal clerks from the archdiocese of York in the fourteeenth century', *Northern History*, 5 (1970), pp. 12–33; see also A. J. Musson, 'The king's own law in God's own county' (forthcoming).
144 Higgins, 'Judges in government', pp. 148–59.
145 *Roll and Writ File of the Berkshire Eyre of 1248*, ed. M. T. Clanchy, SS, 90 (London, 1973), pp. xlvi–xlvii, lxxvii; Clanchy, *Memory*, pp. 272–3.
146 Adams and Donahue, *Select Canterbury Cases*, pp. 22, 38–9; Rigby, *Chaucer in Context*, pp. 8–9, 87–8.
147 C. R. Cheney, *Notaries Public in England in the Thirteenth and Fourteenth Centuries* (Oxford, Oxford University Press, 1972), pp. 34–6, 40, 68–70.
148 N. Ramsey, 'Scriveners and notaries as legal intermediaries in later medieval England', in J. Kermode (ed.), *Enterprise and Individuals in Fifteenth Century England* (Stroud, Alan Sutton, 1991), pp. 118–19, 123, 127.
149 Brand, *Making*, pp. 174–8.
150 *YB 17 Edward III*, pp. 554–6; *York Memorandum Book, part 1 (1376–1419)*, ed. M. Sellers, Surtees Society, 120 (York, 1912), p. 40.
151 R. C. Palmer, *The County Courts of Medieval England, 1150–1350* (Princeton, NJ, Princeton University Press, 1982), pp. 89–112.
152 Musson, *Public Order*, pp. 87–8, 92–3, 116.
153 R. B. Pugh, *Imprisonment in Medieval England* (Cambridge, Cambridge University Press, 1968), pp. 257–60; Musson, *Public Order*, pp. 11–122.
154 Higgins, 'Judges in government', p. 9; Maddicott, 'Law and lordship', p. 30.
155 N. Saul, *Knights and Esquires: the Gloucestershire Gentry in the Fourteenth Century* (Oxford, Clarendon Press, 1981), pp. 64, 156–7; Musson, *Public Order*, p. 156.
156 See 10 Edward II (*SR*, vol. 1, p. 174).

157 For example, in Gloucestershire: William Bradewell, steward of abbot of Winchcombe and keeper of the liberty of the abbot of Westminster (PRO MS JUST 3/20/3 m1, 1d, 214/3 m1); Richard Foxcote, steward of the abbot of Hailes (PRO MS JUST 3/20/3 m1, 214/3 mm1, 15, 17d); Robert Aston, keeper of the liberty of Cirencester (PRO MS JUST 3/20/3 m1, 214/3 mm2, 14–18); John Clivedon, steward of the abbot of Glastonbury and later steward of the bishop of Bath and Wells (PRO MS JUST 3/120m4d, 121 m5, 127 m24d).
158 Saul, *Knights and Esquires*, pp. 64, 156.
159 *CPR 1345–8*, p. 182; Musson, *Public Order*, pp. 71 n.161, 81 n.230.
160 Peter Denardeston from Suffolk studied civil law at Cambridge in about 1275 when he was eighteen, but does not appear to have taken it any further (A. B. Emden, *A Biographical Register of the University of Cambridge* (Cambridge, Cambridge University Press, 1963), p. 181).
161 M. J. Bennett, 'Provincial gentlefolk and legal education in the reign of Edward II', *BIHR*, 57 (1984), pp. 203, 205–6.
162 J. H. Baker, 'Oral instruction in land law and conveyancing, 1250–1500', in *Learning the Law*, pp. 160–7.
163 N. Denholm-Young, *Seignorial Administration in England* (Oxford, Oxford University Press, 1937), pp. 66–85.
164 *Placita Corone, or La Corone Pledee devont les Justices*, ed. J. M. Kaye, SS, Supplementary Series, 4 (London, 1966).
165 D. C. Skemer, 'From archives to the book trade: private statute rolls in England, 1285–1307', *Journal of the Society of Archivists*, 16 (1995), pp. 194–9.
166 A. Harding, 'The revolt against the justices', in R. H. Hilton and T. H. Aston (eds), *The English Rising of 1381* (Cambridge, Cambridge University Press, 1981), pp. 165–93.
167 *YB 14 Edward III*, pp. xliii–xlvii, 324–31.
168 For example: *SCCKB*, vol. 6, pp. 76–7, 115.
169 For discussion of literary motives see Musson and Ormrod, *Evolution*, pp. 161–75.
170 *SCCKB*, vol. 4, p. xxii–xxv.
171 William Langland, *Piers Plowman*, ed. A. V. J. Schmidt (London and New York, 1995), p. 19, C text, ll. 160–4. 'Meten' means 'measure'; 'mum' means 'murmer'.
172 *SCCKB*, vol. 7, p. xxxvii; Rigby, *Chaucer in Context*, pp. 43–5 (summarising the views of others).
173 *SCCKB*, vol. 1, p. lxxvii; Higgins, 'Judges in government', p. 213; R. C. Palmer, *The Whilton Dispute, 1264–1380* (Princeton, NJ, Princeton University Press, 1984), pp. 10–11.
174 N. Fryde, 'A medieval robber baron: Sir John Molyns of Stoke Poges, Buckinghamshire', in R. F. Hunnisett and J. B. Post (eds), *Medieval Legal Records Edited in Memory of C. A. F. Meekings* London, HMSO, 1978), pp. 197–222.
175 A. P. Baldwin, *The Theme of Government in Piers Plowman* (Woodbridge, D. S. Brewer, 1981), pp. 24–38.
176 Musson and Ormrod, *Evolution*, pp. 171–3.
177 *Adae Murimuth Continuatio Chronicarum. Robertus de Avesbury de Gestis Mirabilibus Regis Edwardi Tertii*, ed. E. M. Thompson, RS (London, 1889),

p. 245; *Political Poems and Songs*, ed. T. Wright, RS, 4 vols (London, 1859), vol. 1, pp. 193-4. Perjury was also addressed in legislation in the 1350s and 1360s (see Chapter 5).
178 *SCCKB*, vol. 7, p. xxxiii; D. Carpenter, *The Reign of Henry III* (London, Hambledon Press, 1996), pp. 83-4.
179 Matthew Paris, *Chronica Majora*, vol. 4, p. 49; vol. 5, p. 138.
180 *State Trials of the Reign of Edward the First, 1289-1293*, ed. T. F. Tout and H. Johnstone, Camden Society, 3rd series, 9 (1906), pp. 95-9.
181 Vale, 'Profits of law', pp. 100-1.
182 PRO MS C66/186 m31; *YB 12 & 13 Edward III*, pp. cxxvii-cxxviii.
183 Dobson and Taylor, *Rymes of Robin Hood*, p. 253.
184 Baker, *Serjeants at Law*, pp. 70-2; Vale, 'Profits of law', p. 93.
185 Brand, *Origins*, pp. 140-1.
186 Higgins, 'Judges in government', p. 216.
187 *RP*, vol. 3, pp. 101-2.
188 Powell, *Kingship*, p. 43.

3

Pragmatic legal knowledge

THE acquisition and development of legal consciousness among those who were not themselves lawyers or judges is a significant feature of the political history of the period 1215–1381. The political ramifications of this phenomenon will be explored in Chapters 5 and 6. In this chapter it is argued that from childhood through to adulthood legal relationships, duties and obligations impinged on the mind. All ordinary people acquired some legal knowledge, even if rudimentary or unfocused, through their experiences both within the family and household and as members of the communities in which they lived and worked. Even those (such as criminals, vagrants, outlaws) who by choice or accident or for whatever reason lived (at least in jurisdictional terms) outside these groups must have had some legal awareness, if only of their own standing in terms of the law. Regular attendance at local courts and other meetings provided a direct opportunity for both men and women to become acquainted with the processes of law and legal concepts. This was matched by regular attendance at church. These institutions each had both spiritual and secular elements, and in their different ways fostered ideas of law and justice. At all levels of the court system, legal knowledge was a concomitant of experience gained from, and in many cases a necessary requirement for, employment as a court official and service as a juror. Finally, an understanding of the law could be acquired either directly or indirectly from the growing documentary culture, from book learning and/or from exposure to literature (either reading it for themselves or listening to it being read) relating to legal matters.

This chapter underlines the incremental nature of legal experience. Knowledge was acquired throughout a person's life concomitant with the level of his or her exposure to legal processes. Moreover, legal experience was gained not in the vacuum of one particular jurisdiction, but from an appreciation of the advantages to be gained in pursuing legal actions in a variety of courts in often overlapping, sometimes competing jurisdictions, be they royal, urban, ecclesiastical or manorial. As people became increasingly familiar with legal processes and concepts, so in turn they influenced the character and development of law in that they were able to ease and adapt it as well as circumvent and subvert it.

Family and household

The initial stimulus to the individual's development of some form of legal consciousness derived from an awareness of his or her own situation and standing in the world. The family and the household provided the most immediate source of information about, and education in, the nature of legal relations. Social relationships and natural occurrences (such as birth or death) could all have profound legal implications and in many cases were related to financial interests or triggered payments (to the king or the lord). Sexual relations outside marriage, childbirth within or outside wedlock, entering into marriage, and death could have legal consequences. Death especially affected the extended family with importance attached to whether the deceased possessed property, whether they had any heirs, and if they did, whether those heirs were male or female, of full age or minors. This is, of course, a complex area and one that cannot be fully explored in the present work.[1] The following paragraphs nevertheless are intended to provide some insight into the role of what anachronistically would be termed 'family law' in the context of legal consciousness.

It was in their interests for historical actors to know how best to deal with the situation in the circumstances in which they were placed. The legal position surrounding the circumstances of a birth, for instance, was of prime importance because it affected the major medieval consideration of inheritance. The canon-law doctrine on illegitimacy was followed (at least with regard to inheritance) at common law and in customary law, which meant that generally bastards could not inherit property from or through their parents, nor have co-laterals as heirs, although this did not prevent gifts being made to the illegitimate child by the parents during their lifetime. On some manors, however, the inheritance disability extended to a woman who bore an illegitimate child. At Cranfield in Bedfordshire in *c.*1312, for example, Dulcia Telat was prevented from inheriting nine acres of land that had been held by her father when it was found that she had given birth outside marriage.[2] In practice, the situation rested on proof of bastardy: an issue that was frequently determined not in the church courts, but in the royal and manorial courts by a jury or the suitors of the court. However, even if proved illegitimate, in practice the legal fact did not induce further incapacities (other than in inheritance matters) for the child.[3]

There were also legal implications for a minor whose parents had died, either because he or she was an orphan or because the child was the heir or heiress to property. The protection of the child's legal interests, maintenance and nurture (support and sustenance) could be entrusted to guardians, who might be other family members or strangers. In 1349, for example, Thomas of Eyxherst came to the manor court of Boxley in Kent to seek permission to take on the nurture of Juliana and Sarah, daughters and heirs of John of Hokynbury, who were minors.[4] A guardian's actions, however, could not legally bind an infant and so anything done in the child's name could be renounced when they came of age.

The status and legal interests of a person of any age could be affected by their state of mind.[5] Someone such as Robert son of Adam Sumay of Methley, who either as a result of mental problems or grave illness was deemed by jurors to be not of sound memory and of unsound mind (*non fuit sane memorie neque compos mentis*) would be regarded as legally incapable of making property transfers.[6] Proof of insanity could also excuse a person from liability for committing serious crimes. A jury testified to Geoffrey Riche's madness which was apparent when he tried to have intercourse with Agnes Fuller and then cut off her head with a sword when she would not permit him. Following this, he proclaimed to the neighbours that he was a pig and hid under a trough, before going back home, where he found a needle and thread and sewed the head back onto the body.[7]

An individual's legal position or rights under the law were in many ways profoundly affected by gender and unfree status. Awareness of this flowed not just from the limitations that the law imposed on women and villeins, but also as a result of the safeguards, remedies and opportunities for them that the law created and facilitated. We should therefore think in terms of how the legal consciousness of women was formed and changed (depending on their circumstances) and how it differed from that of men.

While positions of control may have been in male hands, and women's public service as jurors limited to tests of pregnancy in criminal trials and testimony of impotence in matrimonial cases, women heads of households were not unusual in some peasant or artisan communities. Single or widowed women in particular enjoyed a certain amount of freedom under the law. It was the married woman who was theoretically disadvantaged since she was subject to the doctrine of coverture: in becoming one person with her husband she was deprived of a separate legal capacity and had to appear with him in court. As many married women found out, however, any disability at law was in fact qualified since she retained rights in relation to her dower and, when land transfers took place, she was supposed to be examined separately to ensure her assent had been given.[8] If the marriage was declared a nullity she could recover property from her former husband by court action.[9] A woman's married status does not seem to have hindered her ability to seek and secure employment away from her home village. Margaret, the wife of John le Bere of Wantesdene (Norfolk) was engaged to serve Alexander in the nearby village of Butley. She nevertheless left her job there to gain higher wages in Ilketilshale, much further away.[10]

The protection of a woman's rights after the death of her husband were enshrined in both the Decretals of canon law and in Magna Carta.[11] Significantly, in spite of (or perhaps in compensation for) a married woman having no right at common law to hold chattels, the Church and ecclesiastical law supported the right of a married woman to make bequests (usually of jewels and clothing) or otherwise dispose of property. For example, at the death of Agnes de Condet in 1223, where those chattels belonging to her (*omnium que mea sunt*) were directed to be sold.[12]

The restrictions placed on those who were villeins by birth (and therefore personally unfree) or who held land by unfree tenure also engendered a particular way of thinking about the world. Villeins had subordinate status in the eyes of the common law as 'unfree' persons subject to the lord's jurisdiction, which impacted on property holding and marriage as well as restricting geographical mobility and access to the royal courts. A lord's jurisdiction, however, was not absolute. Although personal property could be seized by the lord, from the late thirteenth century it is apparent that a number of villeins made wills and executed them, receiving probate both in the church courts and the manor courts.[13] While villeins were constrained in certain respects we should not think of their unfree status as inhibiting entirely opportunities for legal action. Again, they could learn of exceptions and opportunities to gain advantages.

A villein could try and prove free status by seeking a writ *de libertate probanda* or *monstravit*. There were also opportunities to assert their free status as result of having been pressed into service on juries in the royal courts. There were also advantages to be gained from claiming that they resided in a royal borough or that the manor of which they were tenants was in fact part of the ancient demesne of the Crown (and they were the 'villein sokemen') because it meant that they could not be ejected from the land as along as they performed the services owed, services which could not be changed or extended. Villeins on royal manors enjoyed enhanced access to the courts since manorial jurisdiction was overseen by the court of king's bench.[14] In terms of the options and protections available to them it is apparent that villeins often received a benevolent glance from Church and state. As Professor Hyams puts it: 'Chattels they might be to their lord; they were also human beings whose survival concerned both church and king.'[15]

At all levels of society, circumstances and situations within the family and the household played a significant role in informing both adults and children of their legal position in the world and their immediate duties and responsibilities.

Communal obligations

An individual's obligations within a particular community and his or her awareness of those obligations contributed further to the level of consciousness of the law. Legal relations were formed (altered and re-established) on the basis of property holdings, commercial activities and interpersonal behaviour. Even at the lowest levels of society it was understood that property was held in relation to the property of others. Buying and selling goods involved the formation of contracts and the establishing of debts. Interaction with other people in the community could have repercussions if physical force were used or words were directed vituperatively against another person. This nexus of obligations is illustrated in the surviving manorial and urban court rolls and in the Crown pleas of the sheriff's tourn and the eyre where it is clear that people's legal duties were made explicit: in agriculture and pasturage as much as in the control of local violence.

The court rolls of the Hallmoot of the prior of Durham, for instance, contain injunctions directed to the various villages under the prior's jurisdiction. No one is to enter the pastures of Hilden with their animals without licence from the reeve. Cows, horses, pigs, geese and [any] livestock are not to go out of the vill without sufficient guard. The village of Walleshend is to have a common shepherd to look after the sheep. In Acley, no one is to take land to build except in a place called 'le M'spot'. No one should repudiate others by word or deed. All women are ordered to constrain their tongues and not defame without litigating, while no man is to draw his knife or raise his staff and all men are to come and help the constables if any foreigner comes within the vill to do wrong. No tenants or servants of the vill are to assault another with bow or arrow.[16] Those who breached these orders were presented at the court sessions and, if found guilty, were amerced. Newly admitted 'natives' swore touching the sacred gospels (*tactis per ipsum sacrosanctis Ewangeliis*) that they would be justiciable to the prior and convent of Durham and serve the community and thus swore to uphold these obligations.[17]

The articles of the sheriff's tourn overlapped substantially with many of the areas investigated by the eyre (see Chapter 4). Local people were required to identify (among others) those taking part in criminal activities (particularly traitors, murderers, robbers, thieves, arsonists, housebreakers and ravishers of women) and those in the community who were receiving and helping them. There was also concern for those who evaded arrest, escaped from prison, turned outlaw, or abjured the realm. Investigations were to be made of people who abused royal rights (counterfeiters of the royal seal or money and finders of treasure), those who committed offences relating to animals and animal products (in the form of meat and hides), and those who were trespassers in parks. Non-observance of the assizes of ale, bread and measures was reportable and attention was directed towards those who caused various public nuisances such as falsifying or removing landmarks, diverting watercourses, hindering, restraining or narrowing the highway and having buildings that were dangerous to passers-by. Notification was also required of people who took amends without leave of the court (a process known as *thefbote*) and those who gave lodging to strangers for more than two nights. There were also particular questions concerning the spilling of blood and the raising of 'the hue and cry'.[18]

People involved in trades or commercial activity were required to know and follow regulations that highlighted their obligations to the customer, their employees and the general community. Price levels were governed by national and local restrictions, and similar controls were in operation concerning the quality of goods and foodstuffs. Employing servants, labourers or apprentices involved contracting for their services and a recognition from both parties of the mutual obligations and wider duties. This was particularly pertinent after the Black Death when there was fierce competition for skilled workers and the terms of employment swung in favour of the employee. The processing, preparation, selling and delivery of goods and foodstuffs could also involve wives and children (depending on the levels of skill and the market returns), who would need to be aware of the prevailing standards.[19]

Practising a particular trade or industry could create a public nuisance and dangers to public health and safety.[20] In towns such as Exeter, trading itself could only take place in sanctioned 'public' places, such as the market place or sites like the 'Fishfold' or the 'Fleshfold'. Trading was therefore banned from 'private' or 'suspicious' places, such as private houses, taverns, or outside the city gates.[21] Concerned about sanitation, officials in towns laid down rules concerning the slaughtering of livestock and a specific period in the day for the selling of meat and fish.[22] Pollution of watercourses and the atmosphere was also recognised as being a problem. In London there was investigation of 'the many obnoxious dumps and private encroachments in the public lanes which ran down to the Thames',[23] while in Exeter, a bowyer was charged with 'producing bad odours with grease resin and other instruments to the harm of his neighbours'.[24]

These communal obligations were institutionalised and encouraged through the frankpledge system and the watch. The organisation of men over the age of twelve into groups of ten (known as tithings), which in principle went back to Anglo-Saxon times and developed under the laws of Athelstan, Edgar and Cnut, was designed to provide mutual security and a collective sense of responsibility for good behaviour. The geographical ambit of the tithing system lay with the counties south of the Trent (so Yorkshire and other northern counties such as Derbyshire, Nottinghamshire, Lancashire, Northumberland, Westmorland and Cumberland were excluded) and to the east of the Welsh marches (and so did not apply in Herefordshire and Shropshire). The system applied predominantly to those of villein status, and by the fourteenth century exclusively to those who were unfree. It required its members to pledge themselves to serve the tithing faithfully (*fideliter servandi ... totam tethingam*), to pursue and capture felons and to appear in court as a group. The group was led by a head man or chief pledge, who was often a constable of the peace for the vill. It was expected that upon reaching the age threshold dependants would be introduced into the tithing. Any male remaining outside the group once they had reached the requisite age was liable to be punished.[25] The watch, which was intended to complement this system and enhance external security, was a nocturnal vigil undertaken by at least four watchmen, who under various provisions of 1233, 1242 and 1253 were required to challenge, and either keep in custody or find pledges for, strangers and vagrants approaching the town or village.[26]

The communal solidarity built up through these systems was also encouraged through the device of the 'hue and cry'. Public attention was drawn to thefts, violence or suspicious acts by someone raising a shout, blowing a horn or ringing the church bells, as a result of which the community was required to respond by pursuing the culprit or suspected offender. Taking part in the hue and cry helped inform people of the nature of crimes and their details. Indeed, it was considered important that all should know who in particular had been suspected of criminal activity and that the hue should be, or had been, raised on them. Those who were unwilling to follow the hue and cry, or who raised it needlessly or maliciously, or who did not report the facts, would find themselves amerced unless they could provide a suitable excuse.[27] The equipping of members of the watch with light arms and provision of expenses for the keepers of the peace of the hundred (at least in hundreds in Essex and Hertfordshire in the 1320s) provided a shared financial obligation to local policing.[28]

Communal pressures were placed on those who stepped out of line, to conform or settle their differences in an amicable manner. Arbitration and 'lovedays' in particular were familiar expressions of – and recognition of – a sense of community. Arbitration entailed disputing parties choosing their arbiters (who were not exclusively members of a particular affinity) and reaching a fully worked-out, mutually convenient settlement. It marked a 'cross-over' point between the formal and informal judicial processes and was a popular method of dispute resolution since, in achieving settlement, it usually balanced flexibility with economy and speed. In one late fourteenth-century case in Lancashire the arbitrators were expected to have reached a settlement within two weeks, after which time the chief steward of the duchy of Lancaster, Sir John de la Pole, was to render a decision as umpire.[29] Arbitration was often used as a matter of course, sometimes in tandem with litigation, but could be most effective in easing seemingly intractable disputes. In 1219, for example, an award was made in an attempt to settle a long-running inheritance dispute between two members of the Percy family (uncle and nephew), which also involved the abbot of Fountains on the side of the elder relation, Richard Percy.[30]

Arbitration was not a resource restricted to one particular group of people, rather a universal phenomenon, occurring at every level and among all orders of society. While it is difficult to provide an accurate idea of how frequently there was recourse to arbitration, since it generally falls outside the remit of the judicial records, it was an activity which was viewed with seriousness by contemporaries of all stations and was endowed with time and consideration. Participation itself could occur on different levels (as one of the parties, as a negotiator, as an impartial umpire, as a supporter, or as an onlooker) and with varying degrees of connection to and understanding of the process. The employment of arbitration and its effectiveness as a method of resolving disputes relied to an extent on an acceptance and understanding of its integral position within the continuum of dispute resolution. Agreement and reconciliation naturally allowed for reintegration within the value systems, network of relations and power structures that formed part of everyday life and work. It depended upon there being an awareness among all people (litigants, non-litigants or potential litigants alike) of its particular advantages in a given social context.[31]

In the trade and business context arbitration could provide clear advantages, especially in debt cases or contractual disputes where misunderstandings and inadequacies could be brought into the open and the adversarial nature of the court diminished. It also made sense to have the complexities of a dispute (which might be international in scope) evaluated by a group of experts who were familiar with the practices and issues, but hailed from outside the legal profession.[32] Parties were able to appoint their own arbitrators (usually one or more for each side), which extended to drawing them from a party's own nationality, and an additional unanimous choice to act as referee. Generally, though, commercial litigants had great confidence in English arbitrators, who were at pains to verify and assess pieces of evidence and the testimony of witnesses, but did so in a more flexible manner than was possible in court.[33] In Exeter, merchants or artisans with knowledge of the matter normally served as arbitrators, but it was quite usual to have as an impartial umpire a respected local figure or a man of the cloth. For instance, Philip Courtenay, the uncle of the earl of Devon was chosen as umpire by the parties in one case, while in another, Master Walter Robert performed the function.[34]

In London, fraternities provided testimony and support for their members where necessary, while the aldermen of the City, who were drawn from the most prominent guilds, were often called upon as negotiators and arbitrators.[35] In fact in the City there was an efficient system of referral by the Mayor's Court, which was useful in instances where there was a considerable amount of disagreement and possibly out-of-court altercation or background violence. Sometimes it was necessary to ensure that parties took the process seriously either by requiring an oath or a bond. In 1364, the parties in a dispute were 'sworn upon a book' to submit to six mediators.[36] In 1375, Thomas Gisors, a vintner, and his agent, William Misseburgh, similarly swore an oath to assist those mediating in every possible way.[37]

Arbitration was not restricted to mercantile and trade disputes. Since it had its roots in Roman law, it is not surprising that ecclesiastics were familiar with arbitration proceedings.[38] In 1294, for instance, the bishop of Ely and the abbot of Ramsey met at Wenelingham to try and re-establish friendly relations between the two churches.[39] As several historians have shown, it was also a resource that was utilised considerably by the nobility and gentry.[40] It was equally favoured by peasants and actively encouraged by the manorial courts. At Havering in Essex, the parties were expected to choose two or four arbitrators from among the respected men of the community so that the legal issues could be defused and an amicable solution reached, generally one requiring the parties to exchange something for their mutual benefit.[41] Akin to submitting one's case to referees (and sometimes a path towards arbitration) was the involvement of mediators or negotiators. In 1267 a dispute pending judicial action in the county court was settled through the mediation of friends of the parties. It would be impossible to establish statistically the extent to which such 'lovedays' were held, but many court rolls include entries where the parties did not turn up for the hearing or indicate officially that they had come to an agreement. In fact, in medieval minds, while they might appear as opposites, compromise or 'love' complemented the processes of 'law'. Again, lovedays were staged in the full public gaze so that social pressure could be exerted if the harmony faded and might incorporate an oath on the Gospels to solemnise the affair.[42]

If more peaceable methods failed, stripping a person of the right to hold land or exclusion from the village community were sanctions that could be channelled through the collective opinion of the manorial court. Deliberate shunning or ridiculing could also be employed against those who strayed from certain moral, ethical or religious codes.[43] In 1259, for example, an inhabitant of the borough of Scarborough who had refused to pay his share of a tax that was being levied was 'put out of the community of Scarborough vill and banned by the whole vill, nor was anyone to communicate with him in making sales and purchases, and they prevented his having fire and water in his house'.[44] The tradition of 'ridings', placing a person backwards on an animal, belonged to a universal repertoire of symbolic punishment and usually signalled public disapprobation, either for offences committed and otherwise unpunished, or for conduct that went against popular mores.[45] Evidence of such a riding may be contained in a curious presentment at the 1305 Lincolnshire Trailbaston sessions which reveals an otherwise inexplicable scenario in which a certain canon was riding a horse the tail of which had been deliberately cut off and a boy made to kiss its rear.[46] While the presentment does not reveal whether the canon was riding backwards, acting out or parodying the behaviour that had given rise to the demonstration was a common feature of a riding and it may be that the humiliating performance was highlighting some form of transgressive sexual behaviour.[47] That this was a familiar topos in the 'popular' consciousness is illustrated by the late thirteenth-century poem, *The Lay of Havelock the Dane*, which contains a vivid portrayal of a shameful riding to Lincoln undertaken by two alleged traitors,[48] and by the carvings on fourteenth-century misericords in Hereford and Wells cathedrals.[49]

Public humiliation was also meted out for professional misconduct: a baker in the city of London, who had not baked bread to a sufficient standard was drawn on a hurdle through crowded streets with the incorrectly-baked loaf around his neck,[50] while in 1382 a physician who had been revealed as a charlatan was forced to ride backwards in the city and paraded with two urinals (the symbol of doctors) which were hung about his neck.[51] Butchers in Norwich who sold putrid meat had their meat burned and earned themselves a spell of humiliation in the pillory,[52] while traders in Exeter who used false measures had their measures publicly broken and burned.[53] Although not everyone participated or necessarily shared the same views, the imposition of community norms on individuals who appeared out of line through the physical demonstration of expectations regarding acceptable behaviour is a significant exhibition of a collective legal consciousness. Members of the community could, however, act in their own interests to prevent punishment when ordered. Forty-eight people in Suffolk, for example, were said to have intervened to prevent the ritual humiliation of certain brewers when they were assigned the tumbrel. The brewers (who were likely to have been women since the tumbrel was usually reserved for them) were saved by the crowd, who assaulted the abbot of Bury's bailiff and prevented his servants from carrying out the judgment of the manorial court.[54]

More formal processes of exclusion, such as excommunication and outlawry, which acted as forms of judgment on individuals whose behaviour failed to come within acceptable norms and who refused to submit to the law, were supplemented by the informal judgment of a community. In certain circumstances or in particular areas, summary judgment could be carried out by individuals or groups on outlaws, traitors and 'hand-having' thieves (those caught red-handed). The action of members of the community towards these people may in fact have incorporated notions of justifiable excuse arising from the manifest guilt of persons who came into these categories and was no doubt intended to reinforce royal (or local) justice by acting on the spot. There was undoubtedly a change in attitude, however, towards such formally unsanctioned behaviour in that those who killed an outlaw, for instance, were required to attend court and exonerate themselves before the judges by putting themselves 'on the country'.[55] It may also have been a realisation that such action could exacerbate conflict by encouraging violent behaviour. The use of such methods suggests that notions of judgment and punishment were complex and that they sometimes inhabited a grey area between legitimate and illegal violence, self-help and 'misrule'.[56]

Court attendance

Attendance at public courts was an important way of acquiring legal knowledge. It is important to outline briefly the nexus of courts that formed the basis of many people's experience of law and which were adjunct to the royal court system outlined below in Chapter 4. Some tribunals met on a regular and continuing basis, others were more *ad hoc*. The various local courts operating within a shire met on a regular, periodic basis. All tenants were expected to attend the manorial court and the heads of tithings and usually four villeins from each vill were required to be present at the court of the hundred. Both courts were held on a three-weekly basis.[57] The manor court was the primary focus of tenants and the organ through which their tenurial relationship (the rights and obligations in land that derived from a villein's relationships with his lord and with his customary land) was maintained. It also facilitated a villein's own claims to and transfers of land, and governed relations with other tenants. Peasants viewed the manor court as an important institution because of its power to uphold the custom of the manor thereby balancing the lord's interests against rights asserted by the villeinage.[58]

The sheriff's 'tourn', which was a biennial gathering, was (in theory at least) attended by all the suitors of the court, all the tenants who were free in status, the reeve and four men from each vill and (where they were not coincident) the men of the tithings (as well as litigants). Hundreds in private hands experienced twice-yearly 'Great Courts' or courts leet (known as 'lawdays' in Suffolk).[59] At these twice-yearly sessions the view of frankpledge took place (a routine check of the functioning of the tithing system) and probably the assize of arms (a review of the weaponry and functioning of the local militia). It was also an occasion for the presenting of serious crimes that had occurred in the hundred over the previous six months and other offences under the 'Articles of the Tourn'.[60] Married women were also personally involved because as brewers and bakers they were frequently required to answer for defaults under the assizes of ale and bread.[61]

Sessions of the county court were regulated by Magna Carta and met once a month.[62] Although most shires met on a twenty-eight-day cycle, Lancashire, Lincolnshire, Yorkshire and Northumberland customarily held sessions every six weeks.[63] The day for meeting was usually a calendar fixture and ingrained in the memory, while the sessions themselves were normally held in the major county town.[64] The suitors of the court were those who were lord of a manor or even part of a manor or possessed a number of manors, though the burdens of suit of court could be transferred to tenants. Indeed, the reeve, priest and four men of the vill could go in place of the lord.[65]

Urban courts, the mayor's and the bailiffs' courts, sat on a fixed day each week, while pie-powder courts (a corruption of the French for 'dusty feet'), held for itinerant merchants, were summary courts held on the days of the relevant fairs or markets.[66] The payment of fines by way of licensing fees brought various types of merchants, tradesmen and craftsmen to the courts. Taverners and innkeepers (by the nature of the job and their premises) were particularly liable for court attendance. Members of the important occupations such as bakers, brewers, butchers, cooks and fishmongers regularly appeared in court since they came under the assessment of the assizes of bread and ale, and other regulations. Although the fines for breach of the assizes were assessed on the heads of households, women were frequently listed as brewers, for instance, because they did most of the work. Married women also attended court regularly if they were involved in marketing malt (because of the debts built up), as retailers of fish, as cooks and as part of the baking trade. Municipal authorities were keen to regulate the unenfranchised cloth and textile workers (many of whom were widowed and single women) and they too were required to pay sometimes quite substantial fines.

The church courts provided another dimension of legal experience. Under ecclesiastical jurisdiction, the diocesan Consistory court usually sat for three days at three-weekly intervals, while the archdeacon's court went on circuit through the rural deaneries holding a mixture of common (or solemn) sessions and private (or informal) sessions. The latter type of rural chapter enabled visitations of three or four parishes at a time (sometimes in remote places) to be held with the local priest and leading peasants or a few family groups attending. These localised sessions provided information both for parishioners and for the archdeacon and rural deans.[67] Even if they were not themselves suing in the courts, villagers were frequently drawn in to act as witnesses in all sorts of cases. Indeed, where the church courts were particularly active, it has been commented that 'scores [of litigants] seem to be peasants attached to manors in the countryside'.[68]

There was therefore a clear legal context operating of which people even at the lowest levels of society had experience. Attendance at the various courts either as a litigant or a witness or merely an onlooker provided a firm basis for the expansion of legal consciousness. As part of the general climate whereby knowledge could be acquired, royal statutes and other legal concerns were frequently proclaimed in market places and in other public places with the intention that people would listen, be informed, think about and discuss them (see Chapter 6). The use of proclamation also extended to the public notification of a litigant's appearance in court. Before the thirteenth century, the standard method for giving parties notice to appear in court was through an oral summons rather than service of a royal or viscontiel writ. The task of summoning was performed by 'criers' (*criatores*), who according to *Glanvill* were required to inform the parties openly and proclaim the summons itself in a public place. However, this practice was not confined to the twelfth century. The voicing of a summons, which made people (both the parties concerned and others) aware of court action and possibly even provided (or encouraged individuals to find out) the details of the case, appears to have continued at least until Edward I's reign.[69]

Court attendance could educate people in a quite specific way. The acquisition of legal concepts and their use in a judicial context is especially revealed in the pleas and arguments put forward by people in actual trials. A person arrested and charged with an offence may sometimes have had access to professional legal advice.[70] Those who were not so fortunate may have relied on a mixture of common knowledge and what they could glean informally while awaiting trial. This might come from discussion with friends and neighbours, if the offender had been mainprised (allowed bail), or with officials in the gaol.[71] Conversation with other prisoners could also provide a source of useful, though not wholly reliable information. Much of it was probably a mixture of misinformation and mythology, but some criminals obviously built up a store of knowledge and 'tricks of the trade' possibly as a result of a pooling of legal information and their own observation from previous appearances in court. Information about obtaining pardons was one area in which the justices' clerks could be particularly useful.[72]

A speculative, though compelling, example of defendants using information either imparted or overheard comes from the early thirteenth century, at a time when the Fourth Lateran Council's prohibition on clerical participation in ordeals had effectively removed the ordeal as a method of proving guilt or innocence.[73] Discussions in council had taken place over alternative methods of proof in criminal cases, but the justices in eyre in Yorkshire (1218–19) were not instructed until 26 January 1219 as to the way to proceed in cases (such as approver's appeals) where physical combat remained a possibility. Three men were appealed and came to trial sometime before 13 December 1218. The approver did not specifically offer proof by combat (offering instead to prove 'as the court will consider'); nevertheless the first appellee pleaded that he could not take part in physical combat because he was old and maimed. He duly asked for an inquest to decide whether the appeal had been made out of hate and spite (a necessary preliminary to the award of combat for judgment). The second and third put themselves upon the jury for a decision on the hate and spite issue, but significantly also placed themselves on the jury 'for good and ill' (*de bono et malo*) – possibly the first recorded instance of this phrase. Since no decision had formally been made on the method of judgment and the instructions (when they arrived) did not include trial by jury, the advice or opinion must have derived from someone who had a vague knowledge of what had been discussed at Westminster or of what was perhaps a topic of conversation among the company of the eyre justices in York. The precise connection is difficult to make and prove. The social standing of the defendants themselves was not high, though they did serve a significant local lord who was implicated in the appeals. It cannot be refuted, however, that the notion that trial by jury could be offered as a substitute for physical proof had been presented in court, suggesting the informal acquisition and subsequent use of legal knowledge.

An awareness that in the royal court strict procedural rules had to be followed – and that as a result of this observance various pleas and procedures could be used tactically to achieve an adjournment of the hearing – is demonstrated in a number of late thirteenth- and fourteenth-century cases. In 1326 John Adam of Stamford was indicted for the theft of two horses from a park at Austeley. At his trial (oyer and terminer sessions in Leicestershire), he raised a technicality, saying that Austeley Park was in Warwickshire and not in Leicestershire and so it did not show that he should be prosecuted on indictment in the latter county. The presenting jury confirmed this and he was mainprised as it was not possible to arraign him on this.[74] John Wapurnet, a tenant of the prior of Ely at Swaffham, demonstrated at the Cambridgeshire eyre of 1263 that, although 'he was at the bottom of the social scale, he was far from ignorant either of legal niceties or political realities'.[75] Accused of robbery during the civil war by Alan of Kirkebi (a castellan on the king's side), he made the defence that he ought not to answer the accusation since 'in the time of the disturbance' they were on opposing sides. Wapurnet had come forward to answer (after Alan's attorney had put the case against him) because he was aware (and Kirkebi clearly was not) that under the terms of the Dictum of Kenilworth anyone who paid a redemption fine was not liable for damage inflicted on those 'who fought in the time of the disturbance'. Only those who remained neutral were held liable. Warpurnet's knowledge duly saw him acquitted.

By the later decades of the thirteenth century the defendant's right to an alternative mode of trial (such as an ordeal) was a fiction;[76] nevertheless, a few defendants deliberately remained mute, refusing to submit to put themselves 'on the country'.[77] It is not clear what advantage was being sought, since refusal of trial by jury was in effect a refusal of the common law. Sometimes defendants possessed a disability preventing them from speaking.[78] In other instances individuals may not have spoken up because they did not understand the jury system, or perhaps were scared to entrust their fate to the chosen twelve. Alternatively they may have remained mute deliberately either through malice or (in the case of the manifestly guilty) because they were aware that even if they died as a result of the *peine forte et dure* (which was the statutory retribution for failing to plead),[79] technically they would not have been convicted and so any chattels they possessed would not be forfeit to the Crown.

The possibility of challenging the jury may have been well known. In 1333 three defendants accused of robbery and homicide placed themselves on eight of the jury, but challenged the rest and all others who came, with the result that they were returned to prison.[80] At a Norwich gaol delivery session in 1351 John Munch challenged twenty-nine of the jurors and secured respite until the next delivery. A little knowledge could be taken to extremes. In sessions at Northampton in 1333, John Dounedale of Geytington challenged the jury to such an extent that he exhausted three dozen of them. Since he had showed himself unwilling to place himself on any of the thirty-six men who had been summoned, the justices asked him whether he wished to place himself on a jury at all. He declined (perhaps erroneously thinking he would not then be tried),[81] but the justices decided to try and persuade him and he was sent back to prison on a starvation diet (*ad dietam*) for refusing to put himself 'on the country'.[82]

Challenging the jury could be followed up by employing other procedural delaying tactics. William of Shouldham, arrested on suspicion of theft, challenged a jury at gaol delivery sessions held in Norfolk in June 1321.[83] It is not clear what the outcome of this ploy was, but someone of the same name appeared before the justices at similar sessions five years later, this time under indictment for theft. He was convicted by the jury, but promptly claimed benefit of clergy. Not surprisingly, no bishop's ordinary came to acknowledge him as being in holy orders and he was sent back to prison.[84] In June 1325, Agnes Roger, accused of homicide, challenged the jury sitting to try her. She appeared again a month later, but had not been able to obtain from chancery a writ *de bono et malo* to enable her trial for homicide to proceed.[85] Usually only a few members of the jury were challenged, but further rejection might secure an adjournment.

In March 1324 Adam Patrik secured an initial respite from trial upon challenging the jury. When he next came before the justices after six months in prison, he decided to earn himself a further breathing space by turning king's evidence or becoming what was known as an 'approver' (see Chapter 4).[86] This apparently adroit, but ultimately ill-conceived, move offered a number of avenues: immediate postponement of his trial (so that his confession could be taken), the hope of freedom if his appellees, when apprehended, were convicted by the jury or were vanquished by him in battle, and the possibility of escape from prison while all this was taking place.[87] For the approver, a further stay of execution could be gained either by challenging the jury pronouncing the verdict on his appeals,[88] or by pleading benefit of clergy. Benefit of clergy was invoked by many defendants, though some were unable to fulfil the literacy test or, if they passed, were unable to provide the relevant charters proving ordination, or their recent tonsure or lay habit aroused suspicion.[89] This suggests that such prisoners, even if not thoroughly conversant with the full requirements of the system, were at least familiar with methods of obtaining release from royal criminal jurisdiction.[90] Self-confessed felons who had been allowed to abjure the realm, but had subsequently returned (itself a felony), on recapture tried to play the system and prolong their lives by turning approver again. Walter Blowewberne, for example, turned king's evidence in 1249 and having defeated ten of his appellees in battle was allowed to abjure the realm. A year later he was arrested once more, became an approver and accused another twenty people.[91]

The excuses put forward by approvers when retracting their confessions, namely that they were made under duress, through maltreatment or on account of diminished responsibility (*non compos mentis*), sound plausible and the details provided in evidence may give an indication of what life was like in medieval gaols. Yet, first, the coroner's record testified as to how the confession was made and generally demonstrated that the approver was of sound mind.[92] Secondly, the remarkable similarity among the stories offered by those approvers who alleged foul play, suggests that duress of imprisonment had become a standard excuse used by approvers keen to be let off the hook. Indeed, the employment of this particular plea followed closely a statute of 1340 which provided that, if it was found that prisoners were forced to become approvers against their will through duress of imprisonment or by pain, the gaoler (or whoever) would be liable to judgment of life and member.[93] The shadowing of the wording suggests that approvers were aware of this statute and deliberately invoking its provisions. Following allegations of duress, inquiries had to be set in motion and the approver's trial adjourned.[94] In specimen cases, the jury returned that the confession was not obtained as a result of any coercion, but was voluntarily spontaneous.[95] An indication that this had become a standard plea among the criminal fraternity comes from entries made in the rolls from the mid 1370s, which betray the Crown's desire to pre-empt the approver's plea of duress: the clerk records from the outset that the approver turned king's evidence spontaneously of his own will without any coercion in a meeting of the full county court with the coroners and named knights present as witnesses.[96] In an attempt to prevent any adjournment, efforts were clearly made to have the evidence before the court in advance of the hearing, before the approver could withdraw his confession and claim duress of imprisonment.

The above cases illustrate that some knowledge of legal procedure and the way the courts operated, even if rudimentary and misconceived, was in some way obtained, shared and utilised by defendants. In many instances it proved insufficiently founded to achieve much advantage, but where appropriate to the situation, it could prove beneficial. The criminal underworld may have always been a useful source of legal 'titbits'. As the legal procedure became more complex so the need to counteract or take advantage of loopholes increased. Experience of the judicial system and some legal knowledge could therefore help those appearing in the courts, whether innocent or manifestly guilty.

Church attendance

Attendance at church, required by the 1215 Lateran Council, provided various opportunities for the acquisition of legal knowledge. The tenets of divine law and biblical ideas of how justice should operate in the world were at the root of the Church's teaching. Notions of morality, law and justice could be conveyed visually by examples of obligations, sin and judgment (especially the Last Judgment or the Judgment of Solomon) depicted by artists and craftsmen on church walls or in intricate woodcarvings. Such notions could be inculcated aurally by priests, both from the pulpit and through the confessional. Sermons were ideal vehicles for putting across moral stances, standards of conduct and Christian obligations. They could also provide an insight into the world of law. In one sermon, the current legal procedure in the central courts was the subject of a simile, while in others there were passing references to a criminal being led to the gallows and to seals and charters.

Sometimes the focus of a sermon was the law itself. In the 1350s, for example, sermons were preached by the vicar of Aldbury (Hertfordshire) and Robert of Fulham, a hermit, against the Statute of Labourers. On other occasions legal imagery was employed as a metaphor for Christ's sacrifice and redemption.[97] In the late thirteenth century, Archbishop Pecham ordered that Magna Carta should be explained to congregations during mass.[98] As surviving confessional manuals show, clergy offered guidance (and imposed penances for sinfulness) on how girls and boys should behave and on matters such as marriage, infanticide and prostitution.[99] The Church used these methods in particular to bring to public attention the so-called 'rules' of Pope Alexander III regarding marriage formation – what constituted a valid marriage.[100] The clergy were also prime motivators in respect of mediation, since they were urged to encourage their parishioners towards amity: disputants were to be 'brought together by love' and priests were to exhort people not to let 'the sun go down upon the[ir] anger'.[101]

The churchyard and the church itself provided venues for much secular business. Court sessions were sometimes convened inside the church, and in some the composition of judicial writs and the solemnising of arbitrations took place.[102] Churches were also used as meeting-places to discuss common action.[103] Churchyards could be used to hold fairs and markets (particularly on a Sunday) and sessions of the hundred court or to make proclamations,[104] while church doors were utilised to publicise laws and important public information. By the late fourteenth century (at least) church doors were the showcases for defamatory bills or 'libels'.[105] In a more general way attendance at church may have encouraged literacy or at least some familiarity with the written word.

Experience of office-holding

Medieval administration and office-holding was often conceived of in jurisdictional and legal terms, either in the type of tasks men were appointed to do or with regard to the special knowledge of the person who was appointed to an office. The appointment of local men (as opposed to royal bureaucrats or household officials) to county and borough offices and their employment by the Crown for judicial work in the shire was a significant step, which not only expanded the enterprise of royal administration, but also broadened the outlook and experience of men in the regions. Those who took on the major judicial and administrative posts in the shires, boroughs and liberties (sheriff, coroner, mayor, bailiff, steward, keeper of the peace) required some legal know-how to fulfil the ordinary tasks of the office, which entailed a significant amount of judicial administration. Experience of the judicial processes of the courts, though, was not restricted to particular levels of society, but rather permeated all levels during the period stretching from Magna Carta to the Peasants' Revolt. The above officials were assisted at the level of hundred, ward, vill and manor by numerous underlings. Many of the routine tasks, however, had to be carried out by the more senior officials alone, and even those duties that they were able to delegate, they remained answerable for.[106]

The period witnessed shifting patterns in the nature of local officials' judicial or quasi-judicial responsibilities and in the knowledge that was required to fulfil them. The multiplication of judicial agencies, and a growth in the volume of legal business over the course of the thirteenth and fourteenth centuries generally, placed a heavier burden upon those entrusted with duties in judicial administration. As the tasks themselves increased in number and complexity, the type of service for which people were engaged, the levels at which they operated, or the form of employment they were willing to undertake accordingly altered. The onerous nature of the duties of sheriff, coroner and mayor are implied by their citation in claims for exemption. This was partly a consequence of royal policy. The Crown allowed the purchase of exemptions from office-holding and jury service, which at times were eagerly sought, not only because of the burdensome nature of service, but because people could take them as a precaution against having to hold office when it was inconvenient to do so.[107] The Crown's demands for military service, though fluctuating in their pressure, could remove many administrators and jurors from the county for indefinite periods of time. Demographic and socio-economic changes, such as increased mobility (both social and geographical), economic shortage, the plague and population shortage, also influenced the availability, recruitment and status of personnel.[108]

In addition to fiscal duties, there were important legal and executive aspects to the shrievalty. The sheriff presided over the county courts and the courts of the royal hundreds within his bailiwick and he was the executive officer for royal writs, judgments in the royal and county courts, and all orders for summons, distraint or attachment. The sheriff's work associated him with the assizes, though he was linked more closely to gaol delivery sessions.[109] Coroners heard confessions and abjurations of the realm made by felons and held inquests concerning homicides and suicides. They recorded indictments in the sheriff's tourn, and in the county court kept a record of the pleas of the Crown, where they were also involved with appeals and the process of outlawry. Constant attendance at both local and royal court sessions, where the record of the rolls was vital, must have enabled both officers not only to acquire legal knowledge, but also to learn much about local jurisdictions.[110]

The majority of towns were not self-governing and did not have the right to a chartered mayor during the period covered by this book, but in places that were autonomous, the mayor and bailiffs played a key role in urban judicial affairs. In some cases formal jurisdictional independence was not confirmed until a date considerably after it was being exercised. Grimsby, for instance, had a mayor by 1216 even though this privilege was not explicitly recorded in a charter until 1319.[111] The scope of the mayor's jurisdiction depended to a large extent on the borough's charter, though much of the law involved was customary.[112] The urban courts were generally responsible for specialised civil litigation – mainly cases of debt, breach of covenant and trespass – as well as the enforcement of local regulations and (sometimes) property disputes. The courts might have different names, such as Guildhall, Hustings, Portmoot, or Burgharmoot, but generally the mayor sat in the main borough court (usually called the mayor's court), while the other court, known as the provost's court in Exeter, for instance, was presided over by the town 'stewards' or bailiffs (sheriffs in London).[113] Where the town was a designated Staple town (under the 1353 ordinance), there was another important local judicial post to be filled, that of mayor of the Staple. Possessing civil jurisdiction over his Staple and exercising jurisdiction in Law Merchant over contracts and trade disputes which occurred there, like his counterpart, it was vital, and indeed a prerequisite of the post, that he knew mercantile law. The mayor of the Staple was also a royal official for the purposes of sealing and executing recognisances of debt.[114]

The task of maintaining the peace in a town also fell to the mayor and other borough officials, although formal appointments to peace commissions were not issued in chancery until Edward III's reign and then usually in response to specific royal or local concerns.[115] The mayor's role in criminal justice appears to have extended to taking indictments of felonies,[116] while some mayors sat on the gaol delivery panel with the royal justices and tried felons from the borough. The Mayor of London often delivered Newgate during the early fourteenth century.[117] Judicial work could also qualify the individual for a civic post. John Hall, for instance, frequently appeared as an attorney in the Colchester borough courts and was employed by local landlords for various types of legal work. His legal knowledge was no doubt regarded as valuable as he was appointed a member of the Colchester council in 1381–82.[118]

Liberties were administered by a steward or bailiff and, like boroughs, had their own coroner. Changes in agricultural practices and the growing complexity of the law in the thirteenth and fourteenth centuries saw the employment of special officials to oversee landowners' business affairs. The stewards of monastic or lay landowners were not only responsible for the administration of their great estates, but presided over the courts of the manor and hundred within the landowner's control. The employment opportunities for such a man of law were especially numerous in the fourteenth century as a result of the laicisation of the law and displacement of clerks.[119] For some, the job of steward could involve them in the service of several landowners either consecutively or concurrently.[120] The prominence of a steward in a particular locality and his obvious legal expertise meant he was an ideal candidate for employment in judicial and administrative tasks carried out on behalf of the king.

The responsibilities associated with all these offices did not remain static over the period. The purview of each official altered in scope to match both the expansion of royal justice over the thirteenth and fourteenth centuries and the relative vitality of business in the urban and manorial courts. Although this might imply in a general way that the responsibilities devolving to a particular office were greatly enlarged over the period, such a blanket generalisation masks the variety and divergence occurring. In addition to changes in the status and nature of the shrievalty,[121] the sheriff witnessed a decline in the business at his tourn (though it was still functioning in the later fourteenth century) with the evolution of the office of justice of the peace.[122] The duties undertaken by coroners in the field in fact differed in scope and extent from those ascribed to them in contemporary treatises and by modern historians.[123] In individual cases a steward might find himself underemployed or indeed, unemployed, where the business of a manor court diminished or disappeared. The mayor of a borough that was designated a Staple town in 1353 might have felt his jurisdiction was diminished.

It appears that, at least by the fourteenth century, there was remarkable continuity in county office-holding, measured either through individual length of service or through the service of subsequent generations of the same family. Yet, although the group of office-holders might alter in composition, as families grew to prominence or waned in influence, the burden was shouldered by a smaller group in the thirteenth century than was correspondingly the case by the late fourteenth century. This was partly because of an expansion in the number of posts and an increase in the size of commissions, but also because of the prestige that was attached to a place in the *cursus honorem* and to certain offices, in particular, holding the shrievalty and a place on the peace commission.[124] The creation of office-holding dynasties was not confined to the shire: three generations of the Selby family, for example, were between them mayors of York for at least seventeen years over the period 1217–89.[125]

Experience of shire government and local justice, therefore, was not only achieved by growing numbers of people over the course of the period, but, equally significantly, it was something people aspired to.[126] The business of judicial administration which was carried on by many individuals probably gave rise to its own ethos and consciousness about their work and service, especially where duties were carried out in unison or over a long period of time. The trio of Northamptonshire men, John Willoughby, John Longueville and Eustace Bruneby, carried out delivers of Northampton gaol for eight consecutive years (1316–21), during which time they also sat on the county bench.[127] It brought many different sorts of people together, some of whom met while engaged in different capacities, perhaps as sheriff or steward, coroner or justice of the peace, and encouraged a familiarity that was important for administrative workability. This was enhanced through private connections, such as family ties or kinship or those built up by being landowners in the same area. Just as much as less formal venues and meetings, the courts provided opportunities for discussion, exchange of views and information on law and politics (among other things).[128]

Below shire level, a network of lesser officials operating in towns, hundreds and liberties across the countryside performed duties as under-sheriffs, bailiffs, constables, haywards and reeves and undertook much of the day-to-day executive business and policing of the hundreds, towns and villages. At the lowest levels the churchwarden was required to report matters occurring within the parish, while the tithingman had a part to play, patrolling at night with his wandstaff (*cum werstaf*).[129] The most obviously onerous or controversial tasks at the local level were enforcing the provisions of the Assize of Arms, which was updated and recast in the form of the Statute of Winchester in 1285, and the labour legislation as enshrined in the Statute of Labourers (1351). Under the Statute of Winchester, two constables in each hundred were entrusted with the view of arms and on two occasions each year were to check that the men of tithings (the smallest grouping) were arrayed according to their competence.[130] Under the latter, local officials were directed to compel labourers to take an oath to uphold the requirements of the statute. It empowered the local officials to imprison any who refused to take the oath or who disobeyed and broke their agreements. Workers who left their village could also be arrested.[131]

In addition to their involvement in other areas of the judicial system, there is evidence that (during the first half of the fourteenth century at least) keepers of the peace in towns and at hundred level were regularly hearing indictments. The constables of the peace and bailiffs of the towns of Oxford, Bishop's Stortford and Worcester, for instance, certainly did so,[132] while there are examples of indictments taken before constables/ keepers of the peace in Northamptonshire in 1299, before John Randolf, a keeper of the peace in the hundred of Copthorne in Surrey in 1316 and before William Henry one of the constables of the peace for the hundred of Happing in Norfolk in 1344.[133] The practice was neither occasional, nor restricted to a particular geographical area and may have been a reflection of other work these men undertook, perhaps as local stewards.

The assumption of judicial tasks by men operating at this level was regarded by some judges as unwarranted and was at best controversial. In 1310, for instance the Norfolk gaol delivery justices decided that the constables of the hundred did not have the jurisdictional or written authority (*potestatem et warantum*) to inquire of felonies. This was underlined by their successors on the circuit twenty years later, when the court ruled that an indictment taken before the constables was not sufficient to bring persons to trial in a judgment of blood (*ad deducendum in iudicium vite seu membrum*). Clearly, however, the message had not filtered through or was deliberately being ignored as the practice continued. In 1371 the justices decided that John Lomere and Roger Upham, constables of the peace for the hundred of Munstoke in Hampshire, did not have the requisite authority to hear an indictment and ordered a diligent inquiry as to whether the men charged were guilty of felony. Despite these instances of court rulings, many justices were content to allow such indictments and there appears to have been no legislation against it, nor a decided policy on the matter. It serves to underline the measure of participation in the administration of justice that was afforded those operating below the level of the shire.[134]

Service in judicial administration was not without its drawbacks or hazards. In 1236, twenty-five Devon residents refused to acknowledge the authority of the serving sheriff (either because they did not like him personally, or because they objected to his holding pleas of the Crown) and walked out of the county court.[135] In 1326 John de la Pennes' sessions as a keeper of the peace were disturbed by an intrusion of armed men,[136] while a decade later the work of one of the Kent coroners, John Pricket, was impeded by someone hiding the dead body he had come to view.[137] Many local officials had their work severely hindered in 1381[138] (see Chapter 6). There were also reactions against local law enforcement officers while they were trying to carry out their duties (*quia ipsi constabularii fecerunt officium suum*) which frequently took the form of physical intimidation and accusations of malicious prosecution: one constable of the peace was allegedly killed; others were assaulted or had their attempts to arrest offenders resisted or their efforts to obtain oaths from labourers rebuffed.[139] In the case of local officials, some of this may have arisen out of a conflict of perceptions on the part of the official and the individual. There was often a difficulty in distinguishing between legitimate arrests and an excuse for an assault, between justified distraint of goods and outright robbery.[140] Yet it was not easy to maintain a perfect balance when an official might have his commission disbelieved and the warrant torn up in his face. When a distraint of chattels was carried out by local officials in Lakenheath in Suffolk in 1371, a bailiff's wand of office was broken in defiance as the villagers tried to recapture their chattels.[141]

It is difficult to know how such manifestations of dislike and defiance affected attitudes towards office-holding and whether they had their origins in the post-Black Death economic and social problems. The willingness to undertake public office was undoubtedly reduced when people were being vilified in court actions against them or being subjected to violence. The ability to juggle the needs and requirements of the community and those of royal government was obviously a key quality in an official. Moreover, personal relationships probably counted for much in the enclosed life of a town or village. Such relationships, however, could become strained as a result of continuing royal or seigneurial demands.

This was particularly true following the Statute of Labourers and with the advent of poll taxes and searching judicial inquiries, which made life increasingly difficult for the 'middle men', whose loyalties were being stretched in opposing directions. An unwillingness exhibited by constables of Lakenheath 'to answer for certain articles' at the king's bench visitation of Suffolk in 1379 exemplifies this dilemma.[142]

The sources for such examples tend to be documents of the later fourteenth century, but we should not assume this dislike and defiance is a post-plague phenomenon purely on the basis of records (such as sessions of the peace) whose survival is patchy before the mid-fourteenth century. Indeed, we should be cautious of trying to isolate a particular cause since it is likely that the prevailing influences, whether political, social or economic, were interconnected. It does, however, reflect the growth of legal consciousness, a change in understanding of the implications (among local officials on the one hand and villagers on the other) concerning the nature of their duties and a rise in the expectations associated with office-holding.

The use of sworn inquests provided the mainstay of judicial business in both royal and seigneurial jurisdictions by the time of the Peasants' Revolt. The range of legal and administrative responsibilities with which jurors were entrusted was enormous, encompassing all manner of calls for inquiries and decisions. In addition to providing answers to the articles of the eyre, trailbaston, and sheriff's tourn, in preparation for provincial visitations of the king's bench and at peace sessions (see Chapter 4), jurors were required to provide verdicts in civil litigation (including the petty assizes) and in criminal trials. The coroner was aided in his duties by a sworn inquest, the members of whom had to be able to pronounce on aspects of the death. The escheator required inquests based on the articles of his office. Jurors were used for deciding aspects of a trial (whether the case had been brought out of hate and spite)[143] and to report on and decide issues of economic status in preparation for distraint to knighthood as well as providing evidence concerning an heir's age in wardship cases.[144] Verderers required a jury of twelve 'regarders' to answer questions relating to the forest.[145] Jurors with specialised knowledge were empanelled to try instances of lawyers' professional misconduct[146] and for mercantile cases, where half the jury was made up of fellow merchants. Mercantile cases might also require a jury 'of the half-tongue', those of the defendant's nationality,[147] while in maritime disputes, juries consisting of masters of ships, travellers, merchants and those making a living by or from the sea were usually summoned.[148] When a woman claimed pregnancy at gaol delivery, her trial would be delayed until the justices had a decision on the question of her physical state, which was entrusted to a jury of matrons (the only royal jury on which women could serve).[149]

Increased familiarity with the jury system (a product of the period 1215 to 1381) significantly altered the attitudes and experiences of those involved in jury service (though of course it is something that is difficult to measure). The following section will nevertheless examine the knowledge acquired by – and the mental processes that were required of – members of at least some juries, and assess in general terms changing perceptions over this period of their reliability.

The introduction of the jury involved a move away from the ordeal as a form of judgment in the royal courts and from the system of collective judgment in the local courts, which in turn brought in new concepts which had to be broached and accepted by people familiar with the older forms.[150] Jury trial gave rise to different concerns for jurors depending on whether the cases were civil or criminal in nature. The increasing complexity of issues within disputes and the corresponding development of the substantive law, pleading and legal exceptions meant that jurors had to be aware of the legal principles pertinent to the given situation. Further, juries should not be thought of as homogeneous entities, consisting of twelve individuals of the same character, status, knowledge and experience. The customary-law and common-law procedures drew upon the 'neighbourhood' and the 'locality', but the neighbourhood (*visnetum*) was not a definite administrative unit as such: it had no firm boundaries. Similarly, 'the country' (*patria*) appears as a fluid term. It may be equatable with 'community', but it refers not to a single community but rather a number of communities.[151]

The adoption of the jury system in the manorial courts during the thirteenth century signalled important changes in the participation of justice (and thus in perceptions of justice) at the local level. Traditionally, offences were prosecuted by individual suitors and manorial officials. The lord's steward or a royal bailiff presided over the court, but, where necessary, any judicial function was undertaken by the whole court, the suitors. All the tenants on the manor were thus obliged to come and take part in proceedings, shouldering responsibility for deciding factual issues in land litigation, for example (in something akin to the grand assize), and for interpreting aspects of manorial life according to local custom. A bifurcation of the main responsibilities occurred with the introduction in the manorial courts of presentment and judgment by panels of jurors. In turn, the role of president of the court shifted from being purely managerial, acquiring instead more of a judicial flavour.[152]

If we are looking for reasons for this new departure, the viability of communal participation was undoubtedly affected by social and economic factors, such as the growth and decline of settlement areas and fluctuations in mobility and migration. Nevertheless, legal, administrative and financial factors, such as the need for greater efficiency in dealing with the increasing number of civil cases brought by individuals and a desire for stricter enforcement of the lord's rights, may equally have precipitated the change. It is noticeable, however, that this revolution in procedural practices did not occur uniformly across the country. Thus, on the abbot of Bec's manors, juries were in use before the mid-thirteenth century, while the manors belonging to the abbey of St Albans continued to rely on the judgment of the whole court well into the fourteenth century.[153]

For many people this alteration of practice brought a reduction in direct personal involvement in local court matters since their responsibilities had devolved upon two smaller groups (the presenting and trial juries).[154] To some extent this may have depended on whether jury service was spread out among all eligible people, who thus took it in turns, or whether it took the form of regular employment of a smaller pool of people. Although the former may have been favoured as an ideal, the latter was probably the norm in practice. The courts also granted suitors the right of essoin (excuse) in a relaxation of the need to attend. The new direction, therefore, was probably not unacceptable in that it provided relief from the onerous and time-consuming duty of suit of court.

The shift from communal participation to a discrete group acting on the wider community's behalf not only altered the practicalities of court attendance, but also redrew some of the conceptual boundaries of participation. No longer was investigation of a matter linked to giving judgment in it. Nor was the rendering of a verdict necessarily associated with the interpretation and application of customary law. Moreover, for those engaged in jury work, the restriction of the panel to twelve members[155] dictated a change in attitude towards the tasks undertaken. It meant that people's involvement became deeper and more focused, as their group was solely responsible for the duty entrusted to them. But it also made them more exposed, in that they were open to public scrutiny and in effect forced to put their reputations on the line, especially over the accuracy of their fact-finding and with regard to the correctness of the decision-making.

As mentioned above, the new procedures not only introduced different forms of service but demanded different ways of thinking. Moreover the legal system's dependence on the jury system, which increased exponentially with the rapid expansion in royal justice during the thirteenth and fourteenth centuries, spawned a proliferation of legal and administrative uses to which sworn inquests were committed. This in turn engendered changes in the knowledge base and in the personnel of the jury, but also gave rise to concerns as to the way juries operated and their reliability.

What legal knowledge was required or could be acquired by a juror? Did jury service simply entail reporting facts or did it involve a more reflective process of thinking, deciding and utilising knowledge and experience? In many instances a manorial juror needed a thorough grasp of the prevailing customs and local affairs. In 1321 the steward of the bishop of Ely's court at Littleport, while accepting the jurors' version of the facts in a case, did not agree with their interpretation of custom.[156] Obviously, where a special jury had been convened it was the inside knowledge and understanding of the profession or trade that was important.[157] Where recognition of landholding, age, or economic status were concerned, a good memory and an ability to ascertain the correct type of information from other people and other sources was a prerequisite.

Experience in the day-to-day running of administrative affairs was an important element in the empanelling of jurors. It is not surprising, therefore, to find that manorial officials such as haywards and reeves usually served on local juries.[158] Town officials were also involved as jurors, sometimes presenting offences, sometimes rendering verdicts on them. Of the forty-seven presenting jurors mentioned in the rolls of sessions of the peace held in Lincoln in 1351–54, for example, seven had at one time served as mayor and two were bailiffs of the city. Peter Bellassise, a former mayor, was among a number of men who also appeared on a trial jury panel.[159] Their previous (or current) legal experience in an official post may have been useful, if not influential, in bringing offenders to account and determining thorny issues.

For some cases knowledge of the law was essential. At common law, jurors in land litigation needed to be aware of the doctrine of livery of seisin in order to fulfil their role correctly. It is unclear, however, whether a jury was specifically told what to look for by the justices/officials or whether they were co-ordinated or informed by a foreman or the most experienced members of the panel. The group was clearly not always aware of its legal duties. A Derbyshire jury in 1304 was described disparagingly by a second jury as comprising 'simple persons who were not cognizant with English laws and customs', because they assumed that a charter was adequate proof of a conveyance. They were unaware that under the doctrine of seisin, in order for a gift of property (such as a house or messuage) to take legal effect the donee had to have had the property properly delivered to him and had to have taken seisin (possession) of it. Irrespective of whether there was a genuine, correctly drafted and valid charter conveying the property in documentary form, physical symbols of possession or control of the property remained paramount in establishing livery.[160]

The resolution of wardship cases also necessitated not only careful deliberation of the facts but a clear knowledge of the prevailing rules and customs. Where there were conflicting rules a decision might need to be taken as to which should obtain. In one case, the issue raised was that of priority of feoffment. But since the jurors did not know whose lands were covered under the rule which favoured the most ancient feoffment, they relied instead on another rule which stated that in 'whosoever fee the heirs are found after the death of their ancestor, to him the marriage is always accustomed to pertain'. The resulting decision may be evidence of the consultation of legal treatises or at least a good working knowledge of the law. *Bracton* and the second Statute of Westminster offer priority of feoffment as the basic rule, but, interestingly, the later treatise *Britton* confirms the legitimacy of the path taken by the jury: since they could not establish the priority of feoffment then right went to whoever had hold of the heir.[161] The complexity of civil litigation might necessitate a number of juries being called upon to decide different issues. As we noticed above, jury knowledge was not infallible. Occasionally, as in a case on a plea of waste (an action concerning the destruction or treatment of property in a way that was prejudicial to the heir or to those possessing an interest in the land), jurors returned a verdict that was in fact contrary to statute law.[162]

In criminal trials, too, the jury had to be able to formulate within certain strict rules the defences (presumably) offered by the accused. In cases of homicide where the defendant acted in self-defence or the killing was accidental the trial jury had explicitly to exclude felonious intent and give an account of the circumstances. In the early thirteenth century the novelty of jury work and the inexperience of jurors in approaching such matters becomes apparent from the judges' questions, for they reveal a lack of understanding of the details required for a verdict of accidental death. Moreover, the phraseology of the jury's testimony in this period, frequently couched in terms 'reminiscent of the passages from penitentials and the works of canonists', suggests that they were searching for a particular formula and applying the terminology of a moral or religious stance.[163]

In later years, the introduction of formulae both in the wording of commissions for special inquisitions and in the questions put by justices provided jury members with the necessary signposts and guidelines. Nevertheless they were still required to establish a number of features of the encounter based on their own knowledge or investigation. These features included showing the perpetrator had not started the fight, or it had got out of hand or he was provoked; or the encounter was premeditated and having been tirelessly pursued while trying to escape, he had eventually been forced into a corner; he had been unarmed and picked up a weapon or his weapon was smaller or a blunt instrument; any force used was commensurate with the attack and had been out of desperation to save his life.[164] There were similar legal considerations which jurors entered into in cases of insanity and infanticide.[165] The stock phrases, vivid scenes and embellishments which characterised many verdicts of self-defence or insanity were probably the outcome of previous experience of such cases or consultation with others who had.[166]

In some cases it is difficult to judge whether the jury lacked the requisite knowledge or were deliberately and cleverly misinterpreting their brief. In the thirteenth century, for instance, prisoners seeking release on bail for homicide could apply for a writ *de odio et atia* and a special inquiry would take place accordingly to assess whether the defendant was facing trial out of hate and spite. Jurors serving on such inquisitions often took the 'hate and spite' issue as relating to the offender's state of mind prior to the killing rather than the referring to the possible prejudices of the accuser and so rendered a verdict that underlined his actions as not being determined by felony or preconceived malice. This in effect twisted the purpose of the inquest so as to benefit the defendant wishing to obtain a pardon.[167] This type of verdict was occasionally brought in cases of insanity, where it was found that the defendant had not killed out of hate and spite, but madness.[168]

Sometimes the jury acknowledged that they did not know (*ignorant*) the facts.[169] This might be because they wanted to shield someone, but the ignorance might also be genuine, as in the case of a manorial jury in Methley (Yorkshire) where it was said 'they do not know, because this situation never occurred among them' – in other words, an analogous situation had perhaps not arisen as far as local memory stretched.[170] Where they could not agree, or their collective knowledge or memory was lacking, jurors could consult the court rolls.[171]

Jurors' attitudes to the judicial process were influenced by both the practical and psychological aspects of their work. Depending on the nature and level of the offence they were trying, jury members, either individually or collectively, had to take cognisance of the legal, social and even political ramifications of their decisions. The temptation to temper the harshness of the capital sanction and apply their own notions of justice based on their knowledge of the accused or feelings about a particular situation were undoubtedly strong. In cases of homicide, in particular, the trial jurors' ability to import their understanding of the incident to the final verdict (irrespective of what the coroner's inquest or the presenting jurors had concluded) suggests there were societal forces which the law could not penetrate.[172]

Jury nullification was equally obvious in the trials of people who had been appealed by approvers. Convictions solely on approvers' appeals were rare, amounting to four per cent of all convictions in Norfolk, for example, during the first part of the fourteenth century and less than one per cent of all trial jury verdicts rendered in the county's gaol delivery sessions.[173] The various localities' treatment of approvers' appeals is markedly different from their returns on prosecutions by private appeal or on indictment: ninety-eight per cent of those appealed by Norfolk approvers in the years 1299–1349 were acquitted. The figures for acquittals on indictment are somewhat lower, sixty-three per cent on average for the early fourteenth century.[174] This clear discrepancy reflects a number of concerns at work in the minds of the jury as well as factors about their behaviour that historians need to take into account. There was general public concern for abuses in the system: common petitions in parliament not infrequently complained of false and malicious appeals and the undue pressure exerted on innocent people.[175] That is not to say that all the people whom approvers cited as accomplices were in fact innocent and untainted of any involvement in their crimes. Approvers, themselves, may have been held in low esteem by communities, as disruptive and vindictive elements and this may have contributed to an ingrained attitude of antipathy towards them and prejudiced the decisions on their appeals, which in turn undermined to a certain extent the whole system of turning king's evidence.[176]

In their assessment of damages the civil jury could offer their view on the situation and adjust the damages accordingly, making them more proportionate. But determining a sum was not always an easy job. In a decision which resembled the ideal of the ordeal, an early thirteenth-century jury passed the task on to a higher authority claiming, 'they knew not the damages and no one knew save God alone'.[177] In wardship cases, whether the heir or heiress was still marriageable often proved difficult to answer immediately, as did determining the yearly value of the lands in the inheritance for the purposes of damages. Indeed, two juries might be empanelled and asked to make an award comprising 'damages' and 'additional damages' appropriate to each case. They were not called upon, however, to provide a rationale for their award.[178]

In trying to gauge how jury service affected legal consciousness, it is important to identify how far it permeated the social structure. We should not assume, though, that jury panels themselves represented a cross-section of society or that they were elected freely or all serving of their own free will. Complaints were frequently made by people (including villeins) who had been placed on juries against their will and made to go to London or court venues a good distance from their homes.[179] Jurors in the royal courts in the thirteenth century were expected to be knights or reasonably substantial property owners. The Statute of Westminster (1285) set the official level of standing for service as a juror in the royal courts at having freehold estates of an annual value of 20s within a particular county or 40s for representation outside it, provided he was not incapacitated by age or infirmity.[180] This was altered in 1293 when the rate for those summoned outside their county was increased to lands and tenements to the value of 100s, while the amount for those serving within the county rose to 40s.[181]

In theory the need to meet certain property qualifications may have been a bar to service for those whose income fell below the statutory requirements, but in practice the threshold at which jury service was permitted was considerably lower. Indeed the statutory enactments may have been tacit recognition of the difficulty of getting jurors of a particular standing. Peasants and even villeins were put on juries, in spite of the bars against poverty (instigated on the grounds of perceived corruptibility) and the incapacity of servile status.[182] Indeed, the Statute of Exeter (1285) evidently envisaged that the unfree served as jurors when there were insufficient freemen, since 'bondsmen' were required to have seals in order to validate their written evidence.[183] A petition from the chief pledges in Mildenhall in Suffolk requesting that no villein or customary tenant be appointed a chief pledge and that the steward should not hold a court leet except by the chief pledges, implies that these responsibilities had been taken on by the unfree.[184]

Investigation of the jurors' social background, where possible, and the frequency of their appointment provides two important pointers towards both the communities' attitudes and those of individuals towards jury service. Studies on village communities and on hundred jurors have analysed the people performing jury service in manorial courts and in the eyre. Their findings reveal a marked similarity at both levels in the type of person who was called upon to sit on inquests and the sort of networks in which they existed. At manorial level, there was not a strict attitude towards recruitment, but it certainly was not in any way haphazard. On the basis of analysis of the surviving court rolls from the period 1280–1350 for the village of Ellington on the Ramsey Abbey estates in the East Midlands,[185] it has been suggested that jurors were not simply plucked from the elite families, there was scrutiny of the behaviour of individuals as part of the selection process and conscious attempts at man-management. No single factor necessarily dominated this process; a number of factors affected the choice of a juror. The reputation of his family, their social background and stability, were measured alongside his involvement in running village affairs, his own connections and good standing, long-term residence and ability to keep up with local events.

The composite 'non-juror' was, therefore, perhaps not surprisingly, someone who did not remain long in the village (92 per cent of those who did not serve as juror were highly mobile), did not tend to hold any other official post, was rarely trusted enough to act as a pledge, was implicated in various trespass actions and had a high incidence of disruptive behaviour. Interestingly, the selection process cut across family lines: a disposition towards violence could prevent nomination in spite of the existing service of a brother or cousin. There is evidence that one juror was actually crossed off the list in the court record, probably as a result of a number of antisocial activities in which he was involved. Significantly he did serve as a juror at a later date, by which time his previously tarnished had improved.[186]

The average length of service by a juror in this sample was about eleven years, but individuals acted for as long as twenty years in some cases. The presumed willingness of jurors to continue in this capacity and the extent of their involvement in local life indicate that the manor was able to rely on a reserve of experienced and knowledgeable persons. In the late thirteenth and early fourteenth centuries, temporary poverty does not seem to have operated as a bar to sitting on a manorial court jury. The dramatic fall in population and socio-economic conditions existing after the Black Death also allowed scope for jury service by men whose families had not contributed to the pool of jurors at an earlier date.

Examination of the behaviour of men serving as jurors in the town of Halesowen reveals that concern for the uprightness of jurors was not just a characteristic of the village community. The lack of presentments nominating jurors for anything other than minor offences suggests either a reluctance to present existing jurors (and that cases harmful to their reputation were suppressed) or that in fact they took their responsibilities seriously. Where instances of violence (including bloodshed) are recorded against such people it is a number of years before they were called upon to serve as jurors.[187]

Research into the jurors presenting offences for thirteenth-century eyres has yielded patterns of participation based on particular hundreds in different counties. Information on the composition of juries and how they functioned is vital for ascertaining how jury service was perceived (by those undertaking it and those who for whatever reason were not a part of it) and how it related to life in general. Answers to questions based on these factors can lead on to speculation as to how homogeneous juries were, how members reached decisions and what sort of processes and influences were at work. As we saw with the manorial evidence, however, the paucity of sample means that broad generalisations may not be wholly valid. It could potentially make a difference in which hundred jury service was performed. For instance, the size of hundreds varied from county to county and region to region; some were royal hundreds, others lay in private hands. Calculations of economic status based on variable measures of land and differences in the terminology employed for those holding land make valuable comparison tricky.[188] In the Surrey hundred of Copthorne there were very few knights on the presenting jury: the panels comprised mainly 'sub-freeholders'. In Langtree hundred in Oxfordshire, the jurors were 'sizeable freeholders', while juries in the Cambridgeshire hundred of Armingford were generally made up of 'lesser landowners', some of whom were non-residents. A familiar pattern of continuity and length of service emerges: William Wyke, in particular, appeared on juries at Oxfordshire eyres over a forty-year period (1241–85). Moreover, it was common for successive generations in a family to take up the mantle of jury service.[189]

The concept of the disinterestedness or impartiality of jurors is a difficult one for us to apply wholly to the medieval court system. Jurors were expected to be men 'who bore no relationship to either party',[190] but it would have been virtually impossible to operate the system at the lowest levels without choosing friends and neighbours, though the exact degree of proximity may have been a factor. How impartial were they? During the thirteenth century there was often a close link between the presenting jury and the trial jury because it was felt that the original jury were the ones most likely to know the facts of the case or make judgments accordingly. Were they reliable? Going against the solemn oath would amount to perjury and would jeopardise a favourable destination for the infractor's soul.[191]

There were also procedural safeguards intended to prevent miscarriages of justice, such as the process of attaint, whereby a second jury opinion could review and possibly overturn the first decision, and the system of jury challenges. In the London city courts, both parties were given an opportunity to challenge the jurors. If a challenge was forthcoming a special committee of four had to assess it and report back. The extent to which the court desired a full and accurate verdict is suggested by the summoning of two juries where both plaintiff and defendant demanded one from their respective neighbourhoods.[192] This attitude was still prevalent in the early fourteenth century, though during Edward III's reign there was a shift in views on this point and public opinion became increasingly hostile and sensitive to the notion that a person's indictors should serve on the trial jury. Legislative action (in 1352) acknowledged the feelings on jury behaviour, which was itself increasingly under scrutiny and a feature of complaint (see Chapter 5). The extent to which the legislation was taken seriously and thus impinged on local perceptions can be seen from the rare survival of original jury lists for gaol deliveries in the south-west. The sheriff has crossed through specific names on the existing panel of names and either added a marginal note *'pro indicator'* or a cross, before pricking another name (often the last on the list).[193]

Awareness among jury members of the obligations incumbent upon them is of course difficult to prove. This can be extended to witnesses, who played some part in trials under the common-law system and more extensively under canon law.[194] According to the *Court Baron* a comprehensive oath was sworn that 'for love nor hate nor fear nor anything in this world, nor for price, nor reward tell any falsehood or conceal any truth touching the matter about which I am brought as a witness'. In the ecclesiastical courts, which relied on witnesses as a form of proof, they would be sworn in front of the opposing party and examined on their evidence.[195]

Jurors and witnesses gained first-hand experience of the workings of the courts and must have had some cognisance of the substantive and procedural issues that arose, even if they did not understand them in their entirety. Knowledge of what happened or the ability to become informed of facts was clearly an important function of a jury member and applied to a case that had happened months or even years previously as much as where an event occurred in the presence of the justices, and witnesses were required on the spot.[196] Fitting those facts to be in accord with a defence or to shape a verdict, however, required some legal understanding and/or the persons serving to have experience of such cases, whether they be civil or criminal. The social levels which jury service (both inside and outside the courts) permeated and the length of time that jurors usually spent in office suggests that there were a substantial number of people capable of having informed views on legal matters.

Book learning and literacy

Participation in the legal culture was influenced by the spread of literacy and the written word. Despite the continued acceptance of older methods of proof (such as symbolic mementoes, tally-sticks and the memory of members of the community),[197] a growing requirement for documentary evidence led to an understanding of the significance of record-keeping, while the increasing use and availability of documents not only widened familiarity with the written word, but broadened people's confidence in – and expectations of – a literate culture. The importance of documents and record-keeping, which was recognised by the royal government during the twelfth century, gradually filtered down the social scale over the course of the thirteenth century, so that by the beginning of the fourteenth century it is apparent that the majority of peasants were familiar with writs, charters, written agreements and the like. The documentary culture that fuelled the bureaucracy of royal administration had reached the villages and meant that written records had become integral to the practical purposes of daily life.[198] Indeed, there was a particular desire among peasants for cases to be enrolled where there might be questions at a later date concerning the validity of the marriage, or the legitimacy of the children or concerning the transfer of property at the time of marriage.[199]

For some the introduction to the literary culture may have come from those who were able to write, whose livelihood depended upon a proliferation of documents: clerks and scriveners. As Dr Ramsey puts it: 'The scriveners may have thrived on the law's informality for their inroads into it, but, more importantly, in a more general way it is suggested that they made people familiar with the need to follow set forms, that they helped people to order their lives in accordance with a set of principles which readily resorted to legal machinery when matters did not turn out satisfactorily, and that they thus contributed to the expansion of the law's role in people's lives'.[200]

The extent to which legal documents were a familiar part of everyday life is exemplified by 'testimonials of trustworthiness' which vagrants or individuals travelling around the country carried about their person in order to placate the eye of suspicion which fell on such people. A case from the 1260s demonstrates that the mere possession of a certificate of good character could inspire in the bearer confidence in its power, even if its contents were later ignored by another lord. The use of legal documents among people dwelling in the towns and countryside can also be seen in the requirement for warrants of lawful purchase following the sale of horses, cattle and other animals. Without such receipts, as cases from 1241, 1258 and 1292 demonstrate, a villager could be apprehended for unlawful possession of goods or animals.[201]

Transactions in the land market increasingly necessitated recourse to written instruments. Indeed, from the beginning of the thirteenth century (and probably earlier) the royal courts were unwilling to accept symbolic mementoes alone as sufficient title to land. All classes were encouraged to do business with charters, but the familiarity and confidence with which the peasantry approached such documents, including (very probably) the so-called 'natives', unfree tenants, is quite remarkable. The survival of *cartae nativorum* in the cartulary of Peterborough Abbey in fact may well represent the tip of the iceberg in terms of the number and frequency with which charters were used by small landholders (free or unfree) for the acquisition and conveyance of property.[202] The possession and deployment of seals is also a significant indication of an understanding of the nature of documents and in some instances of a sense of corporate legal personality. There is evidence that the seals of individual peasants were impressed on written agreements and that a common seal was made for a group of tenants in Wiltshire (though its construction was not tolerated by the lord since it implied a concerted challenge to his authority). The burgesses of Grimsby used a common seal during the thirteenth century. An idea of the chronology and level of this activity can be gained from a surviving chirograph dating from as early as 1230, which records a contract between Gloucester Abbey and Emma, a widow and the holder of an unfree tenement, and was duly authenticated by a seal bearing her name and a device. The seal not only gave the holder a legal identity, but was a marker of her aspirations.[203]

An element of literacy and an awareness of both the practical and archival purposes of documents were essential attributes for office-holding. To be a successful local administrative official (including, by 1300, a manorial bailiff or reeve) necessitated a familiarity with bureaucracy, including court record-keeping, and perhaps a working knowledge of as many as three languages (English, French and Latin).[204] Internal evidence from the manorial court rolls of Cuxham (Oxfordshire) demonstrates that some reeves wrote up their accounts themselves and may have received some education in Oxford.[205] On the basis of an account of jury procedures (written in about 1240) together with surviving jury *veredicta*, linguistic knowledge was also a prerequisite for eyre jurors. They (or at least their foreman) had to be able to read French and Latin and could face imprisonment if the English recitation presented at the bar of the court deviated from the previously written French version.[206] For many of their tasks, jurors probably relied to a large extent on memory, but they too required a familiarity with the details of the court record. Manorial jurors, as noted above, were sometimes required to vouch the court rolls as a proof of the accuracy of their statement, so they needed to be able to recognise what the rolls contained and know where they were kept.[207]

There were many opportunities for people to acquire the knowledge and skills useful for work in county administration, in estate management and in private practice. Schooling could be enhanced or supplemented by reading legal texts, from which informal instruction might also be gained. The thirteenth century witnessed a flourishing of handbooks and treatises on legal and administrative matters. Some, as we saw in Chapter 2, were aimed primarily at the upper end of the professional spectrum; others were designed for the generalist, especially the steward and the county justice. As professional administrators the former required knowledge of land tenures, pleas and the intricacies of estate management.[208] This knowledge could be passed on orally by those already steeped in the necessary customs and practices and equally acquired through 'in-service' training.[209] Indeed, attendance in the county court was probably a vital part of the learning process. By the late thirteenth century, informal instruction by word of mouth could be supplemented through the medium of the written word in addition to the discipline of academic study. Treatises, such as *The Court Baron* (composed c.1265) and *How to Hold Pleas and Courts* (composed in c.1272), provided detailed instructions about local courts and templates for potential administrative and judicial encounters, while practically-based management books such as *Seneschaucy* (also of use to the manorial bailiff and reeve, of whom it assumes an ability to read French) and the 'Estate Book of Richard Hotot', which were equally practical, ensured would-be stewards were suitably educated in their role.[210]

Practising lawyers were not the only possessors of statute books. Owners included various landowners, churchmen, and merchants, among whom were Anthony Bek (bishop of Durham), Isabella de Fortibus (dowager countess of Aumale and countess of Devon) and Sir William Breton (a Lincolnshire knight). Many of the surviving copies of statute books are pocket-sized, lacking marginal illustrations and were clearly intended for practising lawyers and estate officials. However, other extant copies, which made their way into the libraries of cathedrals and people's private collections, demonstrate these books were in fact fashioned in various sizes, including large, de luxe volumes. Significantly, they draw together a number of texts that would previously have been restricted in readership to a small percentage of the population. They achieved dissemination of legal information on a wider scale and benefited numerous landowners, officials, merchants and clergy. Indeed, ownership of statute books during the late thirteenth and fourteenth centuries can be traced to at least 249 people.[211] As a comparatively rare commodity and an important resource, it is likely that the actual recorded ownership of books represents the tip of the iceberg in terms of the number and status of people who might have benefited from their contents. There was also a wider area of participation since the owners of books were not their only readers: volumes could be borrowed or stolen by others, thereby enlarging readership. While the language in which they were written may appear to have provided a barrier to a book's contents, this could be overcome by someone else reading aloud to an individual or a group as required.[212]

Statute books were not the only resource acquired by the 'non-lawyer'. A number of secular and ecclesiastical landowners could boast registers of writs, some of which were illuminated, but in such a way that the drawings were of practical use as a finding aid for those not entirely *au fait* with the detailed texts of writs. In the course of locating the correct writ the reader was educated as to the meaning and power of the legal remedy, encapsulated in the drawing or symbol, by which means it impinged on the mind of the reader.[213] Some literature catered for women, who in the absence of their husband or otherwise, required assistance in managing their estates. Bishop Grosseteste's *Rules* were written for the countess of Lincoln, for example, in the 1230s or 1240s and around the mid-thirteenth century Walter Bibbesworth compiled a treatise for Lady Denise de Mounchensy providing her with the vocabulary of 'husbandry and management'.[214] The cultural interests and achievements of local administrators and their wives have been seriously underestimated.[215]

Some knowledge of legal forms and the court system could be gleaned from literary works such as *An Outlaw's Song of Trailbaston*, where the author's self-asserted knowledge of law is demonstrated by his frequent (and accurate) use of legal terms and his synopsis (albeit satirical) of the workings of the legal system,[216] and *The Tale of Gamelyn* where a scene (within the inverted world of the tale) contains a vivid account of a trial.[217] Langland's *Piers Plowman* also provides numerous instances of legal imagery and scenes of judicial encounters.[218] Although it would be unwise to make too many assumptions about the access to and audience of such texts, it is likely that their subject-matter and treatment enabled them to appeal beyond the gentry and merchant households and, through various forms of transmission, mediation, translation and appropriation, reach at least the upper levels of the peasantry and the relatively less well-off townsfolk.[219]

This chapter has outlined the ways in which legal consciousness was part and parcel of everyday life. It has demonstrated how legal knowledge could be acquired pragmatically and that, once acquired, could be employed in a number of spheres. It also stresses the common knowledge and the common behaviour that was manifested, suggesting that mutual obligations and community service led to a sharing of information and something of a collective consciousness. In relation to this, the chapter has sought to underline the very real and important role that many people in the provinces, from knights to peasants (free and unfree), played in the administration of justice and in implementing notions relating to the complex process of resolving disputes. In particular it has focused on the tasks of officials and jurors and has tried to bring out the way in which their personal legal knowledge, of varying capacity, permeated their activities and played an important part in forming their opinions. The extent to which a jury was often more than simply fact-finding and the extent to which memory and documents played a part in decision-making is clearly significant. As David Carpenter notes, 'the juries of presentment which appeared both before the justices in eyre and the sheriff's tourn … themselves included peasants, indeed occasionally unfree peasants, as well as more substantial landholders. These activities, however lowly, had a significant educative effect, putting the peasants in touch with the processes of royal government and administration'.[220] Experience of the legal culture and of the particular fora (both sacred and secular) in which law was administered or where notions of justice were inculcated was thus a key factor in the growth of the legal consciousness of the general populace.

Notes

1 For a more detailed exploration see A. Musson, *English Law in the Middle Ages: a Social History* (London, London Books, forthcoming).
2 *Select Cases in Manorial Courts*, ed. L. R. Poos and L. Bonfield, SS, 114 (London, 1998), pp. cx, 130.
3 Poos and Bonfield, *Manorial Courts*, pp. clxxxiv–clxxxix.
4 *Ibid.*, p. 150.
5 *Ibid.*, pp. cxxix–cxxxix; E. Clark, 'The custody of children in English manor

courts', *LHR*, 3 (1985), pp. 1–16. These issues are also examined in essays in R. Helmholz, *Canon Law and the Law of England* (London, Hambledon Press, 1987).
6 Poos and Bonfield, *Manorial Courts*, pp. cxxxviii, 151.
7 PRO MS JUST 1/1109 m18, cited in N. D. Hurnard, *The King's Pardon for Homicide before A.D. 1307* (Oxford, Clarendon Press, 1969), p. 166.
8 R. H. Hilton, 'Small-town society in England before the Black Death', *P&P*, 105 (1994), pp. 67–8, 72; Poos and Bonfield, *Manorial Courts*, pp. clxvii–clxviii, clxxviii–clxxix; see generally J. M. Bennett, *Women in the Medieval English Countryside: Gender and Household in Brigstock before the Plague* (New York, Oxford University Press, 1987).
9 M. M. Sheehan, *Marriage, Family and Law in Medieval Europe* (Toronto, University of Toronto Press, 1996), p. 22.
10 M. J. Hettinger, 'The role of the Statute of Labourers in the social and economic background of the great revolt in East Anglia', unpublished PhD thesis, University of Indiana, 1986, p. 29.
11 Magna Carta, cc. 7, 8, 11, 26 (1215); 7, 8, 18 (1225); Sheehan, *Marriage, Family and Law*, pp. 23–4, 36.
12 *Ibid.*, pp. 25–9; R. H. Helmholz, 'Married women's wills in later medieval England', in S. S. Walker, *Wife and Widow in Medieval England* (Ann Arbor, University of Michigan Press, 1993), pp. 165–82.
13 Sheehan, *Marriage, Family and Law*, p. 34; Poos and Bonfield, *Manorial Courts*, pp. 156–60.
14 P. Hyams, *King, Lords and Peasants in Medieval England: the Common Law of Villeinage in the Twelfth and Thirteenth Centuries* (Oxford, Clarendon Press, 1980), pp. 162–83; S. H. Rigby, *English Society in the Later Middle Ages* (Basingstoke, Macmillan, 1995), pp. 30–7.
15 Hyams, *King, Lords and Peasants*, p. 125.
16 *Halmota Prioratus Dunelmensis*, ed. J. Booth, Surtees Society, 82 (Durham, 1886), pp. 116, 128, 140, 143, 144, 153, 154, 156.
17 *Ibid*, p. 123.
18 The Articles of the Tourn are given in the Statute of Wales: 12 Edward I c. 4 (*SR*, vol. 1, pp. 57–8).
19 R. H. Britnell, *The Commercialisation of English Society, 1000–1500* (Cambridge and New York, Cambridge University Press, 1993), pp. 165–6; M. Kowaleski, *Local Markets and Regional Trade in Medieval Exeter* (Cambridge, Cambridge University Press, 1995), pp. 126–68.
20 P. M. Nightingale, *A Medieval Mercantile Community: The Grocers' Company and the Politics and Trade of London, 1000–1485* (New Haven and London, Yale University Press, 1995), p. 102.
21 Kowaleski, *Medieval Exeter*, pp. 180–5.
22 *Leet Jurisdiction in the City of Norwich during the Thirteenth and Fourteenth Centuries*, ed. W. Hudson, SS, 5 (London, 1892), pp. 80–1; Kowaleski, *Medieval Exeter*, pp. 181, 188; S. Rees Jones, 'York's civic administration, 1354–1464', in S. Rees Jones (ed.), *The Government of Medieval York. Essays in Commemoration*

of the 1396 Royal Charter, Borthwick Studies in History, 3 (York, 1997), pp. 123, 126–7.
23 Nightingale, *Mercantile Community*, p. 102.
24 Kowaleski, *Medieval Exeter*, p. 190.
25 H. Jewell, *English Local Administration in the Middle Ages* (Newton Abbot, David & Charles, 1972), pp. 161–3; H. R. T. Summerson, 'The structure of law enforcement in thirteenth century England', *AJLH*, 23 (1979), pp. 315–16; *The Court Rolls of the Wiltshire Manors of Adam de Stratton*, ed. R. B. Pugh, Wiltshire Record Society, 24 (Devizes, 1970), pp. 3–4, 45, 84, 116, 159.
26 Summerson, 'Law enforcement', pp. 316–17.
27 *Ibid.*, pp. 317–18; Pugh, *Adam de Stratton*, pp. 59, 124, 129; Hudson, *Leet Jurisdiction*, pp. 10–15.
28 Jewell, *English Local Administration*, p. 166; A. J. Musson, 'Peacekeeping in early-fourteenth-century Lancashire', *Northern History*, 34 (1998), pp. 42–4.
29 S. Walker, *The Lancastrian Affinity, 1361–1399* (Oxford, Clarendon Press, 1990), p. 155.
30 Cited in E. Powell, 'Arbitration and the law in England in the later Middle Ages', *TRHS*, 5th series, 33 (1983), p. 54.
31 B. A. Hanawalt, *'Of Good and Ill Repute': Gender and Social Control in Medieval England* (New York and Oxford, Oxford University Press, 1998), pp. 35–6, 38.
32 That is not to say that certain judges did not specialise in this area.
33 C. Rawcliffe, '"That kindliness should be cherished more, and discord driven out": the settlement of commercial disputes by arbitration in later medieval England', in J. Kermode (ed.), *Enterprise and Individuals in Fifteenth Century England* (Stroud, Alan Sutton, 1991), pp. 99–103; Kowaleski, *Medieval Exeter*, p. 219.
34 Kowaleski, *Medieval Exeter*, p. 219.
35 Nightingale, *Mercantile Community*, pp. 179, 192.
36 *CPMR 1323–64*, p. 278.
37 *CPMR 1364–81*, pp. 201–2.
38 *Select Canterbury Cases, c.1200–1301*, ed. N. Adams and C. Donahue, SS, pp. 11 and n.6, 28–9.
39 J. M. Bennett, 'The medieval loveday', *Speculum*, 33 (1958), pp. 357–8.
40 E. Powell, 'Settlement of disputes by arbitration in fifteenth-century England', *LHR*, 2 (1984), pp. 21–43; I. Rowney, 'Arbitration in gentry disputes in the later Middle Ages', *History*, 67 (1982), pp. 367–76; C. Rawcliffe, 'The great lord as peacekeeper: arbitration by English noblemen and their councils in the later Middle Ages', in J. A. Guy and H. G. Beale (eds), *Law and Social Change in British History* (London, Royal Historical Society, 1984), pp. 34–54.
41 M. K. McIntosh, *Autonomy and Community: the Royal Manor of Havering, 1200–1500* (Cambridge, Cambridge University Press, 1986), p. 198.
42 *Select Cases concerning the Law Merchant AD 1239–1633*, ed. H. Hall, SS, 46 (London, 1930), vol. 2, pp. 19–21. M. T. Clanchy, 'Law and love in the Middle Ages', in *Disputes and Settlements*, ed. J. Bossy (Cambridge, Cambridge University Press, 1983), pp. 47–67.
43 Summerson, 'Law enforcement', pp. 314–15; Hilton, 'Small-town society', pp. 71–

2. A sensitivity to extra-marital sex was observeable in Halesowen: this was in part a legal concern, based on the need to conform to the prevailing property laws: rules preventing illegitimate children and their offspring from inheriting property were in force from at least 1342.

44 Cited in Summerson, 'Law enforcement', p. 315.
45 R. Mellinkoff, 'Riding backwards: theme of humiliation and symbol of evil', *Viator*, 4 (1973), pp. 153–86.
46 PRO MS JUST 1/509 m7; A. Harding, 'Early trailbaston proceedings from the Lincoln roll of 1305', in R. F. Hunnisett and J. B. Post (eds), *Medieval Legal Records Edited in Memory of C. A. F. Meekings* (London, HMSO, 1978), p. 158.
47 M. Ingram, 'Ridings, rough music and the "reform of popular culture" in early modern England', *P&P*, 105 (1984), pp. 86–7, 93. The tail may also have had some symbolic function here: Mellinkoff, 'Riding backwards', pp. 174–5.
48 Mellinkoff, 'Riding backwards', pp. 157–8.
49 M. Jones, 'Folklore motifs in late medieval art II: sexist satire and popular punishments', *Folklore*, 101 (1990), p. 75–6.
50 Hanawalt, *Gender and Social Control*, p. 28.
51 Thomas Walsingham, *Historia Anglicana*, ed. H. T. Riley, RS, 28 (London, 1864), vol. 2, p. 63.
52 Hudson, *Leet Jurisdiction*, p. 80.
53 Kowaleski, *Medieval Exeter*, p. 189.
54 C. Dyer, *Everyday Life in Medieval England* (London, Hambledon Press, 1994), p. 227.
55 Musson, *Public Order*, p. 217 and n.55; R. B. Dobson and J. Taylor, *Rymes of Robin Hood: an Introduction to the English Outlaw*, rev. edn (Stroud, Alan Sutton, 1997), p. 29.
56 M. K. McIntosh, *Controlling Misbehaviour in England, 1370–1600* (Cambridge, Cambridge University Press, 1998), pp. 24–8.
57 *Close Rolls, 1231–34*, pp. 588–9; H. M. Cam, *The Hundred and the Hundred Rolls* (London, Merlin Press, 1963), pp. 168–9. One exception was the Halesowen borough (or hundred) court which in practice was held monthly (Hilton, 'Small-town society', p. 57).
58 Poos and Bonfield, *Manorial Courts*, pp. lxxii–lxxvii.
59 Cam, *Hundred Rolls*, p. 126.
60 Summerson, 'Law enforcement', pp. 318–20; Jewell, *English Local Administration*, pp. 163–4, 166.
61 J. M. Bennett, *Ale, Beer and Brewster in England: Women's Work in a Changing World, 1300–1600* (New York and Oxford, Oxford University Press, 1996).
62 Magna Carta c. 34 (1225 version).
63 R. C. Palmer, *The County Courts of Medieval England, 1150–1350* (Princeton, NJ, Princeton University Press, 1982), pp. 4–5: being a Palatinate and not affected by Magna Carta, Cheshire met on a variable schedule (including once a fortnight) into the fourteenth century.
64 Palmer, *County Courts*, pp. 5–16. There were exceptions to the set venue in Kent, Middlesex, Sussex and Cornwall.

65 Palmer, *County Courts*, pp. 78–9.
66 Hudson, *Leet Jurisdiction*, p. xxiii; Kowaleski, *Medieval Exeter*, pp. 41–2, 62–5.
67 B. L. Woodcock, *Medieval Ecclesiastical Courts in the Diocese of Canterbury* (Oxford, Oxford University Press, 1952), pp. 31–2; J. Scammell, 'The rural chapter in England from the eleventh to the fourteenth century', *EHR*, 86 (1971), pp. 13–21; P. Hyams, 'Deans and their doings: the Norwich inquiry of 1286', *Proceedings of the Berkeley Congress of Medieval Canon Law, 1980*, Monumenta Iuris Canonici, Series C, Subsidia 7 (Vatican City, 1985), pp. 619–46.
68 P. Hyams, 'What did Edwardian villagers understand by law?', in Z. Razi and R. M. Smith (eds), *Medieval Society and the Manor Court* (Oxford, Clarendon Press, 1996), pp. 78–9; Sheehan, *Marriage, Family and Law*, p. 44 (quotation).
69 Clanchy, *Memory*, pp. 272–3.
70 On one reading the following examples may indicate that lawyers were more involved with defendants at gaol delivery than has hitherto been accepted or disclosed directly by the evidence.
71 C. J. Neville, 'Common knowledge of the common law', *Canadian Journal of History*, 29 (1994), pp. 472–3.
72 Hurnard, *King's Pardon*, pp. 230–2.
73 The following paragraph is based on R. Groot, 'Teaching each other; judges, clerks, jurors and malefactors define the guilt/innocence jury', in *Learning the Law*, pp. 17–23. Note that all dates, *passim*, are based on the year beginning on 1 January.
74 PRO MS JUST 1/470 mm1d, 4d.
75 D. A. Carpenter, *The Reign of Henry III* (London, Hambledon Press, 1996), p. 323. For what follows see pp. 323–4.
76 T. A. Green, *Verdict According to Conscience: Perspectives on the English Criminal Trial Jury, 1200–1800* (Chicago, IL, University of Chicago Press, 1985), p. 15.
77 The testimony of other prisoners was required to ascertain whether the defendant possessed a tongue and could speak if he or she wanted to (PRO MS JUST 3/51/4 m7).
78 For example: PRO MS JUST 3/48 m28d (Henry Raven of Oxburgh).
79 See 3 Edward I (*SR*, vol. 1, p. 29); H. R. T. Summerson, 'The early development of peine forte et dure', in *Law, Litigants and the Legal Profession*, ed. E. W. Ives and A. H. Manchester (London, Royal Historical Society, 1983), pp. 118–20.
80 PRO MS JUST 3/125 m16d.
81 Alternatively, he may genuinely have feared that he would not receive a fair trial.
82 PRO MS JUST 3/123 m22.
83 PRO MS JUST 3/49/1 m38.
84 PRO MS JUST 3/117 m14 (April 1326).
85 PRO MS JUST 3/117 mm8d, 9d, 11d (she still did not have the writ in December 1325, though it is not clear what the difficulty was); J. M. Kaye, 'Gaol delivery jurisdiction and the writ de bono et malo', *LQR*, 93 (1977), pp. 259–72.
86 PRO MS JUST 3/49/1 m56 (March 1324), 117 m2 (September 1324).
87 A. J. Musson, 'Turning king's evidence: the prosecution of crime in late medieval England', *OJLS*, 19 (1999), pp. 472–4.

88 PRO MS JUST 3/99 m7d (1300).
89 PRO MS JUST 3/117 m9d (1325). One such defendant who was not wearing clerical garb claimed that his ordination had occurred 'ten years ago' (PRO MS JUST 3/48 m20).
90 In 1365, two boys were found to have taught elementary reading skills to a prisoner in Carlisle gaol (Neville, 'Common knowledge', p. 473).
91 M. T. Clanchy, 'Highway robbery and trial by battle in the Hampshire eyre of 1249', in Hunnisett and Post, *Medieval Legal Records*, p. 31.
92 I am also leaving aside the possibility that the record was not entirely truthful.
93 See 14 Edward III st. 1, c. 10 (*SR*, vol. 1, p. 284).
94 For example: PRO MS JUST 3/134 m64 (1347).
95 For example: PRO MS JUST 3/156 m3 (1371).
96 PRO MS JUST 3/161 m8d (Worcs.), m13d (Staffs.).
97 G. R. Owst, *Literature and Pulpit in Medieval England*, 2nd edn (Oxford, Blackwell, 1966), pp. 26–31; *SCCKB*, vol. 6, pp. 110–11; *The English Works of John Wyclif*, ed. F. D. Matthew, Early English Text Society, 74 (London, 1880), pp. 182–3, 299; A. Hudson, *The Premature Reformation: Wycliffite Texts and Lollard History* (Oxford, Clarendon Press, 1988), pp. 378–81; A. P. Baldwin, *The Theme of Government in Piers Plowman* (Woodbridge, D. S. Brewer, 1981), pp. 65–7.
98 D. L. Douie, *Archbishop Pecham* (Oxford, Clarendon, Press, 1952), pp. 113–20.
99 L. E. Boyle, *Pastoral Care, Clerical Education and Canon Law, 1200–1400* (London, Variorum Reprints, 1981); P. Biller, 'Marriage patterns and women's lives: a sketch of a pastoral geography', in P. J. P Goldberg (ed.), *Women in Medieval English Society*, rev. edn (Stroud, Alan Sutton, 1997), pp. 60–107.
100 Poos and Bonfield, *Manorial Courts*, p. clxx.
101 Bennett, 'Medieval loveday', pp. 355–8; this well-known quotation comes from Ephesians 4: 26.
102 E. Crittall (ed.), 'Fragment of an account of the cellaress of Wilton Abbey, 1299', in N. J. Williams (ed.) *Collectanea*, Wiltshire Archeological Society, 12 (Devizes, 1956), p. 144; Palmer, *County Courts*, pp. 19–21; P. Brand, *The Making of the Common Law* (London, Hambledon Press, 1992), pp. 175, 180; Rawcliffe, 'Commercial disputes', p. 110.
103 Nightingale, *Mercantile Community*, p. 177.
104 Kowaleski, *Medieval Exeter*, p. 54 n.43; Cam, *Hundred Rolls*, p. 170; A. Gransden, *Historical Writing in England, c.1307 to the Early Sixteenth Century* (London, Routledge and Kegan Paul, 1982), p. 28.
105 S. Justice, *Writing and Rebellion: England in 1381* (Berkeley and Los Angeles, CA and London, University of California Press, 1994), pp. 28–9, 77.
106 Palmer, *County Courts*, pp. 40–55; H. M. Jewell, 'Local administration and administrators in Yorkshire, 1258–1348', *Northern History*, 16 (1980), p. 7.
107 S. L. Waugh, 'Reluctant knights and jurors: respites, exemptions and public obligations in the reign of Henry III', *Speculum*, 58 (1983), pp. 937–86.
108 W. M. Ormrod, 'The politics of pestilence. Government in England after the Black Death', in *The Black Death in England*, ed. W. M. Ormrod and P. G. Linley (Stamford, Paul Watkins, 1996), pp. 152–5.

109 Palmer, *County Courts*, p. 28.
110 R. F. Hunnisett, *The Medieval Coroner* (Cambridge, Cambridge University Press, 1961), pp. 1, 55–70, 75–86; Palmer, *County Courts*, pp. 120–1.
111 S. H. Rigby, *Medieval Grimsby: Growth and Decline* (Hull, University of Hull Press, 1993), pp. 38–41.
112 For the example of York: D. Palliser, 'The birth of York's civil liberties, *c.*1200–1354', and Rees Jones, 'Civic administration', in Rees Jones (ed.), *Medieval York*, pp. 88–107, 108–140.
113 Kowaleski, *Medieval Exeter*, p. 101.
114 *The Staple Court Book of Bristol*, ed. E. E. Rich, Bristol Record Society, 5 (Bristol, 1934), pp. 47–8.
115 PRO MS JUST 3/51/4 m8; *Rolls of the Warwickshire and Coventry Sessions of the Peace, 1377–1379*, ed. E. G. Kimball, Dugdale Society, 16 (1939), pp. xxiv–xxv; E. G. Kimball, 'Commissions of the peace for urban jurisdictions in England, 1327–1485', *Proceedings of the American Philosophical Society*, 121 (1977), pp. 449–51.
116 PRO MS JUST 3/51/3 m20 (Northampton); 156 m37d (Exeter).
117 Musson, *Public Order*, p. 115.
118 R. H. Britnell, *Growth and Decline in Colchester, 1300–1525* (Cambridge, Cambridge University Press, 1986), pp. 111, 128.
119 N. Saul, *Scenes from Provincial Life: Knightly Families in Sussex, 1280–1400* (Oxford, Clarendon Press, 1986), pp. 41–8.
120 For example, Robert Hungerford (see Chapter 5).
121 Carpenter, *Henry III*, pp. 151–82.
122 S. Walker, 'Yorkshire justices of the peace, 1389–1413', p. 291; Jewell, 'Local administration', p. 2. In early commissions of the peace, serving sheriffs were either named on the panel or were members *ex officio* (Musson, *Public Order*, pp. 152–3).
123 R. F. Hunnisett, 'Pleas of the crown and the coroner', *BIHR*, 32 (1959), pp. 117–37.
124 N. Saul, *Knights and Esquires: the Gloucestershire Gentry in the Fourteenth Century* (Oxford, Clarendon Press, 1981), pp. 160–4; Jewell, 'Local administration', p. 16; Musson, *Public Order*, pp. 140–4.
125 Palliser, 'York's civil liberties', p. 101.
126 A place on the county bench should not necessarily be taken as indicating judicial experience, since some members did not actually sit as justices of the peace, preferring a merely honorific position (Musson and Ormrod, *Evolution*, pp. 69–72).
127 Musson, *Public Order*, p. 104. Willoughby was appointed to all the commissions of these years; Bruneby was a keeper of the peace from 1316 to 1320; Longueville was appointed in 1321.
128 Jewell, 'Local administration', pp. 15–16, 18–19; S. M. Wright, *The Derbyshire Gentry of the Fifteenth Century*, Derbyshire Record Society, 8 (Chesterfield, 1983), pp. 57, 59–60.
129 Pugh, *Adam de Stratton*, p. 44.
130 M. Powicke, *Military Obligation in Medieval England* (Oxford, Clarendon Press, 1962), p. 120.

131 B. H. Putnam, *The Enforcement of the Statute of Labourers during the First Decade after the Black Death, 1349–59*, Columbia University Studies in History, Economics and Public Law 32 (New York, 1908); L. R. Poos, 'The social context of Statute of Labourers enforcement', *LHR*, 1 (1983), pp. 27–52.
132 For example: PRO MS JUST 3/115B m3 (Oxford); 126 m1 (Stortford); 172 m4d (Worcester).
133 PRO MS JUST 3/96 m42, 112 m12, 134 m2.
134 For a more detailed analysis see A. J. Musson, 'Sub-keepers and constables: the role of shire officials in keeping the peace in fourteenth-century England', *EHR* (forthcoming).
135 Palmer, *County Courts*, p. 33.
136 PRO MS JUST 1/1395 m13d.
137 PRO MS JUST 1/390 m3.
138 W. M. Ormrod, 'The Peasants' Revolt and the government of England', *JBS*, 29 (1990), pp. 10–14; A. J. Prescott, 'Judicial records of the rising in 1381', unpublished PhD. thesis, University of London, 1984, p. 31.
139 For example: PRO MS JUST 1/1395 m1; *Sessions of the Peace for Bedfordshire, 1355–9, 1363–4*, ed. E. G. Kimball, Bedfordshire Historical Record Society, 48 (1969), 34, 47–8, 73–5; Poos, 'Social context', pp. 31–3.
140 P. C. Maddern, *Violence and Social Order: 1422–1442* (Oxford, Clarendon Press, 1992), p. 72.
141 Dyer, *Everyday Life*, p. 231.
142 *Ibid.*, p. 231.
143 Hurnard, *King's Pardon*, pp. 79–81.
144 J. Bedell, 'Memory and proof of age in England, 1271–1327', *P&P*, 162 (1999), pp. 1–26.
145 Jewell, *English Local Administration*, p. 84.
146 Brand, *Origins*, pp. 131, 136.
147 Rawcliffe, 'Commercial disputes', p. 102.
148 For instance: *Calendar of Early Mayor's Court Rolls, 1298–1307*, ed. A. H. Thomas (Cambridge, Cambridge University Press, 1924), pp. xlii–xliii, 21, 39, 119, 193, 221.
149 PRO MS JUST 3/48 m22; J. C. Oldham, 'On pleading the belly: a history of the jury of matrons', *Criminal Justice History*, 6 (1985), pp. 1–3.
150 P. Hyams, 'Trial by ordeal: the key to proof in the early common law' and C. Donahue, 'Proof by witnesses in the church courts of medieval England: an imperfect reception of the learned law', in M. S. Arnold, T. A. Green, S. A. Scully and S. D. White (eds), *On the Laws and Customs of England: Essays in Honor of Samuel E. Thorne* (Chapel Hill, NC, University of North Carolina Press, 1981), pp. 90–126, 127–58.
151 P. Coss, *Lordship, Knighthood and Locality* (Cambridge, Cambridge University Press, 1991), pp. 8–9.
152 J. S. Beckerman, 'Procedural innovation and institutional change in medieval English manorial courts', *LHR*, 10 (1992), pp. 200–1, 212–13.
153 *Ibid.*, p. 213 n.80.
154 Sometimes the personnel of the two juries overlapped – see below.

155 In practice the figure was sometimes greater or smaller than twelve.
156 Beckerman, 'Procedural innovation', pp. 218–19.
157 Brand, *Origins*, pp. 130–1.
158 K. J. Workman, 'Manorial estate officials and opportunity in late medieval English society', *Viator*, 26 (1995), pp. 223–40.
159 *Sessions of the Peace in the City of Lincoln, 1351–1354 and the Borough of Stamford, 1351*, ed. E. Kimball, Lincoln Record Society, 65 (1971), p. xxix.
160 Clanchy, *Memory*, p. 260.
161 S. Sheridan Walker, 'Wrongdoing and compensation: the pleas of wardship in thirteenth- and fourteenth-century England', *JLH*, 9 (1988), pp. 276–8.
162 S. Sheridan Walker, 'The action of waste in the early common law', in J. H. Baker (ed.), *Legal Records and the Historian* (London, Royal Historical Society, 1978), pp. 190–1.
163 Hurnard, *King's Pardon*, pp. 76–7 (quotation at p. 77).
164 *Ibid.*, pp. 92–3.
165 *Ibid.*, pp. 159–70; See also A. J. Musson, 'Women's violence, violation and vengeance: the evidence of the medieval legal records' (Journal Archives 105, 2001).
166 For example: PRO MS JUST 3/48 mm4d, 6, 10d.
167 Hurnard, *King's Pardon*, pp. 80–1.
168 *Ibid.*, p. 164.
169 PRO MS JUST 3/48 m1.
170 Poos and Bonfield, *Manorial Courts*, p. lxiii.
171 *Ibid.*, p. lxiv.
172 T. A. Green, 'Societal concepts of criminal liability for homicide in medieval England', *Speculum*, 47 (1972), pp. 688–9; and Green, *Verdict According to Conscience*, pp. 28–64.
173 Musson, 'Turning king's evidence', p. 475 (Table 1).
174 Musson, *Public Order*, pp. 210–211 (Tables 6 and 7). Note that Hanawalt achieved different results in her tables through the inclusion of approvers' appeals in her overall figures: see B. A. Hanawalt, *Crime and Conflict in English Communities, 1300–1348* (Cambridge, MA, Harvard University Press, 1979, p. 58 (Table 1). For fuller discussion and a comparison of the methods of calculation see Musson, *Public Order*, pp. 211–14.
175 *RP*, vol. 2, pp. 9 (22), 141 (36); W. M. Ormrod, 'Agenda for legislation, 1322–c.1340', *EHR*, 105 (1990), pp. 15, 26–7, App. A (cc7–10).
176 H. R. T. Summerson, 'The criminal underworld of medieval England', *JLH*, 17 (1996), pp. 202–3; H. Rohrkasten, 'Some problems with the evidence of fourteenth-century approvers', *JLH*, 5 (1984), pp. 14–15. These were not the only factors contributing to the high rate of acquittals: Musson, 'Turning king's evidence', p. 478.
177 *Introduction to the Curia Regis Rolls, 1199–1230 AD*, ed. C. T. Flower, SS, 62 (London, 1943), pp. 332–3.
178 Sheridan Walker, 'Wrongdoing and compensation', pp. 279–81.
179 Musson, *Public Order*, pp. 37, 193.

180 See 13 Edward I c. 38 (*SR*, vol. 1, p. 89).
181 See 21 Edward I (*SR*, vol. 1, p. 113).
182 Hyams, *King, Lords and Peasants*, pp. 153–7.
183 See 14 Edward I (*SR*, vol. 1, p. 211).
184 Dyer, *Everyday Life*, p. 227.
185 S. Olson, 'Jurors of the village court: local leadership before and after the plague in Ellington, Huntingdonshire', *JBS*, 30 (1991), pp. 237–56.
186 *Ibid.*, pp. 249–50. The evidence concerning William Gymber is admittedly drawn from slightly outside our period (1391), but illustrates the choices and considerations operating.
187 Hilton, 'Small-town society', pp. 72–3.
188 I am grateful to Professor Paul Hyams for raising this point in debate.
189 Information from papers on 'The hundred jurors in the thirteenth century' presented at International Medieval Congress, Leeds, 1999, by K. Asaji (Cambridgeshire), A. Lindsay Jobson (Oxfordshire), S. Stewart (Surrey).
190 *CCR 1231–4*, p. 589.
191 Beckerman, 'Procedural innovation', p. 203.
192 Thomas, *Mayor's Court Rolls*, p. 97.
193 PRO MS JUST 3/147 mm10, 16, 17, 32, 41–5.
194 For the use of witnesses in royal courts: Musson, *Public Order*, pp. 202–5; E. Powell, 'Jury trial at gaol delivery in the late Middle Ages: the Midland circuit, 1400–1429', in J. S. Cockburn and T. A. Green (eds), *Twelve Good Men and True: the English Criminal Trial Jury, 1200–1800* (Princeton, NJ, Princeton University Press, 1988), pp. 78–116.
195 Adams and Donahue, *Select Canterbury Cases*, p. 45.
196 Thomas, *Mayor's Court Rolls*, pp. xlii, 15.
197 See Rich, *Staple Court Book of Bristol*, pp. 33–4; J. Cherry, 'Symbolism and survival: medieval horns of tenure', *Antiquaries Journal*, 69 (1989), pp. 111–17; Bedell, 'Proof of age', pp. 1–26.
198 Clanchy, *Memory*, pp. 76–8.
199 Sheehan, *Marriage, Family and Law*, pp. 44–5.
200 N. Ramsey, 'Scriveners and notaries as legal intermediaries in later medieval England', in J. Kermode (ed.), *Enterprise and Individuals in Fifteenth Century England* (Stroud, Alan Sutton, 1991), pp. 118–27 (quotation at p. 127).
201 Clanchy, *Memory*, pp. 48–9, citing H. R. T. Summerson.
202 *Cartae Nativorum: a Peterborough Abbey Cartulary of the Fourteenth Century*, ed. C. N. L. Brooke and M. M. Postan, Northamptonshire Record Society, 20 (Oxford, 1960). Unlike the monastic houses or members of the gentry, peasants did not compile cartularies and their charters tend to be more ephemeral.
203 Clanchy, *Memory*, pp. 50–1; Rigby, *Medieval Grimsby*, p. 43
204 Clanchy, *Memory*, pp. 19, 77–8, 81–3, 98, 199–200, 236.
205 *Manorial Records of Cuxham, Oxfordshire, c.1200–1359*, ed. P. D. A. Harvey, Oxfordshire Record Society, 50 (Oxford, 1976), pp. 36–42.
206 *Ibid.*, p. 207.
207 Beckerman, 'Procedural innovation', pp. 221–3.

208 N. Denholm-Young, *Seignorial Administration in England* (Oxford, Oxford University Press, 1937), pp. 66–85.
209 M. T. Clanchy, 'England in the thirteenth century: knowledge and power', in W. M. Ormrod (ed.), *England in the Thirteenth Century*, Proceedings of the 1984 Harlaxton Symposium (Woodbridge, Boydell Press, 1985), pp. 1–14; Clanchy, *Memory*, pp. 248–50.
210 Clanchy, *Memory*, p. 276; *A Northamptonshire Miscellany*, ed. E. King, Northamptonshire Record Society, 32 (Northampton, 1983).
211 I am grateful to Dr J. Arkenberg for providing me with a list of book owners compiled from his research.
212 A. Bennett, 'Anthony Bek's copy of Statuta Angliae' in W. M. Ormrod (ed.), *England in the Fourteenth Century*, Proceedings of the 1985 Harlaxton Symposium (Woodbridge, Boydell Press, 1986), pp. 1–28; D. C. Skemer, 'Reading the law: statute books and the private transmission of legal knowledge in late medieval England', in *Learning the Law*, pp. 114–15.
213 M. Camille, 'At the edge of the law: an illustrated register of writs in the Pierpoint Morgan Library', in N. Rogers (ed.), *Fourteenth Century*, Proceedings of the 1991 Harlaxton Symposium (Stamford, Paul Watkins, 1993), pp. 1–14.
214 *Walter of Henley and Other Treatises on Estate Management and Accounting*, ed. D. Oschinsky (Oxford, Clarendon Press, 1971); Clanchy, *Memory*, pp. 197–8; R. E. Archer, '"How ladies ... who live on their manors ought to manage their households and estates": Women as landholders and administrators in the later Middle Ages', in Goldberg (ed.), *Women in Medieval English Society*, pp. 149–81.
215 H. M. Jewell, 'The cultural interests and achievements of the secular personnel of the local administration', in *Profession, Vocation and Culture in Late Medieval England*, ed. C. H. Clough (Liverpool, Liverpool University Press, 1982), pp. 130–54.
216 R. B. Dobson and J. Taylor, *Rymes of Robin Hood, an Introduction to the English Outlaw*, rev. edn (Stroud, Alan Sutton, 1997), pp. 250–1.
217 *The Tale of Gamelyn*, ed. W. W. Skeat (Oxford, Clarendon Press, 1884), pp. 33–4.
218 Brown, *passim*.
219 J. Coleman, *English Literature in History, 1350–1400: Medieval Readers and Writers* (London, Hutchinson Education, 1981), pp. 61, 64; S. Justice, *Writing and Rebellion: England in 1381* (Berkeley and Los Angeles, CA and London, 1994), pp. 102–39.
220 Carpenter, *Henry III*, pp. 324–5.

4

Participation in the royal courts

ROYAL jurisdiction through the common law increased exponentially during the period 1215-1381. Participation in the royal courts was therefore an important way in which people became increasingly familiar with the processes of law. The ordinary individual's participation in these processes occurred either as a result of an incident or dispute requiring settlement by mechanisms outside their immediate familial environment and work-based group, or because it was believed that they had committed an offence against the king and they had been summoned to answer the charge before the relevant authorities. This chapter provides evidence for how the law became more familiar, how people could participate in its processes and how these processes could be accessible to the many rather than the few. It examines therefore the mechanics of going to law, the factors facilitating or adversely affecting the prosecution of offenders and the provision of justice.

A mixture of royal policy, experience of litigation and feedback from lawyers and litigants shaped the development of the royal courts. The effects of changes are assessed in this chapter by four criteria: availability, actionability, accountability and accessibility. The first section considers the availability of royal justice and provides the reader with a snapshot of the judicial system, at forty-year intervals during the period 1215-1381, against which can be set contemporary experience and expectations of the administration of justice. This section demonstrates the type of agencies providing royal justice and how their function altered over the period, and gives an indication of how theory met practice in terms of their geographical location, the timing of visits, and the frequency of sessions. The section tries to view the functioning of the system as experienced by users and so to some extent steps outside the historiographical debate on the policies driving judicial administration during these centuries. It does nevertheless aim to compare and contrast the Crown's desires (as shown in statutes) with what contemporaries wanted (as evinced in parliamentary petitions) and to assess the reality: the extent to which any of these expectations was fulfilled in practice.

The second section examines actionability: litigants' options and opportunities arising within the judicial system. It argues that over the period alterations occurred in the scope and nature of actions and in the procedural processes by which relief could be sought. These changes, incorporating not only the growth of new forms of redress, but also the demise of those that were less useful to litigants, demonstrate the flexibility and responsiveness of the system. Participation itself was facilitated either through methods of private prosecution or through a form of public prosecution. Wrongs could be brought to royal attention either by individuals seeking remedy before the royal justices on their own behalf or by groups of jurors constituted to investigate and report to the justices on matters of interest to the Crown. The section therefore outlines the types of offences that the people who served on juries (see Chapter 3) would have learned about, and some of the procedures with which litigants themselves needed to be familiar.

Accountability was an important feature of the Crown's policy towards the administration of justice and one that had political and financial implications as well as purely legal ones. There was an awareness of the shortcomings of legal (and governmental) administration and a determination to monitor the behaviour of officialdom at all levels. As a means of ensuring (or at least instilling notions of) accountability, individuals were encouraged to observe royal officials and bring forward allegations concerning misdeeds. The drive to make people accountable broadened the scope of potential targets from royal to seigneurial officials, while easing the stricture of the procedural requirements accordingly facilitated the making of complaints.

The final section, on accessibility, considers whether participation in royal justice was a socially exclusive phenomenon and investigates the extent to which the judicial system was in fact receptive to litigants of lesser means. Was the provision of legal services to the non-privileged such as to belie the royal courts' traditional image? In order to assess properly the growth of legal consciousness there is a need to understand the extent of participation and the social implications of judicial policy. What factors inhibited access to the courts and to 'justice' (fairness and procedural propriety) within them? The relative accessibility of the system and its continued extensive use (despite its drawbacks) points not only towards high levels of participation, but to a certain amount of confidence in royal justice, even if the attitudes and expectations generated were never quite in line with reality.

Availability

This section will provide an analysis of changes in the availability of royal justice through snapshots of the judicial situation as it would have been experienced by four generations, each of about forty years: 1215–54, 1255–94, 1295–1340, 1341–81. This method is intended to highlight the changes in the judicial system which a person living at the time might observe and how his or her attitudes might fluctuate with alterations in the prevailing legal situation. Attitudes and expectations, however, would have been out of step with the changes because the rate of change was sometimes faster than was comfortably registerable and also because the effect of such changes would usually have taken time to feed into people's perceptions.

From 1215 to 1254

Two important tribunals – later known as the courts of king's bench and common pleas – emerged from the *curia regis* (the highest judicial body under the Normans), and in the opening decades of the thirteenth century there was little to differentiate them. The court of king's bench – or, as it was referred to in the thirteenth century, the court *coram rege* (before the king) – became the judicial body responsible for safeguarding the Crown's civil interests and upholding the monarch's duty to prosecute criminal behaviour or alleged breaches of his peace. The court's close association with the sovereign, which had been developed under King John, derived not only from its distinctive jurisdiction, but its peripatetic accompaniment of the monarch around the country. The court was suspended during the minority of Henry III, but was revived (albeit with little institutional continuity) about 1234 when litigants were required to turn up 'wherever we [the king] then shall be'.[1] Its partner court, which had ceased operating in 1209 and only reopened gradually in 1213, dealt with private litigation under the common law.[2] It was originally known as the 'bench', but came to be called the court of common pleas because of its jurisdiction. In John's reign, litigants were forced to follow the king's peripatetic itinerary because their writs required them to appear before him or his justices. This was amended in Magna Carta when it was established that common pleas ought to be held 'in some definite place' (*in aliquo loco certo*). This did not mean the 'bench' had to remain stationary at Westminster, but rather a place certified or mentioned in the writ, usually an established centre of government. The central courts were in session for about four months of the year, during the four legal terms, Michaelmas, Hilary, Easter and Trinity. Until 1249 the 'bench' did not sit when the general eyre was in operation, owing to an overlap of personnel.[3]

The general eyre was the prime agency of regional justice and in the late twelfth century visited all the counties of England on average once every other year. The eyre justices, who were regarded as holding provincial sessions of the king's court, travelled on distinct circuits, enabling them to cover whole groups of counties during the course of the eyre's peregrination. Following the death of King John, the visitations of the eyre recommenced in 1218 on an almost unprecedented scale,[4] but the frequency of the eyre's provincial visits drastically declined during the reign of Henry III, to the extent that the interval between individual shire visitations had lengthened to about eight years. The obvious delay in reaching counties was not symptomatic of slackness on the part of the royal judicial machine, but rather a reflection of the volume of business being brought before the eyre, for which the justices were forced to assign more time. Added to this, fewer groups of justices were being allocated to each of the circuits, with the result that the scheduled sessions in each county were taking longer to complete.

Separate commissions to hear assizes were issued from the 1220s in order to supplement the work of the eyre and ensure that urgent land litigation did not have to wait until its next visitation. Under Henry III, however, the justices were not assigned to hear all assizes in a specific group of counties: the special commissions assigned them to hear only a single action (assize). The only restriction on places and sessions was the provision in Magna Carta that the assize should be held in the county where the disputed tenement lay. In 1215 it was optimistically envisaged that sessions should be held four times a year, but this was reduced to once a year in 1217.[5] Commissions to try felonies (paralleling the assizes) were sent out from the 1220s (so as to avoid a backlog of prisoners awaiting delivery by the eyre justices) and were usually issued singly for individual shire, borough or franchise gaols. Special commissions could be directed at the delivery of actual named prisoners or certain categories of prisoner, but the general ones were concerned with ensuring delivery of all those available to be tried at the particular gaol. During the late 1230s and 1240s there was a marked increase in the number of royal commissions, especially in the Midlands and East Anglia and regions more remote from Westminster such as Yorkshire, Shropshire and Somerset.[6]

From 1255 to 1294

In theory the king's bench was tied to the availability of the king, but this personal association was weakened in practice during this period, largely because of Edward I's military adventures outside the kingdom. The king's bench, therefore, no longer ceased to function when the king was outside the realm. During Edward I's campaign against the Welsh (1277), the other central court, the 'bench', resided at Shrewsbury and by the 1290s the court had become (at least in the minds of some litigants) the principal location for common-pleas jurisdiction.[7]

A significant change in policy to regularise the eyre's visitations came under Edward I: the practice of arranging eyres throughout England *ad hoc*, either to meet demand or to follow on from wherever the previous eyre left off, was abandoned in favour of two circuits (one covering northern England, one the southern portion) thereby providing what was designed to be a continuous visitation of the whole country.[8] The amount of business that the eyre generated or attracted in some counties (such as Yorkshire, Lincolnshire, Norfolk and Kent) after 1278 forced it to emulate the central courts in dividing up the sessions into discrete terms. The eyre was thus available to litigants within each county for longer periods of time than ever before. Nevertheless, if the eyre's revamp was designed to underline its indispensability and its permanence within the judicial system, as contemporaries envisaged, it was unable to maintain its momentum and predictability. A series of extra-judicial circumstances resulted in the visitations becoming occasional rather than continuous. These culminated in the eyre's suspension in 1294. Ironically, it was the very omnicompetence and thoroughness of the itinerant machine which contributed to its downfall and eventual obsolescence.[9]

Although assize commissions were available under Henry III, it was not until 1273 that the first systematic circuits were set up, initially comprising six county groups covering the whole of England.[10] The number of circuits (and so the selection of counties within them) was flexible and altered over the ensuing twenty years as a result of administrative rationalisations and policy changes (notably in 1285 and 1293). A characteristic feature of general commissions to counties was the frequency of the sessions and the particular venues used by the justices. The majority of sessions were convened in the most important towns of the county, often in turns, with journeys made to various liberties when required.[11] The timing of royal justices' appearances in the shires, however, was governed in part by their responsibilities in the royal courts during the law terms. For those assize justices with court duties, sessions were, therefore, as a matter of practicalities, restricted to vacations.[12] The Church calendar also played a part in determining when sessions could be held and thus their frequency. This was reflected in the first Statute of Westminster (1275), which ordained that special dispensation had to be sought in order for sessions to be held during the important religious seasons of Advent and Lent.[13] A decade later, the second Statute of Westminster permitted the hearing of assizes during three designated periods of the year: between 6 January and 2 February; between 14 September and 6 October; and between 8 July and 1 August.[14]

The statutory frequency of gaol delivery commissions followed that of the assizes in being at least once and not meant to be more than three times a year, though this was frequently exceeded. The number of commissions issued increased during Henry III's last years (possibly through a conscious policy decision), though the distribution to specific prisons was uneven.[15] The geographical distribution of commissions was regularised during the early 1290s when some commissions were issued for a wide circuit consisting of all the gaols within specified counties.[16]

Commissions to hear and determine (*oyer* and *terminer*) civil and criminal offences began to be issued during the reform programme of the early 1270s and were another measure intended to relieve some of the pressure on the general eyre. Modern historians have labelled the two main categories of commissions as 'special' and 'general', though in fact these merely represent the limits of a much broader spectrum. Special commissions of oyer and terminer concerned disputes within a given area, while general commissions could range over a whole circuit of counties. Unlike the assizes and gaol delivery, oyer and terminer commissions did not provide regular judicial sessions. Both special and general commissions of oyer and terminer, therefore, should be viewed as only short-term and mainly reactive expedients. This is not to imply, however, that they did not make significant contributions to dispute settlement and law enforcement.[17]

Men charged to keep the peace in the shires were first appointed during the baronial wars of the mid-thirteenth century. Thereafter commissions directed towards all the counties in England were generally issued when it was felt the internal peace of the realm need to be secured, usually for events or occasions (such as war, marriage, homage or diplomacy) which required the king to be absent from the country. While there were gaps of ten or even thirteen years between the issuing of the first general commissions (1277–1287, 1287–1300), these peace commissions were supposed to run until either they were repealed or superseded by a fresh commission. Unfortunately, few records survive of the earliest sessions held by keepers of the peace so there is no decisive picture of when, where and how frequently inquests were held.[18]

From 1295 to 1340

In 1300 the Articles on the Charters called for the king's bench again to follow the person of the king,[19] but by the fourteenth century the king's literal dispensation of justice through the court was largely a fiction.[20] Consequently, though linked with the king by name, king's bench developed its own identity. The court's importance and superiority within the judicial hierarchy stemmed from its wider functions within the judicial system and the legal and geographical range of its employment, which expanded significantly during the early fourteenth century. In addition to its ability to receive appeals from other courts alleging an error in the judgment (for which the inferior court then had to provide a certified transcript of proceedings – the record and process – for the case to be successfully transferred), in the early fourteenth century, the court enlarged its purview and assumed jurisdiction over all Crown pleas of felony and trespass (including prisoners awaiting trial) in the county in which it was sitting. From 1305 the king's bench also began to accept cases brought by bill, which at an earlier date would have come before the eyre.[21] With confirmation in 1323 of its right to hear informally initiated suits, the king's bench came to act as a court of first instance whenever it sat in the provinces. The itinerant aspect of the court's jurisdiction increased during the later years of Edward II's reign when the court took a more direct approach to the perceived problem of lawlessness. After a rather stable period in Westminster (1305–18),[22] it resumed its provincial visitations, sitting in twenty different counties alone between 1322 and 1330.[23] Although the court of king's bench was deployed successfully as a 'rapid reaction' taskforce, arguably the swiftness of its sessions, the somewhat random nature of its movements and the unevenness of its provincial coverage (there were some counties it never visited) meant that its effectiveness as a 'superior eyre' was limited and decidedly short-term.[24]

The court of common pleas was removed from Westminster during Edward I's and Edward II's Scottish campaigns and relocated in York, which had come to be thought of as a second capital.[25] The establishment of the court 'in some definite place' enhanced its accessibility and increased its business to such an extent that the court expanded to sit in two divisions in the early years of Edward II's reign: issues were joined in one division and tried in the other.[26]

Contemporaries did not consider the eyre's suspension as permanent and assumed it would eventually resume its course.[27] However, after 1294 only individual eyres were held in isolated counties (usually coinciding with a vacant see) over the next thirty years.[28] A full revival of the general eyre (operating on two full circuits again) was planned and initiated in 1328, but the project was aborted in the winter of 1330-31 with only four counties visited. The demise of the eyre is perceived by some historians as having left a void in the judicial system, yet its suspension and eventual passing may not have been noticed at once by contemporaries in the provinces and did not automatically result in an immediate or lasting decline in the provision of royal justice since a number of its functions had already been taken over by other agencies. Indeed, in contrast to the tardiness of the eyre, the specialisation and flexibility offered by the various new types of commissions, whose significance and caseload had increased during the second half of the thirteenth century (probably as a consequence of the hiatuses in itinerations), contributed to their popularity with litigants and encouraged the Crown to expand their availability.

Significantly, after the suspension of the eyre, general assize and gaol delivery commissions became such an indispensable part of the judicial fabric that they continued to be issued on a countrywide basis. The generations following the demise of the eyre, however, witnessed further alterations to the assize circuits, notably in 1305, 1310 and 1328, before they crystallised into a more or less permanent form in the 1330s. During the years 1305-07 the 'trailbaston' justices were authorised to hear assizes and deliver gaols, but the existing circuit justices continued their rounds, with the result that the two sets of commissioners were sometimes holding sessions concurrently. The duplicate sessions held during those years ensured that there was no backlog awaiting the (unbeknown to them now defunct) eyre and enabled people outside London to bring their cases more conveniently.[29]

The extensive list of assize venues available in the later thirteenth century was reduced slightly under Edward II. Then, with the reorganisation of the circuits in the first decade of Edward III's reign, there was a concomitant rationalisation of the justices' itinerary: in order to ensure completion of the circuit within the limited time available (the break between law terms), the focus was now on major towns; separate visitations to liberties became a rarity.[30] By Edward III's reign, too, the number of special assizes enrolled in chancery had fallen significantly, despite their apparent popularity under his father and grandfather.[31]

In 1303 the periods allowed for assizes were restated and there was a stipulation that sessions should not occur more than three times a year.[32] The legislation on the timing of sessions did not of itself ensure regularity, of course, as it merely provided windows of opportunity when sessions could be held. Some of the difficulties in providing regularity of coverage stemmed from geographical location and political concerns. A major problem for the northern counties, for instance, was not only their comparative remoteness from the centre of government (except of course when it had relocated to York), but the unpredictability and danger arising from being a frontier and possible war-zone.[33] A petition from the county of Northumberland in 1304 actually complained that no justices of assize ever came to the county nor did justices of the bench come to hold inquests during the central courts' vacations, unlike the practice in other counties.[34] Westminster's attitude remained unhelpful, though, as in 1313 justices taking assizes on the northern circuit were reprimanded for holding sessions during parliament.[35] Another, though less predictable, reason for a delay to or cancellation of sessions could be the death or illness of one of the justices. A way round this was the insertion in the commission of a *si non omnes* clause (that is, 'if not all are present'), which provided the requisite authority for justices to proceed if one of their colleagues was absent, though it usually specified one member of the commission who had to be present for sessions to be effective.[36] It was not until 1330 that there was legislative encouragement for sessions to be held 'at least three times a year, and more often, if need be'.[37] It is apparent that the statutory minimum, while not always provided, was fairly closely adhered to during the decade.

The link between the assize sessions and the trial of felons in the county gaols, which had been created through the eyre and continued in an *ad hoc* way with the separate commissions, was formally established in 1299. If the statute was intended to ensure gaol deliveries on a more predictable basis, the plan was successful in its immediate aftermath. But the supposed alliance with assize justices grew rather tenuous during Edward II's reign and there was no consistent practice of circuit-style deliveries until the 1330s. The apparent breakdown in the association with the assizes, however, and an absence of strict circuits did not have a profoundly adverse affect on the efficiency or frequency of gaol deliveries. In fact during the early fourteenth century there was a proliferation in the number of gaol deliveries carried out each year, perhaps because the personnel involved were not invariably constrained by the normal law terms.[38] Renewing the statutory link between the two functions in 1328 (underlined again in 1330) ensured that the gaols were visited (in theory) at least three times a year. In practice (as far as the records allow) deliveries of the main gaols during this decade did keep measure with statute or occurred at least twice a year. The reorganisation and rationalisation of the circuits that occurred in the early years of Edward III brought with it the need for expedients such as holding criminal trials at the assize venue if the gaol was not in close vicinity, thereby streamlining the circuit and enabling justices to cut down on excess travel.

Following their introduction towards the end of Edward I's reign, general oyer and terminer commissions became an established part of the judicial machinery and were usually initiated as part of royal law-enforcement drives. Oyer and terminer commissions generally covered most of England: the so-called 'trailbaston' commissions of 1305-07 operated across the country on five circuits of counties.[39] The sets of commissions issued in Edward II's reign (with the exception of those of 1314) were not always so pervasive.[40] Comprehensive commissions covering all the English shires were sent out again in 1331 and 1340-41.[41] Special commissions of oyer and terminer could be purchased from chancery by private persons who wished to receive redress through this mechanism. Barring deliberate curbs on the issuing of commissions, which occurred arbitrarily in Edward II's reign as a result of the influence of the Despensers, or through statutory restriction in the minority regime of Isabella and Mortimer, theoretically as many sessions could be held as the chancery clerks could write out commissions for justices to hold. In reality, after an initial explosive interest during the late thirteenth century, the largest numbers of special commissions were issued during the 1310s and 1320s, when annual totals could rise to over 250.[42]

In spite of the sporadic survival of proceedings held under peace commissions, there is evidence that sessions were held and that significant numbers of people were being brought to trial. Such evidence comes not only from the gaol delivery rolls (where reference is made to the officials), but also from the special mandates issued from chancery during this period, which authorised gaol delivery justices to try prisoners accused of wrongdoing before the keepers of the peace.[43] The absence of trials for Herefordshire, for example, during the period 1316-26 does not reflect inactivity on the part of the keepers. Surviving records of indictments (sworn accusations of wrongdoing – see below) provide some indication of their business and more particularly the venue and frequency of sessions. In 1320, 1321 and 1325 sessions were held twice a year in venues such as Hereford, Weobley, Malvern and Bredwardine. In 1323 the keepers met three times (once at Weobley and twice at Hereford) at intervals of a month, while in 1324 and 1326 indictments are recorded from a single session held at Wyngate and Hereford respectively.[44] Sessions of the peace in the shires continued to be held during the 1330s,[45] but there is no real indication of the frequency until 1338-41, during which time it is clear that the local bench in some counties was fairly active, with as many as seven sessions in Cambridge (August-November 1340) and a minimum of two meetings per year in Somerset.[46]

From 1341 to 1381

The court of king's bench continued to provide an essential interface between the central courts and the regional agencies of justice. The business undertaken by the court of king's bench when effecting first-instance jurisdiction in the provinces has been seriously underestimated, especially during the mid-fourteenth century. In the course of just three terms when sitting at York and Lincoln in 1348-49, for instance, the court dealt with over a thousand bills of trespass, ten times the amount it usually handled at Westminster.[47] The court did not sit because of the plague in the summers of 1349, 1361 and 1368 and was closed during the Trinity term of 1381 'because of the unheard of and horrible disturbances and insurrections'.[48] Regular visitations to the provinces were rarer during this period, but when the court did venture beyond Westminster it not only provided litigants with direct access to justice, but could still be a powerful force in the enforcement of justice, particularly the Statute of Labourers.[49] Even when it was settled at Westminster, the geographical ambit of the court's influence remained wide on account of its supervisory and appellate functions, and notably on account of the frequent transference (for its determination) of indictments made before justices of the peace.[50]

By the mid-fourteenth century the general eyre was definitely a thing of the past, but it remained in people's memory. In fact, on a number of occasions, eyres were 'threatened' by the Crown though never implemented.[51] While there were still some (though perhaps disingenuous) complaints about the assizes,[52] it is a measure of the Crown's willingness to provide opportunities for legal redress that some assize sessions were held in 1348-49 despite the ravaging Black Death. Even with modifications and considerable streamlining to the circuit, though, the sheer volume of business may have made the statutory three times a year a difficult provision with which to comply, given the time allotted. The apparent infrequency and brevity of visits were cited by the parliamentary commons as reasons why the justices of assize would not be effectively employed against the circulation of 'Lusshebournes' (forged currency), though these criticisms should be viewed in terms of the commons' agenda for local justices to enforce such measures.[53] In 1382 the venue was restricted by statute to the major county towns, confirmation of the policies already in action.[54]

The practical reality of gaol deliveries from the mid- to late-fourteenth century was somewhat at odds with the theoretical stance. As far as the gaol delivery records permit a 'full picture' of circuit visitations, it appears that the norm at least for the 1360s and 1370s was probably two deliveries per year rather than the statutory three (though in some years there may have been only the one).[55] The frequency of deliveries was not wholly geographically biased. In the north, it is true that the gaols of Newcastle, Carlisle and Appleby received a single visit, but York sometimes had three. In the south-west, Devon and Cornwall usually enjoyed two, though sometimes Cornwall received only one delivery. The brevity of the judges' visit also meant that unless all the necessary preparations for trial were complete some cases would not get a hearing. If the justices were lacking sufficient information, or the relevant documentary or physical evidence was not there on the day of the sessions, or a jury from another county was required to come and give a verdict, the case would have to be adjourned until the next visitation. If the window of opportunity for the accused had disappeared he or she would be remanded (with or without bail) until the next occasion. The increased effectiveness of the prosecution machinery was providing more prisoners, but rationalisation of the circuits combined with a concentration on tighter procedural matters meant that the justices were not actually able to deliver all those awaiting trial every time. Justices were only able to get through a fraction of the calendar that would have been dealt with earlier in the century.[56] Escapes by prisoners also hindered justice and time was lost in the need to hunt for people and sometimes extradite them from another county. In spite of some drawbacks inherent in the system, county visitations of royal justices provided an important provincially-based forum for land litigation and the opportunity for prisoners to be tried comparatively swiftly, even if expectations could not always be fulfilled.

The regular visitations of the circuit justices provided the shires with an invaluable link to the central courts. The link was in fact reciprocal, for it also gave central government a view of life in the provinces and a valuable channel of communication.[57] This was not only because by the 1340s the personnel of the circuits were drawn from the serjeants and judges working at Westminster (see Chapter 2), but because the assize justices were also entrusted with hearing (though not giving judgment in) cases destined for the central courts, through a process commonly known as *nisi prius*. The name stemmed from a clause inserted in the writs enabling the action to proceed in the central courts 'unless before then' the royal justices were present in the county where the dispute lay. The attractiveness of this opportunity for an expedited hearing was obvious to litigants (and jurors) and ensured availability of common-pleas actions.[58] Although the scheme was initiated in 1285, local approval of the *nisi prius* system is suggested not only by the steady increase in business over the years, but also by petitions in 1350s which requested an extension of the justices' powers.[59]

After the mid-fourteenth century the appointment of general oyer and terminer commissions became more occasional and more limited geographically. When they were issued they were usually sent out for single counties or pairs of counties. The counties of Yorkshire, Lincolnshire, Staffordshire and Shropshire received visitations by the oyer and terminer justices in 1373 and three more, Oxfordshire, Essex and Cambridgeshire in 1375.[60] Significantly there was a revival on a countrywide basis in 1381–82.[61] A steady decline in the numbers of special commissions of oyer and terminer is also observable across the 1340s and 1350s, with a brief flurry of activity in the 1360s, before interest dwindled rapidly during the 1370s.[62]

The irregularity that characterised special and general commissions of oyer and terminer could be seen as a drawback. Yet it was this very feature which highlights their significance within the array of judicial agencies. Like the itinerant king's bench, they had the capacity to strike quickly and supply within a comparatively brief space of time the necessary remedial course for the individual litigant and/or government regime. They were thus an important adjunct to the sessions held in the shires on a more regular basis.

The sessions of the keepers/justices of the peace represented a significant contribution to the regular provision of royal justice locally. The close association that developed during the fourteenth century between the assizes and the quarter sessions made for further integration of different agencies within the judicial system. Indeed, their sessions sometimes overlapped, especially when the trial of indictments made before the keepers/justices was carried out at gaol delivery. Unlike the assize circuits there was no obvious concern to regulate the frequency of peace sessions until the late 1340s. In the Lent parliament of 1348 it was requested that justices of the peace swear (in parliament) to hold sessions at least three times a year.[63]

The Statute of Labourers of 1351 (which initially the justices of the peace, and later special justices of labourers, were to enforce) provided that sessions were to be held four times a year and prescribed the dates as being the feasts of Lady Day (25 March), St Margaret (20 July), Michaelmas (29 September) and St Nicholas (6 December).[64] The session venues were not specified and were presumably left to local custom and the convenience of the justices' schedule. Although only a handful of records of peace proceedings remain for the 1350s, it is possible to glean some information as to counties' adherence to the statutory dates. In Devon in the early 1350s sessions were usually held at least twice a year, but there is no strict pattern and only one of the dates accords with the statutory ones.[65] In Bedfordshire during the late 1350s sessions were held at least three times a year (usually in the spring, summer and autumn), but here, too, they did not keep to the statute.[66] In fact none of the other surviving sessions of the decade 1351–61 appears to have done so.[67] One reason for this could be that these dates did not wholly coincide with the periods when the assizes and gaol delivery took place.

In 1362 the dates were altered by statute to the Octave of the Epiphany (6–13 January), the second week in Lent (a variable period depending upon the date of Easter), between Whitsunday and the Nativity of St John the Baptist (a variable date in May/June up to 24 June) and the Octave of St Michael (29 September to 6 October).[68] The new dates were obviously more flexible and to a certain extent accorded more than the previous statute with existing practices in the holding of judicial sessions. Sessions in most counties seem to have coincided with the Lenten and Whitsun periods, though many counties continued to hold sessions in December near the old statutory date.[69] The Warwickshire justices (including the justices of the peace for the town of Coventry) generally sat four times a year (sometimes more often, as for example, in 1381–82). Although some dates of sessions accorded with the statutory periods, they clearly did not feel bound to hold them at those times.[70] The rolls for Essex and Lincolnshire similarly point to little regard for the statutory dates.[71] Indeed the justices in Lincolnshire were ordered in 1369 'to hold their sessions at the times ordained'.[72]

Disregard for the statutory dates does not in itself point towards a deficiency in the provision of judicial sessions. While justices of the peace may not have sat at the designated 'quarter sessions', there is ample evidence that they did in fact provide 'non-statutory' sessions at frequent intervals and in a variety of locations. The geographical spread of venues and the number of sittings by justices in counties such Yorkshire, Lincolnshire and Essex is quite remarkable and testimony to the availability of justice in the provinces. In 1360, for instance, sessions were held by the Lindsey (a subdivision of Lincolnshire) justices in seven different places.[73] On occasions (as in 1360 and 1373) the justices may even have split into two groups and held duplicate sessions at different venues.[74] In 1374 the Kesteven (also Lincolnshire) justices met in March (twice), April, June, July, August (three times) and September (four times).[75] Between 1377 and 1379 the Essex justices sat, on average, seven times a year, in no fewer than eleven locations.[76]

The general picture of central and local justice in the thirteenth and fourteenth centuries then is one of shifting uses and provision of judicial agencies within the legal system. Even the general eyre in the thirteenth century was an evolving creature and in turn spawned many satellite bodies which themselves developed significantly after its demise. The innovation, extemporisation and experimentation taking place during the fourteenth century, even if it was at times confusing or awkward for contemporaries to digest, may nevertheless have been beneficial. In the short term it ensured the continued provision of justice (albeit manifested in several forms) and in the long term it (almost) guaranteed its predictability and availability.

Actionability

The array of judicial agencies capable of entertaining litigants' pleas and their regular (and irregular) deployment in the shires demonstrate how the opportunity for legal action was provided initially by the prevailing superstructure of the legal system. Cases actually came to be heard in one of the court settings as a result of two forms of initiative: through investigations made on behalf of the Crown or through a suit brought privately by an individual. This section examines, first, the Crown's role in bringing people to court and then, secondly, the methods by which individuals sued. While nowadays most cases sued privately are civil cases and those publicly prosecuted are for criminal offences, the distinctions between public and private prosecution and civil and criminal trials were not so clear in medieval England. Although there were some differences in concept, there were in fact considerable overlaps between methods of prosecution and the type of case they initiated.[77]

Public prosecution
A public prosecuting agency (in the sense of a body of officials responsible for investigating offences and bringing them to court) was not established

until Tudor times.[78] Nevertheless a form of prosecution operating on behalf of the state emerged as a result of the findings of specially constituted juries, who supplied answers to various series of questions. Articles of inquiry were utilised by a number of different agencies, notably the general eyre, the trailbaston commissions, peace sessions, the itinerant court of king's bench and the hundred court as part of the sheriff's tourn (or court leet in the case of a liberty). The designated articles provided the offences upon which jurors were empowered to investigate and report. The jurors themselves needed some understanding of the nature of these areas in order to perform the task properly.

The Articles of the Eyre formed a codified body of questions known as the *capitula itineris*. Representing the 'pleas of the Crown', they were the most comprehensive set of questions with which a jury had to contend, covering criminal matters, royal rights, the observance of economic regulations and the conduct of officials. The presenting juries for the eyres of the early thirteenth century were required to respond to sixty-nine articles. By 1278 a new body of articles (or *nova capitula*) had been formed, comprising thirty-nine articles which had been used to form the basis of the 1254–55 'Hundred Rolls' inquiries, and another thirty-five which were based on provisions in recent statutes. The number of articles for the combined chapters stood at 143. As well as criminal business, the jurors were concerned with such diverse areas as royal escheats (lands that had come into the king's hands), lands held of the king by serjeanty, infringements of royal lands and waters, treasure trove and wrecks, the keeping of the assizes of measures and cloth, the forging and clipping of currency, outlaws and fugitives, poachers, customs levied, the holding of markets and the levying of prises.[79] The articles of the sheriff's tourn, in preparation for his twice-yearly visitation of the hundreds in his bailiwick, overlapped substantially with many of the areas investigated by the eyre.[80]

When considering the 'Articles of Trailbaston' juries were required to investigate problems of organised violence and concerted abuse of legal procedure. Following the Ordinance of Trailbaston of 1305, the jury questions duly targeted people who threatened jurors, who maltreated those who told the truth, who attacked others in fairs, markets and public places out of spite and with prior planning, or who impeded the duties of arresting constables, bailiffs, coroners and exchequer officials. Additionally within the jurors' remit were those who hired or sheltered such wrongdoers, incited or aided their acts, or abused their own power and lordship by protecting them.[81] The articles were also directed (following the Ordinance of Conspirators of the same year) at those who made agreements to pervert the course of justice by making false or malicious accusations or bringing in false verdicts, and included those who retained people in their employ (providing liveries or fees) in order to carry out their vindictive schemes.[82] In preparation for sessions held under general oyer and terminer commissions (as part of the comprehensiveness of their commissions) juries were usually charged with investigating 'ordinary' criminal activity as well, especially homicides, robberies, arsons and other serious crimes.[83]

Juries empanelled in preparation for a visit to the shire by the court of king's bench had to respond to a series of at least thirty articles, some of which overlapped with the concerns of the trailbaston commissions and others which investigated the conduct of officials. Additionally, the charge for the jurors included matters of a political nature or related to recent local incidents. The 1323 visitation to Lancashire, for example, monitored major felonies, conspirators and confederacies, the retaining of men for unlawful enterprises, oppressions by officials and acts which derogated from the king's profit. Anyone who hindered the work of the sheriff or coroner was identified. Jurors were then directed towards discovering the identities of those in Thomas of Lancaster's retinue at Boroughbridge and the names of men from the region who had accompanied Andrew Harclay.[84] They were also to investigate the taking of ransoms following the overthrow of Adam Banaster and look into disturbances occurring at Chaddock.[85]

The set of articles used for peace sessions bears a strong resemblance in many respects to areas covered by the eyre, trailbastons and the local juries before king's bench. Primarily they were related to the statutes of Winchester (1285), Northampton (1328) and Westminster (1361) and so covered questions on felonies, housebreaking and assaults, riding armed against the peace or before the justices or other ministers of the Crown and similar affronts or breaches of the peace. By the later fourteenth century, jurors were also required to investigate areas based upon provisions in other statutes, many of them concerned with economic and social matters. Not only were the jurors empowered to inquire concerning the labour legislation (those taking excessive wages, selling inferior goods and breaches of the compulsory service clause),[86] but also abuses of purveyance. Economic offences (such as the falsifying of weights and measures, regrating and forestalling) and instances of forcible entry were included in the charges by the later fourteenth century.[87]

One thing that is immediately striking is the thoroughness of the Crown's approach and the wide range of matters which local juries were required to grasp intellectually in order to launch investigations. In terms of potential actions, the articles provided a theoretical basis, a resource from which to prosecute people. This was not necessarily how it worked in reality. First, there were far more prosecutions initiated than people who were brought to trial or actually convicted.[88] Second, although a return of every single article would not be expected, it also appears that in practice jurors were selective. This may have arisen because the jurors' *veredictum* (not a verdict in the sense of conclusions reached after trial, but the facts truly presented) had to be completed and delivered to the court within a predetermined time-scale.[89] Written memoranda and other details relating to the veredicta of the 1294 Surrey eyre indicate that jurors prepared their *veredicta* in the hundred court prior to the eyre, discussing there what they were going to include and what they would leave out.[90] The Cambridgeshire jurors in the 1260s concealed some offences and tried to avoid presenting their neighbours.[91] In 1281, out of the 143 articles of the eyre, the jurors of Chippenham hundred brought returns on five questions in the 'old chapter' and sixteen in the 'new chapter'. In general, presenting jurors of the eyre put forward the pleas of the Crown that were within the purview of the coroner: the other matters (given the overlap between their respective articles) were brought up at the sheriff's tourn and, if the accused had been arrested, could be tried at gaol delivery.[92] Presenting jurors at peace sessions could be equally selective in their accusations.[93]

The presenting jury's findings or accusations became indictments when duly sworn and endorsed before a judicial official competent to hear them. They would then go forward to await trial at gaol delivery or oyer and terminer sessions. In the days of the eyre (and into the early fourteenth century) the terminology for prosecution ('presentment', 'indictment', 'appeal') was fluid and often regarded as interchangeable.[94] By Edward III's reign, however, indictments had to conform to certain requirements and include not only details of the accused and the offence itself, but also the date the offence was allegedly committed, the date of the accused's indictment and before whom the indictment was taken. If the formalities were not complied with, the indictment could be challenged and rejected by the justices presiding at trial.[95] In such cases, the person thus charged could go 'without day' (no date was assigned for trial) and the sheriff was forced to redraft the indictment.[96] At high-powered judicial sessions, such as the eyre or those held under general oyer and terminer commissions or by the king's bench, the presenting jurors' findings were scrutinised by a group of 'triers', a jury drawn from the whole of the county, sometimes called a 'grand jury' (*magna inquisicio*). This body, which examined and put forward particularly serious crimes (such as homicide and rape), allegations of interference in the administration of justice, or offences committed by high-status individuals, could include one or two members of the hundred juries, but tended to comprise significant administrators drawn from the county hierarchy to ensure that sufficient weight was behind the prosecution process.[97]

The Crown's role in the prosecution of individuals was not restricted to the identification of offenders through the use of local juries. It was able to take advantage of the inside knowledge gained from criminals who turned king's evidence and became an 'approver'.[98] From at least the twelfth century it was recognised that a man (and very occasionally, in spite of prohibition, a woman) accused of a crime could confess his guilt and turn king's evidence: provide the Crown with full details of his criminal activities, including the names and whereabouts of his accomplices.[99] Under Henry II the system was fairly mercenary and huge sums of money were paid to special 'king's approvers', some of whom seem to have been retained on a professional basis.[100] Although this had changed by the thirteenth and fourteenth centuries, there was no shortage of people willing to 'grass' on their associates in order to save themselves. The Crown's willingness to barter for information by offering the hope of discharge to self-confessed felons lay at the heart of the approver system. The provision of such information offered the Crown the means of prosecuting crimes which otherwise might have gone undetected. The plea rolls provide graphic evidence of the number of approvers and the types of crimes to which they admitted or of which they professed knowledge.[101] Fluctuations in the volume of appeals can perhaps be linked to the Crown's law enforcement drives during the fourteenth century.[102] Approvers were actively used in 1381–82 in the aftermath of the Peasants' Revolt to identify those who had threatened officials and tried to usurp royal authority.[103]

The Crown was not solely reliant on the formal methods of prosecution by presentment or indictment or appeal to initiate proceedings against offenders. Certain officials were allowed to use their discretion to arrest individuals without prior warrant from the sheriff if they were suspected of having committed a crime or were caught red-handed carrying away goods. In the days of the eyre the names of people already suspected of offences were sent to the sheriff before presentments were made. The list of names was compiled secretly (hence it was known as the *privata*) and had to be delivered to the sheriff before the latest day appointed for the return of the jury's *veredictum* so that his officers could make the necessary arrests before the names were read out in court.[104] Constables and keepers of the peace for hundreds and towns could arrest suspicious strangers under the Statute of Winchester and the statute of 1331, but special powers to arrest notorious suspects for public-order offences were also accorded peace-keeping officers in an ordinance of 1336 and in the Statute of Gloucester (1378), the chapter in the latter, although short-lived, enabling those who caused disturbances to be arrested 'without waiting for indictment or other process of law'.[105]

Private prosecution

The legal system also offered the opportunity for private individuals to seek redress before the royal justices. Actions could be initiated by obtaining a royal writ, or less formally, by providing a written bill or oral 'plaint'. The other mechanism by which private suits could be brought to court was by making an appeal of felony. The effectiveness of these methods was dependent upon the plaintiff (the person wanting relief) fulfilling correctly the procedural requirements for bringing their case to trial and judgment. The attractiveness for litigants of these methods lay in the fact that they were directed towards delivering some form of compensation (usually in damages) either through the operation of legal process or through an out-of-court settlement. Again we should not draw too much of a distinction between civil and criminal cases (suits against another individual and offences against the king) since appeals of felony could be made by private individuals with compensation in mind. While this section elaborates on the complaint mechanisms and provides a sample of wrongs covered, it is important to grasp the flexible and evolutionary nature of the processes and the possibilities envisaged by litigants anxious for remedies in ways not hitherto provided. The responsiveness to litigants, and the provision of whatever was most appropriate to their needs, is a significant feature of the period. The story is therefore one of expansion in some areas and decline in others.

An appeal of felony was essentially a private prosecution which could be brought by the victim of a serious crime. If the victim was no longer alive to bring it personally, their widowed spouse, heir or relations could sue on their behalf. An appeal of felony could be initiated by making an oral complaint in the county court, duly witnessed and recorded by the coroner. The appellee was then attached to respond to the allegation at the next judicial sessions. The facts of the appellor's case were woven into a formulaic structure which had to be recited before the justices in eyre or at gaol delivery in the exact words used. Deviations or ambiguities could cause it to fail on technical grounds. Omissions such as failing to raise the hue and cry immediately after the felony was committed or not providing 'fresh suit' (publicising the alleged crime in the four nearest villages) could also prove detrimental to the action. Technically, under Magna Carta, a woman was barred from making an appeal of homicide except where the victim was her husband. Jurisprudential treatises and thirteenth-century judges, however, regarded her legal ambit as wider, encompassing not only the death of her husband (if 'killed in her arms'), but also the deflowering of her body and even the death of an unborn child. In practice, in both the central and local courts, women were given further latitude and brought appeals for the death of relations (son, brother, nephew, mother, daughter) and for robbery and theft.[106]

Despite the dangers and restrictions inherent in prosecution by appeal of felony,[107] the advantages of such an appeal were fourfold. Firstly, it was intended as a judicial means of securing from the party inflicting the wrong a monetary payment or some other form of compensation. If successful in obtaining assurances for this, usually the parties were able to come to terms before the day of reckoning.[108] Indeed, thirteenth-century sources show that fifty-four per cent of appellors dropped their prosecution before it came before the eyre justices.[109] Secondly and linked to the first, the appeal was a useful tactical device. Many appeals of rape, for instance, were begun with the sole intention of forcing a marriage or some form of material settlement following cohabitation or seduction.[110] Thirdly, because of the criminal sanction attached to the action, if the appellee was unwilling to settle and arrived in court, retribution for the wrong might be achieved if the jury found for the appellor and the appellee was hanged.[111] Fourthly and finally, if there were difficulties in indicting a particular wrongdoer, an appeal offered another way of bringing the crime to the attention of the royal courts. For even if the appellor were non-suited, in other words failed to prove their claim to the satisfaction of the court (especially if exception to an appellatrix were taken on legal grounds), the claim then would not necessarily be rejected by the court: it could be taken up at the king's suit and the defendant re arraigned accordingly.[112]

In contrast to approvers' appeals, which were common during the period, and at times actively encouraged by the Crown, the appeal sued by a private individual appears to have declined in use over the course of the thirteenth century. The decline itself was not straightforward: the counties with extant records point towards a dramatic drop during the first three decades of the thirteenth century and then a resurgence of use until the early 1250s, before a period of decline again over the next ten years. From the early 1260s until the suspension of the eyre in 1294 the number of appeals levelled out, but the trend thereafter was a slow, downward one.[113]

The long-term decline in bringing private appeals has been accorded several explanations: the archaic nature of the appeal, judicial discouragement because of exploitation of the technicalities, the rise of presentment, the availability of trespass actions and the recasting of some felonies as trespasses. Although these elements may have been contributory in some respect, they do not satisfactorily account for the fluctuations (rather than decline) in use. The most recent investigation, however, has concluded that the phenomenon can best be accounted for by changes in judicial policy towards the settlement of appeals.[114] A study based on surviving eyre rolls of course can be flawed and does not take into account appeals siphoned off through supplementary gaol deliveries, which were commoner in the later thirteenth century, nor the use of bills and oral complaints which began during the 1250s.[115] Whatever the reasons for this gradual shift in prosecution methods during the thirteenth century, the goal delivery rolls indicate that it still remained an option throughout the fourteenth century, even if appeals were rarer than in the previous hundred years. Continued use of the private appeal – though no longer the preferred choice of judges and/or litigants indicates favourable expectations of its prosecuting power.[116]

For many private litigants a writ was the most frequent recourse for bringing an action in the king's courts. An 'original' writ (one from which proceedings were originated) could be obtained from chancery by a legal adviser, the plaintiff in person, or through a courier.[117] Writs, in a fixed and stereotypical form covering a large number of frequently recurring cases (which had been approved by the king and council, and collected together in the chancery in registers of writs) were issued as a matter of course (*de cursu*) and without the need for special authorisation. If the prospective litigant knew the name of the particular writ he or she required it could be supplied accordingly. If not, he or she could explain the facts of the case and ask to be furnished with the appropriate one.[118] Getting the correct writ and one that accorded with the desired action was a vital prerequisite for bringing a case. A writ not framed or devised in the appropriate chancery form, or one alleging matters not contained in the correct writ, would not be answered.[119] Some writs may have been drafted by practitioners in advance and then set before the chancery clerks for their approval.[120]

In its basic form, a writ was a document giving instructions. It was addressed to the sheriff and authorised the instigation of proceedings (in whatever was the subject-matter of the writ) in the court to which the writ was 'returnable'. The sheriff then had to provide a report (written on the back of the writ) to the justices as to the action he had taken; where applicable the report included the defendant's statement. On receipt of the sheriff's report the justices took cognisance of the case and could issue further writs themselves ('judicial writs') governing later process. In the period 1215–1381 there were three main classes of originating writ. One form of writ, embodying the command (*praecipe*) of the sheriff, enabled a plaintiff to recover what he considered to be his right. The writ demanded certain action from the defendant, such as handing over land claimed by the plaintiff or debts or chattels that had been withheld, or (in a variation) allowing him to take timber from the wood (as his right) or removing something causing a nuisance. If the defendant refused to do so, he was then required to present himself before the justices. Under another form which allowed the plaintiff to sue retrospectively for a wrong, the sheriff had to instruct the defendant to attend the court to show why (*ostensurus quare*) he had committed the wrong alleged by the plaintiff. In practice, the latter proved a speedier and more effective form of writ and by Edward I's time had largely superseded the writ *praecipe*. Between these two categories came a form instigating the possessory or petty assizes (which could be entertained in the provinces by eyre justices or justices of assize). The most popular and wide-ranging of these was the action of novel disseisin, which provided remedy for a tenant (in the feudal sense) 'unjustly and without judgment' ejected from his freehold, but other possible actions were mort d'ancestor (determining the transmission of seisin of a dead man to the true heir) and darrein presentment (determining who exercised the right of patronage to an ecclesiastical benefice). The common basis to the petty assizes was the summoning of a jury to provide recognition (*recognitionem*) of the matter in dispute.

Writs were available to remedy a multitude of different situations. They covered possession of land and inheritance issues, the enforcement of covenants and various property rights, recovery of debts and goods unjustly confiscated, problems of deceit, negligence and nuisance, and various sorts of trespass. In the early thirteenth century there were about fifty actions in use.[121] A century later the figure had risen to nearly 900. Large numbers of new types of writ were also added to the registers in the reigns of Edward III and Richard II. In part this explosion was a result of the considerable number of remedies provided by statute during the reigns of Edward I and his grandson.[122] It nevertheless offered litigants considerable choice of actions and ensured that they brought their disputes into the royal courts, as they did in growing numbers. Indeed, it has been calculated that in the early part of the fourteenth century as many as 200 or 300 writs *de cursu* were sealed each day.[123] Calculating on this basis, 200 writs sealed per day would amount to at least 1,000 sealed per week; 1,000 per week would yield 50,000 writs in a year. Such a total would theoretically allow for one writ per year (on average) for every head of a free family: a figure that would signify a very high rate of participation.

The new remedies were designed to appeal to and benefit people across the social spectrum. Indeed, Chief Justice Bereford commented on the advantages of replevin (an action whereby the owner or person entitled to repossession of goods or chattels could recover them from the person who had wrongfully distrained or detained them) compared to the cumbersome proprietary action *ne injuste vexes*: 'For twenty years past there has not come to England so good a law for poor folk'.[124] Actions for trespass, which developed over the thirteenth century, increasingly gained in popularity over the period and along with debt litigation accounted for a significant proportion of cases initiated in the central courts. Writs of trespass bore some similarity to criminal actions in that a breach of the king's peace or an allegation that injury was caused by force and arms (*vi et armis*) was required in order to bring the action. The need for violence to accompany a trespass as a prerequisite for admissibility in court, however, had become purely notional by the fourteenth century and was omitted by chancery clerks issuing writs from the 1360s. Writs of trespass *vi et armis* proved an important concession for litigants who were able to sue for wrongs done to land, to chattels and to the person – areas not otherwise covered under criminal jurisdiction.

Some writs developed because of the advantages to be obtained by bringing an action in the king's courts, especially in one of the benches. An important advantage in this respect was the level of damages that could be awarded. The county court and other local courts (unless they had royal permission) could not entertain certain pleas (those in debt-detinue) where the sum asked for in damages was greater than forty shillings.[125] While some litigants may have been content with this ceiling, and continued to use the local courts to remedy situations (particularly trespass actions) using existing options,[126] others may have wanted more substantial damages and (through their lawyers) attempted to 'bounce' the central court judges into accepting actions for which there were as yet no formal writs. This was particularly significant in relation to allegations of breach of duty and negligence (prototype actions of *assumpsit* and trespass on the case) which were 'smuggled into court' by using writs designed for already established actions (such as covenant and detinue) combined with analogy and argument regarding the special nature of the case. The chancery eventually began to issue special writs in these areas, writs of *assumpsit* for injuries experienced as a result of the negligence of someone carrying on their profession or trade (such as providing medical treatment, shoeing horses, or transporting goods or persons) and writs of trespass on the case for injuries caused by the negligent behaviour of ordinary people (through their lack of control of animals or natural elements such as fire).[127]

The flexibility of the legal system and its responsiveness to the needs of litigants is also apparent in the possibility of initiating suits through oral complaint or by means of a written bill.[128] Until the mid-thirteenth century, private proceedings in the king's courts could not be instigated without a writ.[129] Initial encouragement to sue by plaint or bill was given wherever there was a drive against administrative abuses, and the wrongs dealt with by the justices were mostly those involving officials. Within a short time, though, all manner of misdemeanours, petty trespasses, nuisances, and debt cases were being accepted by the eyre, business that would normally have been handled in the local courts.

The lack of formalities in suit by bill or plaint was an important advantage over bringing proceedings by writ.[130] Unlike a writ, a bill did not have to be written in Latin: it could be in French. They were not required to be as precise and as accurate in spelling and grammar as a writ and, although many bills were relatively concise, litigants could get away with long, rambling sentences.[131] Moreover, the legal substance of a bill did not have to be as clearly defined as a writ. As Professor Harding puts it, '[T]he plaintiff who took his bill to the justices was relying less on definite rights in private law than on the king's known concern for justice and public order'.[132] This significant leeway facilitated the birth of new actions through their introduction as test cases.[133] The benefits of this means of prosecution lay in its simplicity for poorer litigants, in the lack of definition required in the legal wording, in the chance for plaintiffs to obtain remedy for a 'new' range of wrongs, which enabled lawyers and litigants to push to their limits the possibilities of the legal system and the opportunities for redress.

A hearing before the king's justices could also be obtained by procedural means: cases could be transferred from a lord's court to the county court using a procedure known as *tolt*; from the county court to one of the royal courts through the writ *pone*; and any case could be reviewed in the court of king's bench following a writ of *certiorari*.[134]

Our cognition of legal matters and, in particular, the conceptualisation of areas of prosecution have tended to be influenced by modern categorisations. The distinction between public and private prosecution was blurred through the ability of the king to step into the plaintiff's shoes and continue the suit if the latter withdrew from the case prematurely. This could occur in appeals of felony or at general oyer and terminer sessions when 'enormous' trespasses (serious offences rather than 'light and personal' ones) were alleged.[135] The late thirteenth and early fourteenth centuries in particular represent a period of transition in the use of legal process. There is evidence of duplication, for instance, occurring between modes of prosecution: some early written bills in eyre correspond to entries in rolls of oral complaints; the substance of a private suit could become enrolled in an indictment, while an offence brought on appeal of felony might equally be presented by a jury.[136] Bills coming before the eyre justices (and later the justices of oyer and terminer and justices of the peace) which were not regarded as private suits, though prosecuted by an individual, were usually passed on to the presenting jurors who would then endorse it *billa vera* (true bill) and include it in their statement of findings. Further insight into approaches to and use of litigation can be gained from the writs of conspiracy and writs of abetment brought by anxious litigants, often previously defendants in cases. Writs of conspiracy were issued both as original and judicial writs for actions based on the Ordinance of Conspirators of 1293,[137] which offered a focus for concerns about abuse of judicial procedure that had hitherto been restricted to the articles of the eyre.

Accountability

The function of the royal judicial system was to uphold both royal and individual (or a corporation's) personal rights and to ensure that the king's peace was not broken. Prosecution by the state or a private person suing someone else in court was a way of making people accountable for their actions and for wrongs of varying types perpetrated against the Crown and their fellow beings. Vigilance over royal interests, however, was not restricted to the conduct of its ordinary subjects. Linked closely to the need for efficiency and dependability in royal government was a deep-seated concern for the behaviour of the mass of officials in royal service at all levels. They were obliged to face up to their shortcomings and could expect physical or financial punishment (and probably moral censure) for their misdeeds.

Serious investigations into corruption and extortion became an important feature of judicial business from the mid-thirteenth century onward with the inclusion of many new articles for the eyre. Despite the demise of the eyre, which had been pushed beyond the scope for which it was intended, kings maintained pressure on erring officers of all kinds during the fourteenth century through the use of general commissions of oyer and terminer, which inquired into oppressive behaviour, extortion, excesses and general corruption among an extensive list of officials (including those entrusted with law-enforcement duties), fiscal officials, those responsible for customs and the forests, keepers of horses and purveyors attached to the royal household, arrayers of troops and also a number of ecclesiastical officials. In addition to commissions focusing on perhaps one aspect, such as the exaction and use made of prises, there were major investigations into official corruption planned and (as some surviving proceedings testify) carried out in 1274, 1298, 1314, 1318, 1321, 1326 and 1331. The most comprehensive inquiries came in the 1340s. The articles of these commissions not only included the trailbaston-type concerns (those believed to be perverting the course of justice or engaged in organised violence), but also inquiry into the fees taken by officials to perform their duties, the amounts of cash they took for the king's use and did not return, those who weighed wool unjustly and who shipped wool illegally without the relevant customs licences. Indeed, the main focus was on wartime supplies: whether taken illegally, whether taken and not paid for, whether they were taken but never sent off or never reached their destination as ordered.[138]

Declining use of general oyer and terminer commissions in the later fourteenth century did not in reality signal a retreat from royal investigations into county administration. Commissions of this type continued to be issued both regionally and nationally when there was a need, but not on a regular or predictable basis. Coincident with a publicly stated dislike of eyres and trailbastons, it marked a significant shift, in responsibility for examining the misbehaviour of local officials, to the assize justices and the court of king's bench.[139]

While regular scrutiny of the operation of central and local government may have enhanced expectations of its reliability, the king's desire for accountability in officialdom did not mean that the interests of the individual who suffered wrong were entirely neglected. From Edward I's reign, parliament provided an important central forum for private complaints about the corruption of officials. Indeed, private petitions were regarded as a useful vehicle for bringing to the king's attention miscellaneous judicial matters.[140] The reviews of official conduct held locally offered the opportunity for individuals to bring actions in the courts to remedy the grievances which they themselves harboured against both royal and seigneurial officials. Indeed, an important by-product of the royal drive against corruption was the introduction of articles of inquiry that suited (or could be adjusted to suit) the person of lesser status. This reflected a concern for those probably most affected by the predatory and unjust behaviour of officials and who undoubtedly felt intimidated about complaining against the king's representatives.

Of the nineteen articles added to the eyre's remit between 1246 and 1254, seven were particularly advantageous to the 'small tenant'. These focused on, for example, sheriffs who stirred up lawsuits in order to gain lands, wardships and debts; officials who took payments from both parties (*ambisinistris*); officials who took the same amercement twice, or who took more than the proper amercement; bailiffs who extorted gifts of crops at harvest or who had distrained a group of people with the same name. Significantly it was not just the royal bailiffs upon whom the spotlight was turned, but the lesser bailiffs, whose oppressions (though comparatively small) were probably more frequent and whose ways were possibly more insinuating.[141] Penetration of the lower levels of officialdom was thus a significant achievement.

Interestingly, the records of the general eyre held in Shropshire in 1256 reveal that the scope of the juries' presentments ranged outside the confines of the articles of the eyre. For instance, questions designed to elicit cases of unjust imprisonment against the interests of the Crown brought into the open injustices suffered by the men of Hales at the hands of the abbot of Hales (such as having their cattle seized by his bailiffs) in the latter's unwarranted assumption of criminal and forest jurisdiction.[142] Juries also bent the strict terms of the article that was inquiring into abuses by officials of their powers of imprisonment. In theory it was directed towards those who released people who had been properly indicted, but it is clear from the findings presented that jurors were looking beyond this not only at arrest and confinement carried out by people who were not royal bailiffs, but also at the nature of imprisonment as a wrong in itself when not justified by indictment.[143]

The second feature stemming from the anti-corruption stance and benefiting the ordinary person was the development of a method of initiating an action that did not require the purchase of a writ and was both inexpensive and easy to facilitate. The justices' acceptance of informal accusations either as written bills or as oral 'plaints' (*querelae*) encouraged large numbers of individuals to come forward with their grievances. Although in fact oral complaints had been sought against officials at least thirty years earlier (during investigations held at Dunstable in 1224 into the behaviour of Fawkes de Breauté and his colleagues)[144] the eyre of 1259 launched by the baronial reform movement against the evils of Henry III's administration rekindled the initiative when it urged the justices 'to hear all complaints of trespasses by whomsoever they had been committed'.[145] In 1340–41 Edward III urged people to hand in written bills secretly if they thought that officials in office would inhibit their presentation.[146]

The Crown's desire for effective governance, one that was increasingly echoed in parliament during the fourteenth century (particularly during periods when the country's resources were channelled into war), not only highlighted the existing bureaucratic and administrative shortcomings, but also heightened awareness of the operation of government among the king's subjects.[147] The king aimed to correct and purge these shortcomings and, by facilitating the making of complaints, he was able to encourage his subjects to give voice to their grievances and point the finger at those who were helping themselves (rather than the king) and/or abusing others on account of their position. The significance of the growth of bills and plaints as a medium for action against officials (evidenced by the special membranes of complaints sewn into the eyre, trailbaston and king's bench rolls) lies in the way it highlights the kinship of interest in this matter between the Crown and its subjects – an affinity that was given physical expression in the outbursts against officials (including summary executions) in 1381. Both sides felt threatened by – and suffered from – (though of course in very different ways) the over-extension and misuse of official powers. Both wanted to make officials accountable for their actions. This also underlines one of the driving factors behind judicial development, one that was concerned not only with ensuring due process, but maximising participation in judicial processes.

Accessibility

The notion of accessibility provokes questions which strike at the heart of the traditional picture of medieval justice. As we have seen so far in this chapter, the availability of royal justice (in terms of the frequency of court sessions) increased over the thirteenth and fourteenth centuries, along with a kaleidoscopic choice of remedies and amelioration of the means of initiating suits. This section looks at the extent to which the royal courts were open to litigation from all classes of people, not just the elite, and examines the possible financial and psychological factors inhibiting access to justice.

The word 'justice' itself has an inherent duality, referring both to the system of rules and procedure within which the law operates and to notions of fairness and procedural propriety. Theoretically there were safeguards within the system, which were intended to enhance its inclusiveness. Although Magna Carta did not herald a 'judicial Utopia' its provisions set a benchmark against which the operation of the legal system in the fourteenth century was increasingly measured. The twenty-ninth chapter of the 1225 version proclaimed: 'to no one will we sell, to no one will we deny or delay right or justice'. Although this was initially directed at a specific group, the tenants-in-chief, it was arguably interpreted to have more general application.[148] By Edward III's reign, Magna Carta was regularly confirmed in statute legislation and there were additional guarantees that, irrespective of his estate, no man would be condemned or made to answer accusations without the correct procedures being followed.[149] Emphasis was also placed at a judicial level on the fair treatment of everyone regardless of their status, particularly during the reforming years of the mid-thirteenth century.[150] Although slightly after 1381, it is significant that in a late-fourteenth-century case it was argued that the cost of a long trial would be prohibitive for the plaintiffs and that to deny them justice because they were poor and unable to afford the cost was 'against law and conscience'.[151]

Even with the manifest availability of judicial arenas and legal remedies one of the main considerations for any potential litigant, let alone the less well-off, was affordability. In the normal course of events the poor plaintiff might find it difficult to purchase the writs necessary to bring an action, or might be unable to meet the fees expected for legal advice and assistance (let alone representation in court). Costs could escalate if a suit was unnecessarily protracted. Moreover, if the plaintiff was unsuccessful or failed to turn up, he might be liable to pay a fine to the Crown for a false claim. There is nevertheless clear evidence that considerable allowance was made for the fact that the cost of litigation (with its attendant expenses) might prejudice potential suits from the lower orders. Indeed, various forms of 'legal aid' existed and efforts were made by parliament and the judiciary to ensure that people were not denied an opportunity for justice purely on economic grounds.

Obtaining the services of a lawyer was a vital factor when pursuing court action by at least the fourteenth century (if not earlier). In order to have a chance of success the plaintiff needed to be appraised of the legal position, had to obtain the correct writ and follow the necessary procedures. A defendant also required expert assistance and had to traverse the charges made against him without omitting a denial or making a verbal error. Finding an attorney was therefore a necessary first step. Legal advice did not usually come cheap. How were the less well-off able to cope? In the thirteenth century, *ad hoc* advice and assistance could often be obtained from the clerks of royal justices travelling in the provinces.[152] By the early fourteenth century, men of law whose work lay predominantly outside London were increasingly available for advice or representation and, judging by the number of suits brought in the court of king's bench by peasants using an attorney, the fees they charged cannot have been unduly exorbitant or prohibitive.[153] Although it is difficult to be sure of the prevailing standard fee (if indeed there was such a thing), it has been suggested that the figure of 3*s* 4*d* quoted in a City of London ordinance of 1356 can be equated with a 'reasonable fee' and was probably near enough the amount charged by a late-medieval attorney operating in the provinces.[154] Payment did not have to be wholly in cash: some attorneys accepted payment in kind (for example in cheese and butter).[155]

For the majority of litigants, the services of a pleader (arranged by their attorney) might also be required. In comparison with attorneys, the fee-scale for serjeants was generally higher, but a modest remuneration was all that was levied from some litigants and it was not unknown for serjeants to undertake work *pro bono*. In Edward I's reign, for instance, the sum of 3*s* 4*d* is known to have been paid to some serjeants operating in the royal courts – and a similar sum was payable to serjeants practising in the City of London courts about half a century later. Clients too poor to pay the required amount for legal representation were sometimes assigned a pleader by the justices free of charge.[156] In 1292, Alan son of Alan Plotman, for example, on behalf of himself and his mother claimed that they were poor folk and asked the justices 'so that they lose not their right' to grant them a serjeant.[157]

Once the attorney had advised on court action, the economically disadvantaged plaintiff faced further financial barriers. As outlined earlier, to bring litigation at the assizes or in the court of common pleas a plaintiff required an 'original' writ to initiate proceedings and, once the writ had been returned to court, a series of 'judicial' writs to control later stages. The prospective litigant could qualify for help with these charges if he or she were poor since, in spite of a reputation for overcharging, chancery clerks waived the fee of 6*d* for an originating writ if the applicant could swear to poverty.[158] In the thirteenth century and into the early-fourteenth century no major outlay was usually required for judicial writs. At least prior to 1285 they were probably issued free of charge and even after the second Statute of Westminster of that year they cost only one penny.[159] By Edward III's reign, however, the fee for a judicial writ had outstripped the cost of an original writ, having risen to 7*d*; and a further increase of 3*d* had occurred by 1350.[160] Although this inflated price would appear to endorse claims that justice was becoming more exclusive, the cost of litigation did not go uncriticised. The parliamentary Commons petitioned for a reduction in the price of original writs to 3*d*, and for a withdrawal of extra charges (often included for land litigation) which were considered to be unreasonable.[161] The Commons were unsuccessful in reducing the cost of an original writ, but they managed to secure some concessions, including the proviso that any extra costs would not be levied if the writ were granted as an act of charity or by favour of the court.[162]

Suits could also be brought by purchasing from chancery a special commission of oyer and terminer. Issued under letters patent, they were eagerly sought by litigants of various backgrounds from the late-thirteenth century and reached a peak of popularity during the early-fourteenth century.[163] The fee paid to chancery was normally £1. Though it represented a one-off payment (and attracted none of the hidden extras characteristic of judicial writs), such a sizeable sum, considerably in excess of the cost of a writ, would appear to have placed the purchase of such commissions beyond the reach of poorer litigants. Interestingly, however, a variable fee scale appears to have operated, (possibly) controlled by the ability to pay. Charges towards the upper end of the spectrum graduated from 2 marks (equivalent to £1 6*s* 8*d*) through to £2 and could even reach 5 marks (£3 6*s* 8*d*), levels which at times may have scorched the pockets of some gentry families. Towards the lower end applicants were allowed to pay reduced rates, ranging from one mark (13*s* 4*d*) to as little as half a mark. While even these lesser sums may have been difficult for members of the peasantry to raise (half a mark represented twenty-seven days' wages or more), it is nevertheless clear that the relative poverty of some of those applying for commissions was taken into consideration. Indeed, it is apparent that not infrequently special oyer and terminer commissions were issued 'for God' as an act of Christian charity and accordingly the requirement for payment was dropped altogether.[164]

The cheapest method of bringing an action was to go before the justices with an oral complaint (*querela*) or present a written bill outlining the injury suffered. It would appear that no charge was payable for this facility and it enabled ordinary people to bring with relative ease their cases before the group of royal justices visiting their county.[165] The suspension of the eyre in 1294 did not end the opportunity for cheap and easy access to the courts. Jurisdiction over oral complaints and bills passed initially to justices holding general commissions of oyer and terminer and the itinerant king's bench. Despite the latter's pre-eminent position in the hierarchy of courts, peasants were not inhibited from initiating proceedings in king's bench, as a social analysis of lawsuits coming before the court when sitting in Lincolnshire (1291-1339) has indicated.[166] New cases brought by 'villagers' never accounted for less than 70 per cent of the total business generated in the shire, while the average for the period was an impressive 81 per cent. The comparative frequency with which the court of king's bench visited Lincolnshire (once every eighteen months on average during the sixteen years 1323-39) may have been a relevant factor not only in encouraging this group to use the court, but to continue to have recourse to the king's bench when it was no longer in the county.[167]

In addition to fees for the services of a lawyer and payments to get the case off the ground there were other expenses attendant on private litigation. A person who initiated an action had to be able at the outset to satisfy the court that he would turn up and prosecute the case. A claim, therefore, had to be supported by two people who were duly required to ensure the plaintiff's presence in court, and who were liable to imprisonment or to pay a fine if he defaulted. Here, again, special consideration was given to those who lacked the necessary economic wherewithal. If the complainant was poor and unable to find anyone to back his claim he could take an oath and pledge his faith instead. Suitors who could not find personal pledges were also allowed to substitute items of clothing or property, such as a cloak or a horse.[168] If, at some later date, the claim was not pursued and the plaintiff withdrew his suit (perhaps because the case had been settled out of court) or he failed to substantiate the whole claim, he might then find himself liable for further expenditure: suffering an amercement for a false claim or having to pay for a licence to come to an agreement. Accepting the financial hardship that would be incurred by a person of slender means, the court might remit the fine where the litigant was poor.[169]

If the outcome of litigation was favourable, some (or all) of the expense involved in bringing the action might be recouped in the damages awarded. Although the justices and their clerks were usually entitled to a share of the sum recovered, the proportion was not fixed. In any case the assignment of a fraction of the award was probably not obligatory for poorer plaintiffs nor necessary when the sum itself was insignificant.[170] Generally defendants were kept in custody until they satisfied the required sum, although in 1300 a losing litigant who had been committed to prison was released when the justices discovered that he was penniless.[171] The justices obviously had some sympathy for, or were realistic about the chances of satisfaction from, a defendant with little or no income as there is evidence that the impoverished were excused payment altogether.[172]

When the parties finally arrived in court, how intelligible were events there? Given the somewhat arcane and technical language, court proceedings inevitably took on an air of mystery and exclusivity, and litigants faced potential barriers in comprehension, both cognitively and linguistically. The legal records appear to reinforce this: the plea rolls of royal (and even manorial) courts are in Latin; the legal treatise known as *Bracton* employs Latin dialogue in its examples, as does the earliest report of a cross-examination by a judge,[173] while the Year Books, which often seem to be convincing reports of actual proceedings in the eyre and Westminster courts, are in French.[174] Could the informed layman understand what was going on? Was the poor litigant able to grasp anything of what was occurring?

To answer this we need to consider both the nature and content of trials. The question of comprehension can be broached initially by querying whether it was necessary for a litigant to be fully conversant with the pleadings and procedures. The extent of any personal involvement would have depended upon whether professional representation was appropriate or available, upon the judicial forum and the nature and complexity of the particular case. Suits which revolved around difficult points of law would necessarily require expert presentation and certainly after 1259 obtaining the services of a serjeant was compulsory in pleas of land and of replevin in the City of London courts.[175]

In order to appreciate the extent to which the system possessed (or acquired) an element of 'user-friendliness' we must first distinguish between the language(s) used to record details of the court proceedings and the language(s) actually spoken in court. A further distinction should then be made between the language of the formal pleadings and that used in the later proceedings. Surviving lawyers' manuals show that the rehearsal of issues before the court was carried out in French, rather than in Latin, certainly from the mid-thirteenth century.[176] This linguistic preference probably continued for at least another hundred years, until it was decreed by the City of London in 1356 that pleadings should be in English,[177] a move that was extended to all courts of law by royal statute six years later.[178] Such a change (if indeed it occurred) would not, of course produce instant transparency, or remove the opportunity for confusion arising out of the complexity of legal language. Nonetheless, a measure of accessibility may have been achieved through the introduction of the vernacular in that it would have enabled those who were unrepresented and had little or no knowledge of law French to put (as effectively as they could) their claims before the justices.[179]

Focus on the language of pleadings inevitably obscures the extent of language exchange that took place.[180] Jurors presenting their responses to the 'articles of the eyre' at the Kent eyre of 1313-14, for instance, were apparently required to submit orally in English (through their foreman) answers which, before their acceptance by the court and subsequent enrolment in Latin, had to correspond exactly with the same words previously recited in French by the court clerk. The oral use of vernacular was not limited to simple statements. Where the mother tongue of court participants was English (and as early as Henry III's reign the judges were native Englishmen) it would be reasonable to suppose, indeed it would be common sense in the case of a poor villager, that the vernacular was used if a meaningful and effective exchange were to take place between the bench and parties or witnesses. There is evidence of French and English being used in cross-examinations in the church courts in 1271[181] and English may have been used when questions were asked of witnesses or parties in the royal courts (even the central courts).[182] Dr Brand, however, raises some doubt as to the extent to which use of vernacular English obtained in the benches and argues on the basis of internal evidence in the rolls that (in the thirteenth century at least) proceedings were normally conducted in French.[183]

While the full implications of proceedings may have eluded many litigants, their general understanding of events may have been enhanced during the later fourteenth century by the use of English in spite of the illusion provided by the surviving records. The opportunity to employ a man of law, whose level of standing (particularly compared with a poor litigant) and expertise in the language of the law enabled a case to be steered through court, was also a powerful means of overcoming both the technical and psychological barriers to bringing litigation in the royal courts. The ability of the lower orders to obtain legal advice and use the judicial system to their advantage has long been underestimated. Indeed, some peasants can be shown to have been experienced litigators, at times bringing cases in the royal courts, at other times pursuing (often lengthy) disputes in the manorial courts.[184] Some peasants contributed to a common purse in order to finance litigation.[185] Even the unfree (who technically had no rights to sue in the royal courts, certainly for matters concerning tenure) appear to have employed lawyers and achieved a measure of access, particularly during the later fourteenth century.[186] The fact that the system was so obviously stacked against the unfree does not mean that justice was perceived as a closed shop: access to the royal courts was clearly regarded as an important advantage to be preserved or acquired.[187]

The thinking within government and judicial circles concerning treatment of the indigent at law may have arisen from a heightened consciousness about the poor combined with new attitudes towards the moral character of poverty. From at least the twelfth century there was much debate among jurists and theologians (and particularly between the Church and the mendicant orders) on the nature of poverty and how relief might best be given to the poor. This involved identifying what have subsequently been called the 'deserving poor' – those who, it was felt, could be distinguished from the general mass of poor folk for the receipt of charity because they were not capable of working (possibly through sickness or injury or other weakness) or had been respectable but were now experiencing difficult times. Donors were advised to avoid giving charity to those likely to resort to crime or sin, or to able-bodied idlers or mere vagrants – an attitude that was echoed in the labour legislation of the mid-fourteenth century. The *pauperes verecundi* or shame-faced poor, however, those who had been used to a measure of comfort but through circumstances were now reduced to poverty, did merit charity. Indeed, they were regarded as doubly needy since they had not only suffered physically through shortage and need, but also mentally through social dislocation and the associated shame.[188]

Some examples of bills presented to the justices in eyre seem to bear this out. John Feyrewin told how he had been forced to become a pauper begging his bread 'for God's sake' and ended up by saying 'I have not a halfpenny to spend on a pleader'. William son of Hugh of Smethumilne's request placed emphasis on the personal spiritual benefits of allowing aid: 'And I pray you, for your soul's sake, that you will give me remedy for this, for I am so poor that I can pay for no counter'. Edith, widow of Richard Darlaston, made similar claims, praying 'remedy for your charity and for God's sake, for she is poor'. She may in fact have fitted into the category of shame-faced poor and thus regarded as truly deserving of help, since she claimed that 'by these things [the legal misfortunes she relates] she has been brought to beggary'.[189]

The practice of aiding the litigation of poor persons was not confined to the royal courts, but was mirrored in the ecclesiastical courts. Indeed, from the late thirteenth century it was regarded as the ethical professional duty of canon lawyers to act without remuneration for impoverished clients.[190] The first official indication of the English Church's practice appears in a statute of Archbishop Winchelsey of 1295, which provided that it was the duty of the judge presiding in the Court of Arches to grant advocates and proctors to clients who claimed poverty.[191] This was also the tenor of regulations promulgated by the bishop of Durham in 1312.[192] The phenomenon of legal aid, however, was not limited to the English court system, as legislation from northern Italy demonstrates. What is interesting from this point of view is, firstly, the capacity for such a provision to transcend national and jurisdictional boundaries. Secondly and more significantly, while the general duty to aid the poor may have derived from canonist doctrine, the initiative and responsibility did not remain purely with the Church. Although the English state, unlike some of its continental counterparts,[193] issued no formal, all-encompassing legislation on this issue during this period, it is clear that its more piecemeal and *ad hoc* discretionary measures nevertheless pre-empted considerably the *in forma pauperis* provisions of Henry VII's reign.[194]

While there appears to have been no clearly defined or articulated 'policy' as such, there was definitely a feeling within government and judicial circles and among the more privileged members of society that royal justice was an area in which discretion should operate. The Commons persistently argued throughout the fourteenth century that the royal courts should be equally accessible to the less well off (if not also to the genuinely poor). As we have seen, litigants frequently requested help in purchasing writs or special commissions of oyer and terminer and in obtaining legal representation and were duly awarded them in terms that describe this as an act of charity. The very fact that poor people were granted this legal aid must say something about the approachability of the judicial system, but we can only speculate about how they came to seek it in the first place. How did they know that they could receive help to bring a suit unless this was by some means communicated to the lower classes? Perhaps the poor who were given help to settle their problems in the royal courts received information from persons to whom they were connected in some way, either through kinship or friendship or to whom they were linked through clientage, as tenants or servants.

One deliberate method of exclusion occurred through the process of outlawry, which put outside the law defendants who did not turn up to the fifth county court after a summons to appear before the justices. The process was frequently cited in complaint literature as unjust and maliciously engineered by the defendant's enemies.[195] Viewed in its legal context, the onus was clearly on the individual to respond to the accusation (either civil or criminal) against him or her[196] within the required time period, so there was not necessarily anything sinister about it. It was purely a matter of process: the status of outlaw was proclaimed in default of an answer. Seeing the outlaw's exclusion as unduly harsh also takes no account of the fact that once outlawry had been pronounced there were in fact many ways of reversing it, not least by having a reasonable excuse for not being able to turn up on the occasion of the final summons.[197] Moreover, at the time the poem *An Outlaw's Song of Trailbaston* was written (in the first decade of the fourteenth century), the system of outlawry, like the contemporary legal institutions themselves, was in a state of flux. From the government's point of view, up to the late thirteenth century, outlawry was a useful process whereby criminals were identified and information about them communicated. Its effectiveness derived from its use of the sanction of exclusion as a means of preventing crime. By the fourteenth century, however, partly as a result of demographic changes, exclusion from the community had become less meaningful to the individual and more difficult to enforce. Consequently outlawry no longer possessed so much bite.[198] Alterations in the rules and practices surrounding it over the course of the century also lessened its direct effect.[199]

This chapter has demonstrated the gamut of legal agencies and the range of litigation options that were available in the royal court system. It has stressed the flexibility and responsiveness of the system and the way in which royal justice relied for its operation both on the demands of litigants and the service (as jurors) of members of local communities. Some historians have favoured the notion that the supposed new cultural and political values of the post-plague era necessarily brought restriction to the legal system and oppression in the administration of justice. These views rest mainly on arguments that the emergence of the justices of the peace (as a replacement for the eyre and for oyer and terminer commissions) eroded the climate of participation and opportunity which the older agencies had fostered, and that in the wake of the Black Death royal justice was effectively appropriated by the propertied elite in the shires. In administering the law (especially the labour legislation of 1349–51) along class lines, the JPs were, in the words of Steven Justice, a 'local judiciary more concerned to oppress than redress'.[200]

The medieval judicial system, as we have seen, did not operate deliberately to the exclusion of the disadvantaged in society, provided they remained within the boundaries of the legal world. In many ways it went out of its way to make its services available for those with little money or influence, and waived fees or abrogated strict rules of procedure when approached. It was keen to make it known that it followed the ideal that justice should be equally favourable to the poor and to the rich and that its officers were bound to uphold this maxim. Although we should not idealise the medieval world, in order for the poor to move beyond the manorial courts, and use and *reuse* the mechanisms of royal justice, they evidently possessed a certain level of confidence in the system and in its capacity to embrace all estates. Far from bringing alienation from the king's courts, the widening scope of royal justice observable over the course of the thirteenth and fourteenth centuries (in terms of opportunities for redress and in the range of legal remedies available) not only provided greater access at the local level, but also catered for the litigious tendencies of at least some sections of the peasant and urban communities. In the majority of the cases brought before the justices of the peace and justices of gaol delivery, both plaintiffs and defendants were men and women of low rank. Their business was uncontentious to the political elite and unlikely to suffer interference. Even in the case of the labour laws, where an action could be brought by the employer, who was normally of higher social status than the defendant (the employee) the idea of blatant class interests and prejudice being worked out through litigation tends to be undermined by the fact that a significant number of employers seeking redress through this mechanism were themselves of peasant status. Individuals were not necessarily restricted to membership of one economic class: in fact they often had multiple class locations.[201]

Participation in the royal courts should not necessarily be viewed in isolation from involvement in the courts of other jurisdictions (see Chapter 3) since suits in the royal courts could go hand in hand with cases brought elsewhere. Nor should the legal knowledge acquired through experience as an office-holder be artificially separated from other aspects such as involvement in litigation. Officials could serve as jurors, jurors could become officials, and both could prosecute offenders or initiate private litigation in the courts or themselves be subject to complaints both for their public business and as part of their private lives. Experience of litigation could benefit employment as a juror or official, while familiarity with the law and the judicial machine gained from royal or seigneurial service could enhance prospects in personal disputes. Moreover, an appreciation of the range of options both for initiating and concluding a case and an understanding of the interaction of the law with alternative methods of dispute settlement were important factors in the tactics of litigation and in the channelling of resources. The understanding of judicial processes arising out of experience in the courts encouraged reflection on improvements in the workings of the law. Experience and reflection led to the development of new attitudes towards the administration of justice, with new opinions that insisted on being heard.

Notes

1. R. V. Turner, *Judges, Administrators and the Common Law in Angevin England* (London, Hambledon Press, 1994), pp. 17-33; P. Brand, *The Making of the Common Law* (London, Hambledon Press, 1992), p. 136.
2. J. C. Holt, *Magna Carta*, 2nd edn (Cambridge, Cambridge University Press, 1992), pp. 323-4.
3. Magna Carta c. 17 (1215), c. 11 (1225); M. T. Clanchy, 'Magna Carta and common pleas', in H. Mayr-Harting and R. I. Moore (eds), *Studies in Medieval History Presented to R. H. C. Davies* (London, Hambledon Press, 1985), pp. 219-32.
4. Clanchy, 'Common pleas', pp. 224-5.
5. Magna Carta c. 18 (1215), c. 12 (1225); Holt, *Magna Carta*, pp. 324-5.
6. R. B. Pugh, *Imprisonment in Medieval England* (Cambridge, Cambridge University Press, 1968), pp. 255-60.
7. Clanchy, 'Common pleas', pp. 226-7.
8. Brand, *Origins*, pp. 14-15, 20-1 (see especially Table 2.1 showing the total number of eyres over the period 1189-1307); Brand, *Making*, pp. 137-8.
9. Brand, *Making*, p. 138; D. Crook, 'The later eyres', *EHR*, 97 (1982), pp. 241-3, 248; D. Crook, *Records of the General Eyre*, Public Record Office Handbooks, 20 (1982), pp. 144-5, 170-1.
10. *CCR 1272-9*, p. 52.
11. For example in Buckinghamshire, assizes might be held in Aylesbury, Buckingham, Edlesborough, Colnbrook, Denham, Wycombe, Stony Stratford, Southcote, Wendover or Crendon.
12. This restriction was not applicable of course when the assize justices were not drawn from the ranks of central court personnel (see Musson, *Public Order*, pp. 93-4).
13. See 3 Edward I c. 51.
14. See 13 Edward I c. 30.
15. Pugh, *Imprisonment*, pp. 260, 266, 278.
16. Musson, *Public Order*, p. 95.
17. Musson and Ormrod, *Evolution*, pp. 48-9, 53-4.
18. A. Harding, 'The origins and early history of the keeper of the peace', *TRHS*, 5th series, 10 (1960), 85-109; H. M. Cam, 'Some early inquests before "custodes pacis"', *EHR*, 40 (1925), pp. 415-19.
19. See 28 Edward 1 c. 5 (*SR*, vol. 1, p. 139).
20. The king's right to hear cases in person was usually exercised through the court of the verge, though both Edward II and Edward III occasionally presided over king's bench (see Chapter 6).

21 See below, 'Actionability', pp. 159–60.
22 Although in 1305 the court was involved in hearing and determining offences as part of the 'trailbaston' proceedings in the counties forming the 'home' circuit (*CPR 1301-7*, pp. 354–5).
23 For the sessions and itineraries of the court of king's bench during this period see the table in the appendix in Musson and Ormrod, *Evolution*, pp. 197–8.
24 The term 'superior eyre' was coined by Professor Bertha Putnam. For comments on this see Powell, *Kingship*, pp. 63–4.
25 M. Hastings, *The Court of Common Pleas in Fifteenth Century England* (New York, Columbia University Press, 1947), pp. 21–2; W. M. Ormrod, 'York and the Crown under the first three Edwards', in S. Rees Jones (ed.), *The Government of Medieval York*, Borthwick Studies in History, 3 (York, 1997), pp. 14–33.
26 *CCR 1307-13*, p. 231; D. J. M. Higgins, 'Judges in government and society in the reign of Edward II', unpublished DPhil thesis, University of Oxford, 1987, p. 39.
27 *RP*, vol. 1, p. 178; *SCCKB*, vol. 2, p. cl ('avant la venue de noz iustices erranz serra comme beverage devant medecine').
28 Cambridge (1299), Cornwall (1302), Durham (1303), Kent (1314–14), London (1321): Crook, 'Later eyres', pp. 245, 248–9.
29 Musson, *Public Order*, pp. 88–92, 98–100, 107–110.
30 *Ibid.*, pp. 118–21.
31 This apparent decline may have stemmed from the regularity of general commissions and procedural advances, although of course it may be a reflection of the clerk's failure to enrol them rather than any real drop in interest. For important changes in the assize of novel disseisin see Musson and Ormrod, *Evolution*, pp. 122–5; and more generally D. W. Sutherland, *The Assize of Novel Disseisin* (Oxford, Clarendon Press, 1973).
32 *CCR 1302-7*, pp. 89–90.
33 *Ancient Petitions Relating to Northumberland*, ed. C. M. Fraser, Surtees Society, 176 (Durham, 1966), pp. 115–16.
34 *RP*, vol. 1, p. 161. The response was that Lambert Threekingham would expedite them.
35 Higgins, 'Judges in government', p. 60.
36 Musson, *Public Order*, p. 117; Higgins, 'Judges in government', pp. 52–3.
37 See 4 Edward III, c. 2 (*SR,*, vol. 1, p. 261).
38 Musson, *Public Order*, pp. 102–14.
39 *CPR 1292-1301*, p. 338; *CPR 1301-7*, pp. 352, 354, 542–3; *CPR 1307-14*, pp. 243–4.
40 For 1321 (17 counties) and 1328 (16 counties) see *CPR 1317-21*, pp. 548–9; *CPR 1327-30*, p. 297.
41 *CPR 1330-4*, pp. 133–4; *CPR 1340-3*, pp. 106, 108, 111–13, 204.
42 R. W. Kaeuper, 'Law and order in fourteenth century England: the evidence of special commissions of oyer and terminer', *Speculum*, 54 (1979), pp. 734–84.
43 The number of mandates relating to a particular county may not be entirely representative of the keepers' apparent activity (or inactivity), though they provide some indication of government response to requests for deliveries.
44 PRO MS JUST 1/309 m2, 2d.

45 Musson, *Public Order*, pp. 17, 56–74.
46 *Proceedings before the Justices of the Peace in the Fourteenth and Fifteenth Centuries*, ed. B. H. Putnam (London, Ames Foundation, 1938), pp. 149–77 (for Somerset, 1338–41); *Some Sessions of the Peace in Cambridgeshire in the Fourteenth Century, 1340, 1380–3*, ed. M. M. Taylor, Cambridge Antiquarian Society, 55 (Cambridge, 1942), pp. 1–40 (for Cambridge, 1340). Complaints were made in Suffolk (PRO MS SC 8/73/3605), which resulted in two commissions (*CPR 1338–40*, p. 279).
47 W. M. Ormrod, 'Edward III's government of England, *c.*1346–1356', unpublished DPhil thesis, University of Oxford, 1984, pp. 189–93.
48 PRO MS KB 27/482 m3.
49 *SCCKB* vol. 6, pp. x–xii; B. H. Putnam, *The Place in Legal History of Sir William Shareshull* (Cambridge, Cambridge University Press, 1950), pp. 70–5.
50 Putnam, *Proceedings*, p. lxiv; A. Harding, 'The revolt against the justices', in R. H. Hilton and T. H. Aston (eds), *The English Rising of 1381* (Cambridge, Cambridge University Press, 1981), pp. 182–3.
51 For instance, eyres proclaimed in Kent and Durham in 1333: Crook, 'Later eyres', p. 265; F. Bryant, 'The financial dealings of Edward III with the county communities', *EHR*, 83 (1968), pp. 763–4.
52 For example: PRO MS SC 8/327/E832: claimed that no assizes had been held in Gloucs., Herefs., Salop, Worcs., or Warks. for twelve years since last held by Henry Spigurnel. His last commission appears to have been 24 October 1324. Contrary to the petition, over the next decade eleven commissions were issued for assizes in the region (PRO MS C 66/161–186). Confirmation of assize sessions held in these counties between 1326 and 1340 can be found in PRO MSS JUST 1/1394, 1403, 970, 292, 310, 1406 and 1413.
53 *RP,* vol. 2, 167 (19); A. J. Verduyn, 'The attitude of the parliamentary commons to law and order under Edward III', unpublished DPhil thesis, University of Oxford, 1991, pp. 103–4.
54 See 6 Richard II c. 5 (*SR*, vol. 2, p. 27). This provision was criticised in 1388 (*RP*, vol. 3, p. 247(33)).
55 The following analysis is based on PRO MS JUST 3/145, 150, 151, 152, 153, 156, 166, 172.
56 R. B. Pugh, 'The duration of criminal trials in medieval England', in E. W. Ives and A. H. Manchester (eds), *Law, Litigants and the Legal Profession* (London, Royal Historical Society, 1983), pp. 104–15.
57 Powell, *Kingship*, p. 56; G. L. Harriss, 'Political society and the growth of government in late medieval England', *P&P*, 138 (1993), pp. 33–4.
58 M. M. Taylor, 'Justices of assize', in J. F. Willard, W. A. Morris and W. H. Dunham (eds), *The English Government at Work, 1327–1336*, 3 vols (Cambridge, MA, Medieval Academy of America, 1940–50), vol. 3, pp. 240–1.
59 Verduyn, 'Attitude', pp. 129–30.
60 *CPR 1370–4*, pp. 310–11, 388, 487; *CPR 1374–7*, pp. 141, 144, 150. The patent roll is missing for the first half of 1372.
61 E. Powell, 'The administration of justice in late-medieval England: peace sessions

and assizes', in R. Eales and D. Sullivan (eds), *The Political Context of Law* (London, Hambledon Press, 1987), pp. 54-5.
62 Kaeuper, 'Special commissions', pp. 746-7; Musson and Ormrod, *Evolution*, pp. 120-1.
63 Verduyn, 'Attitude', p. 103.
64 See 25 Edward III st. 2, c. 7.
65 Putnam, *Proceedings*, p. 82. The date of the first session recorded on the roll is 22 July 1351.
66 Gaol delivery sessions were, however, held on or near the feastday of St Margaret in 1356-9: *Sessions of the Peace for Bedfordshire, 1355-1359, 1363-1364*, ed. E. G. Kimball, Bedfordshire Historical Records Society, 48 (1969), p. 15 n.7; Putnam, *Proceedings*, p. 58.
67 *Essex Sessions of the Peace, 1351, 1377-1379*, ed. E. C. Furber, Essex Archeological Society, 3 (Colchester, 1953), p. 27; *Some Sessions of the Peace in Lincolnshire, 1360-75*, ed. R. Sillem, Lincoln Record Society, 30 (Lincoln, 1937), p. xxviii; Putnam, *Proceedings*, pp. 195 (Somerset), 289 (Staffs.), 378 (Suffolk). The nearest to a statutory date is a session held at Taunton on 4 December 1357.
68 See 36 Edward III st. 1, c. 12.
69 Kimball, *Bedfordshire Sessions*, p. 14; Putnam, *Proceedings*, pp. 122-3 (Norfolk), 208 (Hants.), 289 (Staffs.), 378 (Suffolk); *Rolls of the Gloucestershire Sessions of the Peace, 1361-1398*, ed. E. G. Kimball, Transactions of the Bristol and Gloucester Archaeological Society, 62 (Gloucester, 1940), pp. 33, 54-5.
70 *Rolls of the Warwickshire and Coventry Sessions of the Peace, 1377-1397*, ed. E. G. Kimball, Dugdale Society, 16 (1939), app. 2, pp. lxxxix-xci.
71 Furber, *Essex Sessions*, p. 28; Sillem, *Lincolnshire Sessions*, pp. xxviii-xxix.
72 *CPR 1367-70*, p. 265.
73 Scotter, Burton on Stather, Epworth, Louth, Partney, Wragby and Lincoln.
74 Sillem, *Lincolnshire Sessions*, pp. xxvii-xxviii.
75 *Ibid.*, p. xxix. Some sessions may have been continuations since they were held a week later at the same venue.
76 Furber, *Essex Sessions*, p. 28: Braintree, Brentwood, Chelmsford, Coggeshall, Colchester, Dunmow, Manningtree, Saffron Walden, Thaxted and Witham.
77 Powell, *Kingship*, pp. 48-50.
78 J. H. Langbein, 'The origins of public prosecution at common law', *AJLH*, 17 (1974), pp. 131-5.
79 *Crown Pleas of the Wiltshire Eyre, 1249*, ed. C. A. F. Meekings, Wiltshire Record Society, 16 (Devizes, 1960), pp. 27-33; R. E. Latham and C. A. F. Meekings, 'The veredictum of the Chippenham hundred, 1281', in N. J. Williams (ed.), *Collectanea*, Wiltshire Archeological Society, 12 (Devizes, 1956), pp. 50-1. The Articles of the Eyre are also printed in *SR*, vol. 1, p. 232.
80 The Articles of the Tourn are given in the Statute of Wales: 12 Edward I c. 4 (*SR*, vol. 1, pp. 57-8). See also J. Beckerman, 'The articles of presentment of a court leet and court baron in English, c. 1400', *BIHR*, 47 (1974), pp. 230-4; and see (above) Chapter 3.
81 *RP*, vol. 1, p. 178; A. Harding, 'Early trailbaston proceedings from the Lincoln roll

of 1305', in R. F. Hunnisett and J. B. Post (eds), *Medieval Legal Records Edited in Memory of C. A. F. Meekings* (London, HMSO, 1978), pp. 144-5.

82 *RP*, vol. 1, p. 183; *SR*, vol. 1, p. 145; A. Harding, 'The origins of the crime of conspiracy', *TRHS* 5th series, 33 (1983), p. 97.

83 *The 1341 Royal Inquest in Lincolnshire*, ed. B W. McLane, Lincoln Record Society, 78 (Woodbridge, 1988), pp. xiii, xxviii–xxix.

84 Importance was attached to finding out whether Harclay made them affirm their vow by oath or in writing, no doubt with a view to prosecuting for treason.

85 *South Lancashire in the Reign of Edward II*, ed. G. Tupling, Chetham Society, 3rd series, 1 (Manchester, 1949), pp. xli, 2–6. For the relevance of the local concerns see pp. xlii–li.

86 Ordinance (1349) and Statute of Labourers (1351), and as amended by the Statute of Cambridge of 1378.

87 Putnam, *Proceedings*, pp. 10–20, 23; Kimball, *Gloucestershire Sessions*, p. 47; Kimball, *Warwickshire Sessions*, pp. lvi–lxv.

88 For some discussion of the phenomenon (of non-appearance at trial and prosecutions that did not lead to a conviction) and further references see Powell, *Kingship*, pp. 77, 181–8.

89 Latham and Meekings, 'Chippenham hundred', p. 54.

90 University of Leeds, International Medieval Congress, 1999, unpublished paper by S. Stewart, 'The hundred jurors of Surrey in the thirteenth century'.

91 K. Asaji, 'The Barons' War and the hundred jurors in Cambridgeshire', *JMH*, 21 (1995), pp. 163–4.

92 Latham and Meekings, 'Chippenham hundred', pp. 56–7.

93 J. B. Post, 'Some limitations of the medieval peace rolls', *Journal of the Society of Archivists*, 4 (1973), pp. 633–9.

94 A. Musson, 'Twelve good men and true? The character of early fourteenth-century juries', *LHR*, 15 (1997), pp. 118–20.

95 Musson, *Public Order*, pp. 176–8.

96 PRO MS JUST 3/156 m21.

97 D. Crook, 'Triers and the origin of the grand jury', *JLH*, 12 (1991), pp. 103–16; Musson, 'Twelve good men', pp. 123–6.

98 A. J. Musson, 'Turning king's evidence: the prosecution of crime in late medieval England', *OJLS*, 19 (1999), pp. 467–79.

99 F. C. Hamil, 'The king's approvers', *Speculum*, 11 (1936), pp. 238–58; H. R. T. Summerson, 'The criminal underworld of medieval England', *JLH*, 17 (1996), pp. 197–224.

100 M. H. Kerr, 'Angevin reform of the appeal of felony', *LHR*, 13 (1995), pp. 356–9.

101 See Musson, 'Turning king's evidence', p. 475 (Table 1). Naturally their confessions should not be taken wholly at face value by researchers: H. Rohrkasten, 'Some problems of the evidence of fourteenth century approvers', *JLH*, 5 (1984), pp. 14–22; J. B. Post, 'The evidential value of approvers' appeals: the case of William Rose, 1389', *LHR*, 3 (1985), pp. 91–100.

102 Musson and Ormrod, *Evolution*, pp. 78–81, 84–5, 102–6.

103 A. J. Prescott, 'Judicial records of the 1381 rising', unpublished PhD thesis,

University of London, 1984, pp. 234-40; S. Justice, *Writing and Rebellion: England in 1381* (Berkeley, Los Angeles and London, University of California Press, 1994), pp. 64-5, 68.
104 Latham and Meekings, 'Chippenham hundred', p. 54.
105 See 2 Richard II st. 1, c. 6 and st. 2 (repeal of c. 6); (*SR*, vol. 2, pp. 9-10, 12)
106 *SCCKB*, vol. 3, pp. lxxii-lxxiv; D. Klerman, 'Settlement and decline of private prosecution in thirteenth-century England', (forthcoming). I am grateful to the author for an advance copy.
107 Proof for an appeal of felony originally had to be trial by battle (see below).
108 N. Hurnard, *King's Pardon for Homicide in England to A.D. 1307* (Oxford, Clarendon Press, 1969), pp. 172, 194.
109 Klerman, 'Settlement and decline': it is possible that this reflects settlement of at least a quarter of all cases.
110 J. B. Post, 'Ravishment of women and the statutes of Westminster', in J. H. Baker (ed.), *Legal Records and the Historian* (London, Royal Historical Society, 1978), pp. 152, 158.
111 For some fourteenth-century evidence, see Musson, *Public Order*, pp. 170-1.
112 *SCCKB*, vol. 3, pp. lxxii-lxxiv.
113 Klerman, 'Settlement and decline'; Musson, *Public Order*, pp. 171-2.
114 Through regression analysis Professor Klerman has achieved a correlation between respect for settlement and the rate of appeals.
115 A. Harding, 'Plaints and bills in the history of English law', in D. Jenkins (ed.) *Legal History Studies 1972* (Cardiff, University of Wales, 1975), pp. 74-6.
116 Powell, *Kingship*, pp. 71-2.
117 *SCCKB*, vol. 2, pp. lxxxvi-lxxxviii.
118 *Early Registers of Writs*, ed. E. de Haas and G. D. G. Hall, SS, 87 (London, 1970), pp. xviii-xix, cxxvii-cxxviii.
119 *SCCKB*, vol. 1, pp. 173-4, 175-6.
120 See below concerning writs of trespass on the case.
121 Under the Provisions of Oxford of 1258 the chancery clerks were not allowed to issue writs that had not been authorised by the king and council.
122 *Early Registers of Writs*, pp. xxi, cxxii.
123 H. C. Maxwell-Lyte, *Historical Notes on the Use of the Great Seal of England* (London, HMSO, 1926), p. 296.
124 *YB 3 & 4 Edward II*, p. 162.
125 See 6 Edward I c. 8 (Statute of Gloucester); J. S. Beckerman, 'The forty-shilling jurisdictional limit in medieval English personal actions', in Jenkins (ed.), *Legal History Studies*, pp. 110-17.
126 A. Musson, 'New labour laws, new remedies? Legal reaction to the Black Death "crisis"', in N. Saul (ed.), *Fourteenth Century Studies* (Woodbridge, Boydell Press, 2000).
127 A. Kiralfy, *The Action on the Case* (London, Sweet & Maxwell, 951); R. C. Palmer, *English Law in the Age of the Black Death, 1348-1381: a Transformation of Governance and Law* (Chapel Hill, NC, University of North Carolina Press, 1993), pp. 169-293.

128 *Brevia Placitata*, ed. G. J. Turner, SS, 66 (London, 1951), p. xliv-xlvii; R. C. Palmer, *The County Courts of Medieval England, 1150-1350* (Princeton, NJ, Princeton University Press, 1982), pp. 225-6; *Calendar of Early Mayor's Court Rolls, 1298-1307*, ed. A. H. Thomas (Cambridge, Cambridge University Press, 1924), pp. xxvii-xxviii.

129 An oral complaint based on an established original writ was sometimes admitted if the injury alleged occurred 'within the summons of the eyre' (see *Select Cases of Procedure Without Writ under Henry III*, ed. H. G. Richardson and G. O. Sayles, SS, 60 (London, 1941), p. 137; Harding, 'Plaints and bills', p. 57).

130 A. H. Hershey, 'Justice and bureaucracy: the English royal writ', *EHR*, 113 (1998), pp. 829-51.

131 *Select Bills in Eyre, AD 1292-1333*, ed. W. C. Bolland, SS, 30 (London, 1914), *passim*; Harding, 'Plaints and bills', p. 75. It is not clear whether oral plaints were made in English.

132 Harding, 'Plaints and bills', p. 75.

133 Kiralfy, *Action on the Case*, pp. 45-8. For example: PRO MS KB 27/354 m. 85 (Yorks.) – the well-known Humber Ferryman Case (1348).

134 Brand, *Making*, pp. 98-101; J. H. Baker, *An Introduction to English Legal History*, 3rd edn (London, Butterworths, 1990), pp. 170-1.

135 Harding, 'Early trailbaston', pp. 144-5.

136 Powell, *Kingship*, pp. 71-2. The enrolment of appeals as indictments was a way of ensuring that the appeals were not made maliciously.

137 *SCCKB*, vol. 3, pp. lvii-lxxi; *Early Register of Writs*, pp. cxxxiv-cxxxv; Harding, 'Origins of conspiracy', pp. 95-7.

138 McLane, *1341 Royal Inquest*, pp. xiii-xiv, xxvii.

139 Verduyn, 'Attitude', p. 97; Musson and Ormrod, *Evolution*, pp. 180-1.

140 J. R. Maddicott, 'Parliament and the constituencies', in R. G. Davies and J. H. Denton, *The English Parliament in the Middle Ages* (Manchester, Manchester University Press, 1981), pp. 64-9.

141 *The Roll of the Shropshire Eyre of 1256*, ed. A. Harding, SS, 96 (London, 1980), pp. xxii-xxiii.

142 *Ibid.*, p. xxiii.

143 *Ibid.*, p. xxiv; see also A. Harding, 'The revolt against the justices', in Hilton and Aston (eds), *English Rising*, pp. 169, 173-4.

144 Richardson and Sayles, *Procedure without Writ*, pp. 49-57.

145 Harding, *Shropshire Eyre*, p. xliii: *ad audiendum omnes querelas de transgressionibus quibuscunque factis*.

146 N. M. Fryde, 'Edward III's removal of his ministers and judges, 1340-1', *BIHR*, 48 (1975), pp. 148-9.

147 G. L. Harriss, 'Political society and the growth of government in late medieval England', *P&P*, 138 (1993), p. 32.

148 Holt, *Magna Carta*, pp. 1, 149-3, 327.

149 See 25 Edward III c. 4, 28 Edward III c. 3, 42 Edward III c. 3 (*SR*, vol. 1, pp. 321, 345, 388).

150 D. Carpenter, *The Reign of Henry III* (London, Hambledon Press, 1996), pp.

328-9. See also Chapter 2.
151 *SCCKB*, vol. 7, pp. lxv-lxvi. The plaintiffs were clearly asking for an equitable remedy, but it was felt that since they could afford serjeants to act for them their alleged poverty was a fiction.
152 Brand, *Making*, p. 184.
153 Brand, *Origins*, pp. 91-4; B. W. McLane, 'Changes in the court of king's bench, 1291-1340: the preliminary view from Lincolnshire', in W. M. Ormrod (ed.), *England in the Fourteenth Century: Proceedings of the 1985 Harlaxton Symposium* (Woodbridge, Boydell Press, 1986), pp. 159-60.
154 *CLBCL: Letter Book G*, p. 74; P. Tucker, 'London's courts of law in the fifteenth century', in C. W. Brooks and M. Lobban (eds), *Communities and Courts in Britain, 1150-1900* (London, Hambledon Press, 1997), p. 33.
155 Bolland, *Select Bills in Eyre*, p. 119.
156 Brand, *Origins*, pp. 104-5.
157 Bolland, *Select Bills in Eyre*, p. 21.
158 J. C. Davies, 'Common law writs and returns, Richard I to Richard II', *BIHR*, 26 (1953), pp. 139-42; B. Wilkinson, *The Chancery under Edward III* (Manchester, Manchester University Press, 1929), pp. 60-2.
159 See 13 Edward I (Statute of Westminster) c. 44 (*SR*, vol. 1, p. 93); Brand, *Making*, p. 183 and n.81: Dr Brand points out that the sum of 7*d* per writ was paid by the prior of Norwich in 1283, and hence the 'rise' may in some cases have been illusory.
160 Wilkinson, *Chancery*, p. 60.
161 *RP*, vol. II, pp. 170, 229-30, 241, 261, 305; Verduyn, 'Attitude', pp. 133-4.
162 *RP*, vol. 1, p. 376; *CCR 1341-3*, p. 633; Wilkinson, *Chancery*, pp. 61-2.
163 Kaeuper, 'Special commissions', pp. 734-84.
164 Based on an analysis of *Calendars of Patent Rolls 1377-99*.
165 The common form and language of some bills suggests that some legally skilled person drafted them: payment might then have been required, but the evidence is lacking.
166 McLane, 'Court of king's bench', pp. 158-9.
167 The unusually high frequency of visitations may have created special conditions in Lincolnshire which would mean these findings are not necessarily applicable to other counties.
168 *Selected Rolls of the Chester City Courts*, ed. A. Hopkins, Chetham Society, 3rd series, 2 (Manchester, 1950), pp. lv, 41, 54; Harding, 'Plaints and bills', p. 70.
169 PRO MS KB 27/272 *Rex* m21 (Northamptonshire – Emma Watecok).
170 Kaeuper, 'Special commissions', p. 757; Brand, *Making*, p. 184.
171 S. Sheridan Walker, 'Wrongdoing and compensation: the pleas of wardship in thirteenth and fourteenth century England', *JLH*, 9 (1988), p. 289.
172 For example: PRO MS JUST 1/1395 m10: John Whyshele of Abingdon, found to have assaulted Walter Godusglade, was liable to pay one shilling in damages until he was excused.
173 *Bracton on the Laws and Customs of England*, ed. S. E. Thorne, 4 vols (Cambridge, MA., Harvard University Press, 1968-77); *The London Eyre of 1244*, ed. H. Cam, London Record Society, 6 (London, 1970), p. 134 (no. 345).

174 Some of the early law reports may not in fact have been based on discussions in the courtroom: P. Brand, 'The beginnings of English law reporting', in C. Stebbings (ed.), *Law Reporting in Britain* (London, Hambledon Press, 1995), pp. 1–14.
175 Brand, *Origins*, p. 67.
176 For example: Turner, *Brevia Placitata*; see also *Four Thirteenth-Century Law Tracts*, ed. G. E. Woodbine (London, Oxford University Press, 1910), p. 162.
177 *CLBCL: Letter book G*, p. 73.
178 See 36 Edward III st. 1, c. 15 (*SR*, vol. 2, pp. 375–6).
179 This is a matter upon which I am currently engaged in further research.
180 For what follows see Clanchy, *Memory*, pp. 206–9.
181 *Select Canterbury Cases, c.1200–1301*, ed. N. Adams and C. Donahue, SS, 95 (London, 1981), pp. *48–9*, 119, 390.
182 For example: *YB 2 Edward II*, pp. 11, 36; *YB 12 & 13 Edward III*, p. 274. We should, however, be wary of reading too much into the law reports since some early ones ascribe dialogue to the parties rather than to the serjeants who must have spoken for them: Brand, 'English law reporting', p. 4.
183 P. Brand, 'Inside the courtroom: lawyers, litigants and justices in England in the later Middle Ages', in P. Coss (ed.), *The Moral World of the Law* (Cambridge, Cambridge University Press, 2000), pp. 107–11.
184 P. R. Schofield, 'Peasants and the manor court: gossip and litigation in a Suffolk village at the close of the thirteenth century', *P&P*, 159 (1998), 1–42.
185 Harding, 'Revolt against the justices', p. 191.
186 P. Hyams, *King, Lords and Peasants in Medieval England* (Oxford, Oxford University Press, 1980), pp. 125–51; Kaeuper, 'Special commissions', p. 752; R. Faith, 'The "great rumour" of 1377 and peasant ideology', in Hilton and Aston (eds), *The English Rising of 1381*, pp. 43–73.
187 M. K. McIntosh, 'The privileged villeins of the English ancient demesne', *Viator*, 7 (1976), pp. 325–6; Carpenter, *Henry III*, pp. 229–32.
188 B. Tierney, 'The Decretists and the "deserving poor"', *Comparative Studies in Society and History*, 1 (1958–9), pp. 360–73; M. Rubin, *Charity and Community in Medieval Cambridge* (Cambridge, Cambridge University Press, 1987), pp. 68–74; C. Dyer, *Standards of Living in the Later Middle Ages* (Cambridge, Cambridge University Press, 1989), pp. 236–40.
189 Bolland, *Select Bills*, pp. 6, 44, 47.
190 Brand, *Origins*, pp. 153–4; J. Brundage, 'Legal aid for the poor and the professionalization of law in the Middle Ages', *JLH*, 9 (1988), pp. 174–5.
191 D. Wilkins, *Concilia Magnae Britanniae et Hiberniae*, 4 vols (Brussels, Londini, 1964), vol. 2, p. 206.
192 *Ibid.*, p. 418.
193 Statutes from Modena, Bologna and Ferrara indicate a willingness on the part of civic authorities to provide public lawyers for the poor, financed out of tax revenues (Brundage, 'Legal aid', 174–5).
194 J. M. Maguire, 'Poverty and civil litigation', *Harvard Law Review*, 36 (1923), pp. 361–404.
195 See for instance 'An outlaw's song of trailbaston' in R. B. Dobson and J. Taylor

(eds), *Rymes of Robin Hood: an Introduction to the English Outlaw*, rev. edn (Stroud, Alan Sutton, 1997), pp. 251-4.
196 Technically, a woman was 'waived' rather than 'outlawed'.
197 Hastings, *Common Pleas*, pp. 180-3.
198 H. R. T. Summerson, 'The structure of law enforcement in thirteenth century England', *AJLH*, 23 (1979), pp. 313-27.
199 See 18 Edward III st. 2, c. 5 (no *exigent* to go out unless felony or trespass against the peace); 25 Edward III st. 5, c. 17 (process of *exigent* in debt detinue and replevin); 37 Edward III c. 2 (indemnity for injustices and mistakes because of outlawry) (*SR,* vol. 1, pp. 301, 322, 378).
200 See for example: G. L. Harriss, *King, Parliament and Public Finance in Medieval England* (Oxford, Clarendon Press, 1975), pp. 354-5; R. W. Kaeuper, *War, Justice and Public Order* (Oxford, Clarendon Press, 1988), pp. 386-7; R. H. Hilton, *Class Conflict and the Crisis of Feudalism*, rev. edn (London, Hambledon Press, 1990), pp. 49-65, 173-9; Palmer, *English Law*. The quotation is from Justice, *Writing and Rebellion*, p. 62.
201 E. Clark, 'Medieval labor law and English local courts', *AJLH*, 23 (1983), pp. 330-53; M. J. Hettinger, 'The role of the Statute of Labourers in the social and economic background of the great revolt in East Anglia', unpublished PhD thesis, University of Indiana, 1986, pp. 171-2, 198, 204; S. H. Rigby, *English Society in the Later Middle Ages: Class, Status and Gender* (Basingstoke, Macmillan, 1995), pp. 37-8.

5

The role of parliament

THE emergence of parliament as an important forum for legal and political matters was a significant feature of the period 1215–1381. Parliament provided a focal point where views were expressed on issues of constitutional import connected to the Crown's jurisdiction and the nature of royal governance, on problems of law and order and on many other issues within a judicial context. Its essence was discussion and debate, both of which were fostered not only in parliament, but also beyond, in the towns and shires. For those taking an interest in its decisions and law-making business (whether or not they attended in person) parliament acted as a catalyst for legal thought, provoking suggestions for reform and legislative impulses, some of which have been captured in surviving memoranda.[1] Reflection on the rapidly evolving institution and the processes associated with it equally produced the views and attempts at definitions that form the 'quasi-legal treatise' known as the *Modus tenendi parliamentum*.[2]

In the thirteenth century, the idea of national assemblies to discuss the affairs of the realm and the dispensation of justice on such occasions was not novel. Anglo-Saxon 'witans' and Anglo-Norman 'great councils' were well-established features in the conduct of royal government, while the use of such a body to decide complex or significant law suits was a familiar, if not routine, recourse. Over the course of the thirteenth and fourteenth centuries, however, the assembly itself, its purposes, functions and essential personnel altered in nature, scope and rationale. The *ad hoc* meetings known in the early thirteenth century as 'parliament' (describing their purpose, which was discussion) developed an institutional form as both a venue for discussion and an aspect of royal government. The institution, which by the late fourteenth century had expanded its membership, agenda and influence, comprised a distinct body of people who, when assembled and in agreement, offered the support of the 'community of the realm' to designated royal actions. Parliament, therefore, embodied for medieval people a triune nature: an occasion or venue for discussion of royal business (and at times popular concerns), a wing of royal government (possessing a combination of fiscal, judicial and political functions), and a collection of particular people and particular groups of people providing through their pool of knowledge and experience an element of national consciousness.[3]

By the end of the fourteenth century two distinct groups of delegates were clearly visible, the Commons (attending as community representatives) and the Lords (summoned personally by the king). Representatives of the lower clergy were frequently required to attend, as were the archbishops, bishops and prelates, although they also held their own separate 'convocation'. In the thirteenth century the Commons' attendance was infrequent and not necessarily associated with legislative concerns. As early as 1213, though, small numbers of knights were summoned 'to speak with us on the affairs of the kingdom', and in 1227 to expound 'on behalf of all the county' grievances against the implementation of Magna Carta. This trend was consolidated in the 1250s and 1260s – the years of baronial domination – and brought a widening of the representative element required for consent to taxation. Under Edward I the summoning of representatives was regularised and about the 1320s (during Edward II's reign) petitions of general interest purporting to be from the 'community of the realm' were submitted and entertained. In the course of Edward III's fifty-year reign it became standard practice for the knights of the shire and burgesses to assent to taxation in return for the redress of specific grievances, which were presented in the form of common petitions. Elements of these were frequently incorporated in royal statutes. Parliament itself gathered fiscal and political overtones and its sessions became something of a 'sounding-board' for public opinion.[4]

Much has been written on the evolution of parliament and its functioning as an institution, on the legal doctrines and justifications underpinning different types of taxation and notions of consent.[5] This chapter does not seek to duplicate that work, but rather explores the part played by parliament in providing a forum for 'justice', in utilising legal knowledge, in acting as a focal point for legal initiatives and, more generally, in furthering legal consciousness. It considers, firstly, the judicial importance of parliament, which lay in its role as a forum for petitions, as a court of appeal, as a tribunal for the resolution of difficult cases and as a venue for state trials. The main analytical focus, however, is on the personnel summoned to and attending sessions of parliament. It was they who helped shape these occasions, the processes and nature of the institution and, in turn, the attitudes displayed in it. Assessing the extent and impact of the legal expertise among parliament's constituent members (Commons, Lords and officials), it is argued that those with legal know-how and parliamentary experience played an important part in consultative exercises and in the passage of statute legislation (particularly legislation concerning the law and the judicial system) at every juncture. Finally, this chapter looks at the interaction between local and national legislation and assesses briefly the reciprocal influences on its form and content, the growing tendency towards written legislation and its effects on the wider populace.

The high court of parliament

Judicial matters represented a significant element of parliamentary business. As the anonymous legal treatise *Fleta* (*c.*1290) acknowledged: 'The king has his court in his council in his parliaments ... [where] are terminated doubts concerning judgments, and new remedies are devised for new wrongs which have arisen, and justice is done to each one according to his deserts.'[6] Parliament (or a committee of the upper house) heard cases which had been transferred on appeal from king's bench or other courts and dealt with particularly troublesome disputes (in the sense that the common law did not provide a clear remedy or because there was disagreement over procedure) which had been referred to the king in parliament, either by the body hearing the case or by the parties themselves. In a case before the court of common pleas in 1332 the judges were unwilling to give judgment until the 'commune conseil' of parliament had been sought,[7] while in 1339 it was clear that 'the general opinion of the king's council and all the justices' had been obtained.[8]

The king's council, an inner circle of ministers and justices, sometimes had cases of a particular nature reserved for hearings before it, usually those involving serious violence, instances of fraud (forged charters, false claims, counterfeit money, malicious indictments and the like), accusations of heresy, sorcery and witchcraft, maritime and mercantile disputes and litigation concerning 'uses' (precursors to modern-day trusts). Parliament also became the venue for the staging of state trials, which in the fourteenth century were initiated through the process of impeachment (see Chapters 2 and 6). The Good Parliament of 1376 was particularly spectacular in this respect since the Commons forced the Crown to submit various courtiers and financiers to the judicial scrutiny of the Lords.[9]

The dispensation of justice by providing responses to petitions was one of the most significant aspects of parliament. Edward I had originally encouraged petitioning in parliament as a way of providing redress for individuals and as a means of facilitating royal government in the shires.[10] Under Edward II the knights and burgesses attending parliament to assent to taxation began to articulate specific grievances and draw up lists of demands. As a result, petitions containing matters deemed to be of common interest to the realm (in that their contents concerned the law of the land or the welfare of people) came to be an established part of parliamentary procedure outside the normal realm of private petitioning. By the mid-fourteenth century, when parliament had become predominantly a fiscal and political institution, the Commons used their control over taxation to extract concessions from the Crown. The adoption of the complaints and remedies outlined in the common petitions as a basis for the formulation of legislation in turn transformed the nature and content of statutes. While there was sometimes a reluctance on the part of the king to have recourse to parliament, by Edward III's reign parliament came to be seen as the appropriate forum for legislative activity.

Men of law may have helped with the subject-matter and the drafting of common petitions, but there are evidential problems in pinning down specific drafting to specific individuals. In the absence of direct evidence as to who composed the petitions, the context in which petitions originated may provide some pointers. Although we have no particular names, enough research has been carried out on private petitions presented in the parliaments of this period to make it evident that provincial lawyers were crucial to the whole process: the composer of a petition not only needed to be able to write (usually in Anglo-Norman French), but had also to understand the appropriate formulae for such quasi-legal documents. The petitions of towns may have been drawn up by scriveners – men who were often intermediaries between the public and the law and who increasingly in the late fourteenth century were advising on the substance of the law as well as preparing documents that fitted its formal requirements.[11]

There is a difference of course between the ability merely to draft or record ideas and that of coming up with or preparing suggestions. To try to identify those who drafted common petitions, it is worth considering the role of the county court in the articulation of local grievances and the formulation of petitions. The variety of functions fulfilled by this court – judicial, administrative, political and social – made it a natural and regular point of contact between local landed society and provincial men of law. Under Magna Carta, 'four knights' were to be elected in the county court, to join the royal justices sitting at assize sessions and inquiring into the wrongdoing of local officials.[12] Furthermore, since the county court was where that the stewards of lords acted as suitors and parliamentary representatives were selected for the shires, it is reasonable to suppose that it was in and around the monthly meetings that many of those who intended to send petitions to parliament sought out the legal services needed to set such a process in motion and nominated those most likely to represent their concerns effectively. The formal setting of the county courts was by no means, though, necessarily the only place that those interested in submitting petitions might meet and discuss their ideas and drafts: some communication on these matters might take place while performing judicial and administrative services on commissions or juries, witnessing legal documents or, more informally, at feasts and family gatherings, tournaments and hunting parties.[13]

Petitioning had advantages both for the Crown and its subjects. Petitions provided the Crown with a means of monitoring royal government and the exercise of justice as well as offering constructive local feedback on policies and administrative difficulties. The method gave individuals and particular groups the opportunity to vent their concerns, suggest changes, and request new judicial initiatives or a better service. It would be naive to assume that common petitions were unbiased and altruistic in their motives. Nevertheless, we should not lose sight of the capacity of individual petitions to accord with a more general mood or notion, nor for there to be co-operation between corporations or groups of counties. Petitions submitted by the counties in the Scottish and Welsh marches demonstrate that MPs could use parliament as a focal point for issues such as law and order – matters that could be presented as regional concerns.[14] While it was general parliamentary practice that petitions were composed before the parliamentary session, not every petition was compiled outside parliament: some were the product of parliamentary discussion.[15] In such cases there was obviously an immediacy and topicality to the issue and an opportunity (if necessary) for those gathered at the centre to initiate or influence the debate.

The requirement for assent to taxation and the concomitant expansion of the petitioning process did not mean that the king was forced to grant the petitions 'on the nod' or that statutes were dependent upon or forthcoming only after an influx of common petitions.[16] Legislative initiatives and grants of taxation were frequently coincident with bursts of promulgations and it is often difficult to divorce the two. Yet some caution should be used in the way the process is described: the bargaining aspect in particular should not be over-emphasised. Dispensation of justice in parliament was after all part of the monarch's duty.[17] This point is particularly pertinent to the development of the peace commissions during the fourteenth century. In a general sense the fiscal imperatives of war influenced the course of, and changes in, judicial administration and thus the short-term fortunes of the peace commissions. But the process was not driven by the Commons: they possessed no clear idea, consistent pattern, nor agenda on the judicial aspects of peacekeeping until the 1340s. Even then the Commons' developing agenda deviated from royal policy on what were sometimes fundamental points of detail. During the 1350s and 1360s, however, there was an atmosphere of co-operation, which is more adequately reflected in the statutes.[18]

Moreover, we should not assume that the flow of private petitioning had totally dried up by the mid-fourteenth century. In the closing years of the 1370s, for instance there were forty-nine private petitions presented in 1377, sixty-eight in the following year and thirty-seven in 1379. From an analysis of the nature of these requests it appears that the majority were from named individuals regarding property disputes. It is clear, therefore, that in the later fourteenth century parliament continued to be an important forum for obtaining legal redress, especially with regard to difficult cases before the courts, through the medium of the private petition.[19]

The legal personnel of parliament

What was the strength and influence of the legal element in parliament during the fourteenth century? Men of law had a significant impact on the shape and character of legislation at all stages of its creation and gestation. In fact at probably no other time in the evolution of parliamentary processes were men of law so predominant in number and so able to influence the nature of legislation as in the early years of statute-making. The role of the Commons in raising and debating matters of judicial administration – such as commissions to justices of the peace – has already been charted, while the possible lead taken by the legal *cognoscenti* in facilitating approvers' appeals and regulating the conduct of sheriffs and gaolers has also been exposed in published works.[20] The focus here will be on one particular legislative area, namely the concern for the composition and proper functioning of juries. The effectiveness of the jury system underpinned the functioning of the entire judicial system. Although the jury system had been in operation for over a century, the massive expansion in judicial business over the course of the thirteenth and early fourteenth centuries highlighted the pressures placed on justices, sheriffs and jurymen alike.

To facilitate comparisons of attendance and among legislative initiatives, the analysis here is based strictly on attendance at *parliaments*, that is occasions where both Lords and Commons were formally requested to be present and at which both common and private petitions were normally presented. The other main type of assembly where the Lords were augmented by representatives from the boroughs and shires,[21] and on certain occasions petitions were presented and answered, was a great council.[22] However, there were essential differences between parliaments and great councils. It was the king and the royal council who chose the delegates for a great council, not the local community: the personnel of the delegations, therefore, were those from whom the king desired specific advice. Furthermore, there was no guarantee that common petitions would be accorded a response outside a fully constituted parliament. While in time the differences between the two forms were eroded, the great council falls outside this study of personnel. That is not to imply that it was unimportant or that a legal element was insignificant. In some cases lawyers were especially invited to attend great councils, as in 1329 at Windsor where matters of law and order were on the agenda.

Turning now to the legal element itself. The word 'legal' carries the obvious implication that we are talking about 'lawyers', but what 'legal' qualities were apparent among the men attending parliament? In the fourteenth century there was a general view that parliament comprised at least some men possessing legal knowledge: for example, c. 38 of the Ordinances of 1311 stated that any doubtful provisions of Magna Carta and the Forest Charter should be clarified in parliament 'by advice of the baronage and the justices and the other wise men of the law'. Similarly, in 1322 in a letter to Edward II, Walter Stapleton, the bishop of Exeter, intimated that parliament provided the opportunity for obtaining the advice of those 'learned in the laws and customs of England'.[23] These contemporary statements are most obviously referring to the royal judges (those sitting in the courts of king's bench and common pleas) and the king's serjeants and serjeants-at-law who were at times called upon to advise the royal council or bolster the official element in parliament. This group should also include other legal officers such as the barons of the exchequer and the attorney general.

The term 'legal' should not be so narrowly defined as to encompass only those men who had formal legal qualifications or who had a recognised position in the upper levels of royal judicial administration. As emphasised already in Chapter 2, there was a broad culture to the legal profession: it included not only those who possessed a formal legal education or a recognised position in the upper levels of royal judicial administration, but also men whose legal training was gained from a variety of sources, both formal and informal, and whose experience and consequent expertise might be the product of a number of different areas of legal employment. Such a definition results in a considerable overlap between those traditionally labelled as 'gentry' or as 'lawyers'. The following discussion, therefore, looks at men, who in contributing to the development of parliament and in particular to its legislative agenda, were themselves at various levels and stages of professional development, but who had at least some understanding of legal process and administration. The Commons will be examined first, then the Lords, and from them we turn to the legal officers of the king's council and (more particularly) the royal judges.

Commons

What role did the legal element in the Commons play in the making and presenting of parliamentary petitions? It is possible to argue there was an intimate connection between petitioners and men of law. Although there is little direct evidence, four factors advance this connection: firstly, the content of the petitions submitted in parliament; secondly, the legal profile of those who were elected to serve in parliament (as knights of the shire and borough representatives); thirdly, the continuity of service observable among many representatives; and, fourthly, the emergence of the office of speaker.

The parliaments of the 1330s through to the 1360s are renowned for the amount of legislation they produced and their particular concern over matters of law and order and judicial administration. There has been a tendency among historians to view the petitions purely in political terms, but many of the issues raised were in fact technical, procedural points. A number during that period in fact related to the composition and conduct of juries. The abundance of petitions containing such issues implicitly betrays an understanding of workings of the law. Even if they appear in the official language of complaint, they were not just simple grievances, but capable of being positive, constructive documents forming a consistent agenda of reform. In certain cases they contain suggestions of necessary remedial action. Extensive legislation relating to the jury system was enacted in the 1350s and 1360s. It was preceded by some statutes in the early years of Edward III's reign, but came about largely through a sustained bout of petitioning by the Commons, particularly during the 1340s. The statutory measures promulgated in 1352, 1354, 1361, 1365 and 1368 respectively concerned both civil and criminal juries, but focused especially on presenting and trial juries, covering the process of taking indictments, the summoning and composition of jury panels and remedies against alleged instances of corruption.

The petitions received in parliament in this period – both those that were the immediate precursors of these statutes as well as those of previous years – reflected a number of these issues, though it is not appropriate here to go into great detail. The petitions on the empanelling of jurors both stressed the lack of qualifications of jurymen and alleged that sheriffs and justices were unprofessional when dealing with juries. One petition from 1334 made out that sheriffs took bribes to pervert the course of justice.[24] In 1341 it was claimed that the arrayers of juries were not following the statutory guidelines on the qualifications for jury service, nominating non-resident or indisposed men.[25] This theme was picked up again in 1354, maintaining that the jurors summoned were not men of any substance, nor from the vicinity of the claim or incident. This carried an implication that judges were not being careful enough to ensure good and competent juries. In 1354 (a claim repeated verbatim in 1355) it was also said that the sheriff or other royal official was not carrying out the array of jurors, with the result that the task was not done effectively by the bailey or his deputy.[26] Although the complaints seem to be pointing the finger at sheriffs (many of whom were serving or had served in parliament), this may in fact be recognition of the difficulties that local officers were encountering. There was obviously a concern with tightening up the system and an implication that existing practices were straying from some ideal. It is clear that legal consciousness played a large part in the presentation of petitions: representatives did so from their own knowledge and with direct experience of the difficulties in securing well-qualified jurors and of the concomitant changes in juries (see Chapter 3).

The recurring complaint was against members of the presenting jury being present on the subsequent trial jury. In 1341 and 1343 it was urged that indictors should not serve as trial jurors and that the challenge of such persons be allowed.[27] In the early years of the century there had been complaints that jury challenges were often malicious and unreasonable, impeded the prosecution, and were merely a tactical device to ensure procedural delay.[28] Confirmation of the common-law practice of jury challenges was received, but the issue was not resolved by the grant of a statute. It continued into the 1350s, when it was also felt that jurors should not be discouraged from speaking the truth and should remain free from any external influence, be it from justices or anyone else. Petitions concerning corrupt jurors were submitted on occasions from 1334.[29] An indication that the petitions were not simply complaints but sometimes blueprints for reform comes from a novel method of fining corrupt jurors and embracers: it was suggested that the perpetrator would have to pay ten times the bribe and the sum would be shared between the injured party and the Crown. This method had previously been used for economic offences, but was an imaginative suggestion on the part of the Commons as a means of countering the problem of corruption and one that was adopted by the Crown in the statute of 1365.[30]

The content of the petitions reveals an implicit understanding of the workings of the law, and various strands of legal experience are observable in their formation and presentation. Service in local judicial administration appears to have been a significant element since this generally involved contact with both civil and criminal juries through hearing presentments, taking indictments or trying cases. Sheriffs and coroners had important ancillary tasks and required a good working knowledge of procedure (*see* Chapter 3). Holding office as sheriff may not always have preceded parliamentary election, but it frequently dovetailed or coincided with parliamentary service: John Trehampton, sheriff of Lincolnshire 1334–37 and 1345–48, was a knight of the shire for the county in five parliaments in the 1330s and for two sessions in 1348. Similarly, John Engayne (sheriff of Cambridgeshire and Huntingdonshire 1345–47) represented Cambridgeshire in eleven significant parliaments between 1339 and 1362.[31] Both men also had considerable experience as justices of the peace. Sheriffs may simply have returned themselves in some cases (Thomas Swynnerton, sheriff of Shropshire and Staffordshire 1341–43, represented both counties in 1343), but they may have been targeted for parliamentary service if their knowledge and influence were deemed important. An unusually high number of former sheriffs were returned to the parliaments of 1381 and 1382, which suggests that experienced members of local society were considered especially desirable in the aftermath of the Peasants' Revolt. A number of coroners were returned to parliament: Roger Belgrave, a Leicestershire coroner, for instance, was an MP for the shire for three parliaments in the 1320s and again in 1338, following experience gained as a keeper of the peace and a gaol delivery justice in the 1330s. John Hales, one of the Norfolk coroners, was an MP in 1343, 1348 and 1351, while John

Upton, one of the Wiltshire coroners, represented the city of Salisbury in 1355, 1360 and 1363.

Many MPs had experience as keepers and (from the 1330s) justices of the peace, a good proportion of them as 'working justices' rather than as more honorific members of the bench.[32] Indeed, in some parliaments over half the representatives were currently or had previously been commissioned as JPs. Town officials such as the mayor and bailiffs were usually *ex officio* members of the urban peace commission. A number of mayors were MP for their borough including the aptly named Peter Bellassize, sometime mayor, constable and keeper of the peace for Stamford.[33] In Colchester, the local lawyer, John Hall, who was an attorney in the borough courts and one of the town bailiffs, attended more parliaments in the period 1360–72 than the representative of any other borough.[34]

Analysis of the parliamentary returns and plea rolls indicates that stewards of franchise regions (liberties) formed a significant number of the members. Indeed the bulk of MPs in the south-western counties in the 1350s and 1360s were the stewards – those talented men who supervised the complex affairs of lay and eccelsiastical landowners. Thomas Hungerford had a parliamentary career stretching from 1357 to 1393 as an MP for Wiltshire and Somerset.[35] Hungerford was heavily in demand on local commissions and was both a JP and escheator. Over the course of his career he served, in the capacity of steward, the earl of Salisbury, the bishops of Salisbury and Winchester, Queen Philippa, the Black Prince, and the house of Lancaster. While he cuts perhaps an extraordinary figure, he was not alone. Some, such as John Dabernoun, steward of the Black Prince in Devon and Cornwall, and William Luscote, steward of the earl of Devon, were knights of the shire; others, such as Robert James, bailiff of the bishop of Salisbury at Sherborne,[36] John Cary, steward of the earl of Devon's liberties at Wonford, Exminster and Axminster,[37] and John Wyncanton, steward of the liberty of Sydbery in Devon,[38] were borough representatives.

Another way in which relevant experience could be gained was jury service itself. A Buckinghamshire grand jury for oyer and terminer sessions held in 1326 included Roger Tyringham (MP in 1321 and 1327), a man who had considerable experience as sheriff, keeper of the peace and gaol delivery justice, Andrew St Lucio (MP 1325–28 and a keeper of the peace in 1326), James Freysel (MP 1324 and 1328–30, keeper of the peace 1329–32 and steward of the prior of Christ Church, Canterbury at Risborough in the 1330s) and John de la Penne (an MP and keeper of the peace in 1326). In 1336, three grand jurors in Kent sessions later represented their county: Philip Pimpe (1340), Stephen Ashley (1338) and William Moraunt (1334 and 1336),[39] while a third of Lancashire grand jurors in 1365 sessions served as MPs.[40]

The men in the Commons also included some men of law who were already practising in the central courts (or had been on the bench) and others, who were apprentices or future serjeants. A few of Edward I's judges were MPs, including William Ormesby (justice of king's bench, 1298–1303 and variously a justice in eyre and assize justice), who represented Norfolk in 1290 and Great Yarmouth in 1307.[41] During Edward II's reign the two most notable examples (of judges who were MPs) were Robert Baynard and John Cambridge. Baynard was a stalwart in provincial administration in East Anglia for many years and was a knight of the shire for Norfolk on various occasions between 1314 and 1326 before his appointment to the court of king's bench (1327–30). Cambridge, who in fact had been a serjeant-at-law since 1309 and was steward of the abbess of Chatteris from 1305 to 1320, was a member for Cambridgeshire from 1320 to 1327 before his promotion to the court of common pleas (1331–34).[42] Robert Warwick, who was a knight of the shire for Warwickshire in March 1330 and returned for the city of Warwick in the following November, had been an attorney in the court of common pleas and one of the principal pleaders in the county court.[43]

A notable and prominent feature of the 1330s and 1340s (but one that declined after the 1350s) is the number of men serving as MPs who were either already serjeants-at-law or who were then (almost immediately) called to the order,[44] many of them going on to higher positions within the judiciary. The majority attended in the capacity of knights of the shire, but a small number served additionally or solely as burgesses. Assuming they have been correctly identified with the person of that name, in the 1330s ten men were returned to parliament who were already pleading in the central courts,[45] while another seven were awaiting future call.[46] In the 1340s three members had previously been called as serjeants,[47] while another ten members were yet to be called.[48] In the 1350s only two future serjeants represented their constituency.[49] In the 1360s there were five men yet to be called as serjeants who were serving in parliament, a figure which had decreased to three in the 1370s and remained the same for the 1380s.

Given the numbers of men attending any one sitting of parliament and that the attendance of these particular men of law was in most cases not constant throughout the decade, these figures may not seem that impressive. A more decisive profile can be gained, however, from looking at attendance at specific parliaments over the particular decades. In the

1330s, for instance, there is a bunching effect towards the end of the decade, with five men of law returned for the parliament of 1336, four for 1337, and five for both the sessions held in 1339. In the 1340s, three were present for at least one of the two sessions in 1340, five attended the parliament of 1341, possibly four the parliament of 1343, and six the parliament of March 1348.

The significance of these figures lies in the fact that common petitions featuring legal issues were tendered at the majority of these parliaments. They should be taken in conjunction with the attendance of men of law who were stewards and/or royal officials in the shires. An analysis of royal officials who were MPs in Essex, Leicestershire and Shropshire (1330-70) shows that in the decade 1330-40 on average just over sixty per cent of MPs were holding or had held office in these counties. In the parliaments of 1343, 1355, 1361 and 1366, all the MPs of the three counties were professional administrators, while they were dominant among those returned in 1348, 1354, 1357, 1358, 1365 and 1368. It is highly probable this pattern was duplicated in other counties across the country.[50]

The predominance of stewards of lay and ecclesiastical landowners in the ranks of the Commons has political ramifications that go beyond the scope of this present work. It may be thought that such a convergence points towards collusion and conspiracy: the stewards were there purely to take the line espoused by their patron and/or that he was attempting to pack the house to achieve an ulterior motive.[51] The stewards may have been in the service of a powerful individual or corporation, but it does not necessarily follow that their choice or voice in parliament was influenced or compromised by the person by whom they were employed. Fourteenth-century patrons, especially powerful ones, such as the Black Prince or John of Gaunt, recruited from the best available talent: men of law were employed for their knowledge, experience and advice.[52] Given the desire to have the most able people serving in parliament and the fact that there were a lot of landowners in any one county it is not surprising that many stewards sat as MPs. Their attendance was an opportunity for the Crown to take advantage of their legal and administrative capabilities. It was also a chance for different localities to put forward their own views, which they wanted a well-connected person to do.

The tradition of electing 'serjeants' (and sheriffs) to parliament was officially ended by an ordinance of 1372, which forbade the practice in relation to knights of the shire, although there was seemingly no such restriction on borough representatives.[53] The particular terminology used for men of law ('serjeants') has usually been taken to refer to men employed in the central courts, but could also refer to pleaders in the county courts. If the latter, this would appear to be a significant move against the men of law who served in parliament, but was one that was probably government-inspired rather than an initiative from the Commons.[54] It is not exactly clear for what reason this was passed. The reason stated for imposing the ban was that the legal element had been concentrating rather exclusively on private or individual business: 'they procure and put forward many petitions in parliament in the name of the Commons, which are no concern of the Commons, but touch only the particular persons by whom the lawyers are retained'. The measure of its effectiveness largely depends upon the particular definition of men of law. Certainly in the short term it may have been heeded in some quarters since there was a sudden influx of parliamentary novices in the parliament of 1373: in 1372 60 per cent of knights of the shire were old hands, while in 1373 this figure had dropped to 53 per cent. Analysis of the composition of parliaments during the later 1370s and into the 1380s indicates that some practising lawyers continued to be returned and that it had in the longer term as slight an effect on men of law as it did on sheriffs and other royal ministers when a similar ban was suggested in 1337.[55]

Arguably, from the 1340s the Commons matured politically and their legislative agenda possessed a consistency of approach.[56] There is no doubt this was in large part a symptom of the immense continuity that existed in parliaments of this era. Individual members in each county can be cited who put in long, unbroken spells of service. Many of them were men of law, but even those who were not contributed through their experience of parliamentary business. They brought a valuable sense of collective memory to parliamentary proceedings and through their persistence ensured that important legislative provisions made it to the statute book: the prohibition on indictors being on the trial jury, for instance, was first raised in 1341 and eventually became law in 1352. This corporate experience is manifest in the statistics based on the re-election of MPs, which became commoner under Edward III than under his predecessors.[57]

The speaker was important in focusing the Commons' deliberations and in their relay to the Crown. The profiles of the medieval speakers for the Commons in parliament have been traced in detail by J. S. Roskell and since the speakers of the late fourteenth and early fifteenth centuries were frequently lawyers the choice of personnel holding the office had important implications for the promotion of issues of legal interest or the conduct of business in parliament.[58] Although the first speaker, Sir Peter de la Mare, chosen at the Good Parliament of 1376, led debate as well as representing the opinion of the lower house, the speakers of later years were more clearly responsible for supervising the conduct of business in the Commons.[59] De la Mare, who was knight of the shire for Herefordshire in the years 1376, 1377 (acting again as speaker in the October parliament), 1380 (in both January and November), 1382 (in May and October) and in February 1383, was steward of Edmund Mortimer, the earl of March, and had been sheriff of Herefordshire for seven months from December 1372 to July 1373. He may also have been connected to the cathedral authorities in the county in an administrative capacity during the 1380s. He was a Herefordshire justice of the peace (1380–82), a period when the powers of the commissioners were considerably enlarged to allow JPs to determine indictments without the quorum. His immediate successor as speaker in the parliament of January 1377 was Sir Thomas Hungerford.[60] Subsequent fourteenth-century speakers also had interesting legal careers (some of them in civil law). Sir James Pickering was chief justice of Ireland in the 1360s, MP for Westmorland for the four parliaments of 1377–82, and speaker, first in 1378 and then again in 1383.[61]

Lords

If it was the lower house which increasingly provided initiatives for legislation through the submission of common petitions, it was the upper house which provided the main focus of the institution, authority and expertise being vested in the men given individual summonses. Although they certainly played some role, unfortunately evidential difficulties make assessing their precise contribution problematic. The evidential problems concern, firstly, the records of parliament. The rolls of parliament rarely provide any description of the proceedings in the Lords.[62] Although there are records of meetings of great councils, it is difficult to gauge what precisely they discussed and the role they played in legislative solutions. The second problem arises from the actual enrolments of those summoned as peers. Michael Prestwich has demonstrated in particular the unreliability of the lists of men recorded as being summoned to parliaments and councils in the closing years of Edward I's reign. In 1301, for instance, the wardrobe account of payments to royal messengers indicate that ninety-three men were sent writs, not eighty as shown in the Close Rolls.[63]

The lists of those receiving personal summonses may not only be incomplete, but as they stand they may also offer a potentially inaccurate picture of who actually attended a given parliament. A third evidential difficulty that presents itself, therefore, is absenteeism among the Lords.[64] In 1307, for example, summonses were sent out to 167 people, but probably no more than fifty-seven attended. In the York parliament of December 1332 only five of the eleven earls turned up and just over half of the sixty-six 'peers' summoned. A number of peers never turned up for perfectly genuine reasons such as old age, illness, military service or other important royal or personal business, but the failure to attend naturally makes it difficult to be sure who was present when specific deliberations occurred.

Late appearance by magnates at parliamentary sessions also impeded parliamentary business. In the January parliament of 1348 Chief Justice Thorpe could not give his speech declaring the reason for the summons until four days after the scheduled start of proceedings because 'grantz et autres' had not 'pleinement venuz' (fully arrived). From about the mid-fourteenth century the Crown was increasingly unwilling to tolerate excuses for absence, or dilatory attendance among the prelates and magnates, and attempted to limit exemption to infirmity. The recorded instances of those exonerated from attending parliament during Edward III and Richard II's reigns are in fact few given the length of the period: letters from seven lords and seventeen bishops and abbots. Other evidence points towards there being a certain level of attendance in spite of occasional lapses: letters of proxy or attorney notifying the Crown of a lack of personal attendance (although surviving only for the period 1307–39) number just twenty, involving a mere seven lords.

There are two observable groups with a legal character in the Lords. The first one comprised members of the nobility who, while they would never call themselves lawyers as a matter of status or profession, nevertheless exercised some judicial functions in person and possessed knowledge based on experience from several counties. The second one consisted of men who whose social status was lower and whose knowledge and experience might be related more specifically to one or two counties, but whose weighty and conspicuous service and possible influence in the local community made them people whose opinions it was deemed the king ought to take note of when making decisions and discussing legislation. The significance of the summonses to the latter group, therefore, perhaps lies not so much that they should be seen as part of the peerage, rather in what this implied about their relationship to the Crown and the central government.

The involvement of magnates in the administration of justice varied according to the nature of the judicial agency (and perhaps to an extent with their own interest and ability, though it seems unlikely that the most powerful earls and other noblemen would often involve themselves personally in county legal administration).[65] Great lords were often employed alongside central court justices on general commissions of oyer and terminer (as in 1328 and 1340), to which complaints about the operation of the judicial system were addressed, and were regularly appointed to special oyer and terminer commissions on account of their personal standing and political authority within a county. The inclusion of the baronage and titled nobility in commissions of the peace from the mid-fourteenth century equally reflected the need to have the co-operation of those with the greatest wealth and inherent political authority when it came to maintaining law and order, but it is clear that they did not by and large consider themselves to be working justices. Some lesser noblemen and barons, however, did attend peace sessions on a regular basis: the earls of Stafford, for instance, were among the working justices in Staffordshire, Thomas Beauchamp, earl of Warwick, received indictments at Worcestershire sessions in the 1370s, while the earl of Angus (summoned 1332–80) is known to have acted in Lincolnshire (and was even keeper of the rolls for the Kesteven peace commission in 1372). Clearly experiences gained from these forays could be formed into opinions and channelled into debates accordingly.

The career of Roger Chandos is illustrative of the type of person whose judicial service and considerable knowledge of county affairs earned him a position in the upper house. Prior to his summons in 1337, he was sheriff of Herefordshire four times for a total of thirteen years (1312–15, 1322–27, 1328–32 and 1334), a keeper of the peace for a decade (1327–36), and more briefly escheator for the western border counties and the Welsh March (1332–33). His summonses continued until his death in 1353 and he was included in further peace commissions in 1338, 1344 and 1351. Interestingly in addition to parliamentary service in 1318 and 1322, he was an MP for Herefordshire again in 1340 and 1343 after his summonses as a lord.

In fact it was not unusual for men receiving personal summonses to continue to be active in a judicial capacity in their county after their first attendance as a lord. William Botiller of Wemme (summoned from 1308 to 1325) was a keeper of the peace from 1308 to 1332; similarly William Deyncourt (summoned 1332–63) received peace commissions from 1329 to 1351. Robert FitzPayne received a personal summons in 1326 and continued to be required until 1351. During that time he was active in local administration in Dorset and served on fourteen peace commissions between 1316 and 1351. The business of these parliaments and reasons for holding the first (and possibly subsequent) ones to which these men were summoned may (in the absence of precise indications) provide some clue as to why their presence was desired: many were parliaments at which the focus was issues of law and order or judicial administration, for example, though there may be significant political (rather than purely legal) reasons for requiring them.[66] While some of the greater lords may have declined or ignored the summons, there were advantages and incentives for lesser men whose presence was desired because of their legal and administrative know-how. Connections forged through parliamentary attendance might lead to further service and social advancement.

The potential legal input of the upper house was boosted through the practice of appointing proxies or attorneys when a lord was unable to attend parliament as required. As noted earlier there are twenty surviving letters of proxy for seven lay peers for the period 1307-39 (though most of the letters are relevant to Edward III's reign). While a few letters appointed the lord's son, it is significant that men of law were frequently the nominees, among them Robert Cheddworth (whom Robert de Vere, earl of Oxford, described as 'seneschal of our estates'), Robert Hungerford, Simon Drayton, Roger la Zouche and Robert Bousser.[67] Cheddworth was active in judicial administration in Essex, serving on various peace commissions 1330-32. Hungerford was keeper of Henry of Lancaster's lands in Wiltshire and in 1332 was also steward of the bishop of Bath and Wells. He represented Wiltshire nine times between 1324 and 1339 and was a member of the peace commissions of 1332. Drayton was a keeper of the peace for Northamptonshire in 1327 and an MP fourteen times in the period 1321-37. Zouche was sheriff of Leicestershire and Warwickshire on two occasions (1329-30 and 1334-40), keeper of the peace twice (in 1347 and 1351) and an MP in 1324, 1331 and 1337. Bousser was an Essex MP in the two parliaments of 1330, an oyer and terminer justice in 1331 and a keeper of the county in 1332. He was himself summoned to parliament in his own right (1348-49) and in the 1340s was one of the first common lawyers to become chancellor.

The role of men of law among the Lords is something that has been underestimated. Although we cannot be precise about the whole body of the House, an impression can be gained of the experience and interests of at least some of those who attended in response to their summons.

Judges

The most prominent lawyers, the chief justices and the judges of the two benches, as well as the chief baron of the exchequer, the king's serjeants and one or two canon lawyers, were among the official legal element expected to attend parliament (in the fourteenth century) and were probably the most influential group with regard to legislation. The judges were also the ones who were afforded the long view, the wide angle; they could have an idea as to what was going on in the planning of legislation, and in the courts and the country as a whole. As a professional body they were usually men with experience as pleaders in the central courts and veterans of work in judicial administration. During Edward II's reign, royal judges were appointed directly from the ranks of serjeants-at-law and a tradition was established that appointments to the bench were made (or at least announced) in parliament.[68] Generally they were set apart from the body of the Lords, though they likewise found, compliance with the summons was not always possible, especially when one of the benches or, conversely, parliament itself, was sitting in a county outside Westminster. In 1328, for instance, when the court of common pleas was temporarily established at York, Chief Justice Herle alone went to the Northampton parliament, while his fellows attended to their judicial business.[69]

The judges' presence on the king's council meant they could initiate and agree legislation outside parliament, but a vital feature was the expertise they could bring to the discussion of government business and the formulation of legislation in parliament. This fact was explicitly stated by the council in response to a petition in 1318.[70] The judges were influential in five main areas: addressing parliament at the start of a session; serving on committees; reporting on the outcome of legislative enactments and administrative policy; ruling on cases and providing opinions in parliament; and initiating and shaping legislation.

Providing the reasons for the parliamentary gathering and an explanation of the business agenda was a privilege shared between senior judicial figures. In the thirteenth century there is evidence for the king's business being expounded at great councils or parliament by the justiciar, Hubert de Burgh (in 1225), William Raleigh, chief justice of king's bench (in 1234 and 1237) and by Roger Seaton, chief justice of common pleas (in 1275). In the fourteenth century the chief justice of king's bench appears to have given the opening speech in the majority of sessions held between 1327 and 1355. In the second half of the century, apart from 1362, all sessions were opened by the chancellor.[71] To an extent, the task of delivering the opening speech remained in the hands of an important judicial officer since, although the office of chancellor was usually filled by an ecclesiastical dignitary, during the 1340s and the 1370s the great seal was held by common lawyers who had experience as judges. Moreover, with the growth of the chancellor's equity jurisdiction, all incumbents were increasingly required to act judicially.[72]

Judges were regularly included on parliamentary committees and could thus exert influence over the consideration and handling of numerous matters. In the parliament of September 1305, for instance, three royal judges (Brabazon, Hengham and Bereford) liaised with Scottish representatives to draw up a plan for the government of Scotland. In Edward III's reign, committee work became an established feature. In 1331, four judges sat on a committee to discuss relations with the French, while in 1334 seven judges were present to advise on matters of taxation and replies to the common petitions.[73] A special committee of royal advisers – appointed to provide answers to the common petitions of 1344 – comprised the two chief justices, William Scot and John Stonor, and five other leading central court justices: William Shareshull, Roger Hillary, Richard Willoughby, William Basset and Richard Kelshall.[74] The November parliament of 1381, which met in the aftermath of the Peasants' Revolt, received a request from the Commons that a committee of two judges, two serjeants and four apprentices examine the administration of the law.[75]

Judges were also appointed to the committees which considered private petitions. There were two separate committees, one which dealt with petitions from the 'home' countries (England, Wales, Scotland and Ireland) and one which looked at petitions from outside the British Isles (from Gascony and other foreign territories). Some specialisation in handling the complaints of the two regions seems to have developed. In the 1370s and 1380s, for instance, the chief justice of king's bench and the chief baron of the exchequer were appointed exclusively to the committee taking petitions from the British Isles. Other members of the judiciary were equally consistent in their membership of this committee. Roger Belknap of the court of common pleas was appointed on fifteen out of sixteen occasions and his colleague, Roger Fulthorpe, managed nearly three-quarters of the sessions.[76]

The judges appear to have played a vital part in communicating to the king and parliament the success or failure of legislative enactments or administrative policy. Such reports were usually based on their work in the central courts and judicial commissions in the provinces. Bereford's report on work of the so-called 'trailbaston' commissions was probably destined for parliament.[77] In 1316 the chief justices were required to record and then forward to parliament all matters which were outstanding before them and which could only be dealt with in parliament.[78]

The king summoned to parliament personally a number of legal experts. Indeed, the official element varied over the course of the fourteenth century, with as many as forty being summoned in the early fourteenth century, a figure more than halved by Richard II's reign to a core of about eight to fourteen individuals. 'Les Justices et autres gentz de loy de la Terre' were the nucleus of expertise in parliament and were frequently required to assist the king and the Lords in providing rulings on cases coming before the king or their opinions on particular points of law. In 1378, for instance, they ruled that clergymen could not enjoy immunity from prosecution for debt, trespass or any other cause.[79] In the same parliament a question was put to the justices, serjeants and other men of law by Edward III's executors, a matter which was obviously of some difficulty as it was discussed again by the legal experts in the parliament of January 1380.[80] In 1380 it was also recorded that 'les Justices en presence du Roi ... & les Seign[eu]rs' had agreed that the murder of an ambassador was an act of treason.[81]

The royal judges were also instrumental in articulating ideas on the status of statute law and, in particular, the relationship between the law and parliament. At the beginning of Edward I's reign it was well understood that a judicial decision could 'make a law throughout the land'. With the promulgation of Edward I's new statute legislation (much of it technically a codification of existing common law), initially there appears to have been no strict delineation between judicial decisions and statutes. Nevertheless, it is apparent from the late thirteenth century that, as a written body of provisions, the legislative corpus of Edward I was gradually conceptually set apart from the ordinary common law. Just as common law was distinguished from 'the usage of the country' (customary law), so statutory law, referred to as *ley especial* or *novel ley*,[82] had come to be seen as distinct from the *auncien ley*.[83] By the beginning of Edward II's reign it was recognised that a statute could defeat the common law[84] and by his son's there was a realisation that there could be a considerable difference between the two types.[85] Indeed, in Edward III's reign the common law was contrasted with 'the law now in force'.[86]

Given such an acknowledgement in open court and the increasing number of statutes being passed, it is not surprising that the relationship between judicial decisions and statutes, the judicial interpretation of statutes, received re-consideration by leading lawyers, among them, Geoffrey Scrope and William Bereford. The former advocated that when seeking to understand a statute one should not step outside the bounds of its wording,[87] while the latter declared from the bench that in cases where statute law was applicable then that provided the authority and no contrary averment could be accepted.[88] Following the political and judicial crisis of 1340–41, it is surely no coincidence that various judges again urged that a strict line was to be taken when interpreting statutory provisions. Indeed, during the years 1342–43 the maxim *statuta sunt stricta juris* was coined by Robert Thorpe[89] and later endorsed by William Shareshull, echoing the words of Scrope, when he said of a case 'we cannot take the statute further than the words of it say'.[90] This was not a theory developed merely to protect their professional reputations from accusations of leniency or bias. It represented an acceptance of the authority of statute law and provides an indication of the power that a form of words (framed as such for a reason) could invoke. Indeed, it was also about this period (in 1338) that a principle of interpretation which still holds good in modern times, the *eiusdem generis* rule,[91] was enunciated by John Stowford, a serjeant in the court of common pleas, namely that general words placed at the end of a statute do not extend its application, but are governed by the preceding special words of limitation.[92]

The perception of statute legislation as a second tier of law, to be enforced in addition to the existing and evolving common law, was matched by a growing acceptance of a necessary relationship between parliament and statute legislation. In Richard II's reign, it could satisfactorily be declared that 'The law of the land is made in parliament by the king and the Lords .... and the commonalty of the realm'.[93] Such constitutional formulae had their precedents earlier in the century. As early as 1318 it was perceived that a full parliament was the place where adjustments to the law of the land should be deliberated and then declared, while in 1322 emphasis appears to have been placed on parliament as the forum in which the business of the kingdom 'shall be treated, accorded and established' and on these undertakings requiring the consent of the representatives of the whole political community.[94] Even if even these statements were more a form of rhetoric and not to be taken as having precise constitutional implications, there was clearly a growing desire to acknowledge parliament's role in the legislative context.

In Edward III's reign, the royal judges voiced opinions on how laws were passed and the effect of their enactment. In 1348, for instance, Chief Justice William Thorpe (giving judgment on a case in parliament) underlined the idea that the power of the king was the necessary enacting force in parliament when he stated that 'the king makes laws with the assent of the peers and the Commons and not through the instrumentality of the peers and the Commons'.[95] The new role afforded to parliament in the promulgation of legislation was also highlighted and confirmed in a judgment by Chief Justice Robert Thorpe in 1365. In a far-reaching statement that stressed the overriding nature and binding force of statute law he declared that 'as soon as parliament concludes any matter, the law presumes that every person has cognisance of it, for parliament represents the body of the whole realm and for this reason proclamation is unnecessary since the statute takes effect immediately.'[96]

The judges' influence on parliamentary proceedings was probably most profound in their role as architects of legislation. While much of the evidence linking the king's council with the legislative process is fairly circumstantial, the significance of senior lawmen in the formulation of legislation surely cannot be doubted. Direct and incontrovertible evidence of the contribution by senior judges under Edward I and Edward II is provided in the statements made by various chief justices in relation to particular statutes. The famous retort to counsel by Ralph Hengham (chief justice of king's bench, 1274-89 and chief justice of common pleas, 1301-09) 'Do not gloss the statute; we understand it better than you do, for we made it' is indicative of the close relationship with legislation that was possible in a period when statute law did not arise directly or solely from deliberation in parliament. Hengham refers to such discussion, however, when adjudicating whether the second Statute of Westminster allowed receipt of a wife to defend her right if it was not mentioned in the original writ saying, 'We agreed in parliament that the wife, if not named in the writ, should not be received'.[97] Finding a new statutory provision unsatisfactory Roger Brabazon (chief justice of king's bench, 1295-1316) expressed a desire to discuss the matter with colleagues 'who were at the making of the statute'.[98] The preamble to the Statute of Escheators (a product of the Lincoln parliament of 1301) contains explicit reference to legislative advisers, who included about a dozen royal justices and other officials, such as the escheator south of the Trent.[99]

Under Edward III the relationship between lawyers and legislation was rather more complex and ambiguous. The new procedural and political importance of the common petition and the tendency of the Crown to base statutes on the communal grievances thus highlighted (with little alteration to the text) makes any straightforward connection often difficult to perceive. The longevity of tenure exhibited by a number of central court judges would suggest that the benches contained men with considerable judicial experience and administrative ability that could be channelled into the creative processes underlying the production of royal statutes. In particular, the careers of various chief justices of king's bench demonstrate the capacity of senior figures within the judiciary to inform and direct the legislative process: Ralph Hengham was in post for sixteen years (1274-90), Roger Brabazon lasted twenty-one years (1295-1316), Geoffrey Scrope held office virtually continuously for fourteen years (1324–38), William Shareshull was chief justice for eleven years (1350–61) while John Cavendish managed nine years (1372–81).[100] While it would be misleading to credit them with all the legislative initiatives that emerged in their respective periods of ascendancy, their vision and force of personality undoubtedly helped to devise and implement far-reaching legislative reforms.

Statute legislation was in fact the product of a wide range of different legislative initiatives that included decisions from court cases and private petitions as well as the Commons' petitions. While the Commons needed the king to give effect to legislation, the Crown did not require the Commons' petitions to form statutes.[101] The hand of fourteenth-century royal judges is especially discernible in legislative provisions which have no obvious corresponding common petition or where the wording of the petition has been altered slightly or angled to the king's advantage. This is noticeable in the two major bouts of legislation occurring in 1351–52 (the Statutes of Labourers, of Provisors and of Treasons) and 1361 (the Statute of Westminster) and provides convincing evidence that the legal experts on the king's council, including Shareshull and the other senior judges, played an important role in drafting, if not indeed initiating, the key statutes of these years.[102] The coterie of lawyers may have exercised considerable influence over a number of other statutes promulgated in the late fourteenth century for which there are no surviving petitions, notably some highly specialised legal measures in the statute of 1379 and clauses dealing with the reform of exchequer procedure in legislation of 1381.[103]

The regulation of everyday life

The growth in enacted legislation not only affected the substantive law, in the nature of its provisions and in recognition of its status and function as an addition to the common law, but also the degree to which people were subject to government regulation. The volume of legislation in the form of statutes and ordinances stemming from parliament or great councils increased considerably over the period. A somewhat crude impression can be gained from the number of statutes issued during the reigns of the first three Edwards. The legislation of Edward I's thirty-five-year reign represents in the region of forty-eight statutes (with about 270 chapters) and covers 126 pages of the *Statutes of the Realm*, his son's by contrast covering forty-three pages with about twenty-two enactments, while the fifty-year reign of Edward III witnessed fifty statutes and ordinances (running to over 400 separate chapters), which cover 143 pages of the statute book.[104] These figures are based on the enrolled statutes of the first three Edwards since many of the statutes of Henry III's reign were decreed orally and rarely reduced to writing as an archive resource. The bare statistics also do not differentiate the number of chapters within statutes, nor the length and complexity of individual chapters. However, they do serve to indicate the level of regulation that people increasingly came under and, upon closer examination of the texts, how the king was promulgating legislation that was designed to regulate more closely and on a national basis aspects of daily life, such as what people could wear and how much they could earn.

Parliamentary legislation provided another tier to the growing regulation of trade, commerce, agriculture and social conduct that was occurring in the towns and villages.[105] Indeed, the example provided by parliament may have encouraged local communities not only to issue more frequently their own local legislation, but also to reduce to writing their practices, privileges and aspirations. Mirroring collections of statutes and the production of treatises, this took the form of codification of various types of by-laws and customs. In the 1320s and 1330s codices of village by-laws concerning harvest were drawn up in a number of manors.[106] In Bristol the recorder of the city started compiling in about 1344 what is known as *The Little Red Book of Bristol* in an attempt to preserve in written form past ordinances and contemporary trading practices as well as provide a dedicated space for the recording of future decrees.[107] In London, the city's chamberlain, Andrew Horn took much interest in compiling an authoritative collection of the customs, statutes and precedents (*Liber Horn*) in the early fourteenth century,[108] while in York, the common clerk, John Rufford, began the *York Memorandum Book* in the 1370s.[109]

Local legislation and practices could also provide the inspiration and example for important pieces of national legislation. Indeed, Professor McIntosh's comments for a later period are valuable here when she says that 'local communities often confronted new problems first and generated practical responses to them that subsequently served as models for policy at a higher level'.[110] For example, Edward I's legislation on acquiring property, the statute *Quia emptores* (1290), had its origins in practices of the local courts.[111] The decree that legal pleadings were to be in English, which was contained in the statute of 1362, was foreshadowed in an ordinance of the City of London issued six years earlier.[112] Social and economic legislation, particularly the sumptuary legislation, was probably adopted from initiatives in London and elsewhere.[113] The decree of 1363 concerning the 'outrageous and excessive apparel of divers people, contrary to their estate and degree', though difficult to enforce and a legislative failure, was probably reflecting shifting perceptions of identity and status through dress occurring in the fourteenth century.[114] An Oxford decree of 1358, for instance, held that learned men considered it 'both decent and consonant with reason that those whom God hath made eminent over laymen through inward adornments should also be outwardly distinguished from laymen by their habit'.[115] The legal measures adopted in the Ordinance (1349) and Statute of Labourers (1351) had precedents in the by-laws of the countryside and the existing local jurisdiction over litigation on breach of contract.[116] The anti-gaming statute of 1388 (although linked with a requirement to practise archery, intended to strengthen the military machine) was presaged by by-laws (and common law provisions) against gambling (including the game 'prickpeny') and forbidding the playing of 'knuckle bones' and football (*ad pilam*).[117]

The adoption of such measures in programmes of national legislation suggests the initiative or model came from those MPs or burgesses most closely associated with the making and enforcement of local regulations – lords' stewards and mayors and bailiffs – who, as was demonstrated above, featured prominently in many fourteenth-century parliaments. The judges and serjeants who formulated the statutory provisions would also have had some knowledge either through previous experience as a steward or from legal employment in, for example, the City of London. This phenomenon also underlines the complexity of the world behind the statute and the significance of those with legal knowledge being returned to parliament.

As this chapter has attempted to illustrate, there is strong circumstantial evidence that men of law elected as members of the 'Commons' or summoned to parliament as 'peers' played a crucial role in the formulation of at least certain key areas of legislation. Although a proportion of legislation was either devised or reworked by the royal judges on the basis of their own or the royal council's initiatives or as a result of difficult cases appearing in the courts, by the mid-fourteenth century a substantial amount of legislation arose from the contents of petitions submitted to the king and deliberated upon in parliament. A significant number of men of law attended as members of the Commons during Edward III's reign and between them seem to have had considerable experience in local judicial administration and of the jury system among other things. This tends to suggest that the composition of the lower house was not random or left to chance. Returns were designed to reflect the desires and requirements of the represented area.

It should be stressed, however, that although there may have been a significant legal voice in parliament, neither the Commons nor the Lords were monolithic bodies. The knights of the shire and the borough representatives each had their own particular concerns which they wished to voice at the appropriate juncture and their own preferred methods.[118] Indeed, persuasiveness of presentation, the ability to get behind and promote an issue in parliament, may have been a critical factor not only in a petition achieving 'common' status, but also in the communities' selection of their MPs.[119] With ability to give professional opinions, speak in public and see issues clearly, men of law (who usually possessed useful connections with important landowners, merchants and royal officials) were natural choices for representatives.

The implications of the issues arising in this chapter reach beyond the purely legal arena, however, and touch matters of a political complexion. One of the things that a holistic view of the personnel of parliament has revealed is the fluidity between the various groups (or houses) in the institution. There were overlaps between service as a knight of the shire and borough representative, former or serving MPs could receive personal summonses to the Lords, while some men reverted to the Commons after a stint in the upper house. The system of proxies or attorneys enabled men of law of the provinces to contribute occasionally to the debates of the Lords in addition to their more usual forum. Some speakers of the Commons were or had been members of the king's council, while several generations of royal judges had seen life on the other side as members of the Commons.

A sense of cohesion and integration between the composite elements of parliament can also be evoked. The special legislative committee set up in 1340 contained twelve knights and six burgesses in addition to prelates, lords and ministers. Though a bit of a 'one-off' in terms of the mid-fourteenth century, it paved the way for the slightly smaller inter-communing committees of the later fourteenth century and special *ad hoc* committees containing knights and burgesses. Looking at things from the legal and administrative perspective provokes the need for some rethinking of the political aims apparently espoused by the Commons. The concern for particular legislative agenda, and the efforts made to pursue issues to a conclusion as statute law, indicates that the Commons were not just out for themselves, pursuing particular interests peculiar to the 'gentry'. As local officials they knew where the weak links lay. In betraying a genuine concern for the administration of justice it could be said that the Commons were prepared to promote what were effectively national issues as well as parochial concerns.

Consultative exercises, in whatever form they took, may have given the impression that people had a stake in the running of the kingdom, in the formation of policy and legislation even. The opportunity to provide information for the Crown and present concerns or grievances was advantageous in that it brought matters to royal attention and offered the possibility of redress or action. From the corresponding royal point of view, it may have seemed a useful means of receiving information about conditions throughout the kingdom from people well placed to give an authoritative account.[120] The new method for the formulation of statutes gave rise to opinions as to the inherent qualities of statute law and a perceptual differentiation from the common law. This in turn contributed directly or indirectly to parliamentary legislation being given a new legal footing in that it was regarded as a directly enforceable body of rules adjunct to the common law. The concept emerging in the courts of the binding force of statutes combined with an acceptance of the legislative supremacy of parliament to provide a context for the birth and enforcement of legislation. It is from Edward III's reign, therefore, that 'law-giving' in the form of enacted statutes not only gains a new meaning, but itself earns enhanced authority. While this re-definition of 'law' may not have been consciously constructed, it undoubtedly was a by-product of the relationship between Edward III and parliament (both Commons and Lords) and between the king and his advisers (particularly the judges). In turn it influenced the way legislation was thought about, framed and enforced.

Notes

1. W. M. Ormrod, 'Agenda for legislation, 1322–c.1340', *EHR*, 105 (1990), pp. 1–33.
2. W. C. Weber, 'The purpose of the English *Modus tenendi parliamentum*', *Parliamentary History*, 17 (1998), pp. 149–75.
3. D. Carpenter, *The Reign of Henry III* (London, Hambledon Press, 1996), pp. 381–90; G. Dodd, 'Crown, magnates and gentry: the English parliament, 1369–1421', unpublished DPhil thesis, University of York, 1998, pp. 267–9.
4. Carpenter, *Henry III*, pp. 390–406; G. L. Harriss, 'The formation of parliament, 1272–1377', in R. G. Davies and J. H. Denton (eds), *The English Parliament in the Middle Ages* (Manchester, Manchester University Press, 1981), pp. 29–60.
5. See especially, H. G. Richardson and G. O. Sayles, *The English Parliament in the Middle Ages* (London, Hambledon Press, 1981); G. L. Harriss, *King, Parliament*

and *Public Finance in Medieval England to 1369* (Oxford, Clarendon Press, 1975).
6   *Fleta II*, ed. H. G. Richardson and G. O. Sayles, SS, 72 (London, 1955), p. 109.
7   *YB 11 & 12 Edward III*, p. 136 (a case cited by Parving).
8   *YB 12 & 13 Edward III*, p. 366.
9   G. Holmes, *The Good Parliament* (Oxford, Clarendon Press, 1975), pp. 2, 100–58; J. G. Bellamy, 'Appeal and impeachment in the Good Parliament', *BIHR*, 41 (1966), pp. 35–46.
10 For the following paragraph see Harris, 'Formation of parliament', pp. 29–60, and J. R. Maddicott, 'Parliament and the constituencies', in Davies and Denton (eds), *English Parliament*, pp. 61–87; Ormrod, 'Agenda for legislation', pp. 1–33; W. M. Ormrod, *The Reign of Edward III* (New Haven and London, Yale University Press, 1990), pp. 60–2.
11 N. Ramsey, 'Scriveners and notaries as legal intermediaries in later medieval England', in J. Kermode (ed.), *Enterprise and Individuals in Fifteenth Century England* (Stroud, Alan Sutton, 1991), pp. 119, 125–7.
12 J. C. Holt, *Magna Carta*, 2nd edn (Cambridge, Cambridge University Press, 1992), pp. 324–5, 384.
13 J. R. Maddicott, 'The county community and the making of public opinion in fourteenth-century England', *TRHS*, 5th series, 18 (1978), pp. 27–43.
14 Dodd, 'Crown, magnates and gentry', pp. 181–4.
15 *Ibid.*, pp. 125–6, 186.
16 See below; about 140 Commons' petitions were submitted to the Good Parliament in 1376, yet no statutes were issued: A. J. Verduyn, 'The attitude of the parliamentary Commons to law and order under Edward III', unpublished DPhil thesis, University of Oxford, 1991, pp. 171–2.
17 Dodd, 'Crown, magnates and gentry', pp. 34–5.
18 Musson and Ormrod, *Evolution*, pp. 86–9.
19 Dodd, 'Crown, magnates and gentry', pp. 179–80; G. Dodd, 'The hidden presence: parliament and the private petition in the late Middle Ages', in A. Musson (ed.), *Expectations of the Law in the Middle Ages* (Woodbridge, Boydell Press, 2001).
20 Verduyn, 'Attitude', *passim*; Musson, *Public Order*, pp. 240–8.
21 For instance there were great councils called in September 1327, July 1328, September 1336, September 1337, July 1338, October 1342, August 1352, September 1353 and June 1371 (Ormrod, *Edward III*, pp. 208–9).
22 As in 1353 (Verduyn, 'Attitude', p. 5).
23 D. J. M. Higgins, 'Judges in government and society in the reign of Edward II', unpublished DPhil thesis, University of Oxford, 1986, p. 59.
24 *RPHI*, pp. 233–4 (5).
25 *RP*, vol. 2, p. 134 (66),
26 *RP*, vol. 2, pp. 259 (30), 266 (26).
27 *RP*, vol. 2, pp. 128 (14), 134 (67), 140 (30).
28 *RP*, vol. 1, pp. 160, 166.
29 *RPHI*, p. 234 (6).
30 *RP*, vol. 2, pp. 287–8 (29).

31 Engayne was also a JP (1338–44 and 1347). The twinning of counties to be administered by a single sheriff was a regular practice.
32 During the early fourteenth century, when the size of peace commissions was small (usually three, but rarely more than five members) it is highly probable that the men commissioned would have actually attended the relevant judicial sessions. From the middle years of the century, when the size of the peace commissions expanded, service as a JP cannot be taken as conclusive evidence that the commissioner was a man of law.
33 *Sessions of the Peace in the City of Lincoln, 1351–1354, and the Borough of Stamford, 1351*, ed. E. Kimball, Lincoln Record Society, 65 (1971), p. xxix.
34 *Return of Members*, pp. 163–88; R. H. Britnell, *Growth and Decline in Colchester, 1300–1525* (Cambridge, Cambridge University Press, 1986), pp. 111, 128.
35 *Return of Members*, pp. 160, 165, 171, 197, 200, 203, 305, 207, 211, 219, 221, 230, 235, 239, 240, 246.
36 MP for Ilchester in 1352.
37 MP for Totnes in 1358 and for Launceston in 1365.
38 MP for Barnstaple in 1355 and then Dartmouth five times in 1358–63.
39 Ashley and Moraunt went on to serve as sheriffs.
40 Otto Halsale (who was also a grand juror in the early 1350s, was an MP in 1351), John Botiller (1366, 1372, 1377, 1378, 1380, 1388), Richard Radcliffe (1368) and William Atherton (1373, 1381).
41 Musson, *Public Order*, p. 142. Walter Helion, an earlier example, was a king's bench justice in 1273 and of common pleas 1278–81, and represented Gloucestershire in 1283 and 1297.
42 Musson, *Public Order*, pp. 133, 159, 241; *The Cartulary of Chatteris Abbey*, ed. C. Breay (Woodbridge, Boydell Press, 1999), p. 76.
43 R. C. Palmer, *The County Courts of Medieval England, 1150–1350* (Princeton, NJ, Princeton University Press, 1982), pp. 97–100.
44 This includes appointment as attorney-general in a few cases.
45 Kelshall, Parving, Hambury, Pole, Elmedon, Power, Miggley, Derworthy, Trewythisa, Merrington.
46 Chelrey, Middleton, Woodstock, Sadlingstanes, Bret, W. Thorpe, Huse.
47 R. Thorpe, Power, Elmedon.
48 Sadlingstanes, Huse, Ingleby, Skipwith, Gaunt, Gower, Haverington, Chelrey, Middleton, Lavenham (Lavenham in fact was never called and remained 'apprentice-at-law').
49 Percy, Morice.
50 I am grateful to Richard Partington for this information.
51 L. Clark, 'Magnates and their affinities in the parliaments of 1386–1421', in R. H. Britnell and A. J. Pollard (eds), *The McFarlane Legacy, Studies in Late Medieval Politics and Society* (Stroud, Alan Sutton, 1995), pp. 127–53; S. J. Payling, 'The widening franchise: parliamentary elections in Lancastrian Nottinghamshire', in D. Williams (ed.), *England in the Fifteenth Century: Proceedings of the 1986 Harlaxton Symposium* (Woodbridge, Boydell Press, 1987), pp. 172–3.
52 Maddicott, 'Parliament and the constituencies', p. 74; N. Saul, *Knights and*

Esquires: the Gloucestershire Gentry in the Fourteenth Century (Oxford, Clarendon Press, 1981), pp. 153–60, 166; S. Walker, 'Yorkshire justices of the peace, 1389–1413', *EHR*, 108 (1993), pp. 287–8; D. Green, 'The politics of service with Edward the Black Prince', in J. Bothwell (ed.), *The Age of Edward III* (Woodbridge, York Medieval Press, 2001).

53 *RP*, vol. 2, p. 310 (13); *SR*, vol. 1, p. 394; K. L. Wood-Legh, 'Sheriffs, lawyers and belted knights in the parliaments of Edward III', *EHR*, 46 (1931), p. 381.
54 Dodd, 'Crown, magnates and gentry', pp. 38–9, 184–5.
55 *RP*, vol. 2, p. 104.
56 Verduyn, 'Attitude', pp. 77, 107; Musson, *Public Order*, pp. 240–8.
57 Maddicott, 'Parliament and the constituencies', pp. 75–6.
58 J. S. Roskell, *Parliament and Politics in Late Medieval England*, 3 vols (London, Hambledon Press, 1981–3), vol. 1 (ch. IV, pp. 31–52) and vols 2 and 3, *passim*.
59 *Ibid.*, pp. 1–14. From 1384 the Commons were officially instructed to elect their speaker in what could sometimes be a real (i.e. contested, rather than purely nominal) election.
60 *Ibid.*, vol. 2, pp. 15–43.
61 *Ibid.*, vol. 3, pp. 1–25. He was also MP for Yorkshire for the five parliaments of 1383–97.
62 An exception is 1331: *RP*, vol. 2, pp. 60–3.
63 M. C. Prestwich, 'Magnate summonses in England in the later years of Edward I', *Parliaments, Estates and Representation*, 5 (1985), pp. 98, 100–1.
64 The following paragraph draws on Roskell, *Parliament and Politics*, vol. 1, ch. II, pp. 153–204.
65 For what follows see Musson and Ormrod, *Evolution*, pp. 69–72.
66 Musson, *Public Order*, pp. 231–3.
67 PRO MS SC10/14 no. 672, /52 nos. 2, 5, 6, 8, 9.
68 See (above) Chapter 2; Higgins, 'Judges in government', pp. 21–2. This provided an opportunity for prior consultation with the Lords.
69 *CCR 1327–30*, p. 376.
70 Higgins, 'Judges in government', p. 71.
71 *Ibid.*, pp. 63–4.
72 Musson and Ormrod, *Evolution*, pp. 33–5.
73 Higgins, 'Judges in government', pp. 69–70.
74 B. H. Putnam, *The Place in Legal History of Sir William Shareshull* (Cambridge, Cambridge University Press, 1950), p. 49.
75 *RP*, vol. 3, pp. 101–2.
76 Dodd, 'Crown, magnates and gentry', pp. 76–7.
77 *CCR 1302–7*, p. 347.
78 *Parliamentary Writs and Writs of Military Summons*, ed. F. Palgrave, 2 vols (London, Records Commission, 1827), vol. 2, pt 2, p. 156.
79 *RP*, vol. 3, p. 37 (28).
80 *RP*, vol. 3, pp. 60 (25), 61 (26): four serjeants-at-law were among the party of lawyers, although they had not been named in the list of summonses (see *SCCKB*, vol. 7, p. lxii).

81 Dodd, 'Crown, magnates and gentry', p. 78.
82 For example: *YB 1 Edward II*, p. 31; *YB 2 & 3 Edward II*, p. 168.
83 T. F. T. Plucknett, *Statutes and their Interpretation in the First Half of the Fourteeenth Century* (Cambridge, Cambridge University Press, 1922), pp. 22–31 and 165–6.
84 *YB 3 & 4 Edward II*, p. 162.
85 *YB 11–12 Edward III*, p. 142.
86 *YB 13 & 14 Edward III*, p. 24.
87 *YB 5 Edward II*, p. 46.
88 *YB 6 & 7 Edward II*, pp. 148–50.
89 *YB 17 Edward III*, p. 142; *YB 17 & 18 Edward III*, p. 446; *YB 18 Edward III*, p. 131.
90 *YB 20 Edward III*, vol. 2, p. 198.
91 J. A. Holland and J. S. Webb, *Learning Legal Rules*, 2nd edn (London, Blackstone, 1991), pp. 195–6.
92 *YB 12 Edward III*, pp. cxviii–cxx, 50.
93 *RP*, vol. 3, p. 243.
94 Higgins, 'Judges in government', p. 41; Verduyn, 'Attitude', p. 6; W. Holdsworth, *A History of English Law*, 4th edn (London, Methuen, 1936), vol. 2, p. 437. But see also comments in H. G. Richardson, 'The English coronation oath', *Speculum*, 24 (1949), pp. 71–4.
95 *YB 22 Edward III*, p. 3 (Hilary, pl. 25).
96 *YB 39 Edward III*, p. 7.
97 Plucknett, *Statutes*, pp. 51, 94–5.
98 *YB 33–35 Edward I*, p. 585.
99 See 29 Edward I (*SR*, vol. 1, p. 142).
100 J. C. Sainty, *The Judges of England, 1272–1990: a List of Judges of the Superior Courts*, SS, Supplementary Series, 10 (London, 1993), pp. 6–8.
101 Musson and Ormrod, *Evolution*, pp. 155–6; Dodd, 'Crown, magnates and gentry', pp. 36–43.
102 Musson and Ormrod, *Evolution*, pp. 154–5.
103 See 2 Richard II st. 2, c. 3, 5 Richard II (*SR* vol. 2, pp. 12, 17–21).
104 These figures are not entirely accurate since the date of some statutes is uncertain.
105 R. H. Britnell, *The Commercialisation of English Society, 1000–1500* (Cambridge, Cambridge University Press, 1993), pp. 173–5; M. Kowaleski, *Local Markets and Regional Trade in Medieval Exeter* (Cambridge, Cambridge University Press, 1995), pp. 183–90; S. Rees Jones, 'York's civic administration, 1354–1464', in S. Rees Jones (ed.), *The Government of Medieval York. Essays in Commemoration of the 1396 Royal Charter*, Borthwick Studies in History, 3 (York, 1997), pp. 125–7, 138–9; M. K. McIntosh, *Controlling Misbehaviour in England, 1370–1600* (Cambridge, Cambridge University Press, 1998), pp. 37–9.
106 W. O. Ault, 'Some early village by-laws', *EHR*, 45 (1930), pp. 209, 211–12.
107 *The Little Red Book of Bristol*, ed. F. B. Bickley (Bristol, W. C. Hemmons, 1900); G. Martin, 'English town records, 1200–1350', in R. H. Britnell (ed.), *Pragmatic Literacy, East and West, 1200–1330* (Woodbridge, Boydell Press, 1997), pp. 126, 129.

108 J. Catto, 'Andrew Horn: law and history in fourteenth-century England', in R. H. C. Davis and J. M. Wallace-Hadrill (eds), *The Writing of History in the Middle Ages* (Oxford, Clarendon Press, 1981), pp. 367-74, 376-8.
109 Rees Jones, 'Civic administration', pp. 111-12, 115.
110 McIntosh, *Controlling Misbehaviour*, p. 40.
111 P. Hyams, 'What did Edwardian villagers understand by law?' in Z. Razi and R. Smith (eds), *Medieval Society and the Manor Court* (Oxford, Clarendon Press, 1996), p. 81.
112 See 36 Edward III st. 1, c. 15 (*SR* vol. 2, pp. 375-6); *CLBCL: Letter Book G*, p. 73.
113 D. Palliser, 'Towns and the English state, 1066-1500', in J. R. Maddicott and D. M. Palliser (eds), *The Medieval State: Essays Presented to James Campbell* (London, Hambledon, 2000), p. 142.
114 The statute was too prescriptive and did not take account of the fluidity and ambiguities of fourteenth-century society (B. Hanawalt, *"'Of Good and Ill repute: Gender and Social Control in Medieval England* (New York and Oxford, Oxford University Press, 1998), pp. 54, 108).
115 J. H. Baker, *The Order of Serjeants at Law*, SS, Supplementary series, 5 (London, 1984), p. 67.
116 W. O. Ault, 'Open field husbandry', *Transactions of the American Philosophical Society*, new series, 55 (1965); E. Clark, 'Medieval labor law and English local courts', *AJLH*, 27 (1983), pp. 333-4, 337-9; A. Musson, 'New labour laws, new remedies? Legal reaction to the Black Death "crisis"', in N. Saul (ed.), *Fourteenth Century England I* (Woodbridge, Boydell Press, 2000).
117 *Halmota Prioratus Dunelmensis*, ed. J. Booth, Surtees Society, 82 (Durham, 1886), pp. 161, 166, 168, 171; *Proceedings before the Justices of the Peace in the Fourteenth and Fifteenth Centuries*, ed. B. H. Putnam (London, Ames Foundation, 1938), pp. cxviii, 207-8; Hanawalt, *Gender and Social Control*, p. 188; McIntosh, *Controlling Misbehaviour*, p. 98.
118 The boroughs, for instance, may have favoured private petitions over common petitions: Dodd, 'Crown, magnates and gentry', p. 106.
119 *Ibid.*, pp. 129, 180-2.
120 For an examination of the important role played by burgesses in this respect see C. Liddy, 'Urban communities and the Crown: relations between Bristol, York and the royal government, 1350-1400', unpublished DPhil thesis, University of York, 1999.

6

The politicisation of law

LAW had a substantial influence on the lives of people in late medieval England. The very expression of royal authority and administration in terms of law meant that law became inextricably linked with politics and a key aspect of royal governance. Arguably the law's role went beyond this in that it provided not simply a framework, but also a language for politics. Political discourse took many forms in various places, from the 'orderly' parliamentary forum, to the preaching and sermonising of the clergy, the domain of satire and polemic in literary works and oral ballads, through to the 'disorderly' activities of the rebels in the Peasants' Revolt.

This chapter maintains that the key concerns and political debates during the period 1215–1381 invariably rested on issues of legal import, among them ways of defining the legitimate exercise of royal power, matters of jurisdiction, law and order, and the functioning of the judicial system. The chapter examines some of the contexts in which law entered the political arena and the processes by which royal authority was transmitted to, and received by, subjects. The first section focuses on kingship and particularly the use of image and rhetoric in upholding public order and maintaining confidence in the law. The second section considers the attempts on the part of successive monarchs to legitimise their actions on the national and international stage by applying legal concepts and processes. It also examines the conceptual difficulties faced by those who sought a formula for restricting the power of the king and the practical problems of finding a means of enforcing the sanctions. The third and final section looks at 'popular' attitudes towards the law and the assimilation of legal concepts as manifested in the Peasants' Revolt. In seeking to answer the questions posed at the start of this book concerning the articulation of ideas during the Revolt and the background to its eruption, the dynamic role of legal consciousness is stressed. One further question arises from this: did the factors facilitating legal consciousness, including the success of the law in reaching out to all sectors of society and the emergence of lawyers as an identifiable group, actually work against the interests and desires of the Crown and its people?

Seeing and hearing the law

The king's role in justice

As supreme judicial authority in the kingdom, the king – by his attitude and actions – obviously played a decisive part in determining the public perception of the law. Contemporary legal theory held that all law was ultimately derived from God and that while (according to one text) the king could act 'unbound by laws', it was widely considered that he was subject to the principles of divine or natural law.[1] The king's personal relations and private interests as a landowner had necessarily to be reconciled with or subsumed within the matrix of responsibilities relating to his office and to his relations with the people both within and outside his kingdom. Historians have emphasised the recognised 'constitutional' duties of the monarch and shown how these interacted with prevailing concepts of kingship.[2] The development of the concept of the Crown as a distinct legal entity was a means of preserving possessions and powers from derogation or alienation, but it also enabled subjects to perceive, comment upon, uphold or judge the actions of the institution rather than the occupant of the throne.[3] In practice, however, distinctions between the public and private interests of the king – and between the Crown as an intangible entity and the king as a person – were less easy for ordinary people to draw since people rarely, if ever, experienced his personal side or saw him in the flesh. Their perceptions were a fused mass of (sometimes competing) images and feelings associated with their sovereign lord.

The king needed to be able to portray a multi-faceted image – one that enabled him to be feared, respected, and revered – in order to encourage stability and legality. Symbols of authority and justice such as crowns and swords were important purveyors of the royal image. Over the course of the period, concepts relating to the Crown were frequently couched in legal terms and reinforced by associated imagery. The notion that the Crown was what nowadays would be termed a 'corporation sole' (a legal entity in its own right irrespective of the incumbent), that certain rights, lands and possessions were an enduring and inseparable part of the

Crown, had been in circulation since the mid-twelfth century.[4] In the thirteenth century, the powers, lands and rights which belonged 'to the ancient desmesne of the Crown'[5] were symbolised by a physical crown (St Edward the Confessor's crown), which Henry III directed to be handed down to his royal successors.[6] This relationship was later confirmed and verbalised by Edward I, who swore by Edward the Confessor to uphold 'the right of his kingdom and of the crown of Saint Edward'.[7] The perception of the Crown as a distinct legal entity was further underlined in the terminology used to describe the death of the sovereign: *il se demyst*. This was a legal term commonly used to record that the holder of a particular estate had divested himself of his interest or title.[8] A case appearing in the court of common pleas in the 1340s refers to Edward II as *de regimine regni Angliae se demisit* (in other words divesting himself of the government of the kingdom of England) which echoes the words proclaimed with regard to Edward II's abdication and his son's accession, which were similarly *seu est ouste del governement du Roialme* (or its Latin equivalent *se amovit a regimine regni*). In both cases they indicate that the Crown was (or was similar to) a legal interest that could be passed on to successors in title, though the holder had first to renounce his legal entitlement either personally (voluntarily) or, as the theory subsequently came to be applied, simply by dying.[9]

Even in death, the king's role as lawgiver continued to be important. The elaborate burial ceremonies of medieval kings made visual statements about the power and authority of kingship in general and the character of their personal rule.[10] Henry III, for instance, was buried in his coronation robes along with certain insignia. It may be postulated, therefore, that Henry, in David Carpenter's words, 'had thought deeply about his death and the form and meaning of his burial'.[11] For a society alive to iconographic statements, the details would not be lost on contemporaries, either at his immediate burial or at his translation in 1290. Wearing the crown and coronation robes contrasted with the 'crownless' King John, who was buried instead in his coif and shirt of unction, and served to emphasise a distinction between majesty and the priestly character of kingship. Again, unlike his father, whose body the young king may have seen, Henry was buried without a sword. At the coronation ceremony the sword symbolised 'justice', which the king was to exercise against the forces of evil and in protection of the Church. The omission of the sword may have been understood as an emasculation of the royal image and had overtones of the arbitrary actions and injustices carried out in Henry's name.[12] Henry no doubt intended it to be regarded as a positive act, for the sword was deliberately replaced by a rod bearing a dove. Not only was the dove a personal symbol Henry III had adopted during the course of the reign (because it was intimately associated with Edward the Confessor), but in the wider context of his reign, it testified to the lengthy periods of peace he brought to the country and ideologically aligned his rule with the legendary stability and justice that marked the Confessor's reign.[13]

The dual nature of kingship, the man and the monarch, was thus juxtaposed at a royal funeral: the physical body (or its effigy) was draped in the robes and insignia of office, subsuming his individuality within the trappings of kingship. It is significant – given the attempts to legitimise the removal of Edward II – that the burial of the deposed (and murdered) king, which it was envisaged would be watched by sufficient numbers as to warrant the construction of special oak barriers to keep the crowds at bay, was not deliberately played down or carried out in a significantly different style from those of his royal predecessors. Although Edward II was accused of breaking his coronation vows and flouting the laws of the land in his lifetime, the burial ceremony was lavish and the funeral arrangements and imagery, conforming to existing aesthetic traditions, portrayed 'a ritualised image of political normality'. The actual body of Edward was interred dressed in the vestments of his anointing at his coronation, while the funeral effigy, on public view, displayed his actual coronation robes and regalia. The visual element of a funeral procession, burial or translation was important not only for giving observers or mourners something to see, but for underlining a particular view of law and kingly power. The funeral imagery of Edward II's burial contributed to Edward III's desired sense of a normal (legal) accession to the throne and public acceptance of a posthumous rehabilitation of the authority of his father.[14]

As distinct from the iconography of the Crown, the personal aspect of kingship – with its mythology and associated images – was clearly regarded as something to be cultivated. The personality models upon which different kings drew for inspiration were significant (whether or not the individual lived up to them) in their espousal of particular ideals and styles of kingship. Personality models helped in the assimilation of such concepts since they encouraged the identification of right rule with the royal personality rather than mere abstract notions of kingship. Henry III's veneration of Edward the Confessor, for instance, imported implications of the Confessor's sanctity and his reputation for justice through his laws.[15] Edward III's imagination and admiration were drawn to Henry II and Edward I, with their expansionist foreign policies and concern for the workings of the law, arguably, emulated in his own reign.[16] The extent to which it was perceived that a particular king fulfilled his own ideals or the commonly expected paradigms of kingship depended partly on the existing 'low' and 'high' views on kingship, the length of his reign, the nature of the public opinion at his death and the vagaries of memory in order to provide valid comparison with his predecessors.[17]

The manner in which the sovereign was addressed could provide an aural and psychological impression of majesty and law-giving qualities both for the king personally and for the benefit of those around him. Edward I and his grandson were referred to on various occasions by bishops or archbishops as 'Excellentissimo principi' (most excellent prince) a term with strong resonances in Roman law, implying that the king was the emperor incarnate, possessed no earthly superior and enjoyed independent lawmaking powers. This style was later cultivated both by Richard II himself and the writers of those prophetic texts which cast him in the role of Caesar, who after much bloodshed and strife would restore justice and the laws.[18]

The king's personal role in upholding the law and providing justice for his subjects was shown, first, in his attitude towards oaths. The operation of the legal system was underpinned by oaths, whether sworn by judicial officers, jurors or those proving facts or giving evidence. The significance afforded to oaths lay in the corresponding concepts of duty, honour, truth, good faith and their inherently sacred nature. Henry III's oaths of July 1232 to maintain a series of charters granted to senior ministers were taken on the supposed relics of the Holy Cross at Bromholm Priory.[19] In 1318 Edward II's promise to abide by the counsel of his earls and barons was announced by the bishop of Norwich 'by the great cross in the nave' of St Paul's Cathedral in London.[20] The religious overtones and notions of trust made them important political events, especially as markers of behaviour. Repudiating a sacred oath required papal release and absolution.[21]

The oath taken by the sovereign at his coronation was a statement of the Crown's duties, but was regarded as an important symbol of the king's own personal obligations to the realm. The coronation ceremony in fact embodied a form of double contract: one between the sovereign and his people (the king's oath) and one between his great men and the king (their renewal of the bond of homage).[22] In its thirteenth-century form (as found in *Bracton*), the king promised (1) to work for the peace of Church and people, (2) to prevent rapacity and oppression, and (3) to do justice impartially and mercifully. Both Henry III and Edward I swore, additionally, to preserve the rights of the Crown. In a foreshadowing of the recast oath of 1308, Edward I may also have promised to uphold the laws of his predecessors (especially Edward the Confessor).[23]

The oath sworn by Edward II in 1308, which began with a promise to observe the body of law 'grauntées par les aunciens rois d'Engleterre' (with special reference to the Laws of St Edward) and continued with the first and third precepts above, contained a fourth promise that was designed to secure the king's observance of the charters and laws that the community of the realm would determine in the future: a direct response to Edward I's obtaining release from his confirmation of Magna Carta and the Forest Charter.[24] An important and sacramental undertaking, it was one made privately during the coronation service in the chapel of St Edward the Confessor in Westminster Abbey, rather than proclaimed publicly.[25] This does not mean that the king made a secret of the nature of his obligations. Edward II, for instance, on several occasions (including in a writ to sheriffs) used phraseology from the coronation oath.[26] It does suggest, however, that the significance of the 1308 oath has been exaggerated by constitutional historians and that while an important marker of the king's duties, it should also be viewed within the theatrical context of the coronation.

The king's personal dispensation of justice in the court *coram rege* had largely become a fiction, but there is evidence of kings intervening in judicial matters. Edward I was recorded as personally contributing to a case involving the countess of Aumale[27] and several other disputes.[28] In 1323–24, in the aftermath of the civil war, Edward II took a particular interest in expediting judicial business himself, issuing writs to the king's bench, personally examining indictments, and summoning the prior of Llanthony for questioning.[29] Edward III sat in king's bench for the trial of some of the Folville gang in 1332, but he was especially active in judicial matters during the 1340s and 1350s, scrutinising points and issuing instructions personally using the great seal.[30] Richard II ordered the issue charters of manumission to rebels during the Peasants' Revolt, but was also prevailed upon during the Revolt by a man passing near him to act personally to provide satisfaction in a land dispute.[31]

There were of course problems with the king's personal dispensation of justice when it was perceived that justice was carried out in a questionable or arbitrary manner, or even denied. Edward I, for instance, appears to have been impatient with legal technicalities, while Edward III seems sometimes to have influenced court cases in a heavy-handed fashion.[32] A number of unjust disseisins were carried out in Henry III's name in the 1230s, for which he made public admission 'with his own mouth' and charges of denial of justice were raised against him in 1264.[33] Edward I also was accused of blocking an action, which John de Ferrers brought against

Walter Langton.[34] At times, the king's favour could be used to particular advantage. It was generally perceived that Henry III's Lusignan half-brothers were protected from legal actions, though this favour was also seen to extend at times to native *curiales*, such as the earls of Cornwall and Gloucester.[35] Under Edward II, legal process was sometimes abused and cases were prevented from receiving justice during the ascendancy of the Despensers.[36] The fear of Edward II's reprisals for failure in royal endeavours lay behind an example of legal validation of actions and a public act of witness. In 1313, upon failure of the negotiations at St Albans for the return of Gaveston's horses and jewels, the king's representatives wrote an account of the matter and ensured that the document was sealed by a notary public and 'read on two days in the church of St Albans before the prior and senior monks and all the people summoned there' and then sealed with the convent's seal.[37]

Justice was not a straightforward matter when litigation concerned magnates and bishops. In Henry III's reign and probably later, the king's support was vital for success. The king's role as power broker and ultimate arbiter, however, meant that bias in one direction could upset the delicate balance. Political considerations, including the number and identity of magnate supporters and backers could inevitably distort the process. The king's handling of the situation was therefore crucial. Henry III's ineptitude when Roger Bigod, earl of Norfolk, and Simon de Montfort were engaged in litigation in the 1250s had substantial and very obvious political repercussions.[38] Edward I had the authority and gall to put the earls of Hereford and Gloucester on trial in the 1290s.[39] By contrast, Edward III built up a good reputation in the arbitrations he undertook, though he did not shrink from making an example of Thomas de Lisle, bishop of Ely, in his dispute with the king's cousin, Lady Wake.[40] Justice meted out after the civil wars or rebellions in the form of forfeiture of titles or confiscation of estates could be equally devastating. The king's actions not only altered the political balance, but could leave power vacuums, destabilise areas and lead to problems of law and order in local society.[41] It was not only the high-status landowners who enjoyed a special relationship with the Crown and the monarch himself, but also tenants of land designated 'ancient desmesne' and people who lived and worked on one of the royal manors.[42]

Royal propaganda

The monarch's duty to uphold justice was most obviously manifested in the soliciting of petitions from his subjects. Edward I specifically requested that grievances be presented in 1289 and, although no specific royal initiative can be found, a large number of petitions were also presented in the early part of his reign (particularly in 1278).[43] Petitions were actively sought from aggrieved subjects in 1327 following the collapse of Edward II's rule, providing a marked contrast to the inaccessibility exhibited during the final years of his reign. Similar credentials were presented by Edward III on his assumption of personal control in 1330, when he too offered to remedy the grievances arising from the minority regime overseen by his mother and her consort.[44] While there was undoubtedly a genuine need for reconstruction in these instances, the king was able to bolster his credibility and create something of a 'feel-good factor' by appearing to listen to and act on demands for justice.

A potent insignia of the operation of the law and one that was in the public domain was the great seal. Necessarily visually recognisable as an icon of government and officially held by the chancellor, the great seal was, at least in the thirteenth century, also a practical necessity for the issue of royal documents. Illegal use of the great seal (which included its removal and illicit use by the king) for the authentication of charters and writs was regarded in Henry III's reign as fraud. The king's use of the great seal was denounced in the so-called Paper Constitution of 1244, a plan of reform designed to control official appointments and supervise aspects of the operation of government.[45] This had particular relevance to the use of the great seal, which had to follow the person of the king. Indeed, before the separation of the chancery from the household of the king and more frequent use of the privy seal, both of which were evident in the fourteenth century, largely as a result of Edward III's military campaigns, it could be declared that any document bearing the great seal, that did not coincide with the royal itinerary, was a forgery.[46]

Although separation from the king and the increasing use of smaller, more personal seals limited the scope of the great seal, it remained a powerful visual sign of royal government and an expression of the authority of the Crown – one evidently appreciated by provincial peasants eager for documents issued under it.[47] As a symbol of royal will the designs on its two faces were undoubtedly significant. 'The seal's icon of the king enthroned in majesty made his authority present wherever his image was present, like Christ enthroned in Majesty.'[48] Henry III personally issued instructions for the form of the great seal of 1259, which depicted him holding the orb and a doveheaded rod, rather than the sword gracing the seals of his predecessors. The position of the monarch was altered to show him seated on a quasi-imperial throne, rather than a low bench, while leopards or lions were placed at its base and sides invoking imagery of the throne of Solomon, the wise law-giver in the Bible.[49] Impressions of the great seal (and later the privy seal) were sent to all sheriffs whenever a new one was cast so that they could recognise the style of the genuine article. Edward III's new great and privy seals, featuring the new quartered arms of France and England and the protocol *rex Anglie et Francie*, were sent to the county courts for public display in 1340.[50]

Public proclamation provided an important non-visual means of reinforcing the king's authority, spreading ideas and policy, and underlining the power of Crown. Indeed, the medium of the spoken word was familiar to contemporaries as the primary method of communicating to the general public news and other information, royal orders, promulgated legislation, and details of court sessions. Although writs and other documents were circulated to individuals and institutions, proclamation was invariably used for both local and national business. A powerful vehicle for the dissemination of decrees and matters of political and legal import, it offered a valuable means of permeating the consciousness of the individual. In this respect we should consider the type of document proclaimed, the geographical coverage, the language(s) used, and, as far as it is possible to measure, the general effectiveness of the exercise.

Significantly, there is evidence to show that it was intended that Magna Carta (both the original and many of the subsequent re-issues and confirmations), the Provisions of Oxford and – by Edward III's reign – most, if not all, statutes and ordinances, be publicised through oral proclamation.[51] Other legal-political matters for proclamation included general pardons, confirmation of liberties, invitations to confirm individual charters, orders for named individuals to attend court to answer accusations, the commissions of itinerant justices (such as justices of trailbaston) and justices of the peace, summonses to parliament and diplomatic treaties.[52] Much of Henry III's legislation was proclaimed 'by the voice of the crier' (*voce preconia*) rather than recorded on statute rolls. In 1234, for instance, orders were given for the proclamation of regulations regarding the supervision of hundred courts (in line with the revision of Magna Carta that year) and in 1248, it was decreed that the right to castrate another man as a punishment for fornication was to be restricted to a husband in the case of his wife's adulterer.[53]

Proclamations intended for the population at large were delivered to the sheriffs in every county and to the bailiffs of liberties for dissemination in the full county court, in cities, boroughs, market towns and hundreds. Towns and cities generally employed men especially to act as 'criers'. The specification of locations, such as fairs and markets, and the general discretion given to the sheriff ('and in other places where you shall see fit') was designed to enable the message to reach as wide an audience as possible. Usually the standard or designated public place was the town cross or a crossroads. In London, messages were broadcast at a considerable number of points around the city, in the suburbs and at wharves.[54] St Paul's Cathedral was frequently the stage for public proclamations and political propaganda. In 1311, for instance, as the *Annales Paulini* recorded, the ordinances were read out 'at the stone cross' in the churchyard.[55]

The capacity of the populace to understand statutes and act upon government commands depended to a large extent upon the language in which the proclamation was delivered. Although Magna Carta was officially issued in 1215 in Latin (the language of government and record, which served to imbue it with legality), its provisions were required to be recited publicly, implying that it was actually proclaimed in the relevant vernaculars. An early thirteenth-century translation into French survives and it is highly probable that the text was also translated into and recited in English. Indeed, to be effective (since not everyone understood Latin, or even French) the crier or a local official must have been able to switch between languages (either at sight or with the benefit of a crib sheet). There are sufficient thirteenth-century references to the publishing of texts or letters in the native tongue (*patriae lingua*), mother tongue (*materna lingua*) or explicitly in English (*Anglicana*) and French (*Gallicana*) for it to be assumed that steps were taken to ensure they reached the widest possible audience.[56]

On occasion the texts of the proclamations were themselves drawn up in French and English. Letters patent of 18 and 20 October 1258 concerning the Provisions of Oxford were drawn up in both vernaculars and sent to the counties addressed to the king's subjects.[57] Two proclamations of 1330, one publicising the earl of Kent's treasonous behaviour, the other informing the nation of the arrest of Roger Mortimer and Edward III's intention to rule with the assent of his magnates, were written down in French. By the fourteenth century, French had become one of the languages of record, certainly for government documents, and was employed in the Year Books; but even though English was (by statute) to be used in the fourteenth-century courts, tradition still refused to give it official acknowledgement in documents. It was only in the second half of the fifteenth century that this privilege was accorded the vernacular (at least in governmental rather than purely legal sources) and proclamations were issued directly in English.[58] Until then, in the absence of official non-Latin or non-French texts, the traditional form of oral publication in the vernacular probably continued to be employed as a means of disseminating statutes and commands.

How effective was proclamation as a vehicle for raising political and legal consciousness? What advantages did it offer over the written word and how do we know that it actually took place? The proclamation as an oral device offered scope for influencing thinking. Announcements could be read 'straight' or in a deadpan way like a newscast, but if the crier were more like a jongleur, they could also be 'played', read with a degree of emotional charge and given a persuasive, even argumentative, tone. It is conceivable that parts could be stressed and embellished accordingly. The recitation was probably a lengthy one (especially if there was a great deal of news and information) and (assuming it was felt to matter) the people's attention had to be captured and maintained for the duration. It was also something that could be repeated at regular intervals to ensure that people got the message. In 1300, sheriffs were told that Magna Carta and the Charter of the Forest were to be read out in front of the people at quarterly intervals (Michaelmas, Christmas, Easter and Midsummer). The Statute of Winchester was also to be recited four times a year and other statutes were frequently read out at county court meetings.[59] In the 1360s there were calls for the recitation of the articles of the eyre and statutes at peace sessions and for the statute of 1362 in particular to be made freely available to individuals.[60]

As well as supplementing the written word, proclamation could also be backed up by the written word. In 1279, for example, Archbishop Pecham's council affirmed a policy whereby a copy of Magna Carta was to be prominently displayed in a public place in every cathedral and collegiate church, with a fresh copy to be substituted every spring (presumably in case the transcript had faded or become damaged). In addition to the oral publication of Magna Carta in 1300, all judges, sheriffs, civic leaders and cathedral chapters received sealed transcripts.[61] Edward III's manifesto, released as part of his claim as king of France, received publication both in England and in France.[62]

Some measure of the effectiveness of the system and the emphasis placed upon it by monarchs can be seen in the way Philip of Valois, Edward III's rival claimant for the French throne, ordered the latter's manifesto to be torn down from church doors and public squares in France.[63] Similarly, Edward I reacted with hostility to Archbishop Pecham's initiative, ordering him to ensure the removal of copies of the Great Charter from church doors.[64] The Crown's concern to check whether proclamations had in fact been made is demonstrated in the requirement, introduced by Edward I, that the sheriff endorse the writ of proclamation, indicating the task had been carried out. This accountability was further enhanced under Edward III, when the sheriff was asked to provide the date and location of performances. In order to ensure the message got home, the language of the writs sent out under Henry III and Edward I (as well as their successors) is at times couched in terms of insistence on compliance, sometimes with added inducements or threats for failure to proclaim verbatim certain key passages.[65] Another measure of the success of this method of communication (though perhaps attributable rather to the spread of statute books for personal use) can be surmised from the trend for litigants and petitioners to quote excerpts from statutes to back up their claims.[66] This did not mean that they had an exact comprehension of the statutory provision. In 1290, for example, a bill coming before the justices of king's bench pointed to Magna Carta (c. 17) as evidence for common-pleas jurisdiction being synonymous with 'the bench' (the court of common pleas).[67]

The well-established system of issuing proclamations provided the Crown with an unparalleled opportunity for influencing the way people thought about the operation of government and, in particular, about the law and the administration of justice. People could be assured of the king's continuing concern for good order in the realm, even during his absences from the kingdom, by means of special proclamations.[68] Royal propaganda could be effectively disseminated when it was included in the form of a preamble to a statute. By prefacing significant pieces of legislation with rhetoric that highlighted the inadequacy of the system in times past (especially under a previous regime), rulers were able to point to novel solutions to problems and thus present themselves as radical reformers addressing the needs of their subjects.

The introduction or preamble to a statute, setting out the basic reasoning behind the legislative action, became an increasingly important device. The trend was perhaps set by Edward I in the Statute of Winchester (1285), which provided a swingeing denunciation of the state of the peace – complaining that daily there were more robberies, homicides, arsons and thefts committed than formerly – and then proceeded to offer a combination of measures designed to rectify the problem.[69] A similar citation of disorder was included in the commissions to keepers/justices of the peace, justices of oyer and terminer and the letters patent for general inquiries.[70] The tradition was extended and utilised particularly effectively by Edward III and Richard II. Indeed, it is noticeable that during the course of the fourteenth century statutory preambles tended to increase in length and verbosity. The following elaborate exposition contained in Richard II's statute of 1378 is a prime example:[71]

> Because our sovereign lord the king has perceived ... that divers of his liege people in sundry parts of the realm gather together a great number of men at arms and archers in the manner of war, and conspire together by oath and other confederacy, not having consideration to God, or to the laws of Holy Church, or of the land, or to right, or justice, but refusing and setting apart all process of law, ride in great routs in divers parts of England, and take manors, lands and other possessions ... and hold them by force ... ; and in some places, lying in wait with such routs, beat, maim, murder and slay the people, in order to have wives and their goods ... ; and sometimes take the king's people in their own houses and bring and hold them to fine and ransom, as it were in a land of war; and sometimes come before the justices in their sessions in such a guise with great force, whereby the justices are afraid ... to do the law ... ; whereby the realm is in great trouble, to the great mischief and grievance of the people and the hurt of the king's majesty and against the king's crown.

The statute itself offered a fresh offensive against conspirators and grew out of a rather prosaic petition concerning confederacy.[72] The prolonged passage preceding the main body of the text of the statute afforded a good public-relations opportunity and provided a useful preliminary to what was in effect a re-launch (confirmation) of the Statute of Northampton of 1328.

Confirming selected older statutes was itself a clever 'marketing ploy' which had the double advantage of enabling the present incumbent of the throne (or his regent) to capitalise on the reforming initiative of the previous monarch, while at the same time emphasising his own legislative credentials. Edward I's reputation as the 'English Justinian', though posthumously awarded and justifiable to a certain extent, does not take into account the fact that many of the measures promulgated were merely a codification of previous legislative impulses. The Statute of Winchester, for example, was essentially an amalgamation of much earlier initiatives concerning the possession of weapons and preservation of the peace.[73] In the period 1327-30, the regency regime of Queen Isabella and Roger Mortimer, undoubtedly influenced by the disastrous events of Edward II's reign, was concerned to re-establish credibility, particularly on law enforcement matters.[74] Indeed, to Mortimer's credit, in 1330 there was no hint of an indictment against him for his policies on the administration of justice or his handling of law and order.[75] A series of important measures introduced during their brief tenure of authority harked back to Edward I's reign both symbolically and literally. The Statute of Northampton (1328), for instance, stressed that the personnel and organisation of the assize and gaol delivery commissions should accord with the Statute of Fines of 1299 and 'the form of another statute made in the time of the said [King Edward I]'.[76] The resurrection of the general eyre in 1329 and its introduction simultaneously in two counties in the Midlands, reputedly a hotbed of disorder, further signalled the regime's commitment to law and order by evoking the somewhat rose-tinted memory of a golden age of peace under the eyres in the thirteenth century.[77]

The political nature of the rhetoric behind these legislative measures shows not only how seriously some monarchs took their sworn duty to maintain law and order and guarantee justice (or, more cynically, realised that their people desired security and welcomed a show of intent),[78] but also the extent to which even successful medieval kings resorted to propaganda both to bolster the standing of their regime and to justify new statutory measures. By adding what modern political commentators would call the correct level of 'spin' to a preliminary message and by effectively 're-branding' a familiar package of measures, the Crown was able to express a rejuvenated commitment to maintaining public order and social stability. The practice was valuable to fall back on, especially when genuinely faced with a situation of political, social and/or economic unrest. Nevertheless, such actions were not simply a clever public-relations exercise. The nature of the statutes and the hyperbolic language of their preambles should not mask the underlying theme: the continuing need to find effective means to counter public-order difficulties and provide redress for litigants – a problem encountered not merely when governments fell, but when the existing initiatives to combat lawlessness failed or judicial remedies proved ineffective.

Public image and propaganda were particularly necessary in the re-establishment or consolidation of the position of the monarch upon his succession, or for boosting confidence in a regime that was flagging in popularity. We should not of course assume that the policy, the propaganda or the proclamation's essential details registered either in their entirety or as intended. Some measure of scepticism as to the effectiveness of proclamations, be it critical or cynical, should be maintained. Even if some form of publication occurred, we cannot be sure how many people listened to it or that they heard exactly what the Crown wanted them to hear. There was scope for discretion in the release, interpretation and translation of the texts and even the vernacular could have been confusing when there was no such thing as standard English and dialects were so very different. In times of civil stress, however, precise instructions and full translations were deemed necessary to ensure the precise message came across. In 1258, when the sheriffs and their criers could not necessarily be trusted, the reforming barons bypassed the usual mechanisms and paid for the proclamations to be written out in full in French and English so that all the king's subjects would learn the subject-matter.[79]

The Crown's propaganda could be disseminated through other equally effective methods. The Church provided a ready-made infrastructure in this respect. The preaching of sermons or the offering of prayers for a specific cause enabled the king, when he specifically required it, to communicate designs and harness the spiritual endeavour of the assembled congregations. The language of the sermons was English and while they contained theological reasoning, the rhetoric was frequently couched in invective and in terms of prejudice.[80] It was a system that could be manipulated to work as well for the sovereign as against him. Preaching directed against particular legislative measures was obviously a worry. In 1356 Robert Gerard, vicar of Aldbury in Hertfordshire, and Richard Fulham, a hermit, appeared in court for publicly denouncing the Statute of Labourers and allegedly 'setting a dangerous example to the said labourers, artisans and servants' and other tenants who had taken notice of their preaching.[81]

Kings could also employ the visual and participatory aspects of processions, feasts and spectacles for their own benefit and for promoting peaceful order. Although slightly outside our period, Richard II's entrance into London in 1392 and the lavish entertainment could be regarded as a form of 'loveday' in which the on-going dispute between the Crown and the city was replaced with physical expressions of unity, harmony and community.[82] Naturally, in such a situation there was still room for power play between the two parties, respective activity and passivity, competing in their desire for attention, magnificence and spectacle, a form of negotiation for recognition of claims.[83] We should also remember that, for those not actually taking part, such displays could prove to be rituals of exclusion. The lack of identification with the parties and an absence of a sense of community could foment disharmony and lead to disorder. The aims of the propaganda exercise and the apparently uniting features could have the reverse effect, emphasising inequalities and exclusion.[84]

The public exhibition of rebellious or deposed leaders, where they were ritually humiliated, their ambitions parodied and their treasonous behaviour signified to the masses attending, was intended to underline royal supremacy and instil by visual means the authority of the law. This was achieved not only literally through physical punishment, but symbolically through a shared culture of iconography and ritual. Certain high-profile cases exemplify different aspects of this tradition. At his execution in 1305, for instance, William Wallace (who, it was said, claimed that he would wear a crown at Westminster) was made to wear a crown of olive leaves before he was hanged, disembowelled (as a felon) and beheaded (as an outlaw). His entrails were burned (for blasphemy to the Church), his head was stuck on London Bridge and his remains, when the body had been quartered (for sedition), were sent to Newcastle, Berwick, Perth and Stirling, as a deterrent.[85] A similar fate overtook Prince Dafydd ap Gruffydd, upon his capture in 1283.[86] Ritual humiliation, involving popular traditions of reversal common in 'ridings', was meted out on the younger Despenser in 1326. Captured when trying to escape to Wales, he was brought to Bristol and mounted on 'le plus petit et maisgre et chetif cheval' (the smallest, thinnest and most puny horse), made to don a tabard with the Despenser arms reversed (a sign of treason) and wear a crown of nettles (possibly symbolising heresy or that he had 'stung' people). Bringing up the rear of the royal procession from Bristol to Hereford, he had to endure his reduced status being proclaimed by trumpets. On arrival in Hereford, someone wrote six verses of a psalm on his clothes and he was serenaded by a form of 'rough music' (*horridus sonus*) comprising cries, insults and the blowing of horns.[87] The recognition of Richard II's overlordship in Ireland was given symbolic resonance in the public submission of the uncle of Art MacMurrough, king of Leinster, to Richard in 1394 'with a halter round his neck and a drawn sword'.[88]

Legitimacy through the law

If upholding and acting within the law provided the template for political behaviour, then use of the law to provide legitimacy for actions in international and domestic affairs can also be seen to characterise the politics of the period 1215–1381. Being on the right side of the law or setting out a case that justified the position adopted was as important for the king when pursing ambitions at home and abroad as for those who sought to challenge his behaviour or his reading of legality. The constraints of space mean that an exhaustive analysis of this aspect cannot be undertaken here. This section, therefore, provides some representative and important examples stretching over the period. In the international arena, Edward I's claim to the overlordship of Scotland and his grandson's claim to the French throne are considered, while on the domestic front, the *quo warranto* inquiries, treason and impeachment, the deposition of Edward II and the role of Magna Carta in politics are examined.

Law became a weapon in Edward I's claim to overlordship of Scotland and he went to considerable lengths in 1290 in an attempt to provide a watertight case for his actions. Under feudal law, Edward required seisin of Scotland. As a first step, he became seised of the country through a legal fiction, whereby the royal castles in Scotland were handed over to him (as one of the competitors to the throne) by their keepers and then entrusted to him as feudal lord by the other competitors. In order to convince international opinion and some of the Scots, who did not accept his capacity, he sought to back it up with legal proof.[89] This precipitated a diligent search of archival sources to find the necessary evidence. Initially it was monastic records, 'chronicles, registers and other archives, both ancient and modern of whatever shape or date', that were prevailed upon, but this search (albeit at short notice) yielded only a citation of the treaty of Falaise of 1174 by which Henry II accepted the homage of William the Lion. The king then tried the royal archives, instructing that the Chancery records in the New Temple be surveyed. Details of treaties made by Henry III in 1237 (with Alexander II) and 1255 (with Alexander III) were sent to Edward, though neither were sufficient for his cause.[90] In 1300 further justification was required in order to convince the pope, who, besides indicting Edward for his conquest of Scotland in 1296, argued that Alexander III's homage was only for his English estates. To counter this, Edward ordered a comprehensive search of 'all the rolls and remembrances' concerning Scottish business, both royal archives (including repositories such as the exchequer and chancery) and monastic records. He also summoned to parliament academics from both the universities skilled in Roman law.[91] Edward's actions indicate that kings appreciated the importance of documentary evidence and the perception of legitimacy conferred by it.[92]

In addition to the provision of historical material in what was a very full justification, an important element in the evidence presented to Pope Boniface was a copy of the properly authenticated words of John Balliol at his homage in 1292, his renunciation in 1296 and his imprisonment in 1298. Adopting continental jurisprudential practices, rather than those more commonly found in English law, Balliol's words of homage and feudal recognition were given the force of law because they had been drawn up by a notary public. It appears that the particular notary had to alter the document because he had omitted an acknowledgement by Balliol that the English king should direct the affairs of Scotland. It did not matter, however, whether this statement was the truth, since the document itself provided the legal evidence (what could be proved) and so was more important than pure historical fact.[93] Ironically, since Edward was unwilling for it to appear as though he were submitting to the pope for adjudication, he asserted that the letter to Boniface was 'not to be treated in the form or manner of a legal plea' and was sent 'altogether extra-judicially'.[94]

The dynastic and imperialist ambitions of the English monarchs could be presented as merely recovering the lands that were rightfully part of the ancient demesne of the Crown. As early as March 1328, Edward III expressed his desire to recover *noz droiz & noz heritages*.[95] War with France, however, was tricky in the sense that the English king was technically a vassal of the king of France (and acknowledged the fact following the treaty of Paris of 1259) since he held the duchy of Aquitaine from him. By claiming the title 'king of France' Edward III could manoeuvre himself around the problems created under feudal law if he were to be adjudged a rebellious vassal.[96] Despite the fact that Philip of Valois had been anointed as king and was the elected ruler, succession to the French throne was not cut and dried, and the issues surrounding it remained doubtful and contentious. The opinions of English lawyers were a significant vehicle for legitimising Edward III's title to the French throne and his use of war as the theatre for enforcing his claim. Although the legal factors did not impinge greatly on the public consciousness (either in England or France), the immediacy and importance of the legal case underlying Edward III's claim to the French throne has generally been underestimated.[97]

Edward was dependent upon his lawyers and their reading of inheritance laws.[98] On the death of Charles IV in 1328, there were three contenders for the throne, Edward III (the nearest male heir through his mother, Charles IV's sister) and two cousins (direct male heirs), Philip of Evreux and Philip of Valois. The latter became king of France on the basis of his superior age, his prevailing support and political prospects, rather than for any legal reasons. Although the young Edward did homage in 1329, he did not renounce his claim and ten years later, in a letter to the pope he couched his hostilities in terms of a natural right to defend himself against the abuses and injustices of the French, which included usurpation of his rightful position as king of France. The formal declaration of intent, Edward's assumption of the title in January 1340, later enshrined in statute, was backed up by lengthy legal opinions on the Plantagenet claim produced for the pope by English diplomats in 1340 and 1344. The main thrust of English legal opinion did not ignore the principle that women could not inherit the French throne, but focused on the circumstances of exclusion, its chronology and standing as authority. It also attempted to circumvent critique by French lawyers by arguing that Edward's homage did not invalidate his claim since he was a minor at the time.

Significantly, the constitutional separation of the Crowns of the two realms was guaranteed by statute.[99] Some historians see this as a legal curb on the king's ambitions and as a political concession on his part, though the statute in fact may represent a premeditated attempt by Edward to avoid the criticism that his assumption of a new title would be to the detriment of England. The legislative initiative could be seen, therefore, as a conscious measure to achieve the support of the political community in his undertaking. However, the appearance of legality could be to suit his own purposes. The creation of a special receiver and committee of auditors (an initiative of the very same parliament) to deal with petitions from Flanders (technically subsumed into the French title) implies that Edward III was perfectly willing to exercise his rights as king of France in the context of an English tribunal as and when his opinion or the circumstances dictated.[100]

The diplomatic side should not be underestimated when considering the Scottish and French wars. As illustrated above, the use of lawyers and legal forms and precedents was recognised as being an important way of legitimising enterprises or at least securing the moral high ground. These methods were supplemented by creating verisimilitudes of antiquity and mythology (in the case of Edward I) or seeking to show divine approval in iconographic programmes associating the earthly ruler with the powers of heaven (in the case of Edward III).[101] Indeed, the chronicler, Robert of Avesbury, was convinced that Edward III's victories were granted by Christ because he 'is always on the side of justice'.[102] In a wider context, it was evidently recognised that laws promoted and projected a sense of national identity. Abrogating those laws or imposing the common law of England on another territory was a part of the reality of royal subjugation and the quashing of that separate national identity. The laws of Scotland, for instance, were considered and discussed and it was found that 'the laws and customs ... are clearly displeasing to God and to reason'.[103] The fact that a complete substitution was not wholly practical or even effective had already been found in Wales, where the Statute of Wales (1284) only abolished those customs most prejudicial to the Crown.[104] With this in mind, it is significant that Edward III's manifesto, issued as part of his claim to the French throne, stated he would respect the existing laws and customs of France.[105]

In domestic politics equally, the law played a decisive part in both private and public ways. The *quo warranto* inquiries, for instance, were a means by which the king's own legal rights could be investigated and upheld, but also could be represented as a way of stamping royal authority on the nobility and gentry by forcing them to submit their exercise of power to royal scrutiny and prove it to the king's satisfaction. The Crown's concern with the preservation of its rights and the accountability of its subjects was thus a key feature in the inquiries. The underlying rationale to the inquiries was the legal philosophy that all judicial authority derived from the sovereign and that since jurisdictional rights were delegated by him, they could be revoked at any time. The king as a property-holder (both tangible in the form of land and intangible in the form of rights and perquisites) was seeking to uphold his property rights in law.[106] As early as Henry III's reign investigations into the assumption of franchisal rights were launched on a county-by-county basis. Although in some cases the justices responded to usurpations with direct action, such as ordering gallows at 'Aton' (Ayton) in Yorkshire to be pulled down (thereby removing the potent symbol of the lord's criminal jurisdiction), the king was not wholly supportive of their firm and direct approach and so most alleged encroachments were merely noted.[107] Under Edward I the investigations became more systematic following the so-called 'ragman inquests' (hundred rolls inquiries) of 1274-75 and the plans published in the Statute of Gloucester of 1278.[108] The king's attorneys were also more aggressive in their prosecution of the king's claims.[109] The campaign hit 1,600 persons of high status, and perceptions were not favourable. One chronicler noted how a rhyme was circulating among the aristocracy: 'Le Roy cuvayte nos deneres/E la Rayne nos beau maners/E le Quo voranto/Sale mak wus al to do.' ('The king he wants to get our gold/The queen would like our lands to hold/And the writ Quo Warranto/Will give us all enough to do.')[110]

By statute, the *quo warranto* cases could only be pleaded in eyres, so – as the vehicle for the inquires – the eyre became intimately associated with them.[111] During the fourteenth century it became clear that the proceedings initiated by Edward I were not a 'one-off' and that, every time the eyre visited a county, claims had to be resubmitted and tested. In fact the imposition of eyres in individual counties (normally when there was a vacant see) and especially in London (1321) was seen as a blatant assertion of royal authority. The resurrection of the eyre in the Midlands (1328-31) similarly betrayed a concern for the exercise of franchises. The very word 'eyre' could raise the temperature of discussion, and dislike of such visitations was used to the Crown's financial advantage by Edward III.[112] The inquiries also highlighted the growing importance of possessing the requisite legal documentation, and the cultural conflict caused by the king's insistence on written forms of proof at the expense of other older forms of evidence. The psychological difficulties of the transition are rather aptly illustrated in the apocryphal confrontation between Edward I and Earl Warrenne, the latter brandishing his rusty, old sword as proof of his rights.[113]

The search to find sanctions against those who through their actions endangered the Crown (and the Crown was no longer seen as just the individual authority of the king but also as encompassing the community of the realm) engendered attempts to find a legal means of defining, and refining the scope of, what was a political crime. The concepts of treason espoused during the period 1215–1381 depended very much on the ideology or style of kingship adopted.[114] Henry III was merciful to the rebels at the end of the baronial wars and since there were no state trials after the civil war there was no precise judicial construction put on Simon de Monfort's behaviour, though judgment was carried out unofficially on his body with beheading and mutilation. For Edward I, treason had to be against the king's person or his servants, though he was prepared (where Scotland was involved) to accept it could be against the people of the realm. To the general notions of lese-majesty, he added the raising of war against the king (riding armed with banner unfurled), while plotting treasonous acts was taken as seriously as actually carrying them out. The legal procedure against offenders was not the usual indictment or appeal, but the idea of public repute 'on the king's record' (at the word of the king and his advisers).[115] Sometimes this occurred in parliament. Following his capture in 1283, a parliament was held to decide the fate of Dafydd.[116] Although Wallace and Fraser were not tried before parliament, judgment was given in the Scottish parliament held by Edward I at St Andrews in 1304.[117]

The use of conviction 'on the king's record' became linked to the summary procedures under the law of arms, which figured in the cases of Gilbert Middleton in 1317 and Andrew Harclay in 1323. In the same way, the process against Thomas of Lancaster (mirrored for the elder Despenser) precluded any right to 'iugement of his peris' or to answer the charges – the common treatment of outlaws. Appeals (even by Edward II) to Magna Carta c. 39 (c. 29, 1225 version) about the lack of 'due process' which this represented fell on deaf ears.[118] Edward II's reign also witnessed the advent of the offence of accroaching the power of the Crown, which encompassed the infringement of royal rights by subjects, but conversely could be used by the community of the realm against the king if he was seen as failing to protect the rights of the Crown.[119]

After the deposition of Edward II, treason trials of an arbitrary nature and on the basis of notoriety were effectively discredited, though the condemnation of Roger Mortimer in 1330 was also on the basis of public ill-fame, which led to a questioning of its legality by at least one chronicler and retrospectively by parliament in 1354.[120] In the early years of Edward III's reign, the scope of treason remained wide and the courts upheld its extension to accroachment of royal authority and waging private war. The Statute of Treasons of 1352, however, distinguished between high and petty treason, limiting the definition of high treason to a few specific crimes: planning and attempting to kill the king, his consort or his heir; raping his consort, his eldest unmarried daughter, or the wife of his heir; raising war against the king or allying with his enemies; counterfeiting the great seal or the currency; and murdering the senior officials of state when in session.[121] Although largely the work of the royal justices, the statute was nevertheless a reply to a petition on the subject of treason requesting a definition of the offence. The petition implied that vigilance over the abuse of royal power and limitation of the scope of the offence were of concern to the political community.[122] The lack of a clear and coherent policy on the treasonous implications of a popular uprising was revealed in the aftermath of the Peasants' Revolt, when the Crown made no effort to bring the statute of 1352 to the attention of the presenting jurors, who in their uncertainty tended to reduce treasonous actions to felony (such as the execution of the archbishop of Canterbury) or, as in many cases, produce rather vague indictments on the rebels' behaviour. It may of course say something about the ambivalence of jurors' opinions of the revolt.[123]

Impeachment was a variant of the accusation on the basis of notoriety, but because it was channelled institutionally through parliament (in what were in effect state trials) it was regarded as a more legitimate way to proceed than the arbitrary method outlined above.[124] Judges and royal ministers were targeted by the Crown and the Lords in 1289 and 1340–41 (see Chapter 2), but the accountability of ministers was showcased in the impeachment proceedings initiated by members of the Commons in the Good Parliament of 1376.[125]

When it was the king who was at fault, there were distinct political and legal problems in formulating and enforcing a reasonable limitation on the scope of his powers or actions. The legitimacy of such attempts rested upon the appropriateness to the situation of theoretical and jurisprudential grounds and an assumed natural respect among all parties for documents of a legal nature. Although the Magna Carta of 1215 'was a political document produced in a crisis'[126] its power arose from the subsequent reissues, confirmations and glosses that gave it a perspective and set it up as fundamental law. Not only did it provide a measurement of legality, but the sense of its provisions could be reinterpreted to suit the prevailing political and social conditions.[127] The principles enshrined in c. 39, in particular, designed to limit the arbitrary will of the king, were afforded a political context during the early years of Henry III's reign. The royal council's concern in 1234 at Henry's actions was also directly reflected in William Raleigh's writings in *Bracton*, where, while acknowledging the king's position, he propagated the view that the king had to rule in accordance with the law rather than *per voluntatem* and could be challenged if he caused injustice.[128] 'The king has a superior, namely, God. Also the law by which he is made king. Also his curia, namely the earls and barons, because if he is without bridle, that is without law, they ought to put a bridle on him.'[129]

Magna Carta's form and power as a charter – a legal document, formally sealed and witnessed, that bestowed or confirmed rights and privileges – meant that it was difficult to override or ignore. The symbolic nature and binding effect of Magna Carta, though apparent to those who invoked it, was not always certain in practice and became a test of the king's good faith. Edward I prevaricated considerably over confirmation of the charters in 1297–99 and there were differences of opinion expressed over the exact legal form of Edward I's confirmation of Magna Carta and the Forest Charter in 1300. The magnates requested that their seals be appended to the charters when reissued, but the king apparently felt this signified either a lack of trust or that he was a minor. The eventual format for the *Articuli super Cartas* was that of a charter (unlike the 1297 *Confirmatio cartarum*, which took the form of letters patent) and it was duly witnessed and given solemnity by a large group of people.[130]

The methods used by the sovereign to extricate himself from such promises were equally aimed at legitimacy in law. In 1305 Edward I sought papal absolution from the promises of 1297 and received it (in the form of a papal bull) on the basis that they were 'varied and harmful, relating to the forests and other rights belonging of old to the Crown and the honour of your royalty'.[131] When rescinding the Ordinances of 1311, Edward II did not use the precedent of his father, but rather sought to justify his actions on the basis of legal arguments prepared by Roman lawyers. Objection to the Ordinances as a whole and to their articles was made not only on the basis of right and reason, but because many of the points conflicted with the terms of the first and fourth precepts of his coronation oath. Cancelling the original Ordinances, the non-contentious parts were issued as a statute in 1322.[132] The statute of 1341, which in a gloss on Magna Carta (c. 39) had held that 'no peer of the land, either officer or other, shall ... be arrested, imprisoned, outlawed or exiled ... or be judged except by award of the ... peers in parliament' was annulled by Edward III by issuing another statute that repealed the former. He acknowledged, however, that those sections which might be thought 'reasonable and in accordance with law' could be salvaged and, with the advice of the judges, resubmitted at some later date.[133] The king might have sworn generally to uphold the laws and customs of the realm, but ultimately he retained the proviso that in specific instances they could be overruled. If laws or charters were not made with his free consent or were injurious to his position he had the right to repeal them.[134]

The genuine concern for precedent among members of the political community met a challenge in the legality and nature of the action to be taken in the wake of Isabella and Mortimer's successful invasion in 1326 and their presentation of a credible alternative (in the form of the teenage Edward III) to the widely-reviled rule of Edward II. Although deposition existed as a theoretical concept, removal of a reigning monarch had not been carried through in practice. Invoking forfeiture of the Crown and the right to rule brought politics within an unknown dimension. Such a step, while portrayed to those assembled (and future generations) as unanimous, consensual and carefully staged, was in reality characterised by uncertainty, indecision, opposition, fear and haste. Nevertheless, it is the portrayal of the 'deposition' that reveals the attitudes and thought-processes of contemporaries and allows us to 'appreciate the ingenuity of medieval political actors and their concern for legal forms ... and the ageless possibilities of re-creating history'.[135]

The concern for the legality of the actions is revealed in the two stages to the process. Commentators differ as to the chronology of these stages, but according to most sources, it seems that on 12 and 13 January 1327, the reasons for the action taken, the so-called Articles of Deposition (or Accusation), were 'put in writing' and read before parliament; and sermons delivered by three bishops preached the moral rectitude of removing a king who was ineffectual. Having heard the evidence, 'deposition' was adjudged, almost like a sentence, by the archbishop of Canterbury (the official responsible for crowning an anointed king and one of the few people to witness the coronation oath),[136] who announced that Prince Edward would replace his father on the throne. At the time it was stressed that the articles were a *concordia* (agreement) and efforts were made to ensure its legality: they were later described as 'public instruments conceived and dictated' in the presence of John Stratford, bishop of Winchester and 'redacted in public form' by a notary.[137]

In spite of the setting and formal pronouncement, however, the Articles of Deposition themselves were not disseminated to the country as a whole.[138] This apparent failure to capitalise on a propaganda opportunity seems to have coincided with a rapid re-think and a move towards a less controversial stance. This may have arisen from the lack of unanimous support for these actions, particularly among a number of bishops.[139] The 'reverse spin' put on the situation, that in fact Edward had voluntarily abdicated, emerged as the official line and was consciously linked (by most commentators) with a meeting by delegates from the assembly with the king at Kenilworth on 20 or 21 January 1327.

The legitimisation of these moves also occurred in two forms. The first was the attempt to justify the process through the written record. It has been argued that the document providing an official transcript of proceedings, akin to the 'Record and Process' used against Richard II in 1399, is the *Forma deposicionis regis Edwardi Anglie post Conquestum Secundi*, which refers to the action as the 'depriving' of government or 'substitution' of ruler.[140] The second was the proclamation of Edward III's accession, which portrayed the event as a voluntary resignation of the reins of government that accorded with the wishes of all the community of the realm.[141] The appearance after the event was equally important. The new regime sought Edward II's rehabilitation as a rightful monarch in the natural succession of kings because Edward III's position (both in England and in his claim to the French throne) relied on the legitimation conferred by him.[142]

The world turned upside down

Resort to civil disobedience and open revolt (in spite of there being three civil wars between 1215 and 1381) was not a frequent occurrence in medieval England. Yet there were key moments during the period when resistance in one form or another emerged from all orders of society (gentry, clerics, peasants) and took the political stage: when public confidence in an administration waned, when it was felt that the government had lost touch, when voices could not be heard through the normal channels or when a point needed demonstrating. This could take the form of symbolic action, as in 1294, when amid strong feelings in the Welsh Marches, a royal writ was seized and someone 'trampled it in the mud so that it could not be found and the king's command contained therein could not be executed',[143] or as in Edward II's reign, when appearance with an armed retinue (or the threat of one) sometimes sufficed.[144]

In political and legal terms, the Peasants' Revolt of 1381, 'arguably the most serious threat ever posed to the stability of English government in the course of the Middle Ages'[145] emerged from the civil disobedience aimed at the third poll tax. Over the space of about a fortnight it contributed a period of 'misrule' when society was literally 'turned upside down'. Much has been written on the causes of the revolt, and historians have tried to enter the minds of the peasants to provide an ideological perspective for their actions. This is not an occasion to duplicate that work, except in so far as it bears on the designs of this book. This section will concentrate on two separate but related aspects of the revolt: the context of the revolt and the targeting of royal justice. How far does the Peasants' Revolt demonstrate a heightened awareness among the lower orders of society of the law and its operation? Did the attack on royal justice have any specific aim? In examining the first question, it will be suggested that various features in the setting, planning, organisation and behaviour during the revolt – and the demands of the rebels – betrayed a strong appreciation of concepts of law (in their widest sense) and how royal and local administration operated. In assessing the attack on royal justice, it will be argued that the ideas and actions of the rebels (as far as they can realistically be perceived and understood) betray an exasperation and frustration with the law and the judicial system. Their revolution was intended to be a cleansing of the Augean stables rather than an overthrow of the whole system.

In examining the context of the revolt it is necessary to consider the time of year in which it took place and the major gathering points, the organisation and planning undertaken, the behaviour of the rebels during the rising and the nature of their demands. While focusing on the details of the revolt, it is also important to view it from a wide perspective, alive to the multiplicity of examples, precedents and influences that charged and shaped the character of the rebellion and informed and infused the behaviour of the insurgents. The appropriation and manipulation of concepts and images from different cultures and traditions enabled competing and complementary discourses to come together, interweave and re-form. While the following is not intended to be an exhaustive examination of those elements of the revolt with legal connotations, it will be clear from this survey that the rebels possessed a strong sense of how the law operated, how it affected them and how it could be reformed. The assimilation of legal concepts by the rebels and their conscious or subconscious expression during the events of the uprising not only illustrates the growth of legal consciousness, but also demonstrates how the rebels believed they had a fundamental stake in the system.

The Peasants' Revolt of course was not one single peasant disturbance. The epicentre was in the south-east, starting in Essex and Kent and converging upon London, but there were isolated outbursts in Hertfordshire, East Anglia, the West, the Midlands, and the North. A common feature nevertheless was the seasonal timing of the risings, the significance of which historians have often underestimated.[146] The period around the end of May and early June saw the major Church feasts of Whitsun, Trinity and Corpus Christi. This heralded not only a time for religious observance, but associated village and town festivities, processions and traditional summer games.[147] This festive period coincided with the holding of courts leet and 'law days' in the hundreds. The view of frankpledge at Romford in Essex, for instance, was always on the Tuesday after Whitsunday.[148] In many counties, including Essex, the peace sessions were held during the Whitsun period.[149] It also accorded with the central court vacation and the routine county visitations of royal justices to hold assizes and deliver gaols.[150]

The imminent court sessions would require the movement and congregation of large numbers of people: those participating in the view of frankpledge, performing suit of court, those summoned to answer an accusation, private parties, onlookers, witnesses, jurors and lesser officials. Similarly the Ascension Day and Rogationtide ceremonies (including beating the parish bounds), which took place in the preceding weeks, and then the staging of Whitsun and Corpus Christi processions and pageants,[151] brought a need for meetings among participating groups and the gathering of throngs, either watching or taking part. Some of the 'sommergamen' allowed access to the lord's close and even the lord's hall.[152] The legitimate planning, preparing, travelling and assembling by people in villages and towns for legal, religious or festive purposes provided a natural setting for mobilisation for revolt.[153] The sheriff's tourn was also an occasion for the twice-yearly 'view of arms' so peasants would legitimately have been carrying weapons. That does not mean that people were predisposed to social unrest in this context, but the masking effect goes towards explaining the authorities' lack of foreknowledge of the revolt.[154]

Historians are now convinced of the extent to which the revolt in the south-east was planned and co-ordinated, even allowing for the actions of some free spirits and local quarrels, and have marvelled at the logistics surmounted, the sychronicity and speed with which the rebels carried out their plans.[155] The risings in other parts of the country may not have been so pre-determined, but when news of the rising reached them, they were able to mobilise themselves equally successfully. Part of the success lay in the appropriation either consciously or subconsciously of existing mechanisms of dissemination and forms of organisation. These included public proclamations in churches and villages urging revolt, the use of the 'hue and cry' and the ringing of church bells. Local defence structures were utilised in Norfolk and a 'taxation' raised in Kent to maintain the rebellion. Elsewhere, money was forcibly taken from officials responsible for the receipt of the poll tax.[156]

The rebels performed their own form of gaol delivery, by storming castles and prisons up and down the country.[157] In London, prisoners in the Fleet, those in the abbot of Westminster's gaol and in the king's bench prison of Marshalsea were released. These actions had symbolic resonance and added momentum to the rising owing to the identity of some of the personnel released. Robert Belling, who had been claimed as a villein and could not afford the fee demanded for 'enfranchisement', was freed in the first 'delivery', which occurred at Rochester gaol.[158] More significantly, John Ball, believed to be one of the architects of the revolt, was sprung from the archbishop of Canterbury's prison at Maidstone where he had been languishing for preaching heretical doctrines. He was able to continue his exhortations, preaching a highly charged sermon at Blackheath before the assembled multitude.[159]

The burning of documents, which was a major characteristic of the revolt, betrays a familiarity not only with the location of archives, their contents and specific types of document, but also an appreciation of the prevailing symbolism. The courts and most government departments were closed for the vacation and so there were no attacks on Westminster Hall itself, but knowledge of the whereabouts of major repositories in London was clearly demonstrated.[160] The gloss put on events by the chroniclers and those complaining about the state of the archives after the event, however, precludes a clear estimate of the extent or nature of the damage to central records, and whether the spoiling or destruction in these places was highly selective (involving recognition of the type of record, its department, and its date or period) or simply indiscriminate. In at least one clear and significant instance selective destruction is suggested:

the absence of the exchequer receipt roll and its duplicates for the period Michaelmas 1380 to Easter 1381 from what is otherwise virtually a complete series for the fourteenth century implies the rebels were able to identify and destroy a crucial document relating to the poll tax returns. On the other hand, the documents at Lambeth Palace may not have been targeted systematically. Although the rebels may not have known this, they probably related to the ecclesiastical courts (such as the Court of Arches, for which no records survive)[161] rather than representing Archbishop Sudbury's personal government papers.

The destruction of documents in the provinces was a two-pronged affair. It involved the burning of manorial court records and those relating to the operation of fiscal and judicial administration in the shire. The destruction of manorial records was widespread and thorough.[162] The rolls of Havering's manor court, for example, begin only in 1382.[163] The manorial records usually contained customary rights and precedents relating to the lord, charters and other tenurial information. A poor brewer in London tried to burn the Jubilee Book in the Guildhall because it contained ordinances controlling his trade.[164] The rebels clearly had more than an inkling of where they were kept and what they contained. Examples from Cambridge (particularly concerning Corpus Christi College) and St Albans indicate that some rebels could distinguish between types of writing and discern the nature of their contents.[165] They needed to be particularly careful that they did not destroy any documents that enshrined their own rights.[166]

The destruction of documents relating to the shire was generally well-organised and again depended upon the rebels knowing not only the record likely to be kept by a particular official, but the fact that officials usually kept their records with them and, of course, where they actually lived. Exchequer documents sent to the shire were usually visually distinct and clearly identifiable since they were sealed with green wax. As a result 'all writs and summonses of the lord king of the green wax' belonging to John Sewale, sheriff of Essex, were removed from his house. His opposite number in Kent, William Septivans, was captured and taken to his manor near Canterbury and made to hand over 'fifty rolls of the pleas of the county and of the Crown' together with royal writs in his keeping, which were then taken back to Canterbury and burned.[167]

The conflagrations were not themselves attempts at the destruction of a literate culture by an illiterate peasantry (as some chroniclers suggested), nor intended to wipe out all government records. The burnings had symbolic significance in addition to the obvious challenge to royal and seigneurial jurisdiction. On a general level, the bonfires in various locations foreshadowed the festive Midsummer bonfires, which themselves represented autonomy and community.[168] The public nature of the burnings, their specific location and the ceremonial way in which they were carried out, however, suggests they were demonstrative in a more direct and meaningful way. The evidence shows that instead of being burned where they were found, the records were generally carried to important towns, such as Chelmsford or Canterbury. Once in the town they were taken to a cross, public square, or crossroads. This was the venue not only for proclamations but also for the ritual humiliation of offenders, and where in particular false charters, rotten goods or the wares of those who had offended the community were exhibited and publicly burned. The punishment meted out to ordinary people, symbolic in its own right, was here being tactically reversed.

The political backlash was manifested not just in the burning of documents but in the targeting of government and shire officials, which was designed to inhibit or paralyse their administrative operations.[169] The sheriffs of Essex and Kent, Sewale and Stepvans, for instance, were both captured on the same day, 10 June.[170] Although very few lost their lives, attacks in the south-east were made on the persons and property of those who were identified as having associations with the poll tax (particularly the enforcement of its collection). One such unfortunate was John Gildesborough, speaker of the Northampton parliament of November 1380 which voted in the tax and a member of the commission in Essex enforcing its collection in May 1381. Attention was also focused on people as a result of their participation in local judicial, administrative and political roles. John Bampton, an Essex JP and steward of the manor of Havering, was another victim of local anger.[171] While some rebels may have had purely personal grievances, discontent was widely felt and it is unlikely that the attacks were uncoordinated and unconnected. As Brooks puts it, 'the rebels' attacks on properties at this time are not simply a general but random assault on manorial lordship – for they left the vast majority of manors untouched at this time – but a specific and selective assault on the judicial establishment in the two counties'.[172] The upheaval may have provided, too, an opportunity for the settling of old scores.[173]

The beheading of 'traitors' on Tower Hill, a recognised venue for public executions, not only mimicked the spectacles that many of the crowd had probably watched before, but gave the occasion an air of legitimacy. The meeting of the rebels and the king at Smithfield was itself symbolic in its legal status as 'neutral territory': documents refer to it both as 'the king's field' and the city of London's 'common ground'.[174]

While we should not ascribe strategic thinking to all the actions of members of the rebel bands nor a pattern or rationale to every movement they took, the aims and objectives of at least some of them are evident in their letters, oaths and actions. The examples of events during previous disturbances, such as the mob's beheading in Cheapside of Walter Stapledon, bishop of Exeter, in 1326 and the concerted action against the abbot of Bury St Edmunds in 1327, may have been in the minds of some.[175] To arrange and carry their objectives through, the rebels must have depended in many cases upon the knowledge, experience and connections of their own number. The targeting of strategic nerve centres of political and judicial administration, both in London and in the provinces and, just as importantly, identifying the whereabouts of senior members of the government and local officials, such as the sheriff, escheator, coroner or justice of the peace, required the knowledge and understanding of those who had experience of local (perhaps even central) government.

Some gentry were apparently 'forced' to join in and their knowledge would have been of service, but it has also been suggested on the basis of the judicial records that social groups higher than peasantry were more extensively involved than is usually recognised.[176] In addition, many of the leaders of the peasant movements were those who naturally held authority in the village or town localities, men such as John Geffrey, bailiff of East Hanningfield in Essex or John Philip of Brandon, warrener and bailiff of Brandon in Suffolk, whose experience of participation in the nitty-gritty of local justice enabled them to act as co-ordinators both before and during the revolt.[177] The involvement of people drawn from all social levels (including members of the lesser clergy) with their own experiences of justice and royal administration would have created an interesting mixture of ideas, grudges and complaints.

What can the demands and behaviour of the rebels tell us about the way they perceived and thought about royal justice as it stood, the influences on their thoughts and attitudes, and why they thought their vision would be better? From the patterns of behaviour outlined already, we can see that the rebels imitated and appropriated concepts of organisation and administration favoured by royal justice. Such behaviour was not new among disaffected groups. The villeins of Great and Little Ogbourne in Wiltshire clubbed together in 1327 to raise money for their litigation, while the 1377 parliamentary petition against villeins reveals that peasants were acquiring a 'war chest' through levies among themselves to cover expenses arising from resistance to their lords' demands.[178] In 1347 the high price of grain caused social unrest in Boston, Lincolnshire, and prompted some rebels to board ships carrying grain and issue 'quasi-royal proclamations'.[179] If imitation is the sincerest form of flattery, then it is clear that they appreciated the advantages that such a system could bring, if only for the sake of familiarity and convenience. In their eagerness for charters of manumission there is an implicit recognition of the power of a document sealed with the royal impression and a tacit understanding that once they have secured such prizes, they can depart contented, having obtained the freedom to litigate in the king's courts and serve on juries there, although – or, reading it another way, more especially because – these were activities that some villeins already enjoyed (see Chapter 4).

The rebels were concerned with accountability: trying to make those responsible for the poll tax, the corruption of justice and lordly oppression face up to their iniquity and wrongdoing. It seems they did not wish to go through the usual channels. At his first meeting with the rebels, Richard II is supposed to have referred them to the normal methods of redress, through the petitioning process. The rebels preferred to bypass the system and come to the king direct. In seeking to make Sudbury accountable for royal expenditure (mentioned twice by the chronicler Froissart), the Kentish rebels and those in London were probably following the lead given by the parliamentary commons over the previous decade.[180] The exhortation that Hales be 'well chastised'[181] and the subsequent execution of both chancellor and treasurer was probably intended not only to cleanse the system, but to act as a deterrent for the conduct of future government ministers. Ironically, it was the chancellor and treasurer to whom complaints about judicial officials were to be directed under the Ordinance of Justices of 1346.[182]

In the shires, the indiscriminate targeting of justices and judicial officers suggests grievances against the royal administration rather than against local individuals. The declaration by John Braundys in 1374, when informed of forthcoming sessions of the peace in Berkshire: 'Iche defie alle the kinges justices', indicates this attitude was not new.[183] The way justice was administered and, in particular, the enforcement of the labour legislation has generally been regarded as the catalyst in this respect, not only fostering resentment among the lower orders, but allowing class prejudice and the economic needs of the elite to come to the fore: the interests of local gentry (justices and employers) against the lower orders (defendants and employees).[184] Yet such an explanation does not take into account the complexity of the situation. Vigorous enforcement of the labour laws, as on the estates of the bishop of Durham or in the Duchy of Cornwall, did not generate the social tensions that elsewhere led to open revolt in 1381.[185] Furthermore, by the 1370s there were fewer labour cases coming before the courts and no real incentive on the part of the justices to enforce the legislation ruthlessly since the fines no longer offset subsidy payments. Indeed, many employers were responding to market forces and paying over the odds for labour. The link between the labour legislation and the revolt, if there is a direct one, may have been a combination of several strands and had more to do with the aspirations of those peasants who were opportunistic and upwardly mobile, who either felt frustrated by the confines of the legislation, or as employers themselves were keen to enforce it in their own interests, or as bailiffs and constables found it embarrassing and often hazardous to apply the legislation in their locality.[186]

Tyler is said to have asserted that once all men of law were dead, 'all things would be regulated by the decrees of the common people'.[187] Even though this may be Walsingham's phraseology, the gist would suggest that familiar methods of promulgating legislation (through proclamation) would continue to be used. In another context, Walsingham's word for the rebels' issuing of instructions, *statuaverunt* (they decreed), reveals at least in his mind that they had a particular air of command and perhaps that the rebel leaders' orders and watchwords were accepted as if they had the force of law.[188] There is some suggestion that the rebels themselves sought legitimacy or claimed it for their actions. Wat Tyler was recorded as seeking a commission for the extermination of men of law. Geoffrey Lister received bills drawn up by local supporters which contained the names of those considered to be traitors. John Stanford, a London saddler, claimed he had in his possession a casket which contained a commission from the king for the destruction of traitors. John Greyston, a rebel leader in Cambridgeshire, assured people he had the king's full authority (*plena potestas*) to muster troops and eliminate traitors and produced a chancery document to prove it (though it was in fact a letter granting protection).[189] Of course a local constable would have had such powers under the Statute of Winchester. The co-opting of the constable of the peace of the hundred of Hoxne, William Rous, and the activities of the sub-constable for Matishale, John Mounteneye, during the revolt in Norfolk suggest that some rebels relied on their positions for their knowledge, their access to existing forms of organisation and their inherent authority.[190]

The rebel demands concerning the law itself are intriguing, and ambiguously betray both conservative and radical stances. One of the letters attributed to the rebels,[191] circulated before the rising, urges 'let might help right' and 'might go before right', suggesting that the rebels believed violence could usher in a new system (or a return to one) built on concepts of natural justice.[192] The oaths allegedly sworn by the Essex insurgents at the start of the revolt similarly speak of a radical desire to destroy the common laws (*ad destruendum ... communes leges suas*) or – according to another jury – to accept only certain laws which they would put in place (*noluerunt aliquam legem in Anglia habere nisi tantummodo certas leges per ipsos motas ordinandum*).[193] The latter of course relates to Tyler's assertion that, once the lawyers were dead, regulation would be by decree of the common people. It is not difficult to imagine how they would perceive (and react against) the veritable bombardment of new legislation during Edward III's reign and at the beginning of Richard II's, all of it regularly announced in the shires. Closer regulation of ordinary life in villages and towns through both local and national ordinances had become an inescapable part of legal and political developments. It is not surprising that people wanted less of it and called for the laws to be rescinded, torn up, burned or destroyed. Advancing (or retreating) to an age where the density of laws was far lighter, and things were arguably less complex, did not necessarily imply that they wanted to be rid of the legal system entirely. They wanted justice for all, based on their own sense of natural justice, of fundamental principles. They wanted to participate in the legal system, but on their own terms, under laws that they could cope with and respect.[194]

The demand made by Tyler that there should be 'no law but the law of Winchester' provides a more explicit, though enigmatic, idea of their aims. Professor Harding has argued that the phrase refers to the Statute of Winchester (1285), in which the traditional forms of community policing were enrolled and which symbolised the absence of interference from central government. There is much to be said for this view in general, though his analysis depends on a particular reading of the changes in the administration of justice and especially in the growth of commissions of the peace and the powers of their personnel occurring over the ensuing century. It also provokes questions as to whether peacekeeping at grass-roots level was now significantly different from what had gone on within living memory and which of the social groups among the rebels was intended to benefit from this 'reversion'. Further, it may in fact have been felt that the frequent proclamation of Winchester and repeated recitation in the peace commissions (alongside the statutes of Northampton and Westminster, which included the powers of the Statute of Labourers) closely identified its provisions with the royal regime and with the increasing authority of the peace commissions themselves.

Even if Tyler was referring to the Statute of Winchester, he may have been invoking a whole body of law – 'the law of Winchester' – popularly associated with a framework of fundamental principles. It is significant that Magna Carta was not cited by Tyler, even though in the early fourteenth century the tenants of Bocking (or their legal adviser) asserted in a petition to their lord, the prior of Christchurch, Canterbury, that amercements on the manor were 'against reason and Magna Carta'[195] and, by the later fourteenth century, its principles were perceived (certainly among the parliamentary classes) as fundamental symbols of accountability and justice.[196] It is possible, since the Statute of Winchester was proclaimed throughout the country regularly along with Magna Carta and recited as part of the peace commissions, that this invoked a particular paradigm of values, which among the peasantry was accorded special status as a touchstone of good governance analogous to Magna Carta. By the 1380s, therefore, it is possible that an unspecified body of provisions associated with the old royal capital was perceived to be fundamental law.

If Tyler's sights were not set on the Statute of Winchester, what could he have meant? There are some alternative readings of 'the law of Winchester' that might fit in with the 'back-to-basics' approach of the rebels. First, it is important to bear in mind that the rebels were invoking a 'law' they considered fundamental and so by definition it had to be of sufficient antiquity to be revered. The incidents recorded at Bury St Edmunds and St Albans, involving demands for the most ancient charters and the burning of those that they considered new, are particularly indicative of this attitude.[197] At first blush, an enactment of Cnut may fit the bill. A code of laws was decreed by Cnut at Winchester in the eleventh century.[198] It opens with the words:

> I will that just laws be established and every unjust law carefully suppressed and that every injustice be weeded out and rooted up with all possible diligence from this country. And let God's justice be exalted; and henceforth let everyman, both poor and rich, be esteemed worthy of folk-right and let just dooms [judgments] be doomed to him

and contains many provisions (such as the regulations for tithings, and the hue and cry and strangers) of fundamental importance to the local community and to the operation of justice. Indeed, it has been suggested that this code was the 'fullest single record of Anglo-Saxon law and had most influence on perceptions of pre-conquest law post-1066'. The main drawback to this argument of course is the lack of specific evidence as to the general awareness of this code in the fourteenth century, though it is clear that chroniclers and legal historians such as Andrew Horn and the anonymous writer of the *Mirror of Justices* were keen to make people aware of their legal heritage.[199] In general terms, as the former capital under the Saxon kings, the city of Winchester itself possessed symbolic resonance, and pride was increasingly taken in the Anglo-Saxon legal past. There was certainly respect for the laws of Cnut in the twelfth century and for charters reputedly from Cnut and Offa at the time of the revolt.[200]

Another, and perhaps more likely contender, however, must be Domesday Book (in spite of Harding's dismissal). It has been identified with Winchester, it was regarded by many (erroneously) as a statute, it had the necessary antiquity and was clearly revered, and it fits ideally into the context of the Peasants' Revolt. Domesday Book originally resided in the treasury at Winchester and there are references to Domesday as the 'roll of Winchester' or the 'book of Winchester'. While they are few in number and none of them immediately contemporary to the revolt, these grounds alone should not invalidate the argument. The status of the Domesday Book as quasi-law in the minds of many litigants and lawyers is significant. Officials at the exchequer in the late twelfth century associated the result of William the Conqueror's attempt to provide a written record of property-holding rights with 'written law'. The title 'Domesday' connected it with the Last Judgment in the book of Revelation and in symbolic terms this made 'its decisions like those of the Last Judgment ... unalterable'.[201]

From the 1250s there were an increasing number of cases using Domesday Book as a source of proof for claims, not just those of 'ancient demesne' status. The crescendo of requests for exemplification climaxed in 1377 when peasants from at least forty villages were involved in legal proceedings of some sort to try and obtain their freedom. In the context of the Peasants' Revolt a few years later, arguably the key to Domesday Book's invocation was what it had come to represent (to some people at least): the possibility of freedom through a legal claim. We could say it was quasi-law to judges, and in the minds of many peasants the *only* law. The new reign had probably conjured up hopes of a new beginning. We need to appreciate the inflated expectations people had when a clear legitimate method of obtaining freedom had been put to them, and the widespread frustration and exasperation felt when these expectations were suddenly deflated and the government reacted with oppressive judicial commissions. It may have been thought (or suggested) that the lawyers who had helped them in this matter in the end had let them down. Certainly the Commons blamed men of law for putting them up to it. The reaction was not immediate, but it intensified the resentment on the part of those who knew (or had thought) the legal system could benefit them. The 'slow-burn' effect was fuelled by the other aspects of social and economic conditions.[202]

Tyler called for the beheading of all men of law, though any large-scale massacre of common lawyers (if one was truly intended) was avoided because most of them were not in the capital, since it was the central court vacation period. The targeting of men of law illustrates the precarious position in which they found themselves. They were 'go-betweens', both literally and symbolically,[203] working for the community, rich and poor alike. But that was conveniently forgotten: they were regarded as helping themselves (in both senses) and this was extended and overlaid on the judicial system. As a generic group, 'lawyers' were made to account for the forms of litigation being brought in the courts, the nature of the cases, the way they were handled and the failure of some of those using the courts to achieve the satisfaction they desired.

When a court case concerns a passionately espoused cause or the decision has ramifications about one's personal life and future, it is common to praise the system if you win and blame it if you lose. Even today, successful litigants can glibly claim 'a triumph for British justice', while the losing party doubts the existence of British justice and points to failures in the judiciary or their legal representatives. In 1381, and in the invective of many satirists and moralists of the period, judges and lawyers were targeted as convenient scapegoats for the evils and aspirations of the age. While their knowledge and experience may have helped many people personally, as a recognisable 'class' lawyers do not appear to have been *valued*. Whether this was because there were too many of them around, they were not tightly regulated enough, or were simply too successful, it is not possible to know.

While much of the rebels' platform came from their immediate and longer-term experiences, the demands and behaviour during the revolt betray numerous interlinking moral and religious influences as well as themes found in *Piers Plowman* and the genre of outlaw literature. The latter, probably transmitted to them in oral form, provided an impetus for or at least a convenient hook upon which to hang their views of the legal system and in giving a carnivalesque reality to some of the scenes and relationships within this literature, they in turn underlined their familiarity and frustration with it.[204]

At the beginning of this book it was suggested that legal consciousness was the product of a combination of the prevailing culture and a person's knowledge and life experiences. The various chapters have explored the realms which provided a breeding ground for and nurtured legal consciousness, and in which ideas and attitudes were formed and disseminated. They have emphasised on the one hand the professional, intellectual and practical sides to the law and on the other the more general perceptual and participatory elements. This study has shown that law operated in a multi-dimensional context. It took effect in various (and often overlapping) jurisdictions and at a variety of social levels. Even the royal courts were not exclusive: their legal remedies were increasingly available for all sorts of people (even the unfree). The nature of law, its persona and authority, were conveyed not only through its force as custom, through its textual documents and by active enforcement, but also through its intangible images and mysterious practices which could have an equally arresting effect on those caught up in its web. Consequently law meant something (positive and negative) to all persons: it did not simply symbolise oppression for the poor, but carried for them (as much as other subjects) opportunity for remedial action in various everyday situations and even freedom from serfdom. The cumulative effect of broader exposure to concepts of law has been illustrated in the political cameos of this final chapter.

The perceptual significance of the chronological end markers of the book (Magna Carta and the Peasants' Revolt) has also been emphasised. Magna Carta's influence derived from its status (in high culture at least) as the premier statute. Its provisions were appealed to in their detail as well as being looked upon more symbolically as providing models for 'best practice'. In the 1340s petitioners wanted laws that were pleasing to God.[205] Magna Carta continued to be invoked in the fields of politics and law as a benchmark for law-giving and judicial conduct and such attitudes enabled it to transcend the immediate context of its first issue. The Peasants' Revolt demonstrated not only what could be termed the 'Magna Carta effect' (the appropriation of widely revered legal documents as symbolic of fundamental law), but also that royal propaganda was successful in putting across the king's role as head of the judicial system and ultimate earthly arbiter. The rebels were unwilling to overthrow the lordship of the rightful ruler and, in a naive (though understandable) belief that they could circumvent the legal system, looked to him to dispense justice personally – expectations similarly expressed in the outlaw ballads.

The revolt also bears witness to the physical expression of the medieval psyche's ability to entertain the proximity of apparent opposites. Rule and misrule, order and disorder were perceptually closer than modern minds would credit. The alleged misrule of royal officials and apparent peace in the land were briefly swapped for the more festively expressed 'order' of the rebels. The latter's period of 'misrule', however, like the seasonal festivities, did not last long and after the ritualistic (and actual) bloodletting, there was a reassertion of the 'true' legal order. As a monk at Westminster put it 'the royal justices were ... everywhere to be seen in session, inquiring into the activities of the conspirators'.[206] Lawyers were back in business; though people's view of lawyers themselves were also ambivalent: were they servants of justice or injustice? The revolt itself then passed into the legal and political consciousness of all levels of society as a marker of many things, not least of ideological confidence among the peasantry and the need for royal government to listen to that voice (which to some extent was echoed by the Commons in parliament) and heed its attitudes and desires.

Notes

1 J. E. A. Jolliffe, *Angevin Kingship*, 2nd edn (London, Black, 1963), pp. 54–60.
2 Powell, *Kingship*, pp. 25–30; W. M. Ormrod, *Political Life in Medieval England, 1300–1450* (Basingstoke, Macmillan, 1995), pp. 65–7, 72–4.
3 It also provided the possibility for the king to 'live of his own' – for royal and national revenues to be kept separate: M. Prestwich, *Edward I* (London, Methuen, 1988), p. 521; G. L. Harriss, *King, Parliament and Public Finance in England to 1369* (Oxford, Clarendon Press, 1975).
4 E. H. Kantorowicz, *The King's Two Bodies: a Study in Medieval Political Theology*, repr. (Princeton, NJ, Princeton University Press, 1981), pp. 343–58.
5 *Annales Monastici*, ed. H. R. Luard, RS, 5 vols (London, 1864–69), vol. 1, p. 396.
6 D. Carpenter, *The Reign of Henry III* (London, Hambledon Press, 1996), pp. 446–50.
7 Prestwich, *Edward I*, pp. 90–1.
8 The term *il se demyst* could in fact be used to describe any interest of which the holder could disentitle himself and so is relevant not just to an estate.
9 *YB 14 Edward III*, pp. xli–xliii; C. Valente, 'The deposition and abdication of Edward II', *EHR*, 113 (1998), pp. 871–5.
10 E. M. Hallam, 'Royal burial and the cult of kingship in France and England, 1060–1330', *JMH*, 8 (1982).
11 Carpenter, *Henry III*, p. 433.
12 For instance *ibid.*, pp. 38–9; P. Binski, 'Hierarchies and orders in English royal images of power', in J. Denton (ed.), *Orders and Hierarchies in Late Medieval and Renaissance Europe* (Manchester, Manchester University Press, 1999), p. 79.
13 Carpenter, *Henry III*, pp. 447, 457.
14 J. F. Burden, 'Rituals of royalty: prescription, politics and practice in English coronation and royal funeral rituals, c. 1327 to c. 1485', unpublished DPhil thesis, University of York, 2000, part 3.

15 Carpenter, *Henry III*, pp. 440-2, 456; Binski, 'Royal images', p. 88.
16 W. M. Ormrod, *The Reign of Edward III: Crown and Political Society in England, 1327-1377* (New Haven and London, Yale University Press, 1990), p. 44; A. Musson, 'Second "English Justinian" or pragmatic opportunist? A re-examination of the legal legislation of Edward III', in J. Bothwell (ed.) *The Age of Edward III* (Woodbridge, York Medieval Press, 2001).
17 Ormrod, *Political Life*, pp. 62-6.
18 N. Saul, 'Richard II and the vocabulary of kingship', *EHR*, 110 (1995), pp. 854-77; L. Coote, 'Prophecy and public affairs in later medieval England', unpublished DPhil thesis, University of York, 1997, pp. 203-5.
19 Carpenter, *Henry III*, pp. 50-4: Henry sought papal absolution from his oath on the fall of the justiciar, Hubert de Burgh, less than a month later.
20 *Chronicles of the Reign of Edward I and Edward II*, ed. W. Stubbs, RS (1882-83), vol. 1, p. 282.
21 Carpenter, *Henry III*, p. 54; Prestwich, *Edward I*, p. 547.
22 H. G. Richardson, 'The English coronation oath', *Speculum*, 24 (1949), pp. 62-3 n.91.
23 Richardson, 'Coronation oath', pp. 74-5; Prestwich, *Edward I*, pp. 90-1.
24 Richardson, 'Coronation oath', pp. 43-75.
25 Burden, 'Rituals of royalty', part 3.
26 Richardson, 'Coronation oath', pp. 62-3.
27 As told by Chief Justice Bereford (*YB 3 Edward II*, pp. 196-7), the case occurred in parliament, not in the court of king's bench as mentioned by Prestwich.
28 Prestwich, *Edward I*, pp. 294-6.
29 For example: PRO MS KB 145/1/18; PRO MS JUST 1/425 mm12d, 13, 21d, 22; *South Lancashire in the Reign of Edward II*, ed. G. H. Tupling, Chetham Society, 3rd series, vol. 1 (Manchester, 1949), pp. 19, 24; J. C. Davies, 'Common law writs and returns, Richard I to Richard II', *BIHR*, 26 (1953), p. 155; D. J. M. Higgins, 'Judges in government and society in the reign of Edward II', unpublished DPhil thesis, University of Oxford, 1986, pp. 32-3.
30 Ormrod, *Edward III*, pp. 53-5.
31 J. G. Bellamy, *The Law of Treason in England in the Later Middle Ages* (Cambridge, Cambridge University Press, 1970), p. 104. During Richard II's entry into London in 1392 the king was again accosted under the impression that the king could intervene personally.
32 Prestwich, *Edward I*, pp. 294-6; Ormrod, *Edward III*, p. 55 (examples are cited with reference to individual cases).
33 Carpenter, *Henry III*, pp. 38, 42, 80.
34 Prestwich, *Edward I*, p. 550.
35 Carpenter, *Henry III*, pp. 81-3.
36 Bellamy, *Law of Treason*, pp. 64-5; N. Saul, 'The Despensers and the downfall of Edward II', *EHR*, 99 (1984), pp. 1-33; S. L. Waugh, 'The profits of violence: the minor gentry in the rebellion of 1321-1322', *JBS*, 22 (1982), pp. 23-58.
37 *Edward II, the Lords Ordainers and Piers Gaveston's Jewels and Horses (1312-1313)*, ed. R. A. Roberts, Camden Miscellany, 15 (1929), see p. vii and p. 5;

A. Gransden, *Historical Writing in England c.1307 to the Early Sixteenth Century* (London, Routledge and Kegan Paul, 1982), pp. 6–7.
38 Carpenter, *Henry III*, pp. 30–2, 35; J. R. Maddicott, *Simon de Monfort* (Cambridge, Cambridge University Press, 1994), pp. 52–3, 131, 183.
39 Prestwich, *Edward I*, pp. 349–52.
40 J. Aberth, *Criminal Churchmen in the Age of Edward III: the Case of Bishop Thomas de Lisle* (University Park, PA, Pennsylvania State University Press, 1996).
41 Ormrod, *Edward III*, p. 153; J. Bothwell, 'Edward III and the "new nobility": largesse and limitation in fourteenth century England', *EHR*, 112 (1997), pp. 1111–40.
42 M. K. McIntosh, *Autonomy and Community: the Royal Manor of Havering, 1200–1500* (Cambridge, Cambridge University Press, 1986), pp. 27–49; M. K. McIntosh, 'The privileged villeins of the English ancient demesne', *Viator*, 7 (1976), pp. 295–328; R. Faith, 'The "great rumour" of 1377 and peasant ideology', in R. H. Hilton and T. H. Aston (eds), *The English Rising of 1381* (Cambridge, Cambridge University Press, 1981), pp. 48–51.
43 Prestwich, *Edward I*, pp. 459–61, 465.
44 W. M. Ormrod, 'Agenda for legislation, 1322–c. 1340', *EHR*, 105 (1990), pp. 11–13.
45 Carpenter, *Henry III*, pp. 62–4.
46 B. Wilkinson, *The Chancery under Edward III* (Manchester, Manchester University Press, 1929), pp. 10–25. The chancellor's use of the great seal in the absence of the king had to be restricted and defined.
47 Wilkinson, *Chancery*, pp. 16, 24; Faith, 'Great rumour', pp. 47–8.
48 Clanchy, *Memory*, p. 311. For both faces of Edward III's seal of 1340 see Ormrod, *Edward III*, Plate VI.
49 Carpenter, *Henry III*, p. 439; Binski, 'Royal images', p. 77.
50 W. M. Ormrod, 'A problem of precedence: Edward III, the double monarchy, and the royal style', in Bothwell (ed.), *Age of Edward III*.
51 R. L. Poole, 'The publication of great charters by the English kings', *EHR*, 28 (1913), pp. 448–53; Clanchy, *Memory*, pp. 221–3.
52 J. A. Doig, 'Political propaganda and royal proclamations in late medieval England', *Historical Research*, 71 (1998), pp. 254–7; *Proceedings before the Justices of the Peace in the Fourteenth and Fifteenth Centuries: Edward III to Richard III*, ed. B. H. Putnam (London, Ames Foundation, 1938), p. xcvii.
53 Matthew Paris, *Chronica Majora*, ed. H. R. Luard, RS, 7 vols (1872–83), vol. 5, pp. 18, 29, 35; *Close Rolls 1231–4*, pp. 592–3; *Close Rolls 1247–51*, pp. 139, 394; Clanchy, *Memory*, pp. 263–4.
54 J. R. Maddicott, 'The county community and the making of public opinion in fourteenth-century England', *TRHS*, 5th series, 18 (1978), p. 32; Doig, 'Royal proclamations', pp. 259–60.
55 Gransden, *Historical Writing*, p. 28.
56 Clanchy, *Memory*, p. 266; Doig, 'Royal proclamations', p. 264.
57 Poole, 'Publication of great charters', p. 450; Clanchy, *Memory*, pp. 221–3.
58 Doig, 'Royal proclamations', pp. 264–5.
59 *SR*, vol. 1, p. 136; Prestwich, *Edward I*, p. 523; Maddicott, 'County community', pp. 34–5.

60 A. J. Verduyn, 'The attitude of the parliamentary commons to law and order under Edward III', unpublished DPhil thesis, University of Oxford, 1991, p. 145.
61 Clanchy, *Memory*, p. 265.
62 *CLBCL: Letter Book F*, p. 43; *Foedera*, vol. 2, pt 4, pp. 66-7.
63 C. Taylor, 'Edward III and the Plantagenet claim to the French throne', in Bothwell (ed.), *Age of Edward III*.
64 This might seem strange if the Crown caused it to be read publicly anyway, but the king may have been less interested in the benefits of raising public awareness, than in the fact that the archbishop was usurping royal authority in this venture.
65 Doig, 'Royal proclamations' pp. 259, 261-2.
66 Verduyn, 'Attitude', p. 97; Musson and Ormrod, *Evolution*, pp. 165-6.
67 M. T. Clanchy, 'Magna Carta and the common pleas', in H. Mayr-Harting and R. I. Moore (eds), *Studies in Medieval History Presented to R. H. C. Davies* (London, Hambledon Press, 1985), pp. 223-7 (especially p. 226). Robert of Tilbury claimed he did not have to answer in the court *coram rege* on a plea of warranty of charter 'because this would be contrary to the form of the Great Charter, in which it is contained that common pleas should be held in a certain place, that is the Bench' (*SCCKB*, vol. 2, p. 11).
68 Musson and Ormrod, *Evolution*, pp. 83-4.
69 See 13 Edward I (*SR*, vol. 1, p. 96).
70 Musson, *Public Order*, p. 18.
71 See 2 Richard II st. 1, c. 6 (*SR*, vol. 2, pp. 9-10).
72 *RP*, vol. 3, pp. 42-3.
73 H. R. T. Summerson, 'The enforcement of the statute of Winchester, 1285-1327', *JLH*, 13 (1992), pp. 232-50.
74 Musson, *Public Order*, pp. 236-7.
75 D. Harding, 'The regime of Isabella and Mortimer, 1326-30', unpublished MPhil dissertation, University of Durham, 1985, p. 251.
76 See 2 Edward III c. 2 (*SR*, vol. 1, p. 258).
77 *The Eyre in Northamptonshire, 1329-1330*, ed. D. W. Sutherland, SS, 97-8 (London, 1983), vol. 1, pp. xxii, xxvii; Musson and Ormrod, *Evolution*, pp. 105-6.
78 In the statute of 1378 (see especially c. 6) there is even explicit reference to Richard's recently affirmed coronation oath to uphold justice.
79 Clanchy, *Memory*, pp. 220-2.
80 A. McHardy, 'Liturgy and propaganda in the diocese of Lincoln during the Hundred Years War', *Studies in Church History*, 18 (1982), pp. 215-27.
81 *SCCKB*, vol. 6, pp. 110-11.
82 G. Kipling, *Enter the King: Theatre, Liturgy and Ritual in the Medieval Civic Triumph* (Oxford, Clarendon Press, 1998).
83 See L. M. Bryant, 'Configurations of the community in late medieval spectacles: Paris and London during the dual monarchy' and L. Attreed, 'The politics of welcome: ceremonies and constitutional development in late medieval towns', in B. A. Hanawalt and K. L. Reyrson (eds), *City and Spectacle in Medieval Europe* (Minneapolis, University of Minnesota Press, 1994), pp. 3-33, 208-31.
84 M. Twycross, 'Some approaches to dramatic festivity, especially processions', in

85 Bellamy, *Law of Treason*, pp. 31–43; Prestwich, *Edward I*, p. 503.
86 Bellamy, *Law of Treason*, pp. 23–5, 36.
87 *Chronicon Henrici Knighton vel Cnitthon Monachi Leycestrensis*, ed. J. R. Lumby, RS, 2 vols (1889–95), vol. 1, pp. 436–7; N. Fryde, *The Tyranny and Fall of Edward II, 1321–1326* (Cambridge, Cambridge University Press, 1979), pp. 190, 192–3; M. Jones, 'Folklore motifs in late medieval art II: sexist satire and popular punishments', *Folklore*, 101 (1990), p. 76.
88 Jean Creton, *Histoire du Roy d'Angleterre Richard*, ed. and trans. J. Webb, *Archaeologia*, 20 (1824), pp. 334–5.
89 M. Prestwich, 'England and Scotland during the wars of independence' in M. Jones and M. Vale (eds), *England and Her Neighbours, 1066–1453* (London, Hambledon Press, 1989), pp. 182–3.
90 Clanchy, *Memory*, pp. 152–3.
91 Prestwich, 'Wars of independence', pp. 183–5; Clanchy, *Memory*, pp. 153–4, Prestwich, *Edward I*, pp. 490–2.
92 In 1352 Edward III summoned the historian, Ranulf Higden, to come before the king's council 'with all your chronicles and those in your charge to speak and treat with the council concerning matters to be explained to you on our behalf': J. G. Edwards, 'Ranulph, Monk of Chester', *EHR*, 47 (1932), p. 94; Gransden, *Historical Writing*, p. 43.
93 Clanchy, *Memory*, pp. 304–5.
94 Cited in Prestwich, *Edward I*, p. 492.
95 *Foedera*, vol. 2, pt 3, pp. 9, 13 (letter to seneschal of Gascony and constable of Bordeaux).
96 Prestwich, 'Wars of independence', p. 181.
97 For evidence for this reflection and the following paragraph, see Taylor, 'Plantagenet claim'.
98 For some idea of the lawyers working for the English Crown in France see M. Vale, 'England and France and the origins of the Hundred Years War', in Jones and Vale (eds), *England and her Neighbours*, pp. 208–11.
99 See 14 Edward III st. 3 (*SR*, vol. 1, p. 292).
100 Ormrod, 'A problem of precedence'.
101 Binski, 'Royal images', pp. 91–2; E. Danbury, 'English and French artistic propaganda during the period of the Hundred Years War: some evidence from royal charters', in C. Allmand (ed.), *Power, Culture and Religion in France c.1350–1550* (Woodbridge, Boydell Press, 1989), pp. 90–3.
102 Gransden, *Historical Writing*, pp. 67–8.
103 R. R. Davies, 'The peoples of Britain and Ireland, 1100–1400. III Laws and customs', *TRHS*, 6th series, 6 (1996), pp. 1–23; C. Neville, *Violence, Custom and the Law: the Anglo-Scottish Border Lands in the Later Middle Ages* (Edinburgh, Edinburgh University Press, 1998), pp. 15–17.
104 L. B. Smith, 'Statute of Wales, 1284', *Welsh History Review*, 10 (1980), pp. 151–2.

105 See above, p. 227.
106 D. W. Sutherland, *Quo Warranto Proceedings in the Reign of Edward I, 1278–1294* (Oxford, Clarendon Press, 1963), pp. 1–15.
107 For the case of Ayton, see *Close Rolls 1251–3*, p. 169.
108 Sutherland, *Quo Warranto*, pp. 17–29.
109 Abuse of franchises, although taken seriously, was in fact not a major point of the investigations (Sutherland, *Quo Warranto*, pp. 136–45).
110 *The Chronicle of Walter of Guisborough*, ed. H. Rothwell, Camden Society, 3rd series, 89 (1957), p. 216. The translation by H. M. Cam in her *Hundred and the Hundred Rolls* (London, Merlin Press, 1963), p. 237, does not do justice to the sense of outrage. 'Beau maners' could also imply the removal of status and breeding, while the final line of the stanza suggests that it will not only give them a lot of work, but also bamboozle them.
111 See 18 Edward I (*SR*, vol. 1, p. 107): 1290–4 pleas went to king's bench.
112 D. Crook, 'The later eyres', *EHR*, 97 (1982), pp. 245, 248–9; Sutherland, *Quo Warranto*, p. 30; G. D. Hall, 'The frequency of general eyres', *EHR*, 74 (1959), pp. 90–2; W. N. Bryant, 'The financial dealings of Edward III with the county communities', *EHR*, 83 (1968), pp. 762–3.
113 Clanchy, *Memory*, pp. 35–43.
114 For an examination of these concepts from a literary point of view see R. F. Green, *A Crisis of Truth: Law and Literature in the Age of Richard II* (Philadelphia, University of Pennsylvania Press, 1999), pp. 208–37.
115 Bellamy, *Law of Treason*, pp. 4–14, 21, 27; P. M. Lefferts, 'Two English motets on Simon de Montfort', in I. Fenlon (ed.) *Early Music History* vol. 1 (Cambridge, Cambridge University Press, 1981), pp. 203–25; A. Fitz-Thedmar (attr.) *The French Chronicle of London, A.D. 1259–A.D. 1343*, trans. and ed. H. T. Riley (London, 1863).
116 Prestwich, *Edward I*, p. 202–3. His fate is recorded by the Dunstable Annalist in *Annales Monastici*, vol. 2, p. 294.
117 Prestwich, *Edward I*, p. 462 and n.120.
118 F. Thompson, *Magna Carta: Its Role in the Making of the English Constitution, 1300–1629* (New York, Octagon, 1978), pp. 73–5.
119 Bellamy, *Law of Treason*, pp. 49–51, 64. Quotation cited by Bellamy from the chronicle *The Brut*.
120 Adam Murimuth and Robert Avesbury, *Chronica*, ed. E. M. Thompson, RS (1889), p. 62; Bellamy, *Law of Treason*, pp. 54, 83–4. Mortimer's heir succeeded in having the record altered.
121 See 25 Edward III st. 5 c. 2 (*SR*, vol. 1, p. 320).
122 Musson and Ormrod, *Evolution*, pp. 102–3, 154–5.
123 Bellamy, *Law of Treason*, pp. 103–5.
124 T. F. T. Plucknett, 'The origin of impeachment', *TRHS*, 4th series, 24 (1942), pp. 47–71.
125 G. Holmes, *The Good Parliament of 1376* (Oxford, Clarendon Press, 1975), pp. 2, 100–58.
126 J. C. Holt, *Magna Carta*, 2nd edn (Cambridge, Cambridge University Press, 1992), p. 6.

127 *Ibid.*, p. 18.
128 Carpenter, *Henry III*, pp. 39–43.
129 *Bracton on the Laws and Customs of England*, ed. S. E. Thorne, 4 vols (Cambridge, MA, Belknap Press, 1968–77), vol. 2, p. 110.
130 Prestwich, *Edward I*, pp. 515–20, 524.
131 *Ibid.*, pp. 547–8.
132 Sayles, 'Coronation oath', pp. 68–70.
133 See 15 Edward III st. 2 (*SR*, vol. 1, p. 297); *YB 14 & 15 Edward III*, pp. lxi–lxii; Ormrod, *Edward III*, pp. 16, 48, 67.
134 Ormrod, *Edward III*, pp. 47–8.
135 Valente, 'Deposition', p. 853.
136 By 1327 Robert Winchelsea, the presiding archbishop at Edward II's coronation, was of course long dead.
137 Valente, 'Deposition', pp. 857–8, 878–81 (Articles of Accusation).
138 Ormrod, *Edward III*, p. 45.
139 R. M. Haines, *Archbishop John Stratford* (Toronto, Pontifical Institute of Medieval Studies, 1986), pp. 186–7.
140 Valente, 'Deposition', pp. 871–5.
141 This was stressed in a legal case in 1340: see *YB 14 Edward III*, pp. xli–xlii, 24–34.
142 Burden, 'Rituals of royalty', part 3.
143 *CPR 1292–1301*, p. 113; Prestwich, *Edward I*, p. 414.
144 For example: J. R. Maddicott, *Thomas of Lancaster, 1307–1322* (Oxford, Oxford University Press, 1970), pp. 52–3, 65–6, 78.
145 W. M. Ormrod, 'The Peasants' Revolt and the government of England', *JBS*, 29 (1990), p. 1.
146 S. Justice, *Writing and Rebellion: England in 1381* (Berkeley and Los Angeles, CA, and London, University of California Press, 1994), pp. 156–7.
147 M. Aston, 'Corpus Christi and corpus regni: heresy and the Peasants' Revolt', *P&P*, 143 (1994), pp. 4–9; C. Dyer, *Everyday Life in Medieval England* (London, Hambledon Press, 1994), pp. 232–3.
148 McIntosh, *Autonomy*, p. 84.
149 *Essex Sessions of the Peace, 1351, 1377–1379*, ed. E. C. Furber, Essex Archeological Society, 3 (Colchester, 1953), p. 28.
150 Robert Belknap and his fellows heard assizes at Stratford Longthorne in Essex on 30 May, Barnet on 31 May, Brentwood on 2 June and at Dartford on 3 June.
151 The Corpus Christi processions were more common in towns.
152 Dyer, *Everyday Life*, pp. 232–3. The mumming custom (usually a Christmas phenomenon) similarly allowed entry to the lord's private space.
153 Aston, 'Corpus Christi', pp. 9–11.
154 In spite of premonitions and warnings from Gower and others: R. W. Kaeuper, *War, Justice and Public Order* (Oxford, Clarendon Press, 1988), pp. 349–50; Justice, *Writing and Rebellion*, p. 141.
155 N. Brooks, 'The organisation and achievements of the peasants of Kent and Essex in 1381', in Mayr-Harting and Moore (eds), *Studies in Medieval History*, pp. 252–60, 268–70. The secrecy and planning is revealed in the letters collected by

chroniclers, which are instructional and apocalyptic in message: Justice, *Writing and Rebellion*, pp. 13-28.
156 Ormrod, 'Peasants' Revolt', p. 15; Justice, *Writing and Rebellion*, pp. 64-6; A. J. Prescott, 'Judicial records of the rising of 1381', unpublished PhD thesis, University of London, 1984, pp. 16-17, 51-2, 94, 115. In an ironic reversal the rebels had extorted from the officials in whose custody it was the very money they had been forced to pay to the government at an earlier date.
157 Brooks, 'Organisation', pp. 261, 267, 269.
158 *Ibid.*, p. 256.
159 Aston, 'Corpus Christi', pp. 17-23; Justice, *Writing and Rebellion*, pp. 14-28, 103-19.
160 Ormrod, 'Peasants' Revolt', pp. 5-9.
161 *Select Canterbury Cases, c.1200-1301*, ed. N. Adams and C. Donahue, SS, 95 (London, 1981), p. 37. There may of course be other reasons for the non-survival of the court's records.
162 Dyer, *Everyday Life*, p. 224.
163 McIntosh, *Autonomy*, p. 84. Some manorial courts used a dating formula 'during the time of the uproar and burning of the court rolls' to refer to 1381 (Justice, *Writing and Rebellion*, p. 40; Dyer, *Everyday Life*, p. 236).
164 P. M. Nightingale, *A Medieval Mercantile Community: the Grocers' Company and the Politics and Trade of London, 1000-1485* (New Haven and London, Yale University Press, 1995), p. 265.
165 Justice, *Writing and Rebellion*, pp. 42-5, 47-8.
166 J. S. Beckerman, 'Procedural innovation and institutional change in medieval English manorial courts', *LHR*, 10 (1992), p. 226.
167 Brooks, 'Organisation', p. 260.
168 Justice, *Writing and Rebellion*, p. 150-1, 156.
169 Ormrod, 'Peasants' Revolt', pp. 4-5.
170 Brooks, 'Organisation', p. 260.
171 Brooks, 'Organisation', p. 263; McIntosh, *Autonomy*, pp. 78, 82-4.
172 Brooks, 'Organisation', p. 266.
173 For vendettas concerning title to property, see Nightingale, *Mercantile Community*, p. 266.
174 P. Strohm, *England's Empty Throne: Usurpation and the Language of Legitimation, 1399-1422* (New Haven and London, Yale University Press, 1998), p. 56.
175 Gransden, *Historical Writing*, p. 28; S. H. Rigby, *English Society in the Later Middle Ages: Class, Status and Gender* (Basingstoke, Macmillan, 1995), pp. 167-8.
176 Brooks, 'Organisation', p. 267 n.60; Prescott, 'Judicial records', pp. 377-8; M. Bush, 'The risings of the commons in England, 1381-1549', in Denton (ed.), *Orders and Hierarchies*, pp. 112-14.
177 C. Dyer, 'The social and economic background to the rural revolt of 1381', in Hilton and Aston (eds), *English Rising*, pp. 17-19; Prescott, 'Judicial records', p. 100.
178 A. Harding, 'The revolt against the justices', in Hilton and Aston (eds), *English Rising*, p. 191; Ormrod, 'Peasants' Revolt', p. 15 n.77.

179 Rigby, *English Society*, pp. 122–3.
180 Ormrod, 'Peasants' Revolt', p. 17.
181 Justice, *Writing and Rebellion*, pp. 13, 24: the phrase occurs in the letter to Carter; Hales was identified with Hobbe the Robber.
182 *SR*, vol. 1, p. 305.
183 Putnam, *Proceedings*, p. cxviii.
184 See discussion and references in Musson and Ormrod, *Evolution*, pp. 175–6, 179–81.
185 Rigby, *English Society*, pp. 117–18.
186 Musson and Ormrod, *Evolution*, pp. 97–8; M. J. Hettinger, 'The role of the statute of Labourers in the social and economic background of the great revolt in East Anglia', unpublished PhD thesis, University of Indiana, 1987, pp. 154–8, 192; M. Kowaleski, *Local Markets and Regional Trade in Medieval Exeter* (Cambridge, Cambridge University Press, 1995), pp. 190–1.
187 Cited in Harding, 'Revolt against the justices', p. 165.
188 Justice, *Writing and Rebellion*, p. 66.
189 Prescott, 'Judicial records', p. 103; Ormrod, 'Peasants' Revolt', p. 15.
190 Hettinger, 'Statute of Labourers', pp. 191–2, 207–11.
191 Justice, *Writing and Rebellion*, p. 13.
192 Re-establishment of the kingdom on the basis of natural law principles is a theme vividly portrayed in *Piers Plowman*, where animals' family lives are ruled by reason; see A. Brown, *The Theme of Government in Piers Plowman* (Woodbridge, D. S. Brewer, 1981), pp. 22–3. The notion of *ius* or 'right' was strongly held at the manorial level; see *Select Cases in Manorial Courts*, ed. L. Poos and L. Bonfield, SS, 114 (London, 1997), pp. xxx–xxxi. For an earlier use of a similar phrase with reference to the political context of Edward II's reign, see J. R. Maddicott, 'Poems of social protest in early fourteenth-century England', in W. M. Ormrod (ed.), *England in the Fourteenth Century*, Proceedings of the 1985 Harlaxton Symposium (Woodbridge, Boydell Press, 1986), pp. 138–41.
193 Brooks, 'Organisation', p. 252 and n.18.
194 The author of the *Mirror of Justices* writing in the 1290s (after the numerous statutes of Edward I and the dismissal from office of the higher judiciary) appears to have held similar views on the overcomplicated and dysfunctional nature of the law.
195 J. F. Nichols, 'An early fourteenth century petition from the tenants of Bocking to their manorial lord', *Economic History Review*, 1st series, 2 (1929–30), pp. 300–7.
196 Thompson, *Magna Carta*, pp. 1–19.
197 Justice, *Writing and Rebellion*, pp. 47–8; Faith, 'Great rumour', p. 64. The Bury charters were allegedly from King Cnut, the St Albans charter from King Offa.
198 *Ancient Laws and Institutes of England*, vol. 1, pp. 377–430; P. Wormald, *The Making of English Law: King Alfred to the Twelfth Century* (Oxford, Blackwell, 1999), pp. 132, 345. Whether contemporaries used this phrase is not clear, but Wormald continually refers to Cnut's laws as the 'Winchester code' (e.g. p. 362).
199 J. Catto, 'Law and history in fourteenth-century England', in R. H. C. Davis and J. M. Wallace-Hadrill, *The Writing of History in the Middle Ages: Essays Presented to R. W. Southern* (Oxford, Clarendon Press, 1981), pp. 382–7; D. Seipp, 'The

Mirror of Justices', in *Learning the Law*, pp. 104–5.
200 J. C. Holt, *Magna Carta and Medieval Government* (London, Hambledon Press, 1985), pp. 1–22; J. Hudson, 'Administration, family and perceptions of the past in late-twelfth-century England: Richard FitzNigel and the Dialogue of the Exchequer', in P. Magdalino (ed.), *The Perception of the Past in Twelfth-Century Europe* (London, Hambledon Press, 1992), pp. 94–8. The nature of Tyler's knowledge, contacts and discussions with others on this area would be entirely speculative. For further discussion on appreciation of the legal heritage, see A. Musson, 'Appealing to the past: perceptions of law in late medieval England', in A. Musson (ed.), *Expectations of the Law in the Middle Ages* (Woodbridge, Boydell Press, 2001).
201 Clanchy, *Memory*, pp. 25–6, 32. Quotation from FitzNigel's 'Dialogue of the Exchequer'.
202 Faith, 'Great rumour', pp. 43–70.
203 B. Hanawalt, *"'Of Good and Ill Repute": Gender and Social Control in Medieval England* (Oxford and New York, Oxford University Press, 1998), pp. 20–1: in the ritual of the election of the mayor of London the common pleader traversed the area between the low-status space of the commons and high-status space of the existing mayor and aldermen.
204 Powell, *Kingship*, pp. 39–42.
205 *RP*, vol. 2, p. 141 (42).
206 Cited in Prescott, 'Judicial records', p. 45.

SELECT BIBLIOGRAPHY

The most important investigations of culture and the intellect for the medieval period are M. T. Clanchy, *From Memory to Written Record: England, 1066–1307*, 2nd edn (Oxford, Blackwell, 1993) and M. Carruthers, *The Book of Memory: the Study of Memory in Medieval Culture* (Cambridge, Cambridge University Press, 1992). More generally, the following are extremely useful for their comparative perspectives: S. Reynolds, *Kingdoms and Communities in Western Europe, 900–1300*, 2nd edn (Oxford, Clarendon Press, 1997); C. Geertz, *The Interpretation of Cultures* (London, Fontana Press, 1993); R. N. Swanson, *Church and Society in Late Medieval England* (Oxford, Blackwell, 1993); C. J. Neville, *Violence, Custom and Law. The Anglo-Scottish Border Lands in the Later Middle Ages* (Edinburgh, Edinburgh University Press, 1998); and M. Camille, *Image on the Edge: the Margins of Medieval Art* (London, Reaktion, 1992).

The development of the legal profession has been surveyed in P. Brand, *The Origins of the English Legal Profession* (London, Blackwell, 1992); R. V. Turner, *Judges, Administrators and the Common Law in Angevin England* (London, Hambledon Press, 1994); and J. H. Baker, *The Order of Serjeants at Law*, SS, Supplementary Series, 5 (London, 1984). Some recent research on legal education can be found in the essays in J. A. Bush and A. Wijffels (eds), *Learning the Law: Teaching and the Transmission of Law, 1150–1900* (London, Hambledon Press, 1999). G. O. Sayles (ed.), *Select Cases in the Court of King's Bench*, SS, 55, 57, 58, 74, 76, 82, 88 (London, 1936–71) is a mine of information. B. H. Putnam, *The Place in Legal History of Sir William Shareshull* (Cambridge, Cambridge University Press, 1950) provides an authoritative portrait of one of the leading judicial figures of the period. Attitudes towards the law and the legal profession can be found in J. R. Maddicott, 'Law and lordship: royal justices as retainers in thirteenth and fourteenth century England', *P&P* supplement, 4 (Oxford, 1978); and N. M. Fryde, 'Edward III's removal of his ministers and judges, 1340–1', *BIHR*, 48 (1975). A. P. Baldwin, *The Theme of Government in Piers Plowman* (Woodbridge, D. S. Brewer, 1981) considers literary evidence.

How the law affected peasant communities can be reviewed in L. R. Poos and L. Bonfield (eds), *Select Cases in Manorial Courts*, SS, 114 (London, 1998); P. Hyams, *King, Lords and Peasants in Medieval England: the Common Law of Villeinage in the Twelfth and Thirteenth Centuries* (Oxford, Clarendon Press, 1980). M. Kowaleski, *Local Markets and Regional Trade in Medieval Exeter* (Cambridge, Cambridge University Press, 1995) is a case-study of trade and regulation in towns. The structures of local justice are surveyed in H. Jewell, *English Local Administration in the Middle Ages* (Newton Abbot, David & Charles, 1972), though for a more detailed examination of the shire and hundred courts see R. C. Palmer, *The County Courts of Medieval England, 1150–1350* (Princeton, NJ, Princeton University Press, 1982) and H. M. Cam, *The Hundred and the Hundred Rolls* (London, Merlin Press, 1963). In addition to the articles by Powell, Rowney and Rawcliffe on arbitration and out-of-court settlement, social pressures towards conformity are considered in B. A. Hanawalt, *'Of Good and Ill Repute': Gender and Social Control in Medieval England* (New York and Oxford, Oxford University Press, 1998) and M. K. McIntosh, *Controlling Misbehaviour in England, 1370–1600* (Cambridge, Cambridge University, 1998). J. S. Beckerman, 'Procedural innovation and institutional change in medieval English manorial courts', *LHR*, 10 (1992), pp. 198–252, looks at the introduction of juries in the manorial courts, while a study of juror attitudes can be found in T. A. Green, *Verdict According to Conscience: Perspectives on the English Criminal Trial Jury, 1200–1800* (Chicago, IL, University of Chicago Press, 1985).

An overview of developments in royal justice is provided by A. Musson and W. M. Ormrod, *The Evolution of English Justice: Law, Politics and Society in the Fourteenth Century* (Basingstoke, Macmillan Press, 1998). Texts giving insight into procedure and actions are A. Harding (ed.), *The Roll of the Shropshire Eyre of 1256*, SS, 96 (London, 1980); B. H. Putnam (ed.), *Proceedings before the Justices of the Peace in the Fourteenth and Fifteenth Centuries, Edward III to Richard III* (London, Ames Foundation, 1938); B. W. McLane (ed.), *The 1341 Royal Inquest in Lincolnshire*, Lincoln Record Society, 78 (Woodbridge, 1988); R. C. Palmer, *English Law in the Age of the Black Death: a Transformation of Governance and Law, 1348–1381* (Chapel Hill, NC, University of North Carolina Press, 1993); and A. Harding, 'Plaints and bills in the history of English law', in D. Jenkins (ed.), *Legal History Studies 1972* (Cardiff, University of Wales Press, 1975), pp. 65–86. For peasant litigation and their use of royal courts, see P. R. Schofield, 'Peasants and the manor court: gossip and litigation in a Suffolk village at the close of the thirteenth century', *P&P*, 159 (1998), pp. 1–42. Attitudes to the poor can be found in M. Rubin, *Charity and Community in Medieval Cambridge* (Cambridge, Cambridge University Press, 1987).

The rise of parliament and the petitioning process are examined in R. G. Davies and J. H. Denton (eds), *The English Parliament in the Middle Ages* (Manchester, Manchester University Press, 1981); G. L. Harriss, *King,*

Parliament and Public Finance in Medieval England to 1369 (Oxford, Clarendon Press, 1975); and J. R. Maddicott, 'The county community and the making of public opinion in fourteenth-century England', *TRHS*, 5th series, 18 (1978), pp. 27-43. The personnel of parliament are considered in N. Saul, *Knights and Esquires: the Gloucestershire Gentry in the Fourteenth Century* (Oxford, Clarendon Press, 1981); K. L. Wood-Legh, 'Sheriffs, lawyers and belted knights in the parliaments of Edward III', *EHR*, 46 (1931), pp. 372-88; and J. S. Roskell, *Parliament and Politics in Late Medieval England*, 3 vols (London, Hambledon Press, 1981-3). T. F. T. Plucknett, *Statutes and their Interpretation in the First Half of the Fourteenth Century* (Cambridge, Cambridge University Press, 1922) remains an important study of Edwardian legislation.

Issues of kingship are raised in the biographical studies by D. Carpenter, *The Reign of Henry III* (London, Hambledon Press, 1996); M. Prestwich, *Edward I* (London, Methuen, 1988); and W. M. Ormrod, *The Reign of Edward III: Crown and Political Society in England, 1327-1377* (New Haven and London, Yale University Press, 1990); J. R. Maddicott, *Thomas of Lancaster, 1307-1322* (Oxford, Clarendon Press, 1970); and in W. M. Ormrod, *Political Life in Medieval England, 1300-1450* (Basingstoke, Macmillan, 1995) and E. Powell, *Kingship, Law and Society: Criminal Justice in the Reign of Henry V* (Oxford, Clarendon Press, 1989). For the legal case-studies, see especially J. G. Bellamy, *The Law of Treason in the Later Middle Ages* (Cambridge, Cambridge University Press, 1970); D. W. Sutherland, *Quo Warranto Proceedings in the Reign of Edward I* (Oxford, Clarendon Press, 1963); J. C. Holt, *Magna Carta*, 2nd edn (Cambridge, Cambridge University Press, 1992); C. Valente, 'The deposition and abdication of Edward II', *EHR*, 113 (1998), pp. 852-81. There is a vast literature on the Peasants' Revolt, but of particular relevance here are S. Justice, *Writing and Rebellion: England in 1381* (Berkeley and Los Angeles, CA, and London, University of California Press, 1994); N. Brooks, 'The organisation and achievements of the peasants in Kent and Essex in 1381', in H. Mayr-Harting and R. I. Moore (eds), *Studies in Medieval History Presented to R. H. C. Davies* (London, Hambledon Press, 1985), pp. 247-70, and the essays by C. Dyer, R. Faith and A. Harding in R. H. Hilton and T. H. Aston (eds), *The English Rising of 1381* (Cambridge, Cambridge University Press, 1981). A new insight into law and literature is provided by R. F. Green, *A Crisis of Truth: Literature and Law in Ricardian England* (Philadelphia, PA, University of Pennsylvania Press, 1999).

INDEX

Note: 'n' after a page reference indicates a note number on that page.

Alexander III, pope 14, 102
appeals
　approvers 21, 98, 100–1, 115, 153, 155, 189
　of felony 154–6, 160, 180 n136
apprentice-at-law 40, 46, 50, 75, 76 n20, 213 n48
arbitration 16–17, 18, 21, 22, 55, 91–3, 102, 223
Arches, Court of 38, 45, 171, 245
Athelstan, king of England 90

bastardy, issues of 13, 85–7, 120
Bateman, William 38
Bath, Henry of 59–60
Bedfordshire 85, 148
benefit of clergy 13, 100
Bereford, William 15, 40, 43, 56, 62, 64, 68, 158, 203, 204, 256 n27
Black Death 89, 104, 108, 109, 117, 145, 172
Boniface, pope 233–4
Boroughbridge, battle of 151
Bracton 12, 37, 39, 40, 49, 51, 113, 168, 221, 239
Bracton, Henry 37, 46, 53
Bristol 208, 232
　Little Red Book 30 n30, 208
Britton 40, 113
Bromholm, priory of 221
Buckinghamshire 174 n11, 194

　knight of the shire of 194
　sheriff of 194
Bury St Edmunds 251
　abbot of 14, 68, 94, 247

Cambridge 145, 245
　University 38, 64, 82 n160
Cambridgeshire 99, 118, 147, 152, 175 n28
　knight of the shire of 193
　Peasants' Revolt in 245, 249
　sheriff of 193
canon
　law 9, 10, 15, 38, 41, 85, 87, 119, 171
　lawyers 14, 15, 38, 45, 47, 48, 49, 64, 76 n3, 77 n45, 171
Canterbury 245, 246
Canterbury Tales 66, 71, 74, 77 n29
Carlisle 146
　bishop of 14
Cavendish, John 207
Charles IV, king of France 234
Chester
　courts of 13, 19, 127 n63
　justiciar of 52
　palatinate of 127 n63
Colchester 104, 177 n76, 194
Consolato del Mare 11
Continental law 9, 25
Cornwall 146, 194
Court Baron 69, 119, 122

269

INDEX

customary law 9, 10, 12, 13, 24, 85–9, 110–12, 204, 208–9, 254
Cnut, king of the Danes and of England 90, 251–2, 263 n197, 263 n198

Derbyshire 90, 112
Despenser
    Hugh, the elder 144, 224, 237
    Hugh, the younger 144, 223, 232
Devonshire 108, 146, 148, 194
Domesday Book 22, 252
Dorset 200
Durham
    bishop of 14, 122, 171, 248
    judicial sessions in 175 n28, 176 n51
    palatinate of 14
    prior of 88–9

Edward I, king of England 24, 187, 220, 225
    attitude to law and justice 222, 223–4, 227–8, 239
    claim to Scotland 232–4
    coronation oath 219, 221
    legislative legacy 204, 208, 229
    military campaigns 139
Edward II, king of England 40, 190, 221, 238
    coronation oath 222
    deposition 7, 219–20, 233, 240–1
    dispensing justice 174 n20
    King's Hall, founder of 38
    new ordinances 239–40
    tyranny of 27, 223, 224, 229, 237
Edward III, king of England 226, 259 n92
    accession 240–1
    attitude to law and justice 163, 172 n20, 220, 222–3, 224, 228, 237, 240
    claim to French throne 225, 227, 233, 234–6
    dismissal of judges 56, 59–60
Edward the Confessor, king of England 219–20, 221, 222–3
Essex 93, 147, 148–9, 261 n150
    knight of the shire of 196, 201
    Peasants' Revolt in 243, 245–6, 250
    sheriff of 245, 246
Exeter 90, 92, 94, 104
    bishop of 190, 247

Fleta 40, 186
forests
    royal jurisdiction in 10–11, 190, 222, 227, 239
    verderers 109
frankpledge 90, 95, 243

Gaveston, Piers 223
Gest of Robyn Hode 64, 253
Glanvill 38, 39, 65, 97
Gloucestershire 68, 176 n52
    knight of the shire of 213 n41
Green, Henry 42, 60, 61
Grosseteste, Robert 47, 123

Hampshire 107
Harclay, Andrew 151, 178 n84, 237
Havering, manor of 93, 245, 246
Hengham, Ralph 46, 56, 57, 61, 63, 70–1, 203, 206
Henry II, king of England 10, 47, 153, 220, 233
Henry III, king of England 46, 60, 138, 225, 233, 236
    attitude to law and justice 72, 221–3, 228, 236, 237, 239

iconography of 219–20
minority of 137
shortcomings of rule 163, 222–4
Hereford 94, 144–5, 232
Herefordshire 90, 144, 176 n52
    knight of the shire of 198, 22
    sheriff of 198, 200
Herle, William 44, 73, 202
Hertfordshire 102, 231
Horn, Andrew 24, 42, 208, 252
Hungerford, Thomas 194, 198

impeachment 186–7, 233, 238
Inge, John 57, 58, 72
Inge, William 60, 63
inheritance 85–7, 126–7 n43, 234–6
Innocent III, pope 49
Inns of Court 41, 45, 49–50, 68, 73, 233
Isabella, queen of Edward II 144, 229, 240

jury service 20, 51, 54, 72, 84, 86, 89, 95–6, 98, 99–100, 109–20, 121–2, 124, 150–3, 160, 162, 169, 173, 191–3, 194–5, 209, 238

Kenilworth, dictum of 99
Kent 86, 139, 169, 175 n28, 176 n51, 194
    coroner 108
    knight of the shire of 194–5
    Peasants' Revolt in 243, 244, 245–6, 248
    sheriff of 245, 246
King's Champion 26

Lancashire 21, 91, 96, 151, 195
    knight of the shire of 195
Lancaster
    John of Gaunt, duke of 196
    Thomas, earl of 26, 27, 151, 237
Langland, John 72
    Piers Plowman 71, 123, 253, 263 n192
Lateran Council
    third (1179) 47
    fourth (1215) 98, 101
Law Merchant 11, 12, 104
Lay of Havelock the Dane 94
legal costume 19, 20, 49, 73
Leicestershire 98
    coroner of 193
    knight of the shire of 193, 196, 201
    sheriff of 201
Lincoln 93, 112, 145, 177 n73
Lincolnshire 26, 93, 96, 122, 139, 147, 148–9, 167, 200, 248
    knight of the shire of 193
    sheriff of 193
London 24, 90, 94, 175 n28, 208, 221, 226, 231, 236, 256 n31
    arbitration in 21, 92
    Cheapside 247
    city courts 13, 55, 92, 104, 119, 165, 168, 208, 209
    gilds 16, 92
    mayor of 39, 105, 264 n203
    Peasants' Revolt in 243, 244, 246–8, 249
    Smithfield 246–7
Louis IX, king of France 21
Luttrell, Geoffrey 26, 65
Luttrell Psalter 25–6

March
    days of 14, 16
    laws of 11, 12, 21
    Roger Mortimer, earl of 144, 226, 229, 238, 240

INDEX

Mare, Peter de la 197–8
marriage litigation 13, 85–9, 120
merchants, traders, etc. 11, 17, 89–90, 92, 94, 96, 109, 124, 159
Middleton, Gilbert 237
military law 11, 237
Mirror of Justices 24, 40, 252, 263 n194
Modus tenendi parliamentum 184

Newcastle 20, 146, 232
Norfolk 87, 100, 107, 115, 139
    coroner of 193
    knight of the shire of 193, 195
    Peasants' Revolt in 244, 249
Northampton 99, 106, 202, 246
Northamptonshire 63, 106
    knight of the shire of 201
Northumberland 12, 90, 96, 143
Norwich 94, 99
    prior of 181 n159

oaths
    coronation 220, 221–2, 240–1, 258 n78
    judicial 20, 50–2, 55, 74, 79 n81, 93, 221
    quasi-judicial 250
Oleron, Laws of 11, 30 n32
Ordinances 207–8
    1293 (Conspirators) 74, 160
    1305 (Conspirators) 74, 150–1
    1305 (Trailbaston) 150, 190
    1311 (new) 26, 59, 239–40
    1346 (Justices) 52, 53, 60, 71, 248
    1349 (Labourers) 172, 209
    1353 (Staple) 104
    1372 (knights of the shire) 196
    see also Statutes
outlawry 171–2

Outlaw's Song of Trailbaston, An 73, 123, 172
Oxford 107
    business school 68
    University 38, 49, 68
Oxfordshire 62, 118, 121, 147

Paper Constitution (1244) 224
Paris, treaty of 41
peace commissions 14, 67–8, 105, 106, 130 n122, n126, n127, 144–5, 147–9, 172–3, 200–1, 213 n32, 243, 250
Peasants' Revolt 1, 2, 4, 7, 37, 59, 63, 69, 72, 75, 108, 145, 153, 163, 193, 203, 217, 222, 238, 242 *passim*
Philip of Valois, king of France 227, 234
Provisions of Oxford (1258) 179 n121, 225, 226

Raleigh, William 14, 46, 47, 202, 239
Richard II, king of England 221, 228, 229, 231, 232, 256 n31
    coronation 26, 258 n78
    Peasants' Revolt and 1, 2, 53, 222, 246, 248
    tyranny of 27, 241
Roman civil law 10, 12, 14, 38, 39, 41, 78 n60, 82 n160, 93, 221, 233, 239
    civil lawyers 14, 38, 47, 75, 76 n3, 92
Rothbury, Gilbert 38
Roubery Chest 38

St Albans Abbey 11, 111, 223, 245, 251
St Andrews, Fife 237

INDEX

St Paul's Cathedral 221, 226
Salisbury
  burgess of 194
Scarborough 93
Scrope, Geoffrey 42, 62, 65, 70–1, 204, 205, 206
Scrope, Richard 72–3
seals
  common 121, 223
  great 23, 34 n100, 202, 222, 224–5, 248, 257 n46
  personal 23, 102, 116, 121, 224, 239
Shardlow, John 57, 58, 68
Shareshull, William 42, 43, 44, 51, 56, 58, 60, 62, 203, 205, 207
Shrewsbury 139
Shropshire 90, 138, 147, 162, 176 n52
  knight of the shire of 193, 196
  sheriff of 193
Skipwith, William 60, 61, 213 n48
Somerset 145
  knight of the shire of 194
Staffordshire 62, 147, 200
  knight of the shire of 193
  sheriff of 193
statute books 22, 41–2, 69, 122–3
Staunton, Hervey 43, 46, 56, 64
Statutes 205–8, 211
  1215/1225 (Magna Carta) 1, 2, 22, 38, 41, 69, 87, 96, 102, 137, 138, 155, 164, 185, 188, 190, 222, 225–8, 232, 237, 239, 240, 251, 254, 258 n67
  1275 (Westminster) 53–5, 140
  1278 (Gloucester) 236
  1284 (Wales) 235
  1285 (Exeter) 116
  1285 (Westminster) 69, 113, 116, 139, 140, 147, 166, 206
  1285 (Winchester) 22, 69, 107, 151, 228, 229, 249, 250–1
  1293 67, 116, 139
  1299 (Fines) 47, 143, 230
  1300 (Articles upon the Charters) 141, 239
  1301 (Escheators) 206
  1316 (Lincoln) 68
  1322 (York) 240
  1328 (Northampton) 143, 151, 229, 230, 250
  1330 143
  1331 154
  1336 154
  1340 101
  1341 240
  1351 (Labourers) 102, 107, 109, 145, 147–8, 151, 170, 172, 173, 207, 209, 231, 248–9, 250
  1351 (Provisors) 207
  1352 119, 192, 197
  1352 (Treasons) 207, 238
  1354 192
  1361 (Westminster) 151, 192, 207, 250
  1362 148, 168
  1363 208–9
  1365 192, 193
  1368 192
  1378 154, 229
  1382 146
  1384 33, 63
  1388 (Cambridge) 209
  see also Ordinances
Stonor, John 56, 57, 58, 64, 65, 203
Suffolk 82 n160, 94, 95, 108–9, 116
Surrey 107, 118, 152

Tale of Gamelyn 123, 253
Thorpe, Robert 199, 205, 213 n47

273

INDEX

Thorpe, William 43, 60–1, 77 n28, 205, 213 n46
Tyler, Wat 249, 250–1, 253, 264 n200

villeins 87–8, 90, 95, 116, 121, 124, 169–70, 244, 247, 252, 254

Wallace, William 20, 232, 237
wardship 109, 113, 115–16
Warwick 94, 99
    burgess of 195
Warwickshire 148, 176 n52
    knight of the shire of 195, 201
    sheriff of 201
Welsh law 12
Westminster
    Abbey 222
    Great Hall 20, 244
    royal courts 68, 75, 138, 141, 145, 146, 147
Westmorland 12, 90
    knight of the shire of 198
Weyland, Thomas 56, 57, 58
Willoughby, Richard 56, 57, 58–9, 203
Wiltshire 201, 247
    Chippenham hundred 152
    coroner of 193–4
    knight of the shire of 194, 201
Winchester 251–2
    bishop of 78 n60
    'law of Winchester' 250–2
Winner and Waster 19
Wisby, laws of 11, 30 n32
Worcestershire 176 n52, 200
Wycliffe, John 15

Yorkshire 62, 90, 96, 96, 138, 139, 147, 148, 236
York 67, 98, 106, 114, 141, 143, 145, 199, 208
    mayor of 106
    York Memorandum Book 208